PRAISE FOR
*THE CHURCH SPEAKS TO
THE MODERN WORLD*

This is the best collection of Pope Leo XIII's social teachings. Etienne Gilson's short introductions to each document help the reader to grasp the sapiential order and cohesion of Pope Leo's teaching, without getting in the way of the documents themselves.
—PATER EDMUND WALDSTEIN, O.Cist., lecturer in moral theology, Heiligenkreuz, Austria

"The greatest pope since the Reformation" is a towering figure, basking in the light of all that came before him and casting his protective shadow over everyone who recognizes his greatness. Here, bound in a single volume, are the principal acts of his pontificate introduced and explained by one of the greatest figures of the revival Leo accomplished. Every citizen, every statesman, every parent, every student should read and ponder this book a hundred times.

"The Christian is born for combat", says Leo XIII. Let us arm ourselves with his golden wisdom before entering the field. Here is the blueprint for Christendom, this is the antidote to modernity, the strategikon of Christ's legions on earth.
—ALAN FIMISTER, Ph.D, Assistant Professor of Theology at Saint John Vianney Theological Seminary, Denver CO, Director of the Dialogos Institute, Co-author of *Integralism: A Manual of Political Theology*

The social teaching of Leo XIII covers not only economic questions, but political rights and obligations, marriage and the family, the nature of liberty, and the relation of Church and State. It provides a consistent body of magisterial doctrine that in its range and depth of argument has few parallels in the history of the papacy. Gilson's edition, coming just before the Second Vatican Council, presents this teaching in its entirety, something that has been less usual in the post-conciliar period. This republication will contribute greatly to the recovery of the fullness of Catholic teaching on political, social, and economic questions.
—DR. THOMAS PINK, Professor of Philosophy, King's College London

Now more than ever we need the sobriety and crystal clarity concerning political, cultural, and economic matters that characterize Pope

Leo XIII's social encyclicals, many of which are unjustly neglected today. This welcome reissue will help to remedy that, and thereby contribute to the good of the Church and of society.
 —DR. EDWARD FESER, Professor of Philosophy, Pasadena City College

As a collection of encyclicals from the late 19th century, *The Church Speaks to the Modern World* may seem too antiquated to serve as an adequate guide to our "modern world" of the 21st century. Yet, in republishing this old book for new readers, Arouca Press is not just serving up old wine in a new wineskin, for the Church's social teachings are the wine that is new precisely for being so very old. Founded on the unchanging principles of the social nature of man and its restoration in Christ, the encyclicals in this volume (with its helpful introduction, notes, and reading guides) speak to every age. For, to paraphrase one very old author, in human affairs, there is finally nothing really new under the sun.
 —CHRISTOPHER ZEHNDER, General Editor, Catholic Textbook Project

The writings of Pope Leo XIII mark a decisive turning point in the history of the Church's effort to engage modernity. The encyclicals collected in this volume are essential reading for those Catholics who wish to continue this engagement in our own time. Though occasionally marred by an excessive emphasis on Thomistic scholasticism at the expense of earlier Catholic traditions, these texts make clear Leo's vision of "Christian philosophy": by emphasizing the fundamental continuity of natural and supernatural knowledge, Leo's work provides a powerful corrective to current social Modernists, of the left and right, who seek to carve out a purely "natural" space in social and intellectual life. These writings also make clear that Leo refused to settle for a simple modus vivendi with secular modernity; rather, he saw engagement as but a modern instance of the Church's perennial mission to bring Christ to the world and the world to Christ.
 —CHRISTOPHER SHANNON, Associate Professor of History, Christendom College

THE CHURCH SPEAKS
TO THE MODERN WORLD

The Church Speaks *to the* Modern World
The Social Teachings of Leo XIII

Edited, annotated, and with an Introduction
BY ETIENNE GILSON
*Member of the French Academy Director of Studies,
Pontifical Institute of Mediaeval Studies, Toronto*

Foreword by THOMAS STORCK

Originally published in 1954 as an Image Books edition.
Permission granted by
the Pontifical Institute of Medieval Studies
(Toronto) for this new edition.

Copyright © Arouca Press 2021
Foreword © Thomas Storck 2021

All rights reserved:
No part of this book may be reproduced or transmitted,
in any form or by any means, without permission

ISBN: 978-1-989905-85-2 (pbk)
ISBN: 978-1-989905-86-9 (hardcover)

Arouca Press
PO Box 55003
Bridgeport PO
Waterloo, ON N2J 3G0
Canada
www.aroucapress.com
Send inquiries to info@aroucapress.com

CONTENTS

FOREWORD xi
INTRODUCTION xvii

THE LEONINE CORPUS 1

I. On the Restoration of Christian Philosophy in Schools . . 3
   Aeterni Patris
   On Christian Philosophy: August 4, 1879. 6

II. Human Liberty 31
    Libertas Praestantissimum
    On Human Liberty: June 20, 1888. 34

III. On Christian Marriage 63
     Arcanum Divinae Sapientiae
     On Christian Marriage: February 10, 1880 66

IV. Freemasonry and Naturalism 93
    Humanum Genus
    On Freemasonry: April 20, 1884 97

V. On Civil Government 121
   Diuturnum
   On the Origin of Civil Power: June 29, 1881 123

VI. The Christian Constitution of States 139
    Immortale Dei
    On the Christian Constitution of States:
    November 1, 1885 144

VII. On Socialism 173
     Quod Apostolici Muneris
     On Socialism: December 28, 1878 175

VIII. Rights and Duties of Capital and Labor 187
      Rerum Novarum
      On Capital and Labor: May 15, 1891 193

IX. On Christian Citizenship 235
    Sapientiae Christianae
    On Christians as Citizens: January 10, 1890 239

APPENDIX 267
  I. On the Evils Affecting Modern Society. 269
     Inscrutabili Dei Consilio
     On the Evils of Society: April 21, 1878. 271
  II. On Slavery 283
     In Plurimis
     On the Abolition of Slavery: May 5, 1888 286
  III. Christian Democracy 307
     Graves De Communi Re
     On Christian Democracy: January 18, 1901 310

  CONCLUSION 327
  BIBLIOGRAPHICAL NOTE 331
  INDEX 335
  INDEX OF PROPER NAMES 341

FOREWORD

By Thomas Storck

THIS IS A VERY IMPORTANT BOOK, AND THE reason for that is twofold. On the one hand are its actual contents, Gilson's exposition of the thought of Leo XIII and, the actual text of Leo's encyclicals, and on the other is what the original publication of this work meant and could still mean for the Church's apostolate to the modern world. The book's significance is captured by its title, *The Church Speaks to the Modern World*—to the *modern* world, whatever that strange entity may be. For whatever modernity is, its baneful influence over human life and happiness is recognized by the most diverse groups of people, from ultra-traditional supporters of absolute monarchy to researchers of the Frankfurt School to postmodernist thinkers.

The book's title suggests that the Catholic Church has something of substance to say to this world, the world of modernity or the world of today. And what that is, is quite surprising. This volume was originally published in 1954, and its editor, Etienne Gilson, one hardly needs to say, was one of the most prominent Catholic philosophers and intellectuals of the twentieth century. Yet to his contemporaries, which included such figures as Bertrand Russell, Jean-Paul Sartre, and A. J. Ayer, what Gilson had to offer was "the doctrines of St. Thomas on the divine origin of all authority, on laws, and on all the other fundamental notions in political philosophy." And, Gilson continues, "Catholics should not hope to restore any Christian political and social order on any other foundation" than the philosophy of St. Thomas. He then speaks of what he calls the Fundamental Error, which is nothing other than "the refusal to recognize the existence of God, of a supernatural order, and of the duty we have to submit to it." Taking aim at those he terms naturalists or rationalists, Gilson proceeds on to say that:

Nature stands and falls with the recognition of its supernatural origin. The aim and purpose of these encyclicals are to refute the fundamental error of naturalism and to bring about the recognition of the rights of God through the recognition of the divine authority of His Church.

Speaking of the applications of Leo's principles to the political order, the French Thomist, in a section of his introduction entitled *The Modern Liberties*, summarizes Pope Leo's teaching on these liberties:

There can be no such right as that of thinking anything, of saying anything, of writing anything, of teaching anything, and of maintaining every conceivable position about every possible subject. The true meaning of the criticisms of these so-called "modern liberties" is not that there are no such liberties; rather, it is that these liberties consist in the firm resolve only to think, to say, and to write that which is true, and only to will that which is good according to the prescriptions of the natural law, of the human law, and of their common source, which is the divine law.

Because, Gilson explains, "it is absurd to maintain that error and truth, or evil and good, should have equal rights."

And finally, in what may be Gilson's boldest assertion, he writes that "when [the Church] acquiesces to certain situations in which the fullness of her rights are not recognized, the Church never gives up these rights; she simply waits for more favorable circumstances," and "in no case will she ever admit that Church and State should be kept separate."

Is this what the Catholic Church had to say to her contemporaries in the mid-1950s? No wonder, some might be thinking, that the Church long ago lost any hope of regaining her position as the soul and substance of Western culture. And there were many Catholics who would agree and did agree with this criticism. It was those Catholics who were responsible for the great alteration in the Church's stance vis-à-vis the modern world that took place during and after the Second Vatican Council.

This view, in effect a repudiation of Pope Leo's strategy, was spoken of in a perhaps surprising place, in Pope Benedict XVI's address to the Roman Curia on December 22, 2005. Speaking on the fortieth anniversary of the conclusion of the Second Vatican Council, Pope Benedict stated the following:

> In the great dispute about man which marks the modern epoch, the Council had to focus in particular on the theme of anthropology. It had to question the relationship between the Church and her faith on the one hand, and man and the contemporary world on the other. The question becomes even clearer if, instead of the generic term "contemporary world", we opt for another that is more precise: the Council had to determine in a new way the relationship between the Church and the modern era.

So only ten years after Gilson wrote his uncompromising reassertion of Leo XIII's teachings, it was now somehow necessary "to determine in a new way the relationship between the Church and the modern era." And this "new way" has played out in the subsequent life of the Church and her engagement with the world in the post-conciliar pontificates. It manifested itself for the most part, not so much in an explicit repudiation of Leo's program, but in a continuing series of confused or mixed messages, sometimes affirming doctrines or positions in words while at the same time appearing to deny or repudiate them in practices or symbolic actions. The intentions behind all this would seem to have been good, to update the presentation of the Church's faith, to engage with modernity more effectively, to clear away what was seen as the accumulated accretions from the past. But whether this has been a success or not—I leave that to the judgment of my readers.

But let us return to our original point, the widespread dissatisfaction with modernity. Whence does that arise? While harsh criticisms of the contemporary world have been the staple of moralists for millennia, it seems that a diagnosis of something fundamentally wrong with the social order is relatively new. How did this come about?

The Church Speaks to the Modern World

In the early 1970s, the American philosopher Henry Veatch attempted to call attention to a little-noticed fact: that many of the criticisms then being made of modernity and all its works actually found their best theoretical justification in a surprising source, the ancient Greek philosopher, Aristotle.

> For is it not a singular coincidence that in the confusion worse confounded of what we might call our contemporary youth culture, any number of young people today have begun to insist that they are "turned off" by the entire range of modern science and technology? Not only that, but they would not hesitate to throw out, along with science, the whole philosophical and cultural superstructure that has been erected over our increasingly frenzied and uncritical cults of science and technology as they have been developing over the last three hundred years. Now the irony is that the very rise of so-called modern science and modern philosophy was originally associated—certainly in the minds of men like Galileo and Descartes—with a determined repudiation of Aristotle: it was precisely his influence which it was thought necessary to destroy, root and branch, before what we now know as science and philosophy in the modern mode could get off the ground. Accordingly, could it be that as so many of us today are turning our backs so bitterly on all the heretofore boasted achievements of modern culture, we might find ourselves inclined, perhaps even compelled, to return to the Aristotelianism that both antedated and was considered antithetical to the whole modern experiment in knowledge and living?[1]

And here, of course, we encounter again Etienne Gilson, Pope Leo XIII, and above all, St. Thomas Aquinas himself. This is because St. Thomas was committed in fundamental respects to Aristotle's understanding of society and reality. So if so much of the modern world is disillusioned "by the entire range of modern science and technology," by the whole modern project, in

---

1 Henry Veatch, *Aristotle, a Contemporary Appreciation* (Bloomington: Indiana University, c. 1974), p. 4.

fact, then are not Leo XIII's and Etienne Gilson's prescriptions something to be taken seriously?

One might think that even those who are uneasy with the modernity that presses upon us might nevertheless hesitate to embrace the Pope's proposals for what to do about it. And so it might be for many. But if we were to begin by acknowledging where things began to go seriously wrong historically, is it possible that we would be led, step by step, but inexorably, to the very stipulations that Leo XIII put forward? If, for example, the atomistic conception of social relations that has dominated the West since the eighteenth century is questioned or rejected, then those questioning or rejecting it might find something very attractive in Catholic doctrine and tradition, even if it is first necessary to clear away some unfamiliar expressions of thought as well as jettison some very old prejudices.

Of course, it is the case that since Professor Veatch wrote those words things have changed quite a bit, and are changing still and apparently at an ever-faster rate. So it might not be the case that the fundamental unease with modernity has the same contours as it did in the 1960s or 70s. But does this really matter to the Church's intellectual apostolate? Is it not the case that a confident presentation of her own teachings and traditions is always a *sine qua non* for any effective impact on the world? Catholic doctrine is always the same and so is human nature. Certainly, during the nearly one hundred years that something like the Leonine project guided the policies of the Church, Catholicism did seem to be making an impact upon the contemporary world. Surprisingly enough, it did appear that the cultural trajectory of nineteenth-century secularism was not as sure of itself as it had been. The confident presentation by the Church of her teachings resulted in the conversions of many prominent thinkers and writers, Catholic thought was taken into account and recognized as a legitimate, even if peculiar manifestation on the contemporary intellectual scene. But when we came to believe that we "had to determine in a new way the relationship between the Church and the modern era," this whole endeavor faltered, and, finally, we have arrived at the point where the Church and Catholic thought are pretty much consigned to irrelevancy. For if we have something distinctive to say to the modern world, then why are we not saying it? And if it turns out that all we have to say is what everyone else is saying, then one can get all that much more conveniently elsewhere.

For the specifics of Pope Leo's teaching, I invite the reader to turn to Gilson's Introduction, and then to the text of the papal documents themselves. Here ponder the Church's perennial wisdom, restated to be sure for contemporaries, but in no respect downplaying or leaving out anything essential. For this was the key to the successful Leonine revival, a revival that continued down to the time of the Second Vatican Council: to yield on non-essentials (such as the previous and sometimes unhealthy link between the Church and monarchical government), but never to cease to proclaim what is essential, the whole counsel of God, the entire deposit of faith and tradition committed to and handed down by the Church. This Leo preached in season and out of season, and this Gilson presented in an equally uncompromising manner for his readers. But readers, Catholic and non-Catholic both, might find a refreshing voice here, an unusual message that, if considered with an open mind, can begin to point the way out of the modern morass that right now we are all condemned to dwell within.

INTRODUCTION

I. LIFE OF POPE LEO XIII

Vincent Joachim Pecci was born on March 2, 1810, at Carpineto in the province of Sabina, then part of the Papal States. After studying grammar and humanities at the Jesuit College of Viterbo from 1818 to 1823, he was sent in 1824 to the Collegio Romano, where he completed the humanities and studied natural sciences and philosophy. It is noteworthy that, when chosen to deliver a Latin address at the end of his rhetoric course, young Pecci spoke on "The contrast between pagan and Christian Rome." He was to deal again with this same subject in several of his encyclical letters, especially in *Inscrutabili* (arts. 9–10), where the contributions of the papacy to the welfare and development of Italy are forcefully stressed. After obtaining his doctorate in theology in 1832, he entered the Academy of Noble Ecclesiastics, studied canon law at the Sapienza, and was made a domestic prelate by Pope Gregory XVI on March 16, 1837. He was ordained a priest on December 31 of that year, at the age of twenty-seven.

In 1838, Msgr. Pecci was appointed governor of the pontifical city of Benevento, in the territory of the Kingdom of Naples. When, as Pope Leo XIII, he was to speak of the distinction between the temporal power and the spiritual power, he could do so with full awareness of the political realities at stake. He served as head of police in an area where law and order were at their lowest; he completely reorganized the existing system of taxes; and he carried on diplomatic negotiations with Naples. By the time he became Pope he had, from direct personal experience, acquired wisdom as to political problems and as to the specific nature of temporal authority. When he wrote, the word *State* was to have just as concrete a meaning as the word *Church*.

On July 17, 1841, Msgr. Pecci was entrusted with the still more difficult functions of governor of Perugia, a city where anti-papal feeling was running high. Here again, personal experience was to precede speculation and comment by many years. In January

1843, he was appointed papal nuncio to Brussels. A month later, he was consecrated Archbishop of Damiata, a title he retained when he was consecrated Bishop of Perugia, where he remained for thirty-one years (1846–77).

This was a particularly eventful period in his life. Created a cardinal on December 9, 1853, he was to serve at Perugia with an outlook that often foreshadowed the attitude he was to have as Pope. Among his most remarkable achievements were the founding of an Academy of St. Thomas Aquinas in 1872 and the creation of a group of diocesan missionaries there years later.

Historically, too, these were decisive years. In February 1860, Perugia was separated from the Papal States and annexed to Piedmont. The introduction of new laws by the conquerors gave Cardinal Pecci many occasions to reaffirm the rights of the Church against the encroachments of the temporal power. Particularly to be noted is the influence exercised upon him by the person, attitude, and doctrine of Pope Pius IX, who had succeeded Pope Gregory XVI in 1846.

Pope Pius IX had begun his reign by proclaiming a general amnesty for all political prisoners, by appointing many laymen to high functions in his government, and by introducing many political and administrative reforms. The result was a revolution that obliged him to flee from Rome in November 1848. After his return, on April 12, 1850, he devoted himself for the next twenty years to the task of rebuilding the entire administration of the Papal States. During this period, Cardinal Pecci was a witness to the unyielding stand of Pope Pius IX in refusing to bow to violence and to surrender the rights of the Church. The Vatican Council, which proclaimed the dogma of the infallibility of the Pope in 1869, the publication of the epoch-making encyclical *Quanta Cura* (December 8, 1864), followed by the preparation of the *Syllabus,* or summary list of the main modern errors condemned by the Pope, were to remain as landmarks in the mind of his successor.

After the death of Pius IX on February 7, 1878, Cardinal Pecci was elected Pope thirteen days later, taking the name Leo

XIII. Therewith began one of the longest pontifical reigns in the history of the Church. This is not the place to tell the history of Leo's pontificate. However, we beg to recall that, in dealing with France, he devoted his most constant efforts to persuade the French Catholic leaders of the time that the Republic was a political regime compatible with the loyalty of its citizens toward the Church. This fact should be kept in mind by those among his readers who might be mistaken about the absolute sincerity of his intentions. There is no distinction between Pope Leo XIII as a sovereign and as a supreme teacher of the universal Church. His constant concern was to establish diplomatic relations with all the temporal powers and to re-establish them as soon as possible whenever they were broken. His interest in the United States was always deep and genuine. To refer only to written documents, let us cite his apostolic letter *Longinqua Oceani* (January 6, 1895), to the bishops of the United States and the letter *Testem Benevolentiae,* to James Cardinal Gibbons, Archbishop of Baltimore, on Americanism (January 22, 1899). These afford ample proof of his vigilant care for the future of the Catholic Church in the United States.

Pope Leo XIII died on July 20, 1903, at the age of ninety-three and after a reign of twenty-five years.

II. THE ENCYCLICAL LETTERS

What is an encyclical letter, or, as it is more simply called an encyclical? It is a pastoral letter similar to those which bishops frequently address to the Catholics of their dioceses, but of greater scope. Since the Pope is Bishop of Rome and the successor of St. Peter, he can address some of his pastoral letters to all the Christians now living in all the countries of the earth. As often as not, the Pope will address all men without any distinction of race, language, or even religion.

The primary object of an encyclical is not to define the dogma, that is, the faith, of the Catholic Church. To do so is the proper object of what is technically called the "extraordinary magisterial teaching of the Church." This "extraordinary" teaching enjoys, in each and every one of its parts, without any reservation, the grace of infallibility. This grace belongs to the so-called "ecumenical councils," that is, to councils representing the whole Christian world and, consequently, the preaching of the whole Catholic Church; but, following a decision of the Vatican Council (Session IV, Const. *Pastor Aeternus*), the same grace of infallibility also belongs to the pronouncements of the Pope when, speaking in his capacity as pastor and teacher of all Christians, and by virtue of his supreme apostolic authority, he declares that a certain doctrine concerning faith or moral conduct should be held as true by the whole Church. Such infallible pronouncements, therefore, are final and irreformable by themselves, and not by virtue of the consent of the Church.

The proper object of the "ordinary" teaching of the Church, as given by bishops to their own diocesans and by the Bishop of Rome, that is, the Pope, to all the faithful, is to diffuse this infallible teaching of the Church, to defend it if necessary, and to apply it to some particularly important problems of the day as they arise in social and political life. The encyclical letters are the usual means by which the Popes exercise this definite teaching function. These letters are the highest expression of the ordinary teaching of the Church. To the extent that they restate the infallible teachings of the Church, the pronouncements of the encyclical letters are themselves infallible. Moreover, while explaining and developing such infallible teachings, or while using them as a sure criterion in the condemnation of errors, or even while striving to solve the social, economic, and political problems of the day in the light of these infallible teachings, the Popes enjoy the special assistance of the Holy Spirit, a higher guidance in which the supernatural gift of prudence plays a decisive part.

This is to say, the teachings of the Popes, as found in their encyclical letters, can by no means be considered as expressing mere opinions, which anyone is free to hold or to reject at will. Even though they may not be binding as to faith in all their parts, the teachings of an encyclical are all directly related to

Introduction

faith by the supreme teaching authority of the Church with the special assistance of the Holy Spirit. There always is grave temerity in not accepting the teaching of an encyclical on any one of the points it touches. Pope Pius XII has made clear in his encyclical *Humani Generis* that when some point hitherto under discussion among theologians is expressly settled by the Pope in such a document, everyone should understand that, in the mind and will of the Pontiff, the point at stake should no longer be considered as freely debatable among theologians.

Among the encyclical letters of the Popes, none is more remarkable than those of Leo XIII, especially with reference to the teaching of the Church on social, economic, and political questions. The choice made among them by Leo himself, and which we are here following, finds its justification in the desire to stress that part of the papal teaching which directly concerned the restoration of the social order in the light of the doctrine, and under the guidance, of the Catholic Church. The unity of inspiration of these encyclicals is visible. Although they cannot be said to form a "system," they exhibit the organic unity proper to living bodies as well as to living truth. There is hardly a single one whose general conclusions are not amply confirmed by the teaching of the others, and statements of decisive importance on a certain subject are frequently found in an encyclical primarily concerned with another topic. Such consistency testifies to the important truth that the doctrine of all the encyclicals is fundamentally the same since it consists in solving many different problems in the light of the same principles.

Any attempt to reduce the contents of these encyclicals into a linear system would, therefore, betray their intention, but the following considerations will perhaps help some readers to perceive the deep unity of inspiration that binds together these outstanding documents. Once this unity has been perceived, the reader can but meditate upon their teaching and keep an open mind for the light they shed upon so many problems. He who is firmly resolved never to sin against the light is well ahead on the way to truth.

III. THE MAIN THEMES OF THE DOCTRINE

1. *Christian Philosophy.* In his letter to the prefect of the Sacred Congregation of Studies, dated October 15, 1879, Pope Leo XIII declared that speaking from reflection and from experience, he could see no safer way to end war waged against both the Church and society itself, than "everywhere to restore, by the teaching of philosophy, the right principles of thought and action" (*A. A. S.*, 12, 225). The same letter sought to implement the encyclical *Aeterni Patris* by prescribing that the teaching of the traditional philosophy of the Church should be restored in all schools, especially the doctrine of St. Thomas Aquinas. This means that Leo XIII considered a sound philosophical education the necessary basis for a future restoration of the social order. To consider the teaching of philosophy as a mere intellectual luxury, or as an unpractical method to reform modern societies, would therefore be a complete misinterpretation of his doctrine.

Encyclicals are designated by their first Latin words, not by a title as such; nevertheless, Pope Leo XIII himself has called *Aeterni Patris*: "Our encyclical letter on the restoring in Christian schools of Christian philosophy according to the mind of the angelic doctor St. Thomas Aquinas" (*A. A. S.*, 13, 56). What is "Christian Philosophy"? It is the kind of philosophy or, rather, the philosophical method recommended by the encyclical *Aeterni Patris* as the best way to philosophize there is. It consists of uniting the study of philosophy with a Christian's docility to the teachings of divine revelation. Far from enslaving reason, this "bond of friendship" between reason and faith is for them both a source of many benefits (*A. A. S.*, 13, 57–58).

There will probably be, in the minds of many readers, a tendency to consider this document as only indirectly related to the social and political teaching of Leo XIII. Nothing could be less true. Far from being an unpractical supplement to the doctrine, the teaching of the Christian philosophy of the Scholastics, especially that of St. Thomas Aquinas, is considered by the Pope a necessary prerequisite to any practical scheme in view of restoring the social order.

Introduction

The encyclical *Aeterni Patris* makes this point perfectly clear, especially in arts. 26-29, where the doctrines of St. Thomas on the divine origin of all authority, on laws, and on all the other fundamental notions in political philosophy are said to be, after the grace of God, the best means there are to introduce modern minds to a proper understanding and appreciation of Catholic institutions. "Domestic and civil society even, which, as all see, is exposed to great danger from the plague of perverse opinions, would certainly enjoy a far more peaceful and secure existence if a more wholesome doctrine were taught in the universities and colleges—one more in conformity with the teaching of the Church, such as is contained in the works of Thomas Aquinas." As early as his first encyclical, *Inscrutabili* (April 21, 1878), Leo XIII had expressly declared that "the cause of civilization lacks a solid foundation if it does not rest on the eternal principles of truth and on the unchangeable laws of right and justice." To attempt a political and social reformation without having first ascertained its doctrinal foundations, such as are found in the Christian philosophy of St. Thomas, would therefore be tantamount to erecting a baseless structure. Catholics should not hope to restore any Christian political and social order on any other foundation.

2. *The Fundamental Error.* Practically all the positions rejected by Pope Leo XIII are so many varieties of one and the same error, namely, the refusal to recognize the existence of God, of a supernatural order, and of the duty we have to submit to it. This error is designated by different names according to its different manifestations.

In the field of speculative philosophy, its name is either "naturalism" or "rationalism." The naturalist only recognizes the existence of nature, of natural laws, and of a natural order completely self-sufficient in itself apart from any supernatural cause, such as God. The rationalists apply the same principle to the order of human knowledge. They only recognize as valid such knowledge as can be gathered by the natural reason of man, independent of any supernatural revelation. It is manifest that rationalism is nothing more than naturalism applied to the particular case of natural knowledge, just as naturalism is a direct application of rationalism to the interpretation of nature.

In the fields of practical philosophy, ethics, and politics, the same error is called "liberalism." Taken in the sense which it has in the encyclicals of Leo XIII, this term points out the attitude of those men who refuse to submit their wills to any law prescribed by a higher authority than their own, and, quite especially, by the authority of God. Reduced to its very essence, liberalism is the rejection of any divine and supernatural law. As will be seen, this rejection of the divine law entails the rejection of the natural law.

Those who maintain the self-sufficiency of the natural order (naturalists) end in denying its existence. Nature stands and falls with recognition of its supernatural origin. The aim and purpose of these encyclicals are to refute the fundamental error of naturalism and to bring about the recognition of the rights of God through the recognition of the divine authority of His Church.

3. *The Fundamental Truth.* The teaching of Pope Leo XIII rests upon a certain notion which it inculcates in many ways, but which may sometimes be overlooked because of its very simplicity.

No distinction is more familiar to Christian minds than that of nature and grace. For instance, man is in himself a nature determined by its own definition; nevertheless, if God deems it fit, He can add to this nature any perfection He chooses, provided only that this perfection be not contradictory to human nature. For, instance, since man is endowed with an intellect which, by its own nature, is capable of knowing all that is intelligible, there is no contradiction in admitting that God can elevate man to the beatific vision. There would be a contradiction, however, in saying that a finite intellect, such as that of man, can attain this beatific vision of an infinite being in a *natural* way. For man to attain this end requires a grace super-added to his nature and, consequently, such graces are rightly said to be "supernatural."

Introduction

A less commonly remembered character of the works of God is related to the notion of creation, which is a fundamental one in Christian philosophy. Irrespective of any supernatural grace, created nature necessarily bears the mark of its divine origin. When God created the world, He Himself saw, and said, that His works were "very good" (Gen. 1:31). They were such because they had been created in accordance with the infinitely perfect intellect and will of God. A general consequence of this is that what we call the law of nature is just a particular expression of the divine law.

This fundamental truth is of great importance for a correct understanding of the teaching of Leo XIII. In a divinely *created* universe, nature itself bears the marks of its divine origin because it owes to God both to be and to be that which it is. Consequently, any violation of the law of nature is, by the same token, a violation of the law of God. Conversely, such violations of the divine law are, at the same time, so many violations of the law of nature that threaten it with destruction.

The fact that the Church upholds the rights of created nature (because it is the work of God) justifies the repeated statements of Pope Leo XIII that, if they only knew their true interests, the temporal rulers would realize that the Church is their safest and most sincere ally. This point, however, requires some elucidation.

From the point of view of social and political problems, one of the most striking characters of created nature is the fact that natural beings are unequal in perfection and, consequently, distributed according to a hierarchical order of dignity, of power, and, therefore, of authority. Expressed in terms both simpler and less palatable to the modern mind, this means that one of the most fundamental laws of nature is inequality. Stones are less perfect than plants, plants are less perfect than brutes, brutes are less perfect than man, who exists as the stones, lives as the plants, feels as the brutes, and, moreover, exercises intellectual knowledge owing to his intellect. Even within the human species itself, individuals are unequal both physically and intellectually. These inequalities in perfection entail, as their necessary consequences, other inequalities in power and in authority. Since this is the way the world has been created by God, it is how it should be, and any attempt on the part of man to subvert the natural order of the created universe can only result in catastrophes. It is one of the most constant teachings of Pope Leo XIII that to deny the natural laws, which govern societies is to court disaster. The ceaseless revolutions which threaten modern societies are a clear sign of the peril there is in overlooking the natural order created by God.

The same truth could be expressed differently in saying that overlooking the sacred character of the law of nature is one of the main sources of the evils that threaten modern societies. A striking illustration of this doctrine is found in the first encyclical of Leo XIII, *Quod Apostolici Muneres* (December 28, 1878). Speaking of the domestic authority of husbands over wives, of parents over children, or of masters over servants, the Pope says that it not only takes its origin and force from God but also derives from Him "its nature and character" (*"sed etiam naturam et indolem"*) A. A. S., II, 374). The very authority of the Heavenly Father and Lord of all "flows in the parents and in the masters"; how, then, could it lose a character which it holds from its divine origin? All the modern slogans proclaiming the natural, social, and political equality of all men are irrelevant to the problem. God could have created nature other than it is, but the only question is: Are men naturally equal or not? If they are not, then all the inequalities in wealth, in economic power, and in political power necessarily follow from the natural inequalities first created by God and willed by Him. To rebel against the order of nature is not a way to change it. To deny that things are such as they are is not likely to modify their natures. Were he with us still today, Pope Leo XIII would probably observe that the political regime which has made the strongest bid for the suppression of all social classes, for absolute equality in all domains, and, finally, for the restoration of a society free from all political rulers has brought about the worst social, economic, and political tyranny which the modern world

Introduction

has ever known. The consequences of this point concerning the political authority of the rulers are so important that they deserve special consideration.

4. *Political Authority.* One of the most important among the natural relations created by God between human beings is that which obtains, in political societies, between the rulers and the ruled. We call it a natural relation because it naturally follows from the natural inequalities between men. To the extent that it has been willed by God, and inscribed by Him in the very nature of created beings, political authority is entitled to respect due to its divine origin. Pope Leo XIII has always stressed this point as the safest protection against the perils which, under the form of political crimes and political revolutions, threaten modern societies.

Because, in his own times, most European societies were still monarchies, the doctrine of Leo XIII is often designated as that of "the divine right of kings." For the same reason, that is, because most revolutions were then being carried in the name of democratic ideals, his doctrine has often been interpreted as an attack against the democratic conception of a political society. In point of fact, the teaching of Pope Leo XIII deals with political authority in general. The ultimate meaning of his message on this point is that all established and recognized authority, *whatever its form,* is divine in both origin and character. The political power and authority of a regularly elected president, for the duration of his office, are no less sacred powers, than the power and authority of any king.

The difficulties concerning this point spring from a confusion between two problems that should be kept distinct: the problem of the mode of designation of the sovereign and the problem of the origin of the power and authority exercised by the sovereign. The constant position of Pope Leo XIII is that, whatever his mode of designation, the power of the sovereign flows in him from God. The ruler may be a hereditary king, a self-made emperor, or an elected president; in no case does his mode of designation confer upon him any political authority.

This is eminently clear in the case of hereditary monarchies; to be the heir-apparent to a throne, which is a purely biological relationship, cannot possibly confer upon any human being the right, authority, and power to rule other human beings. The two orders of facts are obviously unrelated. The famous doctrine of the "divine right of kings" simply means that hereditary monarchs do not hold their authority from their ancestors, nor from themselves, but from God.

Despite contrary appearances, the same conclusion applies to the presidents of the various political societies which, whatever their constitutions, bear in common the title of "republics." The president of a republic no more holds his power and authority from his electors than a king holds his power from his ancestors. True enough, presidential elections do make presidents, in this sense, at least, that they determine who is going to be the next president, but they do not give him a political power which his electors themselves do not have. Just as, in hereditary monarchies, the order of succession to the throne points out the future king, so also, in countries where free elections are still possible, the counting of the votes points out the future deputy, the future senator, or the next president of the republic. In the first case, God gives authority to the heir-apparent to the throne; in the second case, God gives authority to the president-elect; in both cases, and exactly in the same sense, authority flows in the ruler from God.

The true meaning of this doctrine is often misunderstood. One of its first characteristics is the intention it betrays to justify the otherwise unjustifiable pretention of certain men to subject other men to their own personal power and authority. Each and every man is endowed with a free will of his own, and no other man, or group of men, has any right to deprive any free will of its freedom and independence. Whatever its particular form, so long as it considers itself a merely human one, no mode of designating the ruler has any right to bend a person's will. In Leo XIII's own words: "No man has in himself or of himself the power of constraining the free will of others by fetters of authority of this kind. This power resides solely in God, the Creator and Legislator of all things; and it is necessary that those who exercise it should do so as having received it from God" (*Diuturnum*, 11; June 29, 1881). Leaving aside, for the present, the duties which it imposes upon rulers, we should understand this doctrine as ultimately resting upon the unconditional assertion of the personal freedom of human wills. No man, only God, has a right to claim obedience from free human wills.

Another way of misunderstanding this doctrine is to interpret it as an attack leveled at democracies on behalf of all forms of authoritarian regimes. Nothing could be less true. Catholic citizens living in democratic countries or, at least, under democratic constitutions, are not only permitted to exercise their political rights but have a duty to do so. The reason why Pope Leo XIII stresses the fact that, even in a democracy, the people are not the source of political authority, is not that he wants to condemn the democratic mode of designation of political rulers. His intention is to denounce the well-known sophism according to which, since the electoral vote *gives authority* to the elected candidate, the same men who have given him political power can take it away from him. And, indeed, if the body politic were the ultimate source of political authority, it would be as free to take it away as to give it. This apparently logical conclusion is, nevertheless, a sophism, because it rests upon the false supposition that the procedure followed to designate the future ruler is, at the same time, the source of his political authority, whereas, on the contrary, whatever the political constitution of a state, authority flows in it from God (*Praeclara Gratulationes*, June 20, 1896).

This is no inference from the words used by Pope Leo XIII. The point has been stated by him in terms so clear that their meaning cannot be misinterpreted. In his encyclical *Diuturnum*, after recalling the fact that the Church has nothing at all against the designation of rulers by way of elections, the Pope added this short but decisive commentary: "And by this choice, in truth, the ruler is *designated, but the rights of ruling are not thereby conferred.* Nor is the authority delegated to him, but the person by whom it is to be exercised is determined upon." Following the constant teaching of the Old Testament, Leo XIII maintains that, since all power comes from God, no human beings or human institutions have any power to give or even to delegate. The New Testament and the Fathers of the Church have taught the same doctrine, whose perfect expression is found in St. Paul's Epistle to the Romans (13:1–2): "Let every soul be subject to higher powers; for there is no power but from God; and those that are, are ordained from God."

The main intention of the encyclicals in teaching this doctrine is to ensure the stability of political authority under all its forms and whatever its mode of designation. That political and social revolutions are evils seldom compensated by whatever good results they may happen to achieve, is a firm conviction of the popes. Nor is this a merely sentimental conviction; it rests upon the principle that the ways of nature are better than those of violence, which is the very negation of natural ways and tendencies. At any rate, the doctrine according to which the people has no authority either to give or to delegate entails this consequence, that the people has no right to unmake rulers whom it has no power to make, or, in other terms, that the electoral body has no justification for taking away from the elected ruler a political power, which it did not give to him on election day. The opposition of the Popes to the doctrine of the "social contract," or covenant, upheld by Jean-Jacques Rousseau, is not directed against any type of democratic constitution; it simply opposes Rousseau's view that the members of the body politic can create political power and, consequently, delegate it or withdraw it at will. God alone, who gives to rulers their authority, can take it away from them before the appointed end of their lives or of their constitutional tenures. Naturally, since they hold their authority from God, rulers should not be obeyed when their orders are contrary to the law of nature and to the divine law. But its refusal of obedience, of which the Christian martyrs gave so many high examples, is very different from any attempt to overthrow by force the established political powers. It is lawful to seek to substitute a better political regime for a bad one, yet the favorite remedy against the abuses of tyranny taught by Leo XIII is the Christian virtue of patience. Here again, the source of the doctrine is to be found in the same text of St. Paul: "Therefore he that resisteth the power, resisteth the ordinance of God. And they that resist, purchase to themselves damnation." Such was the teaching of the Apostle to the Christians at a time when they were subject to the authority of pagan emperors. Read in the light of what is the present plight of several Christian countries, this doctrine is, indeed, "lofty and full of gravity."

This attitude is hard to understand for men who advocate to recourse to violence against injustice, oppression, and tyranny. Two points, however, should be kept in mind with respect to this problem. In condemning the use of violence, Pope Leo XIII has not forbidden subjects to seek peaceful means of obtaining justice from their rulers. Timely reforms are the best safeguards against revolutions. On the contrary, Leo has not a single good word for revolution as an answer to political problems. His doctrine on this point is best understood in the light of his own apostolic letter *Praeclara Gratulationis* (June 20, 1896). Dealing with the problem of slavery, Leo explains there for what reasons, in spite of the fact that she has always condemned slavery and fought against it, the Church has never invited slaves to rebellion. There is nothing to prove that such rebellion would have hastened the disappearance of slavery as an officially recognized institution, but it is a well-known fact that slaves themselves have always paid a heavy price when they resorted to violence in order to achieve their long-hoped-for liberation.

5. *The Modern Liberties.* One of the parts of the doctrine which are most likely to be misunderstood is the notion of liberty developed by Leo XIII in complete agreement with the Christian philosophy of St. Thomas Aquinas. The sore spot, in the minds of many readers accustomed to a different intellectual climate, will be the criticism of the so-called "modern liberties" deduced from this notion by the sovereign Pontiff.

These are the liberties of thought, of speech, of writing, of teaching, and generally speaking, the so-called "liberty of conscience." After distinguishing between the natural liberty of free choice, which belongs to man *qua* knowing being, and the moral liberty, which consists in the power to will the true good known by our reason, Pope Leo XIII establishes that moral liberty presupposes the existence of laws and their recognition by the human will. Since all these laws are finally reducible to the divine law, which prescribes good and forbids evil, the true liberty of man ultimately consists in obeying the divine law (*Libertas Praestantissimum*, 11–12).

On the strength of this conclusion, it would be contradictory to admit that the notion of liberty is complete in itself, independent of that law. There can be no such right as that of thinking anything, of saying anything, of writing anything, of teaching anything, and of maintaining every conceivable position about every possible subject. The true meaning of the criticism of these so-called "modern liberties" is not that there are no such liberties; rather, it is that these liberties consist in the firm resolve only to think, to say, and to write that which is true, and only to will that which is good according to the prescriptions of the natural law, of the human law, and of their common source, which is the divine law. This doctrine is developed in the same encyclical (art. 22–25).

The notion of tolerance raises similar problems and calls for a similar interpretation. There often are reasons to tolerate certain things because, although they may not be good, their suppression would entail still worse consequences. The only reason there is to tolerate evil is the care of the common good. Pope Leo XIII does not deny that there is room for tolerance in the political and social life of the nations. On the contrary, he himself repeatedly calls to our attention the fact that the Church herself often acquiesces to situations of fact, of which she may well disapprove, but which could not be reformed without still more harmful consequences. What is to be condemned is the tolerance born of a complete indifference to the true and

Introduction

the good. Rightful tolerance only tolerates evil, recognized and denounced as such, in view of the common good.

This is so true that, even when she acquiesces to certain situations in which the fullness of her rights are not recognized, the Church never gives up these rights; she simply waits for more favorable circumstances and always hopes that a time will come when the State will do justice to the fullness of her claims. Nothing could be more clear than the statement made on this point by Leo XIII in *Libertas Praestantissimum:* "And although in the extraordinary condition of these times the Church usually acquiesces in certain modern liberties, not because she prefers them in themselves, but because she judges it expedient to permit them, she would in happier times exercise her own liberty; and by persuasion, exhortation, and entreaty, would endeavor, as she is bound, to fulfill the duty assigned to her by God of providing for the eternal salvation of mankind." This is entirely different from granting to all the liberty to do all things, for it is absurd to maintain that error and truth, or evil and good, should have equal rights.

Two outstanding instances of this tolerance are the relations of Church and State and the right of the Church to teach. It may be that, under certain circumstances, such as the exceptional good will of the political powers, the Church deems it preferable to acquiesce to a factual separation of Church and State, but in no case will she ever admit the Church and State should be kept separate. Their separation remains an evil even while, for reasons of expediency, it is being tolerated. The same remark applies to the school problem. The Church is a society to which God has entrusted certain truths necessary for the salvation of man. The Church will never cease to claim the right to teach what it is her duty to teach. There may be "neutral" schools, non-confessional institutions entrusted by the State with the task of educating the youth outside of all religious tradition, particularly that of the Catholic Church. It may be wiser to accept the fact as a lesser evil, so long, at least, as the so-called religious neutrality of such schools is not a front concealing an anti-religious activity. What the Church cannot possibly do is to declare satisfactory a school regime based upon the principle that anybody should be free to teach what it pleases him to call truth, even though it may be error.

This teaching of Leo XIII, that there can be no such thing as unconditional liberty, not even in the teaching of schools, is likely to sound scandalous to two kinds of men: those who are firmly resolved to exclude the Church from all teaching institutions, and those who favor some dictatorial regime in which one and the same State-controlled doctrine is taught in all schools. Before rejecting this position as incompatible with the moral ideal of modern times, it would be simply honest to ask the question: In what country are the schools permitted to teach absolutely all that which their masters may be pleased to teach? Indeed, this is the whole question. Liberty is wholly unconditional or it is not unconditional at all.

6. *Extension of the Problem.* Countless applications of this general doctrine will be found in the encyclicals of Pope Leo XIII. Among these applications, the more important ones concern the natures of marriage, social power, and the right to property.

The case of domestic society and of marriage closely resembles that of political society. Marriage is rightly called a bond because it binds together husband and wife, thus establishing the domestic society made up of one man and one woman together with the children to be born of this union. Strictly speaking, there is nothing in the nature of any human being, considered in itself, to justify such an exclusive privilege as the one which husbands claim to enjoy with respect to their wives, or vice versa. Why should a man be thus bound to only one woman or a woman to only one man, and why should such bonds be considered indestructible? Because many of our contemporaries resent this kind of servitude, they argue that marriage is freely revoked. Hence, the widespread conviction that divorce followed by remarriage is permissible. In countries where these views are sanctioned by law, marriage becomes a mere civil contract and, as all know it, a simple administrative formality.

Introduction

The teaching of Pope Leo XIII is openly directed against these positions, but his reason for attacking them as false remains the same as it was in the case of the authority of rulers. It is true that marriage is a freely contracted mutual obligation. Men are free to choose their wives, and vice versa, just as nations are free to choose their rulers; but, after making this free choice, married people have no more the right to revoke it than nations have the right to take the law in their own hands. And, in both cases, the reason is the same: What is at stake is a *divine* institution.

After relating the creation of man by God, Holy Scripture adds: "male and female He created them" (Gen. 1:27). The first couple thus created by God was composed of only one man and only one woman. However it may have degenerated in later times, the domestic society should remain such as it was first created by God. Domestic society is older than political society, and because there has been marriage at a time when there was not yet any State, it is irrational to conceive marriage as a social institution controlled by the State. Because marriage has been created by God both monogamous and irrevocable, it is an error to consider it as revocable at the will of individuals; and because God Himself has created it, no state has anything to do with marriages. The very notion of "civil marriage" is a contradiction in terms.

This essentially religious nature of marriage has become visible to all since Jesus Christ raised it to the dignity of a Christian sacrament, but even before the coming of Christ, and, in fact, ever since the creation of man, marriage has enjoyed the dignity of a divine institution. In a remarkable text of the encyclical *Arcanum* (February 10, 1880), Pope Leo XIII stressed this point in terms so forceful that they seem to have frightened some of their translators: "marriage has God for its author, and was from the very beginning a kind of foreshadowing of the Incarnation of His Son, and; therefore there abides in it a something *holy and religious;* not extraneous but innate; not derived from men but implanted by nature. Innocent III, therefore, and Honorius III, Our predecessors, affirmed not falsely nor rashly that 'the sacrament of marriage exists amongst both the believers and the unbelievers' [*apud fideles at infidels existere sacramentum conjugii*], that is, amongst Christians and Pagans alike. In short, 'marriage is holy by its very essence [*sua vi*], in its very nature [*sua natura*] and of itself' [*sua sponte*]." It would be difficult to find stronger expressions of the religious and holy character of a nature created by the Christian God.

The same principles apply to the widely debated problem of economic inequality. The unqualified defence of the right of property finds its justification in the *natural* character of the inequal distribution of wealth in a social order whose members themselves are not equal in physical, intellectual, and moral capacities. Since these inequalities are facts of nature such as God has created it, their suppression would imply the suppression of nature itself and, together with it, of man.

These social inequalities follow from many causes. The inequal repartition of wealth is a necessary consequence of purely natural inequalities between human beings. Wealth is power, but so also are physical and mental health, beauty, physical and moral courage, outstanding intellectual abilities, and, in short, all the natural gifts whose unequal repartition is the prime cause of all social inequalities. Even luck, whose importance cannot be denied, only helps those men who are equipped by nature to make good use of it. This perfectly objective view of reality excludes the candid dream of a society of equal citizens composed of naturally inequal beings.

The famous encyclical *Rerum Novarum* can be considered the best effort of Pope Leo XIII to indicate to the Catholics of the world the absolute necessity there is for men to take into account human nature such as it actually is before undertaking any reformation of the social and political order. Faithful to his principle that inequality is a fact of nature and that natural inequality necessarily begets social inequality. Leo XIII inculcates in all possible ways to the rulers of the various nations of the world, *whatever the political regime of their countries may possibly happen to be,* that the only wise governance does not consist in dealing with men and classes as though they were equal, but in devoting to all of them equal care in spite of their factual inequality. The wisdom of this golden rule may not be immediately evident, but it will become more and more clear as the reader becomes more familiar with the teaching of Pope Leo XIII, that is, with principles of the Christian philosophy of Thomas Aquinas.

IV. HOW TO READ THE ENCYCLICALS

A great number of commentaries, explanations, and interpretations of these encyclicals have been written since they were first published. It goes without saying that, when such commentaries are the work of qualified Catholic theologians, nothing can be more useful than to apply to them for help in the study of these important documents. Theology is a science, and no one can hope safely to handle its problems without having first received sound theological training.

Another reason, more proper to the nature of the encyclicals themselves, makes this precaution still more imperative. When a Pope writes such a document, he does so in the full awareness of his spiritual responsibility. He knows very well that each and every sentence, word, noun, epithet, verb, and adverb found in his written text is going to be weighed, searched, and submitted to the most careful scrutiny by a crowd of countless readers scattered over the surface of the earth. And not only this but also the same anxious study of his pronouncements will be carried on by still many more readers, including his own successors, for generation after generation.

This thought should be to us an invitation to approach these texts in a spirit of reverence and of intellectual modesty. The teaching of the encyclicals should not be made either broader in scope or narrower than it is. Dealing as it does with a restatement of the Catholic faith as well as with its applications to definite problems, this teaching must be understood as given. Only a Pope has the authority to complete the teaching of one of his own encyclicals as well as that of the encyclicals of other

Popes, since only a Pope has the authority to write and to publish such a document.

Another rule to observe is not to yield to the temptation of "improving" the doctrine of the Popes.[1] In commenting on the encyclicals, many consider it their duty either to broaden the meaning of the doctrine or, more often still, to tone it down in the hope that, with a few minor adjustments, it will become more palatable to the modern mind. Generally speaking, this well-intentioned desire to better the teaching of the Popes springs from misinterpretation. When it seems to us that an encyclical cannot possibly say what it says, the first thing to do is to make a new effort to understand exactly what it does actually say. Most of the time, it will then be seen that we had missed, not only the meaning of its terms but also the general intention of the document and even, in some cases, the very nature of the problem under discussion.

Although it is true that Catholics are the particularly intended readers of the encyclicals, their teaching is directed to all men without any distinction. Protestants, agnostics, or militant atheists are normally expected to find in these documents, besides the spiritual food they need, various stumbling blocks, usually arising from a common dislike for doctrinal authority. Not much can be done to placate this kind of opposition. It is nevertheless hoped that, before indulging in it, non-Catholic readers will keep in mind a certain number of points on which their own moral responsibility is unavoidably engaged.

Whatever their personal opinions about the Catholic Church, the fact remains that the authority of the Pope does not present itself as a personal one. When one of us objects to the pretention avowed by the Popes to state, with full authority, what is

---

[1] One example of what we have in mind can be found in *Sapientiae Christianae (On Christian Citizenship)*. In a passage where the Pope says: *"Sunt praeterea christiani as dimicationem nati..."* ("Moreover, Christians are born for combat"), Fr. Husslein, S. J., translates: "Some Christians are indeed from their birth formed for battle; and for these the greater their energy,...." Obviously, this translator feels that to say *all* Christians are called to battle is somewhat extreme.

true and what is false, or what is right and what is wrong, he is pitting his own personal judgement, not against the personal judgement of another man, but against the whole ordinary teaching of the Catholic Church as well as against her entire tradition.

Another point to be kept in mind is that, in the conflict which may seem to arise between the pronouncements of the Church and those of today's public opinion, the Church alone represents the point of view of a moral and spiritual authority free from all prejudices, either those of a particular race, of a particular nation, or of a particular social class. Moreover, before claiming the advantage of being "modern" in his judgements, the reader would be well inspired to ask himself who is better placed to solve social and political problems: the man who only sees things through the often distorting light of contemporary experience, or the man who, discussing problems in the light of an experience as old as history itself, can take a broader view of particular situations.

A last remark, which may first sound slightly unpleasant, must nevertheless be made. It is true that certain teachings of the Popes do not agree with what was once called "the affirmations of the modern mind," but it is no less evident that, to a free modern mind, this fact should mean strictly nothing. Indeed, the whole problem is to know, not what the so-called modern mind affirms, but whether what it affirms is true. In order to settle this new problem, it is first necessary to submit these pronouncements of the modern mind to a most exacting criticism. A widely spread conviction may happen to be false, and we all know that it is so, only we do not like to think that this applies to the opinions of our own times. If we subject any one of these to careful criticism, we shall find that our strongest convictions often rest upon weak arguments and flimsy evidence. Why should not the contrary of what we were taking for granted also be given careful consideration? Pope Leo XIII asks for nothing more from those who do not share the Christian faith. It was always his firm conviction, provided only that men consent to face and look upon the reality of Catholic teaching, that they will find in it many reasons for accepting it.

In making a choice of his social encyclicals, we have simply accepted his own selection, as found in the apostolic letter of March 19, 1902, written on the occasion of the twenty-fifth anniversary of his election. The list established by the Pope comprises nine titles. All nine are included in this volume and constitute its core. An appendix includes three other encyclicals dealing with similar topics, but the choice made by the Pope himself of the first nine was a decisive reason to publish them together, as constituting a distinct doctrinal body endowed with a unity of its own. Let us add that, at the time he selected these nine documents, Leo XIII seems also to have suggested the order in which they should appear. It is clearly logical, rather than chronological:

1. On Christian Philosophy (1879): *Aeterni Patris*
2. On Human Liberty (1888): *Libertas Praestantissimum*
3. On Christian Marriage (1880): *Arcanum Divinae Sapientiae*
4. On Freemasonry (1884): *Humanum Genus*
5. On Civil Government (1881): *Diuturnum*
6. On the Christian Constitution of States (1885): *Immortale Dei*
7. On Socialism (1878): *Quod Apostolici Muneris*
8. On the Rights and Duties of Capital and Labor (1891): *Rerum Novarum*
9. On Christian Citizenship (1890): *Sapientiae Christianae*

The first two encyclicals lay down the foundations for the entire structure. After recalling the history of Christian philosophy and defining its nature, the Pope declares that no social reformation is possible except on the basis provided by the doctrine of St. Thomas Aquinas. The exposition of the notion of liberty, in the second encyclical, can be read as an introduction to the problems discussed in the rest of the series. The encyclical on Christian marriage follows because, as the Pope has said, the family is, in a sense, anterior to the body politic. The three following encyclicals deal with predominantly political problems. The discussion of freemasonry comes first because the Pope considered it responsible for the spread of naturalism. In that, on civil government, he determines the original of all political authority, and in the third of this group, the proper relations between the

Introduction

temporal power and the spiritual power are defined. The next two encyclicals deal with predominantly social and economic questions: the refutation of socialism and the definitions of the rights and duties of capital and labor in a Christian society. Since the ninth deals with the duties of Christians as citizens of the City of God, the perfect society and the perfect citizenship it describes rightly make it the crowning piece of the entire structure.

It is to be noted that the encyclicals are, as a rule, written in Latin. Excellent as it is, this humanistic Latin is not always easy to translate. Beyond the problems of language, many difficulties arise from the scrupulous choice of words made by their authors. It is sometimes difficult to find, in other languages, verbal equivalents serving their purpose as adequately as the words used in the original. Authorized or not, all translations fall short of the perfection of the originals.

With only four exceptions[2] all English translations included in this volume are the texts published in pamphlet form by the

---

2   These are the encyclicals *Rerum Novarum (On the Rights and Duties of Capital and Labor)*, for which the basic translation is that published by the Catholic Truth Society of London; *Inscrutabili (On the Evils Affecting Modern Society)*, whose basic text is provided by John J. Wynne, S. J., in *The Great Encyclical Letters of Pope Leo XIII* (3rd ed., New York, Benziger Brothers, 1903); *In Plurimis (On Slavery)*, whose text is from The (London) Tablet; and *Quod Apostolici Muneris (On Socialism)* whose text is from The Catholic World. Grateful thanks are given to these publishers for permitting the use of this material.

Whatever their source, the translations have always been compared with the Latin original of the encyclicals. Modifications have been introduced when the meaning of the document was at stake; the references to the sources of the quotations used have been restored to their original form and, whenever possible, completed; dates have sometimes been added to make chronology more precise. In no case was it considered advisable to insert commentaries of our own in a text over which, to say the least, we had no authority.

The text of the translation followed has been compared with that of other translations and the results are given in a series of footnotes at the end of each encyclical. The abbreviations used here are as follows: P., Paulist Press; W., J. J. Wynne, S. J., *The Great Encyclical Letters of Pope Leo XIII;* H., J. Husslein, S. J., *Social Wellspring;* L., an official Latin text of the encyclicals; F., a text of the French translation published at Paris, with the official Latin text, in *Actes de Léon XIII;* E., Encyclical letter *On*

xli

The Church Speaks to the Modern World

Paulist Press, which we wish to thank for its generosity in placing them at our disposal. Some passages have been revised in order to bring the translation closer to the original. The references have

---

the Christian Constitution of States, Latin text and authorized English translation (London, 1886); NC., pamphlet edition published by National Catholic Welfare Conference. Such variants have been listed only when more than purely literary problems arose.

Problems of another sort are raised by the translations themselves. The encyclicals are not written in mediaeval Latin but in a humanistic variety of classical Latin, which makes for quite a few pitfalls for translators. Such terms as *vis* (which may mean force, but also the import, or meaning, of a word), or *species* (which may mean kind, or sort of, but also beauty), even mere syntactic elegancies, are sometimes enough to throw off balance translators used to a less ambitious, and to us more clear, ecclesiastical Latin. When some of the translations used in this volume contained obvious mistranslations, unnecessary additions, or accidental omissions, we have deemed it preferable simply to recast such sentences, without calling attention to the change. For instance, when the text recommends the study of "St. Augustine and the Angelic Doctor," is it necessary to note that one of the translations omits "and the Angelic Doctor"? Obviously, no one intended to exclude Thomas Aquinas. The only thing to keep in mind on this point is that the whole responsibility for such emendations rests upon their shoulders, and in no way lessens our feeling of indebtedness to the translators whose work constitutes the very body of this book.

Apart from such errors or accidents, these translations, even the most recently revised ones, offered difficulties in terminology, which were inherent in the language itself. They could not possibly be removed. Nevertheless, since we had to compare the text of the translations with the Latin originals if only to remove those among the misinterpretations which had not escaped our attention, it has seemed advisable to publish in footnotes the main results of this comparison. Most readers will be justified in disregarding these footnotes except in the cases when a choice of several different translations is placed at their disposal. As to the Latin words or sentences, with or without tentative English rendering, their only purpose is to invite the reflection of those readers who take an interest in the desperately intricate problems which every translator has to solve.

Among the words that raise such problems, we wish to stress two frequently recurring ones: first, the Latin word which English translations render by "the poor," although the Latin *paupers* is regularly avoided by the encyclicals; second, the series of Latin words used by the encyclicals to express what the English translations uniformly by "the State."

I. THE POOR The encyclicals frequently use the Latin *proletarii.* Its normal translation should be "the proletarians," that is, the men who, taken collectively, constitute the class called the proletariat. In classical

Introduction

been completed whenever it has been possible to do so with the resources at our disposal; a modicum of historical information has been added, especially under the form of dates, but it has

Latin, the *proletarius* (from *proles*, offspring) was one of those men who were "regarded as capable of serving the State only by having children." In current usage, the word signifies "one of the wage-earning class; esp., a laborer for day wages not possessed of capital." All the translations which we have consulted render *proletarii* by "the poor," or by "laboring men," or "workmen," or even by "non-owning workers." It seems obvious that translators feel reluctant to resort to the direct translation, authorized by both the Oxford Dictionary and by Webster, "proletarians."

There is no point in attempting to change usage, but this is one more reason to point out the fact that the Pope has constantly used the Latin equivalent for "proletarians," and never the Latin equivalent for "poor." The reason is apparent. There are, in the Catholic Church, many poor who are, in no sense of the word, "proletarians." The vow of poverty helps place a Christian in a state of perfection wholly unrelated to the condition of what is called the proletariat. Moreover, even actual poverty is not considered an evil by Pope Leo XIII. What he combats is the wide gap there is, in modern societies, between excessive wealth and excessive poverty. Many poor people are not proletarians. The true proletarian is the wage-earner who, having absolutely no access to any kind of private property, is not even assured of finding employment in the future. While preserving the received translation, "the poor," let us remember Bossuet's famous sermon "On the Eminent Dignity of the Poor in the Church."

II. THE STATE From the point of view of the English usage, the word State is correctly employed in most passages of the encyclicals. The word signifies both the "body politic" and that which Jacques Maritain describes as "that part of the body politic especially concerned with the maintenance of the law, the promotion of the common welfare and public order and the administration of public affairs" (*Man and the State*, University of Chicago Press, 1951, p. 12).

On the other hand, the Latin language has several different words to designate the various notions included within the meaning of State. One consequence of this fact is that, while it is usually possible to guess, from the Latin text, how the English translator is going to use State, it is much harder to guess, from the English text, what terms answer the English word in the Latin original.

The Latin terminology related to the notion of State in the encyclicals is as follows:

(1) *societas*, that is, society in general, with a special connotation of the social bond rather than of the political aspect of the collective entity at stake. This term particularly applies to *civilis societas*,

(2) *civitas*, usually polity, that is, "a politically organized community,"

not been our intention to substitute ourselves for those who have authority to interpret and to teach the doctrine. Our own function was, fortunately for us, a more modest one. It consisted in putting these fundamental texts at the disposal of as large a public as possible, in readable form, and in the systematic order adopted by the Pope himself. We have attempted to do this in the spirit so happily defined by the very author of the texts we were editing: "These [laymen], so often as circumstances call for it, may take upon themselves, not indeed the office of the pastor, but the task of communicating to others what they have themselves received, becoming, as it were, living echoes of their teachers in the faith."

---

the body politic. The Latin *civitas* points out the collective entity formed by the "citizens" (*civitas*/city).

(3) *respublica*, that is, the "commonwealth" or body of people constituting a "politically organized community." It often connotes the territory occupied, and the natural resources administered by the commonwealth; for instance, the Commonwealth of Massachusetts, the Commonwealth of Australia. In this sense, it is very near the meaning of *State* (the United States). Unfortunately, the translators use State to render *respublica* as well as *civitas*, and when the two words occur in the same phrase, the situation is awkward. For instance, in *Immortale Dei*: "qualem sit speciem formamque habitura civitas, gubernante christiana philosophia rempublicam." Confronted with this problem, the translator suppresses one of the two words; the English word State stands in his translation for both *civitas* and *respublica*: "what the form and character (*species*) of the State would be if governed according to the principles of Christian philosophy."

(4) *principatus*, the authority and power wielded by the princes (*principes*) that is, the rulers, irrespective of the particular form of government adopted by the body politic. Under the rulers of the commonwealth are the magistrates (*magistratus*) or civil officers administering the law.

(5) *civilis potestas*, a particular application of the notion of *principatus*; designates the political power wielded by the rulers of any denomination, as distinguished from the *ecclesiastica potestas*, that is, the power wielded by the ecclesiastical hierarchy under the supreme authority of the Pope.

THE LEONINE CORPUS

I

On the Restoration of Christian Philosophy in Schools

INTRODUCTION

Published on August 4, 1879, the encyclical letter *Aeterni Patris* prescribes that Christian philosophy, as contained in the works of Thomas Aquinas, should be taught in schools in conformity with the teaching of the Church. The abbreviated title commonly given to it, "On Christian Philosophy," is therefore correct. Its other title, "On Scholastic Philosophy," is correct only to the extent that the scholastic philosophy at stake is that of Thomas Aquinas himself, not a more or less corrupt version of it.

The conclusions of this encyclical were implemented, one year later, by an apostolic letter establishing Thomas Aquinas as the common patron of *all* the Catholic schools (*A. A. S.,* 13 56–59). This letter document explicitly refers to *Aeterni Patris* as to "Our Letter on the Restoring in Catholic Schools of the Christian Philosophy in the Spirit of St. Thomas Aquinas." This doctrine is said to be applicable at all times because of the amplitude of its principles. The remarkable revival of Thomism in modern times has found a powerful incentive in these documents. The critical condition of the complete works of Thomas Aquinas (Leonine edition), the development of historical research work in the history of mediaeval philosophies and theologies, the creation of research centers, collections, and journals devoted to the study of Thomism as well as of its sources and its influence all bear witness to the fecundity of the directives issued in 1879.

In his first encyclical, on the evils that threaten society, Pope Leo XIII had already recalled the warning of St. Paul: "Beware lest any man cheat you by philosophy and vain deceit, according to the tradition of man, according to the principles of the world, and not according to Christ." (Col. 2:8). The safest way to keep false philosophies out of the schools is to have them teach the true one. In defining the method of Christian philosophy or, rather, the Christian way of philosophizing Pope Leo XIII was therefore laying down the doctrinal foundation of the social and philosophical order.

SUMMARY

(1) Doctrinal mission of the Church and teaching office of the Popes. (2) False philosophy has crept into all the orders of the State. (3) Usefulness of philosophy to call back the people to the paths of faith and salvation. (4) Philosophy, if rightly used, is a stepping stone to faith, but, inversely, faith completes and strengthens the light of reason. (5) Services rendered to faith by reason. (6) Philosophy helps theology to assume the nature, form, and character of a science. (7) Philosophy helps in defending divinely revealed truth. (8) Philosophy waits as a handmaid and attendant upon the revealed doctrines which are beyond the reach of human reason; it makes use of its own principles and methods of demonstration in the case of truths accessible to human reason. (9) The best way to philosophize is to unite the study of philosophy to obedience to the Christian faith. (10) This is confirmed by the history of philosophy, especially by the sight of the errors committed by the ancient philosophers who were not guided by the light of the divine revelation. (11) Not so in the case of the apologists, especially Justin Martyr. (12) Contribution of early patristics to the work of Christian philosophy. (13) Outstanding contribution of Augustine and his successors up to Anselm of Canterbury. (14–15) In praise of the Scholastics, especially St. Thomas and St. Bonaventure. (16) This praise of Scholastic theology applies to Scholastic philosophy. (17) Thomas Aquinas, the chief and master of all the Scholastic doctors; characteristics of his method. (18) Because it chiefly dealt with the principles of things, his doctrine contains, so to say, the

seeds of almost infinite truths. (19) Nearly all the founders of religious orders have prescribes to their members to adhere to the teachings of St. Thomas. (20) Many European universities have recognized his authority. (21) Many Popes have praised his teaching as the true and catholic doctrine. (22) The ecumenical councils have held Thomas in singular honor. (23) Heretics have considered him their main adversary. (24–26) Dangers arising from the new systems of philosophy and necessity of a return to Thomas Aquinas as the fountainhead of philosophic truth. (27) Outside of divine grace, nothing is better calculated than the doctrine of the Fathers and the Scholastics to satisfy the minds which claim reason as their sole mistress and guide. (28) It provides the domestics and civil society with the safest guarantee of peace. (29) Not only the social order, but all studies would find the promise of advancement and assistance in the restoration of this philosophic training. (30) The examples of Albert the Great and Thomas Aquinas show that there is no opposition between the study of such a philosophy and that of natural sciences; rather, the reverse is true. (31) Universities should, therefore, restore the wisdom of St. Thomas, without feeling bound to maintain what Scholastic doctors could have said with too much subtlety or that which, in their doctrines, might contradict modern scientific discoveries. (32) This undertaking cannot succeed without the help of the God of all knowledge, who is also the Father of lights. (33) Following the example of St. Thomas, we should beseech God to grant us the gifts of knowledge and of understanding. (34) Apostolic benediction.

I

Aeterni Patris
ON CHRISTIAN PHILOSOPHY
August 4, 1879

1. The only-begotten Son of the Eternal Father, who came on earth to bring salvation and the light of divine wisdom to men, conferred a great and wonderful blessing on the world when, about to ascend again into heaven, He commanded the Apostles to go and teach all nations,[1] and left the Church which He had founded to be the common and supreme teacher of the peoples. For men whom the truth had set free were to be preserved by the truth; nor would the fruits of heavenly doctrines by which salvation comes to men have long remained had not the Lord Christ appointed an unfailing teaching authority to train the minds to faith.[2] And the Church built upon the promises of its own divine Author, whose charity it imitated, so faithfully followed out His commands that its constant aim and chief wish was this: to teach religion and contend forever against errors. To this end assuredly have tended the incessant labors of individual bishops; to this end also the published[3] laws and decrees of councils, and especially the constant watchfulness of the Roman Pontiffs, to whom, as successors of the blessed Peter in the primacy of the Apostles, belongs the right and office of teaching and confirming their brethren in the faith. Since, then, according to the warning of the apostle, the minds of Christ's faithful are apt to be deceived and the integrity of the faith to be corrupted among men by philosophy and vain deceit,[4] the supreme pastors of the Church have always thought it their duty

---

1 Matt. 28:19
2 L. *erudientes ad fidem mentibus.*—P. for the instruction of the faith.—H. to train the minds of men to faith.—Note that the verb *erudire* points out the kind of teaching given to beginners.
3 L. *perlatae leges et decretal.*—H. the sanctioned laws and decrees.
4 Col. 2:8

to advance, by every means in their power, science truly so-called, and at the same time to provide with special care that all studies should accord with the Catholic faith, especially philosophy, on which a right interpretation[5] of the other sciences in great part depends. Indeed, venerable brethren, on this very subject among others, We briefly admonished you in Our first encyclical letter; but now, both by reason of the gravity of the subject and the condition of the time, we are again compelled to speak to you on the mode of taking up the study of philosophy which shall respond most fitly to the excellence[6] of faith, and at the same time be consonant with the dignity of human science.[7]

2. Whoso turns his attention to the bitter strifes of these days and seeks a reason for the troubles that vex public and private life must come to the conclusion that a fruitful cause of the evils which now afflict, as well as those which threaten, us lies in this: that false conclusions concerning divine and human things, which originated in the schools of philosophy, have now crept into all the orders of the State, and have been accepted by the common consent of the masses. For, since it is in the very nature of man to follow the guide of reason in his actions, if his intellect sins at all his will soon follows; and thus it happens that false opinions,[8] whose seat is in the understanding, influence human actions and pervert them. Whereas, on the other hand, if men be of sound mind and take their stand on true and solid

---

5 L. *ceterarum scientiarum recta ratio*. — P. a right apprehension of the other sciences. — H. the proper ordering of the other sciences. — F. la sage direction des sciences. — The word *ratio* is difficult to translate because its meaning covers a wide field. In its wider interpretation, it means that the knowledge of true philosophy is necessary to the proper understanding and interpretation of the other sciences.
6 L. *bono fidei*. — P. which shall respond most fitly to true faith. — H. which shall be suitable and advantageous to faith. — F. qui respecte... les règle de la foi.
7 L. *humanarum scientiarum dignitati*; that is, to the dignity of scientific knowledge possessed by man. — P. with the dignity of human knowledge. — H. to the dignity of human science. — F. la *dignité* des sciences humaines.
8 L. *pravitas opinionum*. — P. looseness of intellectual opinions. — H. Bad opinions, whose seat is in the intelligence.

principles, there will result a vast amount of benefits for the public and private good. We do not, indeed, attribute such force and authority to philosophy as to esteem it equal to the task of combating and rooting out all errors; for, when the Christian religion was first constituted, it came upon earth to restore it to its primeval dignity by the admirable light of faith, diffused "not by persuasive words of human wisdom, but in the manifestation of spirit and of power",[9] so also at the present time we look above all things to the powerful help of Almighty God to bring back to a right understanding the minds of man and dispel the darkness of error.[10] But, the natural helps with which the grace of the divine wisdom, strongly and sweetly disposing all things, has supplied the human race are neither to be despised nor neglected, chief among which is evidently the right use of philosophy. For, not in vain did God set the light of reason in the human mind; and so far is the super-added light of faith from extinguishing or lessening the power of the intelligence that it completes it rather, and by adding to its strength renders it capable of greater things.

3. Therefore, Divine Providence itself requires that, in calling back the people to the paths of faith and salvation, advantage should be taken of human science also—an approved and wise practice which history testifies was observed by the most illustrious Fathers of the Church. They, indeed, were wont neither to belittle nor undervalue the part that reason had to play, as is summed up by the great Augustine when he attributes to this science "that by which the most wholesome faith is begotten... is nourished, defended, and made strong."[11]

4. In the first place, philosophy, if rightly made use of by the wise, in a certain way tends to smooth and fortify the road to true faith, and to prepare the souls of its disciples for the fit reception of revelation; for which reason it is well called by ancient writers

---

9   1 Cor. 2:4.
10 See *Inscrutabili Dei consilio*, 78:113.
11 *De Trinitate*, 14, 1, 3 (PL 42, 1037); quoted by Thomas Aquinas, *Summa theologiae*, I, 1, 2.

sometimes a steppingstone to the Christian faith,[12] sometimes the prelude and help of Christianity,[13] sometimes the Gospel teacher.[14] And, assuredly, the God of all goodness, in all that pertains to divine things, has not only manifested by the light of faith those truths which human intelligence could not attain of itself, but others, also, not altogether unattainable by reason, that by the help of divine authority they may be made known to all at once and without any admixture of error. Hence, it is that certain truths which were either divinely proposed for belief, or were bound by the closest chains to the doctrine of faith, were discovered by pagan sages with nothing but their natural reason to guide them, were demonstrated and proved by becoming arguments. For, as the Apostle says, the invisible things of Him, from the creation of the world, are clearly seen, being understood by the things that are made: His eternal power also and divinity;[15] and the Gentiles who have not the Law show, nevertheless, the work of the Law written in their hearts.[16] But it is most fitting to turn these truths, which have been discovered by the pagan sages even, to the use and purposes of revealed doctrine, in order to show that both human wisdom and the very testimony of our adversaries serve to support the Christian faith—a method which is not of recent introduction, but of established use, and has often been adopted by the holy Fathers of the Church. What is more, those venerable men, the witnesses and guardians of religious traditions, recognize a certain form and figure of this in the action of the Hebrews, who, when about to depart out of Egypt, were commanded to take with them the gold and silver vessels and precious robes of the Egyptians, that by a change of use the things might be dedicated to the service of the true God which had formerly been the instruments of ignoble and superstitious rites. Gregory of Neo-Caesarea[17] praises Origen expressly

---

12   Clement of Alexandria, *Stromata*, 1, 16 (PG 8, 795); 7, 3 (PG 9, 426).
13   Origen, *Epistola ad Gregorium* (PG 11, 87–91).
14   Clement of Alexandria, *Stromata*, 1,5 (PG 8, 718–719).
15   Rom. 1:20.
16   Rom. 2:14–15.
17   Gregory of Neo-Caesarea (also called Gregory Thaumaturgus, that is,

because, with singular dexterity, as one snatches weapons from the enemy, he turned to the defense of Christian wisdom and to the destruction of superstition many arguments drawn from the writings of the pagans. And both Gregory of Nazianzen[18] and Gregory of Nyssa[19] praise and commend a like mode of disputation in Basil the Great; while Jerome[20] especially commends it in Quadratus, a disciple of the Apostles, in Aristides, Justin, Irenaeus, and very many others. Augustine says: "Do we not see Cyprian, that mildest of doctors and most blessed of martyrs, going out of Egypt laden with gold and silver and vestments? And Lactantius, also and Victorinus, Optatus and Hilary? And, not to speak of the living, how many Greeks have done likewise?"[21] But if natural reason first sowed this rich field of doctrine before it was rendered fruitful by the power of Christ, it must assuredly become more prolific after the grace of the Saviour has renewed and added to the native faculties of the human mind. And who does not see that a plain and easy road is opened up to faith by such a method of philosophic study?

5. But the advantage to be derived from such a school of philosophy[22] is not to be confined within these limits. The foolishness of those men who "by these good things that are seen could not understand Him, that is, neither by attending to the works could have acknowledged who was the workman,"[23] is gravely reproved in the words of Divine Wisdom. In the first place, then, this great and noble fruit is gathered from human reason, that it demonstrates that God is; for the greatness of the beauty and of

---

"the miracle worker"), *In Origenem oratio panegyrica*, 6 (PG 10, 1093A).
18   Carm., 1, Iamb. 3 (PG 37, 1045A–1047A).
19   *Vita Moysis* (PG 44, 359).
20   *Epistola ad Magnum*, 4 (PL 22, 667). Quadratus, Justin, Irenaeus, are counted among the early Christian apologists, who devoted their works to the defence of Christian truth against the pagans.
21   *De doctrina christiana*, l, 2, 40 (PL 34, 63).
22   L. *ex illo philosophandi instituto*; that is, from this way of philosophizing.—H. rightly: from this method of philosophizing.—P. from such a school of philosophy; can be maintained with the sense: the school of philosophy which unites the light of faith with the light of reason.
23   Wisd. 13:1.

the creature the Creator of them may be seen so as to be known thereby.[24] Again, it shows God to excel in the height of all perfections, especially in infinite wisdom before which nothing lies hidden, and in absolute justice which no depraved affection could possibly shake; and that God, therefore, is not only true but truth itself, which can neither deceive nor be deceived. Whence, it clearly follows that human reason finds the fullest faith and authority united in the word of God. In like manner, reason declares that the doctrine of the Gospel has even from its very beginning been made manifest by certain wonderful signs, the established proofs, as it were, of unshaken truth; and that all, therefore, who set faith in the Gospel do not believe rashly as though following cunningly devised fables,[25] but, by a most reasonable consent, subject their intelligence and judgment to an authority which is divine. And of no less importance is it that reason most clearly sets forth that the Church instituted by Christ (as laid down in the Vatican Council), on account of its wonderful spread, its marvellous sanctity, and its inexhaustible fecundity in all places, as well as of its Catholic unity and unshaken stability, is in itself a great and perpetual motive of belief and an irrefragable testimony of its own divine mission.[26]

6. Its solid foundations having been thus laid, a perpetual and varied service is further required of philosophy, in order that sacred theology may receive and assume the nature, form, and genius of a true science. For in this, the most noble of studies, it is of the greatest necessity to bind together, as it were, in one body the many and various parts of the heavenly doctrines, that, each being allotted to its own proper place and derived from its own proper principles, the whole may join together in a complete union; in order, in fine, that all and each part may be strengthened by its own and the others' invincible arguments. Nor is that more accurate or fuller knowledge of the things that are believed, and somewhat more lucid understanding, as far as

---

24 Wisd. 13:5.
25 2 Peter 1:16.
26 *Const. Dogm, de Fid. Cath.*, c.3.

it can go, of the very mysteries of faith which Augustine and the other fathers commended and strove to reach, and which the Vatican Council itself[27] declared to be most fruitful, to be passed over in silence or belittled. Those will certainly more fully and more easily attain that knowledge and understanding who to integrity of life and love of faith join a mind rounded and finished by philosophic studies, as the same Vatican Council teaches that the knowledge of such sacred dogmas ought to be sought as well from analogy of the things that are naturally known as from the connection of those mysteries one with another and with the final end of man.[28]

7. Lastly, the duty of religiously defending the truths divinely delivered, and of resisting those who dare oppose them, pertains to philosophic pursuits. Wherefore, it is the glory of philosophy to be esteemed as the bulwark of faith and the strong defense of religion. As Clement of Alexandria testifies, the doctrine of the Saviour is indeed perfect in itself and wanteth naught, since it is the power and wisdom of God. And the assistance of the Greek philosophy maketh not the truth more powerful; but, inasmuch as it weakens the contrary arguments of the sophists and repels the veiled attacks against the truth, it has been fitly called the hedge and fence of the vine.[29] For, as the enemies of the Catholic name, when about to attack religion, are in the habit of borrowing their weapons from the arguments of philosophers, so the defenders of sacred science draw many arguments from the store of philosophy which may serve to uphold revealed dogmas. Nor is the triumph of the Christian faith a small one in using human reason to repel powerfully and speedily the attacks of its adversaries by the hostile arms which human reason itself supplied. This species of religious strife St. Jerome, writing to Magnus, notices as having been adopted by the Apostle of the Gentiles himself; Paul, the leader of the Christian army and the invincible orator, battling for the cause of Christ, skillfully turns

---

27 *Const. cit.*, c.4.
28 *Loc. cit.*
29 *Stromata*, l, 20 (PG 8, 818).

even a chance inscription into an argument for the faith; for he had learned from the true David to wrest the sword from the hands of the enemy and to cut off the head of the boastful Goliath with his own weapon.[30] Moreover, the Church herself not only urges, but even commands, Christian teachers to seek help from philosophy. For, the Fifth Lateran Council, after it had decided that "every assertion contrary to the truth of revealed faith is altogether false, for the reason that it contradicts, however slightly, the truth,"[31] advises teachers of philosophy to pay close attention to the exposition of fallacious arguments; since, as Augustine testifies, "if reason is turned against the authority of sacred Scripture, no matter how specious it may seem, it errs in the likeness of truth; for true it cannot be."[32]

8. But in order that philosophy may be bound equal to the gathering of those precious fruits which we have indicated, it behooves it above all things never to turn aside from that path which the Fathers have entered upon from a venerable antiquity, and which the Vatican Council solemnly and authoritatively approved. As it is evident that very many truths of the supernatural order which are far beyond the reach of the keenest intellect must be accepted, human reason, conscious of its own infirmity, dare not affect to itself too great powers, nor deny those truths, nor measure them by its own standard, nor interpret them at will; but receive them, rather, with a full and humble faith, and esteem it the highest honor to be allowed to wait upon heavenly doctrines like a handmaid and attendant, and by God's goodness attain to them in any way whatsoever. But in the case of such doctrines as the human intelligence may perceive, it is equally just that philosophy should make use of its own method, principles, and arguments — not, indeed, in such fashion as to seem rashly to withdraw from the divine authority. But, since it is established that those things which become known by revelation have the force of certain truth, and that those things which war

---

30 *Epistola ad Magnum*, 2 (PL 22, 666).
31 Bulla *Apostolici regiminis*.
32 Epistola 147, *ad Marcellinum*, 7 (PL 33, 589).

against faith war equally against right reason, the Catholic philosopher will know that he violates at once faith and the laws of reason if he accepts any conclusion which he understands to be opposed to revealed doctrine.

9. We know that there are some who, in their overestimate of the human faculties, maintain that as soon as man's intellect becomes subject to divine authority it falls from its native dignity, and hampered by the yoke of this species of slavery, is much retarded and hindered in its progress toward the supreme truth and excellence. Such an idea is most false and deceptive, and its sole tendency is to induce foolish and ungrateful men wilfully to repudiate the most sublime truths, and reject the divine gift of faith, from which the fountains of all good things flow out upon civil society. For the human mind, being confined within certain limits, and those narrow enough, is exposed to many errors and is ignorant of many things; whereas the Christian faith, reposing on the authority of God, is the unfailing mistress of truth, whom whoso followeth he will be neither enmeshed in the snares of error nor tossed hither and thither on the waves of fluctuating opinion. Those, therefore, who to the study of philosophy unite obedience to the Christian faith, are philosophizing in the best possible way;[33] for the splendor of the divine truths, received into the mind, helps the understanding, and not only detracts in nowise from its dignity, but adds greatly to its nobility, keenness, and stability. For surely that is a worthy and most useful exercise of reason when men give their minds to disproving those things which are repugnant to faith and proving the things which conform to faith. In the first case they cut the ground from under the feet of error and expose the viciousness of the arguments on which error rests; while in the second case they make themselves masters of weighty reasons for the sound

---

33 L. *Quapropter qui philosophiae studium cum obsequio fidei christianae conjungunt, ii optime philosophantur.* — P. Those, therefore, who to the study of philosophy unite obedience to Christian faith are philosophers indeed. — H. Therefore, they who add the study of philosophy to obedience to Christian faith philosophize well.

demonstration of truth and the satisfactory instruction of any reasonable person. Whoever denies that such study and practice tend to add to the resources and expand the faculties of the mind must necessarily and absurdly hold that the mind gains nothing from discriminating between the true and the false. Justly, therefore, does the Vatican Council commemorate in these words the great benefits which faith has conferred upon reason: Faith *frees* and saves reason *from error, and* endows it with *manifold* knowledge.[34] A wise man, therefore, would not accuse faith and look upon it as opposed to reason and natural truths, but would rather offer heartfelt thanks to God, and sincerely rejoice that, in the density of ignorance and in the flood-tide of error, holy faith, like a friendly star, shines down upon his path and points out to him the fair gate of truth beyond all danger of wandering.

10. If, venerable brethren, you open the history of philosophy, you will find all We have just said proved by experience. The philosophers of old who lacked the gift of faith, yet were esteemed so wise, fell into many appalling errors. You know how often among some truths they taught false and incongruous things; what vague and doubtful opinions they held concerning the nature of the Divinity, the first origin of things, the government of the world, the divine knowledge of the future, the cause and principle of evil, the ultimate end of man, the eternal beatitude, concerning virtue and vice, and other matters, a true and certain knowledge of which is most necessary to the human race; while, on the other hand, the early Fathers and Doctors of the Church, who well understood that, according to the divine plan, the restorer of human science is Christ, who is the power and the wisdom of God,[35] and in whom are hid all the treasures of wisdom and knowledge,[36] took up and investigated the books of the ancient philosophers, and compared their teachings with the doctrines of revelation, and, carefully sifting them, they cherished what was true and wise in them and amended or rejected

---

34   *Const. Dogm. de Fid. Cath.*, c.4.
35   1 Cor. 1:24.
36   Col. 2:3.

all else. For, as the all-seeing God against the cruelty of tyrants raised up mighty martyrs to the defense of the Church, men prodigal of their great lives, in like manner to false philosophers and heretics He opposed men of great wisdom, to defend, even by the aid of human reason, the treasure of revealed truths. Thus, from the very first ages of the Church, the Catholic doctrine has encountered a multitude of most bitter adversaries, who, deriding the Christian dogmas and institutions, maintained that there were many gods, that the material world never had a beginning or cause, and that the course of events was one of blind and fatal necessity, not regulated by the will of Divine Providence.

11. But the learned men whom We call apologists speedily encountered these teachers of foolish doctrine and, under the guidance of faith, found arguments in human wisdom also to prove that one God, who stands pre-eminent in every kind of perfection, is to be worshiped; that all things were created from nothing by His omnipotent power; that by His wisdom they flourish and serve each their own special purposes. Among these St. Justin Martyr claims the chief place.

After having tried the most celebrated academies of the Greeks, he saw clearly, as he himself confesses, that he could only draw truths in their fullness from the doctrine of revelation. These he embraced with all the ardor of his soul, purged of calumny, courageously and fully defended before the Roman emperors, and reconciled with them not a few of the sayings of the Greek philosophers.

12. Quadratus, also, and Aristides, Hermias, and Athenagoras stood nobly forth in that time. Nor did Irenaeus, the invincible martyr and Bishop of Lyons, win less glory in the same cause when, forcibly refuting the perverse opinions of the Orientals, the work of the Gnostics, scattered broadcast over the territories of the Roman Empire, he explained (according to Jerome) the origin of each heresy and in what philosophic source it took its rise.[37] But who knows not the disputations of Clement of

---

37 *Epistola ad Magnum*, 4 (PL 22, 667).

Alexandria, which the same Jerome thus honorably commemorates: "What is there in them that is not learned, and what that is not of the very heart of philosophy?"[38] He himself, indeed, with marvellous versatility treated of many things of the greatest utility for preparing a history of philosophy, for the exercise of the dialectic art, and for showing the agreement between reason and faith. After him came Origen, who graced the chair of the school of Alexandria, and was most learned in the teachings of the Greeks and Orientals. He published many volumes, involving great labor, which were wonderfully adapted to explain the divine writings and illustrate the sacred dogmas; which, though, as they now stand, not altogether free from error, contain nevertheless a wealth of knowledge tending to the growth and advance of natural truths. Tertullian opposes heretics with the authority of the sacred writings; with the philosophers he changes his fence and disputes philosophically; but so learnedly and accurately did he confute them that he made bold to say: "Neither in science nor in schooling are we equals, as you imagine."[39] Arnobius, also, in his works against the pagans, and Lactantius in the divine *Institutions* especially, with equal eloquence and strength strenuously strive to move men to accept the dogmas and precepts of Catholic wisdom, not by philosophic juggling, after the fashion of the Academicians, but vanquishing them partly by their own arms, and partly by arguments drawn from the mutual contentions of the philosophers.[40] But the writings on the human soul, the divine attributes, and other questions of mighty moment which the great Athanasius and Chrysostom, the prince of orators, have left behind them are, by common consent, so supremely excellent that it seems scarcely anything could be added to their subtlety and fulness. And, not to cover too wide a range, we add to the number of the great men of whom mention has been made the names of Basil the Great and of the two Gregories, who, on going forth from Athens, that

---

38 Loc. cit.
39 Tertullian, *Apologet.*, 46 (PL 1, 573).
40 Lactantius, *Div. Inst.*, 7, 7 (PL 6, 759).

home of all learning, thoroughly equipped with all the harness of philosophy, turned the wealth of knowledge which each had gathered up in a course of zealous study to the work of refuting heretics and preparing Christians.

13. But Augustine would seem to have wrested the palm from all. Of a most powerful genius and thoroughly saturated with sacred and profane learning, with the loftiest faith and with equal knowledge, he combated most vigorously all the errors of his age. What topic[41] of philosophy did he not investigate?[42] What region of it did he not diligently explore, either in expounding the loftiest mysteries of the faith to the faithful, or defending them against the full onslaught of adversaries, or again when, in demolishing the fables of the Academicians or the Manichaeans, he laid the safe foundations and sure structure of human science, or followed up the reason, origin, and causes of the evils that afflict man? How subtly he reasoned on the angels, the soul, the human mind, the will and free choice, on religion and the life of the blessed, on time and eternity, and even on the very nature of changeable bodies. Afterwards, in the East, John Damascene, treading in the footsteps of Basil and of Gregory of Nazianzen, and in the West, Boethius and Anselm following the doctrines of Augustine, added largely to the patrimony of philosophy.

14. Later on, the doctors of the middle ages, who are called Scholastics, addressed themselves to a great work — that of diligently collecting, and sifting, and storing up, as it were, in one place, for the use and convenience of posterity the rich and fertile harvests of Christian learning scattered abroad in the voluminous works of the holy Fathers. And with regard, venerable brethren, to the origin, drift, and excellence of this scholastic learning, it may be well here to speak more fully in the words of one of the wisest of Our predecessors, Sixtus V: "By the divine favor of Him who alone gives the spirit of science, wisdom, and understanding, and who through all ages, as there may be need, enriches His

---

41 L. *locum.* — P. what height of philosophy. — H. (rightly) topic.
42 L. *investigavit.* — P. reach. — H. (rightly) has he left untouched?

Church with new blessings and strengthens it with safeguards, there was founded by Our fathers, men of eminent wisdom, the scholastic theology, which two glorious doctors, in particular angelic St. Thomas and the seraphic St. Bonaventure, illustrious teachers of this faculty, ... with surpassing genius, by unwearied diligence, and at the cost of long labors and vigils, set in order and beautified, and when skilfully arranged and clearly explained in a variety of ways, handed down to posterity.

15. "And, indeed, the knowledge and use of so salutary a science, which flows from the fertilizing founts of the sacred writings, the sovereign Pontiffs, the holy Fathers, and the councils, must always be of the greatest assistance to the Church, whether with the view of really and soundly understanding and interpreting the Scriptures, or more safely and to better purpose reading and explaining the Fathers, or for exposing and refuting the various errors and heresies; and in these late days, when those dangerous times described by the Apostle are already upon us, when the blasphemers, the proud, and the seducers go from bad to worse, erring themselves and causing others to err, there is surely a very great need of confirming the dogmas of Catholic faith and confuting heresies."

16. Although these words seem to bear reference solely to Scholastic theology, nevertheless they may plainly be accepted as equally true of philosophy and its praises. For, the noble endowments, which make the Scholastic theology so formidable to the enemies of truth—to wit, as the same Pontiff adds, "that ready and close coherence of cause and effect, that order and array as of a disciplined army in battle, those clear definitions and distinctions, that strength of argument and those keen discussions, by which light is distinguished from darkness, the true from the false, expose and strip naked, as it were, the falsehoods of heretics wrapped around by a cloud of subterfuges and fallacies"[43]—those noble and admirable endowments, We say, are only to be found in a right use of that philosophy, which the

---

43 Bulla *Triumphantis*, an. 1588.

Scholastic teachers have been accustomed carefully and prudently to make use of even in theological disputations.[44] Moreover, since it is the proper and special office of the Scholastic theologians to bind together by the fastest chain human and divine science, surely the theology in which they excelled would not have gained such honor and commendation among men if they had made use of a lame and imperfect or vain philosophy.

17. Among the Scholastic Doctors, the chief and master of all, towers Thomas Aquinas, who, as Cajetan observes, because "he most venerated the ancient doctors of the Church, in a certain way seems to have inherited the intellect of all."[45] The doctrines of those illustrious men, like the scattered members of a body, Thomas collected together and cemented, distributed in wonderful order, and so increased with important additions that he is rightly and deservedly esteemed the special bulwark and glory of the Catholic faith. With his spirit at once humble and swift, his memory ready and tenacious, his life spotless throughout, a lover of truth for its own sake, richly endowed with human and divine science, like the sun he heated the world with the warmth of his virtues and filled it with the splendor of his teaching. Philosophy has no part which he did not touch finely at once and thoroughly; on the laws of reasoning, on God and incorporeal substances, on man and other sensible things, on human actions and their principles, he reasoned in such a manner that in him there is wanting neither a full array of questions, nor an apt disposal of the various parts, nor the best method of proceeding, nor soundness of principles or strength of argument, nor clearness and elegance of style, nor a facility for explaining what is abstruse.

---

44 L. *ejus philosophiae, quam magistri scholastici, data opera et sapienti concilio, in disputationibus etiam theologicis passim usurpare consueverunt.* — H. of that philosophy which the Scholastic masters, exercising the utmost industry and consummate wisdom, were accustomed always to employ in theological disputations.

45 Cajetan's commentary on *Sum. theol.*, IIa-IIae 148, 9. Art. 4; Leonine edit., Vol. 10, p. 174, n.6.

18. Moreover, the Angelic Doctor pushed his philosophic inquiry[46] into the reasons and principles of things, which because they are most comprehensive and contain in their bosom, so to say, the seeds of almost infinite truths, were to be unfolded in good time by later masters and with a goodly yield. And as he also used this philosophic method in the refutation of error, he won this title to distinction for himself: that, single-handed, he victoriously combated the errors of former times, and supplied invincible arms to put those to rout which might in after-times spring up. Again, clearly distinguishing, as is fitting, reason from faith, while happily associating the one with the other, he both preserved the rights and had regard for the dignity of each; so much so, indeed, that reason, borne on the wings of Thomas to its human height, can scarcely rise higher, while faith could scarcely expect more or stronger aids from reason than those which she has already obtained through Thomas.

19. For these reasons most learned men, in former ages especially, of the highest repute in theology and philosophy, after mastering with infinite pains the immortal works of Thomas, gave themselves up not so much to be instructed in his angelic wisdom as to be nourished upon it. It is known that nearly all[47] the founders and lawgivers[48] of the religious orders commanded their members to study and religiously adhere to the teachings of St. Thomas, fearful least any of them should swerve even in the slightest degree from the footsteps of so great a man. To say nothing of the family of St. Dominic, which rightly claims this great teacher for its own glory, the statutes of the Benedictines, the Carmelites, the Augustinians, the Society of Jesus, and many others all testify that they are bound by this law.

---

46 P. conclusions.—H. philosophic conclusions with regard to the reasons and principles of things which, being most comprehensive, and containing in themselves the germs of truths almost countless in number, were to be developed by later teachers at a proper time and with abundant fruit.
47 L. *prope*.
48 L. *legiferos*.—H. all the founders and lawgivers of religious orders.—P. all the founders and framers of laws of the religious orders.

20. And, here, how pleasantly one's thoughts fly back to those celebrated schools and universities which flourished of old in Europe — to Paris, Salamanca, Alcalá, to Douay, Toulouse, and Louvain, to Padua and Bologna, to Naples and Coimbra, and to many another! All know how the fame of these seats of learning grew with their years, and that their judgment, often asked in matters of grave moment, held great weight everywhere. And we know how in those great homes of human wisdom, as in his own kingdom, Thomas reigned supreme; and that the minds of all, of teachers as well as of taught, rested in wonderful harmony under the shield and authority of the Angelic Doctor.

21. But, furthermore, Our predecessors in the Roman pontificate have celebrated the wisdom of Thomas Aquinas by exceptional tributes of praise and the most ample testimonials. Clement VI in the bull *In Ordine*; Nicholas V in his brief to the friars of the Order of Preachers, 1451; Benedict XIII in the bull *Pretiosus*, and others bear witness that the universal Church borrows lustre from his admirable teaching; while St. Pius V declares in the bull *Mirabilis* that heresies, confounded and convicted by the same teaching, were dissipated, and the whole world daily freed from fatal errors; others, such as Clement XII in the bull *Verbo Dei*, affirm that most fruitful blessings have spread abroad from his writings over the whole Church, and that he is worthy of the honor which is bestowed on the greatest Doctors of the Church, on Gregory and Ambrose, Augustine and Jerome; while others have not hesitated to propose St. Thomas for the exemplar and master of the universities and great centers of learning whom they may follow with unfaltering feet. On which point the words of Blessed Urban V to the University of Toulouse are worthy of recall: "It is our will, which We hereby enjoin upon you, that ye follow the teaching of Blessed Thomas as the true and Catholic doctrine and that ye labor with all your force to profit by the same."[49] Innocent XII, followed the example of Urban in the case of the University of Louvain, in the letter in the form of

---

49 *Constitutio 5a, data die 3 Aug. 1368*, ad Cancell. Univ. Tolos.

a brief addressed to that university on February 6, 1694, and Benedict XIV in the letter in the form of a brief addressed on August 26, 1752, to the Dionysian College in Granada; while to these judgments of great Pontiffs on Thomas Aquinas comes the crowning testimony of Innocent VI: "His teaching above that of others, the canonical writings alone excepted, enjoys such a precision of language, an order of matters, a truth of conclusions, that those who hold to it are never found swerving from the path of truth, and he who dare assail it will always be suspected of error."[50]

22. The ecumenical councils, also, where blossoms the flower of all earthly wisdom, have always been careful to hold Thomas Aquinas in singular honor. In the Councils of Lyons, Vienna, Florence, and the Vatican one might almost say that Thomas took part and presided over the deliberations and decrees of the Fathers, contending against the errors of the Greeks, of heretics and rationalists, with invincible force and with the happiest results. But, the chief and special glory of Thomas, one which he has shared with none of the Catholic Doctors, is that the Fathers of Trent made it part of the order of conclave to lay upon the altar, together with sacred Scripture[51] and the decrees of the supreme Pontiffs, the *Summa* of Thomas Aquinas, whence to seek counsel, reason, and inspiration.

23. A last triumph was reserved for this incomparable man — namely, to compel the homage, praise, and admiration of even the very enemies of the Catholic name. For it has come to light that there were not lacking among the leaders of heretical sects some who openly declared that, if the teaching of Thomas

---

50 *Sermo de S. Thoma.*—The references inserted in the original text have been restored to their respective places. In this paragraph, the Latin text uses the words *Academiis et magnis Lycaeis* in a sense approximately the same as that of "universities and high schools." It is possible to adhere more closely to the Latin terminology. For instance, P: the academies and great colleges; or H: the great academies and lyceums; but impossible to translate (with P): "the academy of Toulouse," for the document at stake was addressed by Urban V to the university, not to any academy.
51 P. with the code of sacred Scripture.

Aquinas were only taken away, they could easily battle with all Catholic teachers, gain the victory, and abolish the Church.[52] A vain hope, indeed, but no vain testimony.

24. Therefore, venerable brethren, as often as We contemplate the good, the force, and the singular advantages to be derived from his philosophic discipline[53] which Our Fathers so dearly loved. We think it hazardous that its special honor should not always and everywhere remain, especially when it is established that daily experience, and the judgment of the greatest men, and, to crown all, the voice of the Church, have favored the Scholastic philosophy. Moreover, to the old teaching a novel system of philosophy has succeeded here and there, in which We fail to perceive those desirable and wholesome fruits which the Church and civil society itself would prefer. For it pleased the struggling innovators of the sixteenth century to philosophize without any respect for faith, the power of inventing in accordance with his own pleasure and bent being asked and given in turn by each one. Hence, it was natural that systems of philosophy multiplied beyond measure, and conclusions differing and clashing one with another arose about those matters even which are the most important in human knowledge. From a mass of conclusions men often come to wavering and doubt; and who knows not how easily the mind slips from doubt to error? But, as men are apt to follow the lead given them, this new pursuit seems to have caught the souls of certain Catholic philosophers, who, throwing aside the patrimony of ancient wisdom, chose rather to build up a new edifice than to strengthen and complete the old by aid of the new-ill-advisedly, in sooth, and not without detriment to the sciences. For, a multiform system of this kind, which depends on the authority and choice of any professor, has a foundation open to change, and consequently gives us

---

52 Martin Bucer (1491–1551).
53 L. *ejus disciplinae philosophicae.* — P. and H. philosophic system. — We are keeping "discipline" in the archaic sense of "branch of instruction," but without excluding the modern connotation of mental training and intellectual formation acquired through the study of the "discipline" at stake, namely, Scholasticism.

a philosophy not firm, and stable, and robust like that of old, but tottering and feeble. And if, perchance, it sometimes finds itself scarcely equal to sustain the shock of its foes, it should recognize that the cause and the blame lie in itself. In saying this We have no intention of discountenancing the learned and able men who bring their industry and erudition, and, what is more, the wealth of new discoveries, to the service of philosophy; for, of course, We understand that this tends to the development of learning. But one should be very careful lest all or his chief labor be exhausted in these pursuits and in mere erudition. And the same thing is true of sacred theology, which, indeed, may be assisted and illustrated by all kinds of erudition, though it is absolutely necessary to approach it in the grave manner of the Scholastics, in order that, the forces of revelation and reason being united in it, it may continue to be "the invincible bulwark of the faith."[54]

25. With wise forethought, therefore, not a few of the advocates of philosophic studies,[55] when turning their minds recently to the practical reform of philosophy, aimed and aim at restoring the renowned teaching of Thomas Aquinas and winning it back to its ancient beauty.

26. We have learned with great joy that many members of your order, venerable brethren, have taken this plan to heart; and while We earnestly commend their efforts, We exhort them to hold fast to their purpose, and remind each and all of you that Our first and most cherished idea is that you should all furnish to studious youth a generous and copious supply of those purest streams of wisdom flowing inexhaustibly from the precious fountainhead of the Angelic Doctor.[56]

---

54 Sixtus V, Bulla *Triumphantis*.
55 L. *cultores disciplinarum philosophicarum*; that is those who dedicate themselves to the study of philosophy in its various branches.
56 P. That you should all furnish a generous and copious supply to studious youth of those crystal rills of wisdom flowing in a never-ending and fertilizing stream from the fountainhead of the Angelic Doctor. — H. that you all supply for the benefit of young students, plentifully and abundantly,

27. Many are the reasons why We are so desirous of this. In the first place, then, since in the tempest that is on us the Christian faith is being constantly assailed by the machinations and craft of a certain false wisdom, all youths, but especially those who are the growing hope of the Church, should be nourished on the strong and robust food of doctrine, that so, mighty in strength and armed at all points, they may become habituated to advance the cause of religion with force and judgment, "being ready always, according to the apostolic counsel, to satisfy every one that asketh you a reason of that hope which is in you,"[57] and that they may be able to exhort in sound doctrine and to convince the gainsayers."[58] Many of those who, with minds alienated from the faith, hate Catholic institutions, claim reason as their sole mistress and guide. Now, We think that, apart from the supernatural help of God, nothing is better calculated to heal those minds and to bring them into favor with the Catholic faith than the solid doctrine of the Fathers and the Scholastics, who so clearly and forcibly demonstrate the firm foundations of the faith, its divine origin, its certain truth, the arguments that sustain it, the benefits it has conferred on the human race, and its perfect accord with reason, in a manner to satisfy completely minds open to persuasion, however unwilling and repugnant.

28. Domestic and civil society even, which, as all see, is exposed to great danger from this plague of perverse opinions, would certainly enjoy a far more peaceful and secure existence if a more wholesome doctrine were taught in the universities and high schools[59]—more in conformity with the teaching of the Church, such as is contained in the works of Thomas Aquinas.

29. For, the teachings of Thomas on the true meaning of liberty, which at this time is running into license, on the divine origin of all authority, on laws and their force, on the paternal

---

those pure streams of wisdom that flow from the Angelic Doctor as from an inexhaustible and precious fountain.
57 1 Peter 3:15.
58 Titus 1:9.
59 L. *in Academiis et scholis.*

and just rule of princes, on obedience to the higher powers, on mutual charity one toward another—on all of these and kindred subjects—have very great and invincible force to overturn those principles of the new order, which are well known to be dangerous to the peaceful order of things and to public safety. In short, all studies ought to find hope of advancement and promise of assistance in this restoration of philosophic discipline which We have proposed. The arts were wont to draw from philosophy, as from a wise mistress, sound judgment and right method, and from it, also, their spirit, as from the common fount of life. When philosophy stood stainless in honor and wise in judgment, then, as facts and constant experience showed, the liberal arts flourished as never before or since; but, neglected and almost blotted out, they lay prone, since philosophy began to lean to error and join hands with folly. Nor will the physical sciences themselves, which are now in such great repute, and by the renown of so many inventions draw such universal admiration to themselves, suffer detriment, but find very great assistance in the restoration of the ancient philosophy. For, the investigation of facts and the contemplation of nature is not alone sufficient for their profitable exercise and advance; but, when facts have been established, it is necessary to rise and apply ourselves to the study of the nature of corporeal things, to inquire into the laws which govern them and the principles whence their order and varied unity and mutual attraction in diversity arise. To such investigations, it is wonderful what force and light and aid the Scholastic philosophy, if judiciously taught, would bring.

30. And here it is well to note that our philosophy can only by the grossest injustice be accused of being opposed to the advance and development of natural science. For, when the Scholastics, following the opinion of the holy Fathers, always held in anthropology that the human intelligence is only led to the knowledge of things without body and matter by things sensible, they well understood that nothing was of greater use to the philosopher than diligently to search into the mysteries of nature and to be earnest and constant in the study of physical things. And this

they confirmed by their own example; for St. Thomas, Blessed Albertus Magnus, and other leaders of the Scholastics were never so wholly rapt in the study of philosophy as not to give large attention to the knowledge of natural things; and, indeed, the number of their sayings and writings on these subjects, which recent professors approve of and admit to harmonize with truth, is by no means small. Moreover, in this very age, many illustrious professors of the physical sciences openly testify that between certain and accepted conclusions of modern physics and the philosophic principles of the schools there is no conflict worthy of the name.

31. While, therefore, We hold that every word of wisdom, every useful thing by whomsoever discovered or planned, ought to be received with a willing and grateful mind, We exhort you, venerable brethren, in all earnestness to restore the golden wisdom of St. Thomas, and to spread it far and wide for the defense and beauty of the Catholic faith, for the good of society, and for the advantage of all the sciences. The wisdom of St. Thomas, We say; for if anything is taken up with too great subtlety by the Scholastic doctors, or too carelessly stated—if there be anything that ill agrees with the discoveries of a later age, or, in a word, improbable in whatever way—it does not enter Our mind to propose that for imitation to Our age. Let carefully selected teachers endeavor to implant the doctrine of Thomas Aquinas in the minds of students, and set forth clearly his solidity and excellence over others. Let the universities already founded or to be founded by you illustrate and defend this doctrine, and use it for the refutation of prevailing errors. But, lest the false for the true or the corrupt for the pure be drunk in,[60] be ye watchful that the doctrine of Thomas be drawn from his own fountains, or at least from those rivulets which, derived from the very fount, have thus far flowed, according to the established agreement of learned men, pure and clear; be careful to guard

---

60 L. *Ne autem supposita pro vera, neu corrupta pro sinceri bibatur*; that is, But lest a false wisdom be drunk in for the true, or a corrupt wisdom for the pure.

the minds of youth from those which are said to flow thence, but in reality are gathered from strange and unwholesome streams.

32. But well do We know that vain will be Our efforts unless, venerable brethren, He helps Our common cause who, in the words of divine Scripture, is called the God of all knowledge;[61] by which we are also admonished that "every best gift and every perfect gift is from above, coming down from the Father of lights",[62] and again: "If any of you want wisdom, let him ask of God, who giveth to all men abundantly, and upbraideth not: and it shall be given him."[63]

33. Therefore, in this also let us follow the example of the Angelic Doctor, who never gave himself to reading or writing without first begging the blessing of God, who modestly confessed that whatever he knew he had acquired not so much by his own study and labor as by the divine gift; and therefore, let us all, in humble and united prayer, beseech God to send forth the spirit of knowledge and of understanding to the children of the Church and open their senses for the understanding of wisdom. And that we may receive fuller fruits of the divine goodness, offer up to God the most efficacious patronage of the Blessed Virgin Mary, who is called the seat of wisdom; having at the same time as advocates St. Joseph, the most chaste spouse of the Virgin, and Peter and Paul, the chiefs of the Apostles, whose truth renewed the earth which had fallen under the impure blight of error, filling it with the light of heavenly wisdom.

34. In fine, relying on the divine assistance and confiding in your pastoral zeal, most lovingly We bestow on all of you, venerable brethren, on all the clergy and the flocks committed to your charge, the apostolic benediction as a pledge of heavenly gifts and a token of Our special esteem.

---

61 1 Kings 2:3.
62 James 1:17.
63 James 1:5.

II

Human Liberty

INTRODUCTION

The Encyclical *Libertas Praestantissimum*, dated June 20, 1888, deals with the nature of human liberty. No problem has given rise to more controversies, and it is easy to get lost in discussing it since the word "liberty" can be understood in several different senses, which are both distinct and interrelated.

The greater attention shall therefore be devoted to the initial articles of this encyclical, especially art. 5–6, in which the true meaning of "liberty" is defined. There is a fundamental distinction between natural liberty, which belongs to man inasmuch as he is endowed with rational knowledge, and moral liberty, which consists in choosing that good only which is in conformity with the judgment of reason. This encyclical is primarily concerned with moral liberty.

In the light of its definition, moral liberty appears to be inseparable from a certain number of conditions, namely, all the external helps which enable the human will to do the good and to shun evil. Taking up the doctrine of Thomas Aquinas, Pope Leo XIII establishes the necessity of law as a remedy to the defects of the human will and, consequently, a condition for the very possibility of human liberty.

After analyzing the notions of natural law and of human law, the Pope finds their common source in the divine law. The moral liberty of man can then be defined as the submission and obedience of his will to the authority of God commanding good and forbidding evil (art. 11).

This very definition of Christian liberty perfectly agrees with the respect due to established powers, but, for the very same

Human Liberty

reason, it is violently opposed by those whom Pope Leo XIII calls "liberals." Understood as it is in this encyclical, liberalism is in ethics and politics what naturalism or rationalism are in philosophy. Exactly, it means the denial of any divine authority and the refusal to accept it as rule, or law, of the will. We are once more sent back to the fundamental tenet of naturalism, which affirms the supremacy of the human reason (art. 15).

The ensuing examination of the so-called "modern liberties" constitutes one of the most important expressions of the social and political teaching of the Pope. The doctrine has been briefly analyzed above [see pp. xxxi–xxxiv] and will be found in articles 23, 24, 25, 30 of this encyclical. The extreme importance of the determination of the true notion of tolerance contained in art. 34 must be particularly stressed. The temporary acquiescence of the Church to certain necessitates of the times does not mean that she ever compromises on doctrine (art. 41). On the meanings of "liberalism," see the letter of Cardinal Rampolla to the archbishop of Bogota, April 6, 1900, in *Actes de Léon XIII*, Vol. 7, pp. 185–193.

SUMMARY

(1) The Church is not hostile to true liberty. (2) The so-called modern liberties. (3–4) Natural liberty defined and defended by the Church. (5) The good known by the intellect is the object of true liberty. (6) Both intellect and will are liable to error. (7) For this reason, law is necessary to enlighten the intellect and to direct the will; in short, law is a necessary condition for the existence of human liberty. (8) Natural law and its reduction to eternal law. (9) Human law and its reduction to eternal law. (10) Eternal law, the sole standard and rule of human liberty. (11) Obedience to the divine law presupposed by the very nature of human liberty. (12) The civilizing influence of the Church bears witness to the excellence of her teaching on liberty. (13) The duty we have to obey God rather than man is the most effectual barrier opposed to the tyranny of the State. (14–15) Definition of "liberalism" as denying the existence of any divine authority. (16)

Libertas Praestantissimum

The natural consequence of liberalism is tyranny. (17) Moderate liberalism is inconsistent in recognizing that there is a divine law, yet pretending to subtract the human will to its authority. (18) Even the State is bound by the laws of God who is the source of all goodness and justice. (19–21) The so-called liberty of worship cannot be admitted because it would presuppose that the State has no duties toward God. (22) To raise the level of morality is, for the States, the safest way to increase the liberty, the wealth, and the power of their citizens. (23) Considered in the light of this notion, absolute liberty of speech is not a right; there is no liberty to speak against truth. (24) The same remark applies to the liberty of teaching; the liberty to teach error is a contradictory notion. (25–28) Natural truth and divine truth are the proper subjects of teaching; for this very reason, the Church has the right to teach and justly claims the liberty to do so. (30) Liberty of conscience is fully justified when understood as it should be. (31–32) Liberalism results in the all-powerfulness of the State. (33–35) Although evil may have to be tolerated for the sake of the common good, there is no circumstance in which it can be either desired or approved. (36) Summary of the doctrine. (37–40) Liberalism leads to refusing the Church the characters of a true society and to considering as normal the separation of Church and State. (41–42) Because the Church cannot yield on matters of principles, she cannot favor an unconditional liberty of thought, of speech, of writing, or of worship. (43) It is lawful to seek to replace a vicious government with a better one. (44) Or to prefer a democratic form of government, provided this can be done without impairing the rights of the citizens or those of the Church. (45–46) Catholics, unless it be otherwise determined, are recommended to take part in the administration of public affairs, to preserve the independence of their country, and to promote the prosperity of its citizens. (47) Prayer and apostolic benediction.

11

Libertas Praestantissimum
ON HUMAN LIBERTY
June 20, 1888

1. Liberty, the highest of natural endowments, being the portion only of intellectual or rational natures, confers on man this dignity—that he is "in the hand of his counsel"[1] and has power over his actions. But the manner in which such dignity is exercised is of the greatest moment, inasmuch as on the use that is made of liberty the highest good and the greatest evil alike depend. Man, indeed, is free[2] to obey his reason, to seek moral good, and to strive unswervingly after his last end. Yet, he is free also to turn aside to all other things; and, in pursuing the empty semblance of good, to disturb rightful order and to fall headlong into the destruction, which he has voluntarily chosen. The Redeemer of mankind, Jesus Christ, having restored and exalted the original dignity of nature, vouchsafed special assistance to the will of man; and by the gifts of His grace here, and the promise of heavenly bliss hereafter, He raised it to a nobler state. In like manner, this great gift of nature has ever been, and always will be, deservingly cherished by the Catholic Church, for to her alone has been committed the charge of handing down to all ages the benefits purchased for us by Jesus Christ. Yet, there are many who imagine that the Church is hostile to human liberty. Having a false and absurd notion as to what liberty is, either they pervert the very idea of freedom, or they extend it

---

1 Ecclus. 15:14.
2 L. *Sane integrum est homini*; that is, Assuredly it is in the power of man. In this encyclical, there is practically no difference between the translation adopted by H. and the P. text which we are following. One of the most confusing words in this translation, is "State." It should create no difficulty, however, provided it be understood as pointing out the body politic rather than civil government. Exception to this advice should be made when the relationship of Church and State is under discussion. In all the other cases, we have given the various terms used by the Latin original.

Libertas Praestantissimum

at their pleasure to many things in respect of which man cannot rightly be regarded as free.

2. We have on other occasions, and especially in Our encyclical letter *Immortale Dei*,³ in treating of the so-called *modern liberties*, distinguished between their good and evil elements; and We have shown that whatsoever is good in those liberties is as ancient as truth itself, and that the Church has always most willingly approved and practiced that good: but whatsoever has been added as new is, to tell the plain truth, of a vitiated kind, the fruit of the disorders of the age, and of an insatiate longing after novelties. Seeing, however, that many cling so obstinately to their own opinion in this matter as to imagine these modern liberties, cankered as they are, to be the greatest glory of our age, and the very basis of civil life, without which no perfect government can be conceived, We feel it a pressing duty, for the sake of the common good, to treat separately of this subject.

3. It is with *moral* liberty, whether in individuals or in communities, that We proceed at once to deal. But, first of all, it will be well to speak briefly of *natural* liberty; for, though it is distinct and separate from moral liberty, natural freedom is the fountainhead from which liberty of whatsoever kind flows, *sua vi suaque sponte*.⁴ The unanimous consent and judgment of men, which is the trusty voice of nature, recognizes this natural liberty in those only who are endowed with intelligence or reason; and it is by his use of this that man is rightly regarded as responsible for his actions. For, while other animate creatures follow their senses, seeking good and avoiding evil only by instinct, man has reason to guide him in each and every act of his life. Reason sees that whatever things that are held to be good upon earth may exist or may not, and discerning that none of them are of necessity for us, it leaves the will free to choose what it pleases. But, man can judge of this contingency, as We say, only because he has a soul that is simple, spiritual, and intellectual—a soul,

---

3 See pp. 161–163.
4 H. by its own force and of its own accord.

therefore, which is not produced by matter, and does not depend on matter for its existence; but which is created immediately by God, and, far surpassing the condition of things material, has a life and action of its own so that, knowing[5] the unchangeable and necessary reasons of what is true and good, it sees that no particular kind of good is necessary to us. When, therefore, it is established that man's soul is immortal and endowed with reason[6] and not bound up with things material, the foundation of natural liberty is at once most firmly laid.

4. As the Catholic Church declares in the strongest terms, the simplicity, spirituality, and immortality of the soul, so with unequalled constancy and publicity she ever also asserts its freedom. These truths she has always taught, and has sustained them as a dogma of faith, and whensoever heretics or innovators have attacked the liberty of man, the Church has defended it and protected this noble possession from destruction. History bears witness to the energy with which she met the fury of the Manichaeans and others like them; and the earnestness with which in later years she defended human liberty at the Council of Trent, and against the followers of Jansenius, is known to all. At no time, and in no place, has she held truce with *fatalism*.

5. Liberty, then, as We have said, belongs only to those who have the gift of reason or intelligence. Considered as to its nature, it is the faculty of choosing means fitted for the end proposed, for he is master of his actions who can choose one thing out of many. Now, since everything chosen as a means is viewed as good or useful, and since good, as such, is the proper object of our desire,[7] it follows that freedom of choice[8] is a property of the will, or, rather, is identical with the will[9] in so far as it has in its action the faculty of choice. But, the will cannot proceed

---

5   L. *judicio comprehen*sis; that is, knowing by its judgement.
6   L. *facultate cogitandi pollere*; that is, endowed with the power of reasoning.
7   L. *ut proprie appetitionem moveat*; that is, is the proper move of desire.
8   L. *liberum arbitrium*.
9   L. *seu potius ipsa voluntas* est; that is, or rather is the will itself.

to act until it is enlightened by the knowledge possessed by the intellect. In other words, the good wished by the will is necessarily good in so far as it is known by the intellect; and this the more, because in all voluntary acts choice is subsequent to a judgment upon the truth of the good presented, declaring to which good preference should be given. No sensible man can doubt that judgment is an act of reason, not of the will. The end, or object, both of the rational will and of its liberty is that good only which is in conformity with reason.

6. Since, however, both these faculties are imperfect, it is possible, as is often seen, that the reason should propose something which is not really good, but which has the appearance of good, and that the will should choose accordingly. For, as the possibility of error, and actual error, are defects of the mind and attest its imperfection, so the pursuit of what has a false appearance of good, though a proof of our freedom, just as a disease is a proof of our vitality, implies defect in human liberty. The will also, simply because of its dependence on the reason, no sooner desires anything contrary thereto than it abuses its freedom of choice and corrupts its very essence. Thus, it is that the infinitely perfect God, although supremely free, because of the supremacy of His intellect and of His essential goodness, nevertheless cannot choose evil; neither can the angels and saints, who enjoy the beatific vision. St. Augustine and others urged most admirably against the Pelagians that, if the possibility of deflection from good belonged to the essence or perfection of liberty, then God, Jesus Christ, and the angels and saints, who have not this power, would have no liberty at all, or would have less liberty than man has in his state of pilgrimage and imperfection. This subject is often discussed by the Angelic Doctor in his demonstration that the possibility of sinning is not freedom, but slavery. It will suffice to quote his subtle commentary on the words of our Lord: "Whosoever committeth sin is the slave of sin."[10] "Everything," he says, "is that which belongs to

---

10   John 8:34.

it naturally. When, therefore, it acts through a power outside itself, it does not act of itself, but through another, that is, as a slave. But man is by nature rational. When, therefore, he acts according to reason, he acts of himself and according to his free will; and this is liberty. Whereas, when he sins, he acts in opposition to reason, is moved by another, and is the victim of foreign misapprehensions. Therefore, 'Whosoever committeth sin is the slave of sin.'"[11] Even the heathen philosophers clearly recognized this truth, especially they who held that the wise man alone is free; and by the term "wise man" was meant, as is well known, the man trained to live in accordance with his nature, that is, in justice and virtue.

7. Such, then, being the condition of human liberty, it necessarily stands in need of light and strength to direct its actions to good and to restrain them from evil. Without this, the freedom of our will would be our ruin. First of all, there must be *law*; that is, a fixed rule of teaching what is to be done and what is to be left undone. This rule cannot affect the lower animals in any true sense, since they act of necessity, following their natural instinct, and cannot of themselves act in any other way. On the other hand, as was said above, he who is free can either act or not act, can do this or do that, as he pleases, because his judgment[12] precedes his choice. And his judgment not only decides what is right or wrong of its own nature, but also what is practically good and therefore to be chosen, and what is practically evil and therefore to be avoided. In other words, the reason prescribes to the will what it should seek after or shun, in order to the eventual attainment of man's last end, for the sake of which all his actions ought to be performed. This ordination of *reason* is called law. In man's free will, therefore, or in the moral necessity of our voluntary acts being in accordance with reason, lies the very root of the necessity of law. Nothing more foolish can be uttered or conceived than the notion that, because man is free

---

11 Thomas Aquinas, *On the Gospel of St. John*, cap. viii, lect. 4, n. 3 (ed. Vives, Vol. 20, p. 95).
12 L. *rationis judicium*; that is, the judgement of his reason.

Libertas Praestantissimum

by nature, he is therefore exempt from law. Were this the case, it would follow that to become free we must be deprived of reason; whereas the truth is that we are bound to submit to law precisely because we are free by our very nature. For, law is the guide of man's actions; it turns him toward good by its rewards, and deters him from evil by its punishments.

8. Foremost in this office comes the *natural law*, which is written and engraved in the mind of every man; and this is nothing but our reason, commanding us to do right and forbidding sin. Nevertheless, all prescriptions[13] of human reason can have force of law only inasmuch as they are the voice and the interpreters of some higher power on which our reason and liberty necessarily depend.[14] For, since the force of law consists in the imposing of obligations and the granting of rights, authority is the one and only foundation of all law — the power, that is, of fixing duties[15] and defining rights, as also of assigning the necessary sanctions of reward and chastisement to each and all of its commands. But all this, clearly, cannot be found in man, if, as his own supreme legislator, he is to be the rule of his own actions. It follows, therefore, that the law of nature is the same thing as the *eternal law*, implanted in rational creatures, and inclining them *to their right action and end*; and can be nothing else but the eternal reason of God, the Creator and Ruler of all the world. To this rule of action and restraint of evil, God has vouchsafed to give special and most suitable aids for strengthening and ordering the human will. The first and most excellent of these is the power of His divine *grace*, whereby the mind can be enlightened and the will wholesomely invigorated

---

13   L. *Ista vero humanae rationis praescriptio*; that is, nevertheless, this prescription of reason (namely, natural law).
14   L. *nisi quia altioris est vox atque interpres rationis, cui mentem libertatemque nostrum subjectam esse oporteat*; that is, only inasmuch as it is the mouthpiece and interpreter of some higher reason to which our mind and liberty must submit.
15   L. *Vis enim legis cum ita sit*; that is, for, since the scope of law consists in the imposition of obligations and the granting of rights, it wholly rests upon authority, that is, upon the true power of fixing duties...

and moved to the constant pursuit of moral good, so that the use of our inborn liberty becomes at once less difficult and less dangerous. Not that the divine assistance hinders in any way the free movement of our will; just the contrary, for grace works inwardly in man and in harmony with his natural inclinations, since it flows from the very Creator of his mind and will, by whom all things are moved in conformity with their nature. As the Angelic Doctor points out, it is because divine grace comes from the Author of nature that it is so admirably adapted to be the safeguard of all natures, and to maintain the character, efficiency, and operations of each.

9. What has been said of the liberty of individuals is no less applicable to them when considered as bound together in civil society. For, what reason and the natural law do for individuals, that *human law*, promulgated for their good, does for the citizens of States. Of the laws enacted by men, some are concerned with what is good or bad by its very nature; and they command men to follow after what is right and to shun what is wrong, adding at the same time a suitable sanction. But such laws by no means derive their origin from civil society, because, just as civil society did not create human nature, so neither can it be said to be the author of the good which befits human nature, or of the evil which is contrary to it. Laws come before men live together in society, and have their origin in the natural, and consequently in the eternal, law. The precepts, therefore, of the natural law,[16] contained bodily in the laws of men, have not merely the force of human law, but they possess that higher and more august sanction which belongs to the law of nature and the eternal law. And within the sphere of this kind of laws, the duty of the civil legislator is, mainly, to keep the community in obedience by the adoption of a common discipline and by putting restraint upon refractory and viciously inclined men, so that, deterred from evil,

---

16 L. *Juris igitur naturalis*; this translation usually renders *jus* by law, probably its best English approximations. In fact, however, the Latin word just points out the notions of "that which is just" rather that of "law" (*lex*), which points out the binding rule stating that which is just.

they may turn to what is good, or at any rate may avoid causing trouble and disturbance to the State.[17] Now, there are other enactments of the civil authority, which do not follow directly, but somewhat remotely,[18] from the natural law, and decide many points which the law of nature treats only in a general and indefinite way. For instance, though nature commands all to contribute to the public peace and prosperity, whatever belongs to the manner, and circumstances, and conditions under which such service is to be rendered must be determined by the wisdom of men and not by nature herself. It is in the constitution of these particular rules of life, suggested by reason and prudence, and put forth by competent authority, that human law, properly so-called, consists, binding all citizens to work together for the attainment of the common end proposed to the community, and forbidding them to depart from this end, and, in so far as human law is in conformity with the dictates of nature, leading to what is good, and deterring from evil.

10. From this it is manifest that the eternal law of God is the sole standard and rule of human liberty, not only in each individual man, but also in the community and civil society which men constitute when united. Therefore, the true liberty of human society does not consist in every man doing what he pleases, for this would simply end in turmoil and confusion, and bring on the overthrow of the State;[19] but rather in this, that through the injunctions of the civil law all may more easily conform to the prescriptions of the eternal law. Likewise, the liberty of those who are in authority does not consist in the power to lay unreasonable and capricious commands upon their subjects, which would equally be criminal and would lead to the ruin of the commonwealth; but the binding force of human laws is in this, that they are to be regarded as applications[20] of the eternal law, and incapable of sanctioning anything which is not

---

17 L. *civitati*; that is, to the community.
18 L. adds *et oblique*; that is, and indirectly.
19 L. *civitatis*; that is, of the community.
20 L. *manare*; that is, as flowing from.

contained in the eternal law, as in the principle of all law.[21] Thus, St. Augustine most wisely says: "I think that you can see, at the same time, that there is nothing just and lawful in that temporal law, unless what men have gathered from this eternal law."[22] If, then, by anyone in authority, something be sanctioned out of conformity with the principles of right reason, and consequently hurtful to the commonwealth, such an enactment can have no binding force of law, as being no rule of justice, but certain to lead men away from that good which is the very end of civil society.

11. Therefore, the nature of human liberty, however it be considered, whether in individuals or in society, whether in those who command or in those who obey, supposes the necessity of obedience to some supreme and eternal law, which is no other than the authority of God, commanding good and forbidding evil. And, so far from this most just authority of God over men diminishing, or even destroying their liberty, it protects and perfects it, for the real perfection of all creatures is found in the prosecution and attainment of their respective ends; but the supreme end to which human liberty must aspire is God.

12. These precepts of the truest and highest teaching, made known to us by the light of reason itself, the Church, instructed by the example and doctrine of her divine Author, has ever propagated and asserted; for she has ever made them the measure of her office and of her teaching to the Christian nations. As to morals, the laws of the Gospel not only immeasurably surpass the wisdom of the heathen, but are an invitation and an introduction to a state of holiness unknown to the ancients; and, bringing man nearer to God, they make him at once the possessor of a more perfect liberty. Thus, the powerful influence of the Church has ever been manifested in the custody and protection of the civil and political liberty of the people. The enumeration of its merits in this respect does not belong to our present purpose. It is

---

21 L. *juris*; see footnote 16.
22 Augustine, *De libero arbitrio*, lib. I, cap. 6, n. 15 (PL 32, 1229).

Libertas Praestantissimum

sufficient to recall the fact that slavery, that old reproach of the heathen nations, was mainly abolished by the beneficent efforts of the Church. The impartiality of law and the true brotherhood of man were first asserted by Jesus Christ, and His apostles re-echoed His voice when they declared that in the future there was to be neither Jew, nor Gentile, nor barbarian, nor Scythian, but all were brothers in Christ. So powerful, so conspicuous, in this respect is the influence of the Church that experience abundantly testifies how savage customs are no longer possible in any land where she has once set her foot; but that gentleness speedily takes the place of cruelty, and the light of truth quickly dispels the darkness of barbarism. Nor has the Church been less lavish in the benefits she has conferred on civilized nations in every age, either by resisting the tyranny of the wicked, or by protecting the innocent and helpless from injury, or, finally, by using her influence in the support of any form of government, which commended itself to the citizens at home, because of its justice, or was feared by their enemies without, because of its power.

13. Moreover, the highest duty[23] is to respect authority, and obediently to submit to just law; and by this the members of a community[24] are effectually protected from the wrong-doing of evil men. Lawful power is from God, "and whosoever resisteth authority resisteth the ordinance of God";[25] wherefore, obedience is greatly ennobled when subjected to an authority which is the most just and supreme of all. But where the power[26] to command is wanting, or where a law is enacted contrary to reason, or to the eternal law, or to some ordinance of God, obedience is unlawful, lest, while obeying man, we become disobedient to God.[27] Thus, an effectual barrier being opposed to tyranny, the authority in the State will not have all its own way,[28] but

---

23 L. *verissimum officium*; that is, it is a most real duty.
24 L. *cives*; that is, the citizens.
25 Rom. 13:2.
26 L. *jus*; that is, the right.
27 L. *rectum est non parere, scilicet hominibus, ut Deo pareatur*; that is, it is right not to obey men, so that God be obeyed.
28 L. *non omnia pertrahet ad se principatus*; that is, the government

the interests and rights of all will be safeguarded—the rights of individuals, of domestic society, and of all the members of the commonwealth; all being free to live according to law and right reason; and in this, as We have shown, true liberty really consists.

14. If when men discuss the question of liberty they were careful to grasp its true and legitimate meaning, such as reason and reasoning have just explained, they would never venture to affix such a calumny on the Church as to assert that she is the foe of individual and public liberty. But many there are who follow in the footsteps of Lucifer, and adopt as their own his rebellious cry, "I will not serve"; and consequently substitute for true liberty what is sheer and most foolish license. Such, for instance, are the men belonging to that widely spread and powerful organization,[29] who, usurping the name of liberty,[30] style themselves liberals.

15. What *naturalists* or *rationalists* aim at in philosophy that the supporters of *liberalism*, carrying out the principles laid down by naturalism, are attempting in the domain of morality and politics. The fundamental doctrine of rationalism is the supremacy of the human reason, which, refusing due submission to the divine and eternal reason, proclaims its own independence, and constitutes itself the supreme principle and source and judge of truth. Hence, these followers of liberalism deny the existence of any divine authority to which obedience is due, and proclaim that every man is the law to himself; from which arises that ethical system which they style *independent* morality, and which, under the guise of liberty, exonerates man from any obedience to the commands of God, and substitutes a boundless license. The end of all this is not difficult to foresee, especially when society is in question. For, when once man is firmly persuaded that he is subject to no one, it follows that the efficient cause of the unity of civil society is not to be sought in any principle

---

will not appropriate everything to itself.
29 L. *disciplina*; that is, school (of thought).
30 L. *ducto a libertate nomine*; that is borrowing their name from the word liberty, style themselves liberals.

Libertas Praestantissimum

external to man, or superior to him, but simply in the free will of individuals; that the authority in the State[31] comes from the people only; and that, just as every man's individual reason is his only rule of life, so the collective reason of the community should be the supreme guide in the management of all public affairs. Hence, the doctrine of the supremacy of the greater number, and that all right and all duty reside in the majority.[32] But, from what has been said, it is clear that all this is in contradiction to reason. To refuse any bond of union between man and civil society, on the one hand, and God the Creator and consequently the supreme Law-giver, on the other, is plainly repugnant to the nature, not only of man, but of all created things; for, of necessity, all effects must in some proper way be connected with their cause; and it belongs to the perfection of every nature to contain itself within that sphere and grade which the order of nature has assigned to it, namely,[33] that the lower should be subject and obedient to the higher.

16. Moreover, besides this, a doctrine of such character is most hurtful both to individuals and to the State. For, once ascribed to human reason the only authority to decide what is true and what is good, and the real distinction between good and evil is destroyed; honor and dishonor differ not in their nature, but in the opinion and judgment of each one; pleasure is the measure of what is lawful; and, given a code of morality which can have little or no power to restrain or quiet the unruly propensities of man, a way is naturally opened to universal corruption. With reference also to public affairs: authority is severed from the true and natural principle whence it derives all its efficacy for

---

31 L. *potestatem publicam*; that is, political authority.
32 L. *partemque populi majorem universi juris esse officiique effectricem*; that is, and that the majority decides what shall be the rights and the duties for all.
33 L. *omnibus naturis hoc convenit, hoc ad perfectionem singulorum pertinent eo se continere loco et gradu quem naturalis ordo postulat*; that is, and this is fitting for all natures, it is required for the perfection of each and every one of them that it should keep the place and the rank which the order of nature demands, namely...

the common good; and the law determining what it is right to do and avoid doing is at the mercy of a majority. Now, this is simply a road leading straight to tyranny. The empire of God over man and civil society once repudiated, it follows that religion, as a public institution, can have no claim to exist, and that everything that belongs to religion will be treated with complete indifference. Furthermore, with ambitious designs on sovereignty, tumult and sedition will be common amongst the people; and when duty and conscience cease to appeal to them, there will be nothing to hold them back but force, which of itself alone is powerless to keep their covetousness in check. Of this, we have almost daily evidence in the conflict with *socialists* and members of other seditious societies, who labor unceasingly to bring about revolution. It is for those, then, who are capable of forming a just estimate of things to decide whether such doctrines promote that true liberty which alone is worthy of man, or rather, pervert and destroy it.

17. There are, indeed, some adherents of liberalism who do not subscribe to these opinions, which we have seen to be fearful in their enormity, openly opposed to the truth, and the cause of most terrible evils. Indeed, very many amongst them, compelled by the force of truth, do not hesitate to admit that such liberty is vicious, nay, is simple license, whenever intemperate in its claims, to the neglect of truth and justice; and therefore, they would have liberty ruled and directed by right reason, and consequently subject to the natural law[34] and to the divine eternal law. But, here they think they may stop, holding that man as a free being is bound by no law of God except such as He makes known to us through our natural reason. In this, they are plainly inconsistent. For if — as they must admit, and no one can rightly deny — the will of the Divine Law-giver is to be obeyed, because every man[35] is under the power of God, and tends toward Him as his end, it follows that no one can assign limits to His legislative authority without failing in the

---

34 L. *juri naturali*; see footnote 16.
35 L. *totus homo*; that is, the whole man.

Libertas Praestantissimum

obedience which is due. Indeed, if the human mind be so presumptuous as to define the nature and extent of God's rights and its own duties, reverence for the divine law will be apparent rather than real, and arbitrary judgment will prevail over the authority and providence of God. Man must, therefore, take his standard of a loyal and religious life from the eternal law; and from all and every one of those laws which God, in His infinite wisdom and power, has been pleased to enact, and to make known to us by such clear and unmistakable signs as to leave no room for doubt. And the more so because laws of this kind have the same origin, the same author, as the eternal law, are absolutely in accordance with right reason, and perfect the natural law.[36] These laws it is that embody the government of God,[37] who graciously guides and directs the intellect and the will of man lest these fall into error. Let, then, that continue to remain in a holy and inviolable union which neither can nor should be separated; and in all things — for this is the dictate of right reason itself — let God be dutifully and obediently served.

18. There are others, somewhat more moderate though not more consistent, who affirm that the morality of individuals is to be guided by the divine law, but not the morality of the State,[38] for that in public affairs the commands of God may be passed over, and may be entirely disregarded in the framing of laws. Hence, follows the fatal theory[39] of the need of separation between Church and State. But the absurdity of such a position is manifest. Nature herself proclaims the necessity of the State providing means and opportunities whereby the community may be enabled to live properly,[40] that is to say, according to

---

36 L. *ad naturale jus*, see footnote 16.
37 L. *magisterium Dei ipsius*; that is, the teaching authority of God Himself.
38 L. *civitatis*; that is, of the body politic.
39 L. *consectarium*; that is, consequence.
40 L. *oportere civibus in societate suppetere copias opportunitatesque ad vitam honeste ... degendam*; that is, the necessity there is, in a society, to provide the resources and facilities whereby its citizens may be enabled to live properly...

the laws of God. For, since God is the source of all goodness and justice, it is absolutely ridiculous[41] that the State should pay no attention to these laws or render them abortive by contrary enactments. Besides, those who are in authority owe it to the commonwealth not only to provide for its external well-being and the conveniences of life, but still more to consult the welfare of men's souls in the wisdom of their legislation. But, for the increase of such benefits, nothing more suitable can be conceived than the laws which have God for their author; and, therefore, they, who in their government of the State, take no account of these laws abuse political power by causing it to deviate from its proper end and from what nature itself prescribes. And, what is still more important, and what We have more than once pointed out, although the civil authority has not the same proximate end as the spiritual, nor proceeds on the same lines, nevertheless in the exercise of their separate powers, they must occasionally meet. For their subjects are the same, and not infrequently they deal with the same objects, though in different ways. Whenever this occurs, since a state of conflict is absurd and manifestly repugnant to the most wise ordinance of God, there must necessarily exist some order or mode of procedure to remove the occasions of difference and contention, and to secure harmony in all things. This harmony has been not inaptly compared to that which exists between the body and the soul for the well-being of both one and the other, the separation of which brings irremediable harm to the body, since it extinguishes its very life.

19. To make this more evident, the growth of liberty ascribed to our age must be considered apart in its various details. And, first, let us examine that liberty in individuals which is so opposed to the virtue of religion, namely, the *liberty of worship*, as it is called. This is based on the principle that every man is free to profess as he may choose any religion or none.

20. But, assuredly, of all the duties which man has to fulfill, that, without doubt, is the chiefest and holiest which commands

---

41 L. *vehementer repugnant*; that is, it is wholly contradictory.

Libertas Praestantissimum

him to worship God with devotion and piety. This follows of necessity from the truth that we are ever in the power of God, are ever guided by His will and providence, and, having come forth from Him, must return to Him. Add to which, no true virtue can exist without religion, for moral virtue is concerned with those things which lead to God as man's supreme and ultimate good; and therefore religion, which (as St. Thomas says) "performs those actions which are directly and immediately ordained for the divine honor,"[42] rules and tempers all virtues. And if it be asked which of the many conflicting religions it is necessary to adopt, reason and the natural law unhesitatingly tell us to practice that one which God enjoins, and which men can easily recognize by certain exterior notes, whereby Divine Providence has willed that it should be distinguished, because, in a matter of such moment, the most terrible loss would be the consequence of error. Wherefore, when a liberty such as We have described is offered to man, the power is given him to pervert or abandon with impunity the most sacred of duties, and to exchange the unchangeable good for evil; which, as We have said, is no liberty, but its degradation, and the abject submission of the soul to sin.

21. This kind of liberty, if considered in relation to the State, clearly implies that there is no reason why the State should offer any homage to God, or should desire any public recognition of Him; that no one form of worship is to be preferred to another, but that all stand on an equal footing, no account being taken of the religion of the people, even if they profess the Catholic faith. But, to justify this, it must needs be taken as true that the State has no duties toward God, or that such duties, if they exist, can be abandoned with impunity, both of which assertions are manifestly false. For it cannot be doubted but that, by the will of God, men are united in civil society; whether its component parts be considered; or its form, which implies authority; or the object of its existence; or the abundance of

---

42   *Summa theologiae*, IIa-IIae, q. lxxxi, a. 6, Answer.

the vast services which it renders to man. God, it is who has made man for society, and has placed him in the company of others like himself, so that what was wanting to his nature, and beyond his attainment if left to his own resources, he might obtain by association with others. Wherefore, civil society must acknowledge God as its Founder and Parent, and must obey and reverence His power and authority. Justice therefore forbids, and reason itself forbids, the State to be godless; or to adopt a line of action which would end in godlessness—nnamely, to treat the various religions (as they call them) alike, and to bestow upon them promiscuously equal rights and privileges. Since, then, the profession of one religion is necessary in the State,[43] that religion must be professed which alone is true, and which can be recognized without difficulty, especially in Catholic States,[44] because the marks of truth are, as it were, engravers upon it. This religion, therefore, the rulers of the State[45] must preserve and protect, if they would provide—as they should do—with prudence and usefulness for the good of the community. For public authority exists for the welfare of those whom it governs; and, although its proximate end is to lead men to the prosperity found in this life, yet, in so doing, it ought not to diminish, but rather to increase, man's capability of attaining to the supreme good in which his everlasting happiness consists: which never can be attained if religion be disregarded.

22. All this, however, We have explained more fully elsewhere. We now only wish to add the remark that liberty of so false a nature is greatly hurtful to the true liberty of both rulers and their subjects. Religion, of its essence, is wonderfully helpful to the State. For, since it derives the prime origin of all power directly from God Himself, with grave authority it charges rulers to be mindful of their duty, to govern without injustice or severity, to rule their people kindly and with almost paternal charity; it admonishes subjects to be obedient to lawful authority, as

---

43 L. *in civitate*; that is, in the body politic.
44 L. *in civitatibus catholicis*; that is, in Catholic societies.
45 L. *qui rempublicam gerunt*; that is, the rulers of the commonwealth.

to the ministers of God; and it binds them to their rulers, not merely by obedience, but by reverence and affection, forbidding all seditious and venturesome enterprises calculated to disturb public order and tranquillity, and cause greater restrictions to be put upon the liberty of the people. We need not mention how greatly religion conduces to pure morals, and pure morals to liberty. Reason shows, and history confirms the fact, that the higher the morality of States; the greater are the liberty and wealth and power which they enjoy.

23. We must now consider briefly *liberty of speech*, and liberty of the press. It is hardly necessary to say that there can be no such right as this, if it be not used in moderation, and if it pass beyond the bounds and end of all true liberty. For right is a moral power which—as We have before said and must again and again repeat—it is absurd to suppose that nature has accorded indifferently to truth and falsehood, to justice and injustice. Men have a right freely and prudently to propagate throughout the State what things soever are true and honorable, so that as many as possible may possess them; but lying opinions, than which no mental plague is greater, and vices which corrupt the heart and moral life should be diligently repressed by public authority, lest they insidiously work the ruin of the State. The excesses of an unbridled intellect, which unfailingly end in the oppression of the untutored multitude, are no less rightly controlled by the authority of the law than are the injuries inflicted by violence upon the weak. And this all the more surely, because by far the greater part of the community is either absolutely unable, or able only with great difficulty, to escape from illusions and deceitful subtleties, especially such as flatter the passions. If unbridled license of speech and of writing be granted to all, nothing will remain sacred and inviolate; even the highest and truest mandates of natures, justly held to be the common and noblest heritage of the human race, will not be spared. Thus, truth being gradually obscured by darkness, pernicious and manifold error, as too often happens, will easily prevail. Thus, too, license will gain what liberty loses; for liberty will ever be more free and

secure in proportion as license is kept in fuller restraint. In regard, however, to all matter of opinion which God leaves to man's free discussion, full liberty of thought and of speech is naturally within the right of everyone; for such liberty never leads men to suppress the truth, but often to discover it and make it known.

24. A like judgment must be passed upon what is called *liberty of teaching*. There can be no doubt that truth alone should imbue the minds of men, for in it are found the well-being, the end, and the perfection of every intelligent nature; and therefore, nothing but truth should be taught both to the ignorant and to the educated, so as to bring knowledge to those who have it not, and to preserve it in those who possess it. For this reason, it is plainly the duty of all who teach to banish error from the mind, and by sure safeguards to close the entry to all false convictions. From this, it follows, as is evident, that the liberty of which We have been speaking is greatly opposed to reason, and tends absolutely to pervert men's minds, in as much as it claims for itself the right of teaching whatever it pleases — a liberty which the State cannot grant without failing in its duty. And the more so because the authority of teachers has great weight with their hearers, who can rarely decide for themselves as to the truth or falsehood of the instruction given to them.

25. Wherefore, this liberty, also, in order that it may deserve the name, must be kept within certain limits, lest the office of teaching be turned with impunity into an instrument of corruption. Now, truth, which should be the only subject matter of those who teach, is of two kinds: natural and supernatural. Of natural truths, such as the principles of nature and whatever is derived from them immediately by our reason, there is a kind of common patrimony in the human race. On this, as on a firm basis, morality, justice, religion, and the very bonds of human society rest: and to allow people to go unharmed who violate or destroy it would be most impious, most foolish, and most inhuman.

26. But with no less religious care must we preserve that great and sacred treasure of the truths which God Himself has taught us. By many and convincing arguments, often used by defenders of Christianity, certain leading truths have been laid down: namely, that some things have been revealed by God; that the only-begotten Son of God was made flesh, to bear witness to the truth; that a perfect society was founded by Him—the Church, namely, of which He is the head, and with which He has promised to abide till the end of the world. To this society He entrusted all the truths which He had taught, in order that it might keep and guard them and with lawful authority explain them; and at the same time He commanded all nations to hear the voice of the Church, as if it were His own, threatening those who would nor hear it with everlasting perdition. Thus, it is manifest that man's best and surest teacher is God, the Source and Principle of all truth; and the only-begotten Son, who is in the bosom of the Father, the Way, the Truth, and the Life, the true Light which enlightens every man, and to whose teaching all must submit: "And they shall all be taught of God."[46]

27. In faith and in the teaching of morality, God Himself made the Church a partaker of His divine authority, and through His heavenly gift she cannot be deceived. She is therefore the greatest and most reliable teacher of mankind, and in her swells an inviolable right to teach them. Sustained by the truth received from her divine Founder, the Church has ever sought to fulfill holily the mission entrusted to her by God; unconquered by the difficulties on all sides surrounding her, she has never ceased to assert her liberty of teaching, and in this way the wretched superstition of paganism being dispelled, the wide world was renewed unto Christian wisdom. Now, reason itself clearly teaches that the truths of divine revelation and those of nature cannot really be opposed to one another, and that whatever is at variance with them must necessarily be false. Therefore, the divine teaching of the Church, so far from being an obstacle to the pursuit of

---

46   John 6:45.

learning and the progress of science, or in any way retarding the advance of civilization, in reality brings to them the sure guidance of shining light. And for the same reason, it is of no small advantage for the perfecting of human liberty, since our Saviour Jesus Christ has said that by truth is man made free: "You shall know the truth, and the truth shall make you free."[47] Therefore, there is no reason why genuine liberty should grow indignant, or true science feel aggrieved, at having to bear the just and necessary restraint of laws by which, in the judgment of the Church and of reason itself, human teaching has to be controlled.

28. The Church, indeed — as facts have everywhere proved — looks chiefly and above all to the defense of the Christian faith, while careful at the same time to foster and promote every kind of human learning. For learning is in itself good, and praiseworthy, and desirable; and further, all erudition which is the outgrowth of sound reason, and in conformity with the truth of things, serves not a little to confirm what we believe on the authority of God. The Church, truly, to our great benefit, has carefully preserved the monuments of ancient wisdom; has opened everywhere homes of science, and has urged on intellectual progress by fostering most diligently the arts by which the culture[48] of our age is so much advanced. Lastly, we must not forget that a vast field lies freely open to man's industry and genius, containing all those things which have no necessary connection with Christian faith and morals, or as to which the Church, exercising no authority, leaves the judgment of the learned free and unconstrained.

29. From all this may be understood the nature and character of that liberty which the followers of liberalism so eagerly advocate and proclaim. On the one hand, they demand for themselves and for the State[49] a license which opens the way to every perversity of opinion; and on the other, they hamper the Church in divers

---

47 John 8:32.
48 L. *urbanitas*; that is, the civilization.
49 L. *reipublicae*; that is, the commonwealth.

Libertas Praestantissimum

ways, restricting her liberty within narrowest limits, although from her teaching not only is there nothing to be feared, but in every respect very much to be gained.

30. Another liberty is widely advocated, namely, *liberty of conscience*. If by this is meant that everyone may, as he chooses, worship God or not, it is sufficiently refuted by the arguments already adduced. But it may also be taken to mean that every man in the State may follow the will of God and, from a consciousness of duty and free from every obstacle, obey His commands. This, indeed, is true liberty, a liberty worthy of the sons of God, which nobly maintains the dignity of man and is stronger than all violence or wrong — a liberty which the Church has always desired and held most dear. This is the kind of liberty the Apostles claimed for themselves with intrepid constancy, which the apologists of Christianity confirmed by their writings, and which the martyrs in vast numbers consecrated by their blood. And deservedly so; for this Christian liberty bears witness to the absolute and most just dominion of God over man, and to the chief and supreme duty of man toward God. It has nothing in common with a seditious and rebellious mind; and in no title derogates from obedience to public authority; for the right to command and to require obedience exists only so far as it is in accordance with the authority of God, and is within the measure that He has laid down. But when anything is commanded which is plainly at variance with the will of God, there is a wide departure from this divinely constituted order, and at the same time a direct conflict with divine authority; therefore, it is right not to obey.

31. By the patrons of liberalism, however, who make the State[50] absolute and omnipotent, and proclaim that man should live altogether independently of God, the liberty of which We speak, which goes hand in hand with virtue and religion, is not admitted; and whatever is done for its preservation is accounted an injury and an offense against the State.[51] Indeed, if what they say

---

50 L. *principatum*; that is, the government.
51 L. *rempublicam*; that is, against society.

were really true, there would be no tyranny, no matter how monstrous, which we should not be bound to endure and submit to.

32. The Church most earnestly desires that the Christian teaching, of which We have given an outline, should penetrate every rank of society in reality and in practice; for it would be of the greatest efficacy in healing the evils of our day, which are neither few nor slight, and are the offspring in great part of the false liberty[52] which is so much extolled, and in which the germs of safety and glory were supposed to be contained. The hope has been disappointed by the result. The fruit, instead of being sweet and wholesome, has proved cankered and bitter. If, then, a remedy is desired, let it be sought for in a restoration of sound doctrine, from which alone the preservation of order and, as a consequence, the defense of true liberty can be confidently expected.

33. Yet, with the discernment of a true mother, the Church weighs the great burden of human weakness, and well knows the course down which the minds and actions of men are in this our age being borne. For this reason, while not conceding any right to anything save what is true and honest, she does not forbid public authority to tolerate what is at variance with truth and justice, for the sake of avoiding some greater evil, or of obtaining or preserving some greater good. God Himself in His providence, though infinitely good and powerful, permits evil to exist in the world, partly that greater good may not be impeded, and partly that greater evil may not ensue. In the government of States[53] it is not forbidden to imitate the Ruler of the world; and, as the authority of man is powerless to prevent every evil, it has (as St. Augustine says) to overlook and leave unpunished many things which are punished, and rightly, by Divine Providence.[54] But if, in such circumstances, for the sake of the common good (and this is the only legitimate reason), human law may or even should tolerate evil, it may not

---

52 L. *libertatibus quae tanta predicatione efferuntur*; that is, of the very liberties that are so much extolled.
53 L. *in regendis civitatibus*; that is, in governing societies.
54 Augustine, *De libero arbitrio*, lib. I, cap. 6, n. 14 (PL 32, 1228).

Libertas Praestantissimum

and should not approve or desire evil for its own sake; for evil of itself, being a privation of good, is opposed to the common welfare which every legislator is bound to desire and defend to the best of his ability. In this, human law must endeavor to imitate God, who, as St. Thomas teaches, in allowing evil to exist in the world, "neither wills evil to be done, nor wills it not to be done, but wills only to permit it to be done; and this is good."[55] This saying of the Angelic Doctor contains briefly the whole doctrine of the permission of evil.

34. But, to judge aright, we must acknowledge that, the more a State[56] is driven to tolerate evil, the further is it from perfection; and that the tolerance of evil which is dictated by political prudence should be strictly confined to the limits which its justifying cause, the public welfare, requires. Wherefore, if such tolerance would be injurious to the public welfare, and entail greater evils on the State,[57] it would not be lawful; for in such case the motive of good is wanting. And although in the extraordinary condition of these times the Church usually acquiesces in certain modern liberties, not because she prefers them in themselves, but because she judges it expedient to permit them, she would in happier times exercise her own liberty; and, by persuasion, exhortation, and entreaty would endeavor, as she is bound, to fulfill the duty assigned to her by God of providing for the eternal salvation of mankind. One thing, however, remains always true—that the liberty which is claimed for all to do all things is not, as We have often said, of itself desirable, inasmuch as it is contrary to reason that error and truth should have equal rights.

35. And as to *tolerance*, it is surprising how far removed from the equity and prudence of the Church are those who profess what is called liberalism. For, in allowing that boundless license of which We have spoken, they exceed all limits, and end at last by making no apparent distinction between truth and error,

---

55 *Summa theologiae*, Ia, q. xix, a. 9, ad 3m.
56 L. *in civitate*; that is, in a society.
57 L. *civitati*; that is, on society.

honesty and dishonesty. And because the Church, the pillar and ground of truth, and the unerring teacher of morals, is forced utterly to reprobate and condemn tolerance of such an abandoned and criminal character, they calumniate her as being wanting in patience and gentleness, and thus fail to see that, in so doing, they impute to her as a fault what is in reality a matter for commendation. But, in spite of all this show of tolerance, it very often happens that, while they profess themselves ready to lavish liberty on all in the greatest profusion, they are utterly intolerant toward the Catholic Church, by refusing to allow her the liberty of being herself free.[58]

36. And now to reduce for clearness' sake to its principal heads all that has been set forth with its immediate conclusions,[59] the summing up in this briefly: that man, by a necessity of his nature, is wholly subject to the most faithful and ever-enduring power of God;[60] and that, as a consequence, any liberty, except that which consists in submission to God and in subjection to His will, is unintelligible. To deny the existence of this authority in God, or to refuse to submit to it, means to act, not as a free man, but as one who treasonably abuses his liberty; and in such a disposition of mind the chief and deadly vice of liberalism essentially consists. The form, however, of the sin is manifold; for in more ways and degrees than one can the will depart from the obedience which is due to God or to those who share the divine power.

37. For, to reject the supreme authority to God, and to cast off all obedience to Him in public matters, or even in private and domestic affairs, is the greatest perversion of liberty and

---

58   L. *ut restricti ac tenaces in rem catholicam sint: et qui vulgo libertatem effuse largiuntur, iidem liberam sinere Ecclesiam recusant*; that is, it very often happens that they be hard and tight-fisted when it comes to Catholic affairs, and the very same men that readily lavish liberty on all, refuse liberty to the Church.
59   L. *consectariis*; that is, consequences.
60   L. *ut totus homo in verissima perpetuaque potestate Dei sit*; that is, that the whole man be most truly and perpetually subject to the power of God.

the worst kind of liberalism; and what We have said must be understood to apply to this alone in its fullest sense.

38. Next comes the system[61] of those who admit indeed the duty of submitting to God, the Creator and Ruler of the world, inasmuch as all nature is dependent on His will, but who boldly reject all laws of faith and morals which are above natural reason, but are revealed by the authority of God; or who at least impudently assert that there is no reason why regard should be paid to these laws, at any rate publicly, by the State.[62] How mistaken these men also are, and how inconsistent, we have seen above. From this teaching, as from its source and principle, flows that fatal principle of the separation of Church and State; whereas it is, on the contrary, clear that the two powers, though dissimilar in functions and unequal in degree, ought nevertheless to live in concord, by harmony in their action and the faithful discharge of their respective duties.

39. But this teaching is understood in two ways. Many wish the State[63] to be separated from the Church wholly and entirely, so that with regard to every right of human society, in institutions, customs, and laws, the offices of State, and the education of youth, they would pay no more regard to the Church than if she did not exist; and, at most, would allow the citizens individually to attend to their religion in private if so minded. Against such as these, all the arguments by which We disprove the principle of separation of Church and State are conclusive; with this superadded, that it is absurd the citizen should respect the Church, while the State may hold her in contempt.

40. Others oppose not the existence of the Church, nor indeed could they; yet they despoil her of the nature and rights of a perfect society, and maintain that it does not belong to her to legislate, to judge, or to punish, but only to exhort, to advise, and to rule her subjects in accordance with their own consent

---

61 L. *disciplina*; that is, the school.
62 L. *in civitate*; that is, in public life.
63 L. *rempublicam*; that is, the commonwealth.

and will. By such opinion they pervert the nature of this divine society, and attenuate and narrow its authority, its office of teacher, and its whole efficiency; and at the same time, they aggrandize the power of the civil government to such extent as to subject the Church of God to the empire and sway of the State, like any voluntary association of citizens. To refute completely such teaching, the arguments often used by the defenders of Christianity, and set forth by Us, especially in the encyclical letter *Immortale Dei*,[64] are of great avail; for by those arguments it is proved that, by a divine provision, all the rights which essentially belong to a society that is legitimate, supreme, and perfect in all its parts exist in the Church.

41. Lastly, there remain those who, while they do not approve of the separation of Church and State, think nevertheless that the Church ought to adapt herself to the times and conform to what is required by the modern system of government. Such an opinion is sound, if it is to be understood of some equitable adjustment consistent with truth and justice; in so far, namely, that the Church, in the hope of some great good, may show herself indulgent, and may conform to the times in so far as her sacred office permits. But it is not so in regard to practices and doctrines which a perversion of morals and a warped judgment have unlawfully introduced. Religion, truth, and justice must ever be maintained; and, as God has intrusted these great and sacred matters to her office as to dissemble in regard to what is false or unjust, or to connive at what is hurtful to religion.

42. From what has been said it follows that it is quite unlawful to demand, to defend, or to grant unconditional[65] freedom of thought, of speech, or writing, or of worship, as if these were so many rights given by nature to man. For, if nature had really granted them, it would be lawful to refuse obedience to God, and there would be no restraint on human liberty.[66] It likewise

---

64   See pp. 148–149.
65   L. *promiscuam*; that is, indiscriminate.
66   L. *nec ulla temperari lege libertas humana posset*; that is, nor could human freedom be moderated by any law.

follows that freedom in these things may be tolerated wherever there is just cause, but only with such moderation as will prevent its degenerating into license and excess. And, where such liberties are in use, men should employ them in doing good, and should estimate them as the Church does; for liberty is to be regarded as legitimate in so far only as it affords greater facility for doing good, but no farther.

43. Whenever there exists, or there is reason to fear, an unjust oppression of the people on the one hand, or a deprivation of the liberty of the Church on the other, it is lawful to seek for such a change of government as will bring about due liberty of action. In such case, an excessive and vicious liberty is not sought, but only some relief, for the common welfare, in order that, while license for evil is allowed by the State, the power of doing good may not be hindered.

44. Again, it is not of itself wrong to prefer a democratic form of government, if only the Catholic doctrine be maintained as to the origin and exercise of power.[67] Of the various forms of government, the Church does not reject any that are fitted to procure the welfare of the subject; she wishes only—and this nature itself requires—that they should be constituted without involving wrong to anyone, and especially without violating the rights of the Church.

45. Unless it be otherwise determined, by reason of some exceptional condition of things, it is expedient to take part in the administration of public affairs. And the Church approves of everyone devoting his services to the common good, and doing all that he can for the defense, preservation, and prosperity of his country.

46. Neither does the Church condemn those who, if it can be done without violation of justice, wish to make their country independent of any foreign or despotic power. Nor does she blame those who wish to assign to the State the power of

---

67 L. *publicae potestatis*; that is, of public authority.

self-government, and to its citizens the greatest possible measure of prosperity. The Church has always most faithfully fostered civil liberty,[68] and this was seen especially in Italy,[69] in the municipal prosperity, and wealth, and glory which were obtained at a time when the salutary power of the Church has spread, without opposition, to all parts of the State.[70]

47. These things, venerable brothers, which, under the guidance of faith and reason, in the discharge of Our Apostolic office, We have now delivered to you, We hope, especially by your cooperation with Us, will be useful unto very many. In lowliness of heart We raise Our eyes in supplication to God, and earnestly beseech Him to shed mercifully the light of His wisdom and of His counsel upon men, so that, strengthened by these heavenly gifts,[71] they may in matters of such moment discern what is true, and may afterwards, in public and private at all times and with unshaken constancy, live in accordance with the truth. As a pledge of these heavenly gifts, and in witness of Our good will to you, venerable brothers, and to the clergy and people committed to each of you, We most lovingly grant in the Lord the apostolic benediction.

---

68 L. *libertatum*; that is, liberties.
69 L. *civitates italicae*; that is, the cities of Italy.
70 L. *reipublicae*; that is, the commonwealth.
71 L. *ut his aucti virtutibus*; that is, strengthened by these virtues.

III

On Christian Marriage

INTRODUCTION

The encyclical letter *Arcanum Divinae Sapientiae* is dated February 10, 1880. Confirming and developing what he had suggested in his first encyclical on the necessity there was to restore Christian homes in view of restoring Christian education, Pope Leo XIII establishes, with as much force as clarity, the origin of marriage, the true nature of the family union, the indissolubility of the conjugal bond, and the destructive consequences of divorce with respect to social order. The teaching of this encyclical concerning the essentially sacred nature of marriage (art. 19) and the denial that power over Christian marriages has ever lawfully been handed over to the rulers of the State (art. 24) are two doctrinal positions whose importance can hardly be exaggerated. Their far-reaching implications affect the whole social order. The relation between the problem of marriage and the divine nature of all authority has been indicated in the Introduction to this volume and the very text of the present encyclical makes it abundantly clear. The fact that socialism and communism seem to be equally interested in loosening the bond of marriage is a safe indication that its destruction would bring about the destruction of society itself (art. 32). The common belief that marriage is a private affair and that social order is compatible with familial disorder is here exposed as a mere illusion.

SUMMARY

(1–2) Restoration of all things by the Incarnation of Christ. (3) Even the order of nature was elevated by it. (4) Wondrous benefits have accrued to the State as a consequence of this elevation of human nature. (5) Marriage is a point in case. (6–7) Progressive corruption of marriage among both the Jews and the Gentiles. (8) Restoration of marriage by Christ. (9) Catholic tradition concerning marriage. (10) The purpose of marriage is to bring forth children for the Church. (11) Mutual duties of husband and wife. (12) Mutual duties of children and parents. (13) All matters pertaining to marriage have been entrusted by Christ to His Church. (14) Equality of rights in marriage, achieved by the abolition of slavery. (15) The Church protects freedom and personal rights in marriage no less than chasteness and the respect of the religious law. (16) To pervert marriage is to despise the sovereignty of God. (17) This is what is being done by those who subtract marriage from the jurisdiction of the Church in order to subject it to the authority of the State. (18) The contradictory notion of "civil marriage." (19) It is a false notion, since a sacrament of marriage existed even among pagans. (20) Christ has made Christian marriages the noblest of all such unions. (21) The Church has always used her authority in matters of marriage. (22) The Church has never renounced this authority in favor of the emperors. (23) Nor will the Church concede that marriage is subjected to the State inasmuch as it is a contract, while it is subjected to the Church inasmuch as it is a sacrament; in marriage, the contract is inseparable from the sacrament. (24) Moreover, marriage is an image of the mystical nuptials of Christ with the Church. (25) Like all divine and natural institutions, marriage should be preserved unchanged. (26) Marriage instituted by God as a source of individual and of public benefit. (27) Marriage is losing its three main dignities: holiness, unity, and indissolubility. (28) Divorce does not stop immorality. (29) On the contrary, divorce causes many evils. (30) Once tolerated, divorce cannot be kept within bounds. (31–32) It has always caused much misery and it will create social disorder wherever it is introduced. (33) In guarding the indissolubility of marriage the Church is safeguarding the State. (34) The Church has maintained the sanctity of marriage even against powerful rulers. (35) The Church does not deny the right of the States to establish regulations concerning those aspects or consequences of marriage that belong to the civil order. (36) The same fruitful co-operation that obtains between faith and reason in the quest for truth should also obtain between Church and State in all matters pertaining to human life. (37) Both powers should now unite in order to avert the evils by which civil society is no less threatened than the Church. (38) Exhortation to the bishops to preserve the purity of the doctrine. (39) Especially concerning Christian marriage. (40) And the radical difference there is between it and a simple legal formality. (41) Separations are sometimes permitted as extreme cases, but even then marriage remains indissoluble and remarriage is a crime so long as the first one has not been ended by death. (42) Marriages would be more stable if they derived their strength from the virtue of religion. (43) Mixed marriages should be avoided. (44) Irregular unions should be regularized. (45) Invitation to prayer.

III

Arcanum Divinae Sapientiae
ON CHRISTIAN MARRIAGE
February 10, 1880

1. The hidden design of the divine wisdom, which Jesus Christ the Savior of men came to carry out on earth, had this end in view, that, by Himself and in Himself, He should divinely renew the world, which was sinking, as it were, with length of years into decline. The Apostle Paul summed this up in words of dignity and majesty when he wrote to the Ephesians, thus: "That He might make known unto us the mystery of His will ... to re-establish all things in Christ that are in heaven and on earth."[1]

2. In truth, Christ our Lord, setting Himself to fulfill the commandment which His Father had given Him, straightway imparted a new form and fresh beauty to all things, taking away the effects of their time-worn age. For He healed the wounds which the sin of our first father had inflicted on the human race;[2] He brought all men, by nature children of wrath, into favor with God; He led to the light of truth men wearied out by longstanding errors; He renewed to every virtue those who were weakened by lawlessness of every kind; and, giving them again an inheritance of never-ending bliss, He added a sure hope that their mortal and perishable bodies should one day be partakers of immortality and of the glory of heaven. In order that these unparalleled benefits might last as long as men should be found on earth, He entrusted to His Church the continuance of His work; and, looking to future times, He commanded her to set in order whatever might have become deranged in human society, and to restore whatever might have fallen into ruin.

---

1 Eph. 1:9–10.
2 L. *humanae naturae*; that is, on human nature.

3. Although the divine renewal we have spoken of chiefly and directly affected men as constituted in the supernatural order of grace, nevertheless some of its precious and salutary fruits were also bestowed abundantly in the order of nature. Hence, not only individual men, but also the whole mass of the human race, have in every respect received no small degree of worthiness. For, so soon as Christian order was once established in the world, it became possible for all men, one by one, to learn what God's fatherly providence is, and to dwell in it habitually, thereby fostering that hope of heavenly help which never confoundeth. From all this outflowed fortitude, self-control, constancy, and the evenness of a peaceful mind, together with many high virtues and noble deeds.

4. Wondrous, indeed, was the extent of dignity, steadfastness, and goodness, which thus accrued to the State as well as to the family.[3] The authority of rulers became more just and revered; the obedience of the people more ready and unforced; the union of citizens closer; the rights of dominion more secure. In very truth, the Christian religion thought of and provided for all things which are held to be advantageous in a State; so much so, indeed, that, according to St. Augustine, one cannot see how it could have offered greater help in the matter of living well and happily, had it been instituted for the single object of procuring or increasing those things which contributed to the conveniences or advantages of this mortal life.

5. Still, the purpose We have set before Us is not to recount, in detail, benefits of this kind; Our wish is rather to speak about that family union of which marriage is the beginning and the foundation. The true origin of marriage, venerable brothers, is well known to all. Though revilers of the Christian faith refuse to acknowledge the never-interrupted doctrine of the Church on this subject, and have long striven to destroy the testimony of all nations and of all times, they have nevertheless failed not

---

3 L. *societati vero domesticae et civili*; that is, to the domestic society as well as to the body politic.

only to quench the powerful light of truth, but even to lessen it. We record what is to all known, and cannot be doubted by any, that God, on the sixth day of creation, having made man from the slime of the earth, and having breathed into his face the breath of life, gave him a companion, whom He miraculously[4] took from the side of Adam when he was locked in sleep. God thus, in His most far-reaching foresight, decreed that this husband and wife should be the natural beginning of the human race, from whom it might be propagated and preserved by an unfailing fruitfulness throughout all futurity of time. And this union of man and woman, that it might answer more fittingly to the infinite wise counsels of God, even from the beginning manifested chiefly two most excellent properties — deeply sealed, as it were, and signed upon it — namely, unity and perpetuity. From the Gospel, we see clearly that this doctrine was declared and openly confirmed by the divine authority of Jesus Christ. He bore witness to the Jews and to His Apostles that marriage, from its institution, should exist between two only, that is, between one man and one woman; that of two they are made, so to say, one flesh; and that the marriage bond is by the will of God so closely and strongly made fast that no man may dissolve it or render it asunder. "For this cause shall a man leave father and mother, and shall cleave to his wife, and they two shall be in one flesh. Therefore, now they are not two, but one flesh. What, therefore, God hath joined together, let no man put asunder."[5]

6. This form of marriage, however, so excellent and so pre-eminent, began to be corrupted by degrees, and to disappear among the heathen; and became even among the Jewish race clouded in a measure and obscured. For in their midst a common custom was gradually introduced, by which it was accounted as lawful for a man to have more than one wife; and eventually, when "by reason of the hardness of their heart,"[6] Moses indulgently permitted them to put away their wives, the way was open to divorce.

---

4 L. *mirabiliter*; that is, in a wonderous way.
5 Matt. 19:5–6.
6 Matt. 19:8.

7. But the corruption and change which fell on marriage among the Gentiles seem almost incredible, inasmuch as it was exposed in every land to floods of error and of the most shameful lusts. All nations seem, more or less, to have forgotten the true notion and origin of marriage; and thus, everywhere laws were enacted with reference to marriage, prompted to all appearance by State reasons,[7] but not such as nature required. Solemn rites, invented at will of the law-givers, brought about that women should, as might be, bear either the honorable name of wife or the disgraceful name of concubine; and things came to such a pitch that permission to marry, or the refusal of the permission, depended on the will of the heads of the State,[8] whose laws were greatly against equity or even to the highest degree unjust. Moreover, plurality of wives and husbands, as well as divorce,[9] caused the nuptial bond to be relaxed exceedingly. Hence, too, sprang up the greatest confusion as to the mutual rights and duties of husbands and wives, inasmuch as a man assumed right of dominion over his wife, ordering her to go about her business,[10] often without any just cause; while he was himself at liberty "to run headlong with impunity into lust, unbridled and unrestrained, in houses of ill-fame and amongst his female slaves, as if the dignity of the persons sinned with, and not the will of the sinner, made the guilt."[11] When the licentiousness of a husband thus showed itself, nothing could be more piteous than the wife, sunk so low as to be all but reckoned as a means for the gratification of passion, or for the production of offspring. Without any feeling of shame, marriageable girls were bought and sold, like so much merchandise,[12] and power was sometimes given to the father

---

7   L. *quae esse e republica viderentur*; that is, which seemed to emanate from the body politic, not from nature.
8   L. *principum reipublicae*; that is, of the civil authorities.
9   L. *Praeterea polygamia, polyandria, divortium, causae fuerunt...*; that is, Moreover, polygamy, polyandry, divorce, were the causes... P. and H. are not to be trusted for this passage.
10 L. *eamque suas sibi res habere, nulla aepe justa causa juberet*; that is, and would repudiate her, often without any just cause.
11 Jerome *Epist.* 77, 3 (PL 22, 691).
12 Arnobius, *Adversus Gentes*, 4 (sic, perhaps 1, 64).

and to the husband to inflict capital punishment on the wife. Of necessity, the offspring of such marriages as these were either reckoned among the stock in trade of the common-wealth or held to be the property of the father of the family;[13] and the law permitted him to make and unmake the marriages of his children at his mere will, and even to exercise against them the monstrous power of life and death.

8. So manifold being the vices and so great the ignominies with which marriage was defiled, an alleviation and a remedy were at length bestowed from on high. Jesus Christ, who restored our human dignity and who perfected the Mosaic law, applied early in His ministry no little solicitude to the question of marriage. He ennobled the marriage in Cana of Galilee by His presence, and made it memorable by the first of the miracles which he wrought;[14] and for this reason, even from that day forth, it seemed as if the beginning of new holiness had been conferred on human marriages. Later on, He brought back matrimony to the nobility of its primeval origin by condemning the customs of the Jews in their abuse of the plurality of wives and of the power of giving bills of divorce; and still more by commanding most strictly that no one should dare to dissolve that union which God Himself had sanctioned by a bond perpetual. Hence, having set aside the difficulties which were adduced from the law of Moses, He, in character of supreme Lawgiver, decreed as follows concerning husbands and wives, "I say to you, that whosoever shall put away his wife, except it be for fornication, and shall marry another, committeth adultery; and he that shall marry her that is put away committeth adultery."[15]

9. But what was decreed and constituted in respect to marriage by the authority of God has been more fully and more clearly handed down to us, by tradition and the written Word, through

---

[13] Dionysius Halicarnassus, lib. II, chs. 26–27 (see *Roman Antiquities*, tr. E. Cary, Loeb Classical Library, Harvard University Press, 1948, Vol. I, pp. 386–393).
[14] John 2.
[15] Matt. 19:9.

Arcanum Divinae Sapientiae

the Apostles, those heralds of the laws of God. To the Apostles, indeed, as our masters, are to be referred the doctrines which "our holy Fathers, the Councils, and the Tradition of the Universal Church have always taught,"[16] namely, that Christ our Lord raised marriage to the dignity of a sacrament; that to husband and wife, guarded and strengthened by the heavenly grace which His merits gained for them, He gave power to attain holiness in the married state;[17] and that, in a wondrous way, making marriage an example of the mystical union between Himself and His Church, He not only perfected that love which is according to nature,[18] but also made the naturally indivisible union of one man with one woman[19] far more perfect through the bond of heavenly love. Paul says to the Ephesians: "Husbands, love your wives, as Christ also loved the Church, and delivered Himself up for it, that He might sanctify it... So also ought men to love their wives as their own bodies... For no man ever hated his own flesh, but nourisheth and cherisheth it, as also Christ doth the Church; because we are members of His body, of His flesh, and of His bones. For this cause shall a man leave his father and mother, and shall cleave to his wife, and they shall be two in one flesh. This is a great sacrament; but I speak in Christ and in the Church."[20] In like manner, from the teaching of the Apostles, we learn that the unity of marriage and its perpetual indissolubility, the indispensable conditions of its very origin, must, according to the command of Christ, be holy and inviolable without exception. Paul says again: "To them that are married, not I, but the Lord commandeth that the wife depart not from her husband; and if she depart, that she remain unmarried or be reconciled to her husband."[21] And again: "A woman is bound by the law

---

16 Trid., sess. xxiv, *in principio* (that is, Council of Trent, *Canones et decreta*; the text is divided into sessions, chapters, and canons, i.e., decrees).
17 L. *in ipso conjugio*; that is, in the married state itself.
18 Trid., sess. xxiv, cap. 1, *De reformatione matrimonii*.
19 L. viri ac mulieris individuam suapte natura societatem. P. and H. are not to be trusted here.
20 Eph. 5:25–32.
21 1 Cor. 7:10–11.

as long as her husband liveth; but if her husband die, she is at liberty."[22] It is for these reasons that marriage is "a great sacrament;"[23] "honorable in all,"[24] holy, pure, and to be reverenced as a type and symbol of most high mysteries.

10. Furthermore, the Christian perfection and completeness of marriage are not comprised in those points only which have been mentioned. For, first, there has been vouchsafed to the marriage union a higher and nobler purpose than was ever previously given to it. By the command of Christ, it not only looks to the propagation of the human race, but to the bringing forth of children for the Church, "fellow citizens with the saints, and the domestics of God;"[25] so that "a people might be born and brought up for the worship and religion of the true God and our Savior Jesus Christ."[26]

11. Secondly, the mutual duties of husband and wife have been defined, and their several rights accurately established. They are bound, namely, to have such feelings for one another as to cherish always very great mutual love, to be ever faithful to their marriage vow, and to give one another an unfailing and unselfish help. The husband is the chief of the family and the head of the wife. The woman, because she is flesh of his flesh, and bone of his bone, must be subject to her husband and obey him; not, indeed, as a servant, but as a companion, so that her obedience shall be wanting in neither honor nor dignity. Since the husband represents Christ, and since the wife represents the Church, let there always be, both in him who commands and in her who obeys, a heaven-born love guiding both in their respective duties. For "the husband is the head of the wife; as Christ is the head of the Church... Therefore, as the Church is subject to Christ, so also let wives be to their husbands in all things."[27]

---

22 1 Cor. 7:39.
23 Eph. 5:32.
24 Heb. 13:4.
25 Eph. 2:19.
26 Catech. Rom., ch. 8.
27 Eph. 5:23–24.

Arcanum Divinae Sapientiae

12. As regards children, they ought to submit to the parents and obey them, and give them honor for conscience' sake; while, on the other hand, parents are bound to give all care and watchful thought to the education of their offspring and their virtuous bringing up: "Fathers, . . . bring them up" (that is, your children) "in the discipline and correction of the Lord."[28] From this we see clearly that the duties of husbands and wives are neither few nor light; although to married people who are good these burdens become not only bearable but agreeable, owing to the strength which they gain through the sacrament.

13. Christ, therefore, having renewed marriage to such and so great excellence, commended and entrusted all the discipline bearing upon these matters to His Church. The Church, always and everywhere, has so used her power with reference to the marriages of Christians that men have seen clearly how it belongs to her as of native right; not being made hers by any human grant, but given divinely to her by the will of her Founder. Her constant and watchful care in guarding marriage, by the preservation of its sanctity, is so well understood as to not need proof. That the judgment of the Council of Jerusalem reprobated licentious and free love,[29] we all know, as also that the incestuous Corinthian was condemned by the authority of blessed Paul.[30] Again, in the very beginning of the Christian Church were repulsed and defeated, with the like unremitting determination, the efforts of many who aimed at the destruction of Christian marriage, such as the Gnostics, Manicheans, and Montanists; and in our own time, Mormons, St. Simonians, phalansterians, and communists.[31]

---

28 Eph. 6:4.
29 Acts 15:29.
30 1 Cor. 5:5.
31 Gnostics: common name for several early sects claiming a Christian knowledge (*gnosis*) higher than faith. *Manicheans:* disciples of the Persian Mani (or Manes, c. 216–276) who taught that everything goes back to two first principles, light and darkness, or good and evil. *Montanists:* disciples of Montanus (in Phrygia, last third of the second century), condemned marriage as a sinful institution. *Mormons:* sect founded in 1830

14. In like manner, moreover, a law of marriage just to all, and the same for all, was enacted by the abolition of the old distinction between slaves and free-born men and women;[32] and thus, the rights of husbands and wives were made equal: for, as St. Jerome says, "with us that which is unlawful for women is unlawful for men also, and the same restraint is imposed on equal conditions."[33] The self-same rights also were firmly established for reciprocal affection and for the interchange of duties; the dignity of the woman was asserted and assured; and it was forbidden to the man to inflict capital punishment for adultery,[34] or lustfully and shamelessly to violate his plighted faith.

15. It is also a great blessing that the Church has limited, so far as is needful, the power of fathers of families, so that sons and daughters, wishing to marry, are not in any way deprived of their rightful freedom;[35] that, for the purpose of spreading more widely the supernatural love of husbands and wives, she has decreed marriages within certain degrees of consanguinity or affinity to be null and void;[36] that she has taken the greatest pains to safeguard marriage, as much as is possible, from error and violence and deceit;[37] that she has always wished to preserve the holy chasteness of the marriage bed, the security of

---

by Joseph Smith, which favored polygamy. *Saint-Simonians:* disciples of the French philosopher Saint Simon (1760–1825) founder of a "new Christianity" based upon science instead of faith. *Phalansterians:* members of a phalanstery, that is, of a socialist community after the principles of Charles Fourier (1772–1837). *Communists:* supporters of a regime in which property belongs to the body politic, each member being supposed to work according to his capacity and to receive according to his wants; communism is usually associated with the name of Karl Marx (1818–1893).

32 Cap. 1, *De conjug. serv. Corpus juris canonici*, ed. Friedberg (Leipzig, 1884), Part 2, cols. 691–692.
33 Jerome, *Epist.* 77 (PL 22, 691).
34 Can. *Interfectores* and Canon *Admonere*, quaest. 2 *Corpus juris canonici* (Leipzig, 1879), Part 1, cols. 1152–1154.
35 Saus. 30, quaest. 3, cap. 3, *De cognat. spirit.* (op. cit., Part 1, col. 1101).
36 Cap. 8, "De consang. et affin." (op. cit., Part 2, col. 703); cap 1, *De cognat. legali* (col. 696).
37 Cap. 26, *De sponsal.* (op. cit., Part 2, col. 670); cap. 13 (col. 665); cap. 15 (col. 666); cap. 29 (col. 671); *De sponsalibus et matrimonio et alibi.*

persons,[38] the honor of husband and wife,[39] and the sanctity of religion.[40] Lastly, with such foresight of legislation has the Church guarded its divine institution that no one who thinks rightfully of these matters can fail to see how, with regard to marriage, she is the best guardian and defender of the human race; and how, withal, her wisdom has come forth victorious from the lapse of years, from the assaults of men, and from the countless changes of public events.

16. Yet, owing to the efforts of the archenemy of mankind, there are persons who, thanklessly casting away so many other blessings of redemption, despise also or utterly ignore the restoration of marriage to its original perfection. It is a reproach to some of the ancients that they showed themselves the enemies of marriage in many ways; but in our own age, much more pernicious is the sin of those who would fain pervert utterly the nature of marriage, perfect though it is, and complete in all its details and parts. The chief reason why they act in this way is because very many, imbued with the maxims of a false philosophy and corrupted in morals, judge nothing so unbearable as submission and obedience; and strive with all their might to bring about that not only individual men, but families, also—indeed, human society itself—may in haughty pride despise the sovereignty of God.

17. Now, since the family and human society at large spring from marriage, these men will on no account allow matrimony to be the subject of the jurisdiction of the Church. Nay, they endeavor to deprive it of all holiness, and so bring it within the contracted sphere of those rights which, having been instituted by man, are ruled and administered by the civil jurisprudence of the community. Wherefore, it necessarily follows that they attribute all

---

38 Cap. 1, *De convers. infid.* (op. cit., Part 2, col. 587); cap. 5, 6, *De eo qui duxit in matrim.* (cols. 688-689).
39 Cap. 3, 5, 8, *De sponsal. et matr.* (op. cit., Part 2, cols. 661, 663). Trid., sess. xxiv, cap. *De reformatione matrimonii.*
40 L. *religionis incolumitatem.*—P. and H. the security of religion.—H. the Naturalists (they who reject what is supernatural). Cap. 7, *De divort.* (op. cit., Part 2, col. 722).

power over marriage to civil rulers, and allow none whatever to the Church; and, when the Church exercises any such power, they think that she acts either by favor of the civil authority or to its injury. Now is the time, they say, for the heads of the State to vindicate their rights unflinchingly, and to do their best to settle all that relates to marriage according as to them seems good.

18. Hence are owing civil marriages, commonly so called; hence, laws are framed which impose impediments to marriage; hence, arise judicial sentences affecting the marriage contract, as to whether or not it has been rightly made. Lastly, all power of prescribing and passing judgment in this class of cases is, as we see, of set purpose denied to the Catholic Church, so that no regard is paid either to her divine power or to her prudent laws. Yet, under these, for so many centuries, have the nations lived on whom the light of civilization shone bright with the wisdom of Christ Jesus.[41]

19. Nevertheless, the naturalists,[42] as well as all who profess that they worship above all things the divinity of the State, and strive to disturb whole communities with such wicked doctrines, cannot escape the charge of delusion. Marriage has God for its Author, and was from the very beginning a kind of foreshadowing of the Incarnation of His Son; and therefore, there abides in it a something holy and religious; not extraneous, but innate; not derived from men, but implanted by nature. Innocent III, therefore, and Honorius III, our predecessors, affirmed not falsely nor rashly that a sacrament of marriage existed ever amongst the faithful and unbelievers.[43] We call to witness the monuments of

---

41 L. *cum christiana sapientia*; that is, with Christian wisdom.
42 L. *Naturalistae*. — P. all those who reject the supernatural. — H. the Naturalists (they who reject what is supernatural). Maintain the self-sufficiency of the natural order.
43 L. *apud fideles et infidels existere sacramentum conjugii.* — H. substitutes for the text the following gloss: "that a certain sacredness of marriage rites existed ever amongst the faithful and unbelievers. Concerning Innocent III, see *Corpus juris canonici*, cap. 8, *De divort.*, ed. cit., Part 2, col. 723. Innocent III refers to I Cor. 7:13. Concerning Honorius III, see cap. ii, *De transact.*, (op. cit., Part 2, col. 210).

antiquity, as also the manners and customs of those people who, being the most civilized, had the greatest knowledge of law and equity. In the minds of all of them, it was a fixed and foregone conclusion that, when marriage was thought of, it was thought of as conjoined with religion and holiness. Hence, among those, marriages were commonly celebrated with religious ceremonies, under the authority of pontiffs, and with the ministry of priests. So mighty, even in the souls ignorant of heavenly doctrine, was the force of nature, of the remembrance of their origin, and of the conscience of the human race. As, then, marriage is holy by its own power, in its own nature, and of itself, it ought not to be regulated and administered by the will of civil rulers, but by the divine authority of the Church, which alone in sacred matters professes the office of teaching.

20. Next, the dignity of the sacrament must be considered, for through addition of the sacrament, the marriages of Christians have become far the noblest of all matrimonial unions. But, to decree and ordain concerning the sacrament is, by the will of Christ Himself, so much a part of the power and duty of the Church that it is plainly absurd to maintain that even the very smallest fraction of such power has been transferred to the civil ruler.

21. Lastly should be borne in mind the great weight and crucial test of history, by which it is plainly proved that the legislative and judicial authority of which We are speaking has been freely and constantly used by the Church, even in times when some foolishly suppose the head of the State either to have consented to it or connived at it. It would, for instance, be incredible and altogether absurd to assume that Christ our Lord condemned the long-standing practice of polygamy and divorce by authority delegated to Him by the procurator of the province, or the principal ruler of the Jews. And it would be equally extravagant to think that, when the Apostle Paul taught that divorces and incestuous marriages were not lawful, it was because Tiberius, Caligula, and Nero agreed with him or secretly commanded him so to teach. No man in his senses could ever be persuaded that

On Christian Marriage

the Church made so many laws about the holiness and indissolubility of marriage,[44] and the marriages of slaves with the freeborn,[45] by power received from Roman emperors, most hostile to the Christian name, whose strongest desire was to destroy by violence and murder the rising Church of Christ. Still less could anyone believe this to be the case, when the law of the Church was sometimes so divergent from the civil law that Ignatius the Martyr,[46] Justin,[47] Athenagoras,[48] and Tertullian[49] publicly denounced as unjust and adulterous certain marriages, which had been sanctioned by imperial law.

22. Furthermore, after all power had devolved upon the Christian emperors, the supreme pontiffs and bishops assembled in council persisted with the same independence and consciousness of their right in commanding or forbidding in regard to marriage whatever they judged to be profitable or expedient for the time being, however much it might seem to be at variance with the laws of the State.[50] It is well known that, with respect to the impediments arising from the marriage bond, through vow, disparity of worship, blood relationship, certain forms of crime, and from previously plighted troth, many decrees were issued by the rulers of the Church at the Councils of Granada,[51] Arles,[52] Chalcedon,[53] the second of Milevum,[54] and others, which were often widely different from the decrees sanctioned by the laws of the empire. Furthermore, so far were Christian princes from arrogating any power in the matter of Christian marriage that

---

44 *Canones Apostolorum*, 16, 17, 18, ed. Fr. Lauchert, J. C. B. Mohr (Leipzig, 1896) p. 3.
45 *Philosophumena* (Oxford, 1851), i.e., Hippolytus, *Refutation of All Heresies*, 9, 12 (PG 16, 3386D–3387A).
46 *Epistola ad Polycarpum*, cap. 5 (PG 5, 723–724).
47 *Apolog. Maj.*, 15 (PG 6. 349 A, B).
48 *Legat. pro Christian.*, 32, 33 (PG 6, 963–968).
49 *De coron. milit.*, 13 (PL 2, 116).
50 L. *ab institutis civilibus*; that is, with civil laws.
51 De Aguirre, *Conc. Hispan.*, Vol. 1, can. 11.
52 Harduin, *Act. Concil.*, Vol. 1, can. 11.
53 Ibid., can. 16.
54 Ibid., can. 17.

they on the contrary acknowledged and declared that it belonged exclusively in all its fullness to the Church. In fact, Honorius, the younger Theodosius, and Justinian,[55] also, hesitated not to confess that the only power belonging to them in relation to marriage was that of acting as guardians and defenders of the holy canons. If at any time they enacted anything by their edicts concerning impediments of marriage, they voluntarily explained the reason, affirming that they took it upon themselves so to act, by leave and authority of the Church,[56] whose judgment they were wont to appeal to and reverently to accept in all questions that concerned legitimacy[57] and divorce;[58] as also in all those points which in any way have a necessary connection with the marriage bond.[59] The Council of Trent, therefore, had the clearest right to define that it is in the Church's power "to establish diriment impediments of matrimony,"[60] and that "matrimonial causes pertain to ecclesiastical judges."[61]

23. Let no one, then, be deceived by the distinction which some civil jurists[62] have so strongly insisted upon—the distinction, namely, by virtue of which they sever the matrimonial contract from the sacrament, with intent to hand over the contract to the power and will of the rulers of the State, while reserving questions concerning the sacrament of the Church. A distinction, or rather severance, of this kind cannot be approved; for certain it is that in Christian marriage the contract is inseparable from the sacrament, and that, for this reason, the contract cannot be true and legitimate without being a sacrament as well. For Christ our Lord added to marriage the dignity of a sacrament; but marriage is the contract itself, whenever that contract is lawfully concluded.

---

55 *Novel.*, 137 (Justinianus, *Novellae*, ed. C. E. Z. Lingenthal, Leipzig, 1881, Vol. 2, p. 206).
56 Fejer, *Matrim. ex instit.* Chris. (Pest, 1835).
57 Cap. 3, *De ord. cogn.* (*Corpus juris canonici*, ed. Cit., Part 2, col. 276).
58 Cap. 3, *De divort.* (ed. cit., Part 2, col. 720).
59 Cap. 13, *Qui filii sint legit.* (ed. cit., Part 2, col. 716).
60 Trid., sess. xxiv, can. 4.
61 Ibid., can. 12.
62 L. *a regalistis*; that is, by jurists in the employ of kings.—some court legists.

24. Marriage, moreover, is a sacrament, because it is a holy sign which gives grace, showing forth an image of the mystical nuptials of Christ with the Church. But the form and image of these nuptials are shown precisely by the very bond of that most close union in which man and woman are bound together in one; which bond is nothing else but the marriage itself. Hence it is clear that among Christians every true marriage is, in itself and by itself, a sacrament; and that nothing can be further from the truth than to say that the sacrament is a certain added ornament, or outward endowment, which can be separated and torn away from the contract at the caprice of man. Neither, therefore, by reasoning can it be shown, nor by any testimony of history be proved, that power over the marriages of Christians has ever lawfully been handed over to the rulers of the State. If, in this matter, the right of anyone else has ever been violated, no one can truly say that it has been violated by the Church. Would that the teaching of the naturalists,[63] besides being full of falsehood and injustice, were not also the fertile source of much detriment and calamity! But it is easy to see at a glance the greatness of the evil which unhallowed marriages have brought, and ever will bring, on the whole of human society.

25. From the beginning of the world, indeed, it was divinely ordained that things instituted by God and by nature should be proved by us to be the more profitable and salutary the more they remain unchanged in their full integrity. For God, the Maker of all things, well knowing what was good for the institution and preservation of each of His creatures, so ordered them by His will and mind that each might adequately attain the end for which it was made. If the rashness or the wickedness of human agency venture to change or disturb that order of things which has been constituted with the fullest foresight, then the designs of infinite wisdom and usefulness begin either to be hurtful or cease to be profitable, partly because through the change undergone they have lost their power of benefiting, and partly because

---

63 L. *Naturalistarum.*—P. and H. of those who reject what is supernatural.

God chooses to inflict punishment on the pride and audacity of man. Now, those who deny that marriage is holy, and who relegate it, stripped of all holiness, among the class of common secular things, uproot thereby the foundations of nature, not only resisting the designs of Providence, but, so far as they can, destroying the order that God has ordained. No one, therefore, should wonder if from such insane and impious attempts there spring up a crop of evils pernicious in the highest degree both to the salvation of souls and to the safety of the commonwealth.

26. If, then, we consider the end of the divine institution of marriage, we shall see very clearly that God intended it to be a most fruitful source of individual[64] benefit and of public welfare. Not only, in strict truth, was marriage instituted for the propagation of the human race, but also that the lives of husbands and wives might be made better and happier. This comes about in many ways: by their lightening each other's burdens through mutual help; by constant and faithful love; by having all their possessions in common; and by the heavenly grace which flows from the sacrament. Marriage also can do much for the good of families, for, so long as it is conformable to nature and in accordance with the counsels of God, it has power to strengthen union of heart in the parents; to secure the holy education of children; to temper the authority of the father by the example of the divine authority; to render children obedient to their parents and servants obedient to their masters. From such marriages as these, the State may rightly expect a race of citizens animated by a good spirit and filled with reverence and love for God, recognizing it their duty to obey those who rule justly and lawfully, to love all, and to injure no one.

27. These many and glorious fruits were ever the product of marriage, so long as it retained those gifts of holiness, unity, and indissolubility from which proceeded all its fertile and saving power; nor can anyone doubt but that it would always have brought forth such fruits, at all times and in all places, had it

---

64   P. and H. add: individual.

been under the power and guardianship of the Church, the trustworthy preserver and protector of these gifts. But, now, there is a spreading wish to supplant natural and divine law[65] by human law; and hence has begun a gradual extinction of that most excellent ideal[66] of marriage which nature herself had impressed on the soul of man, and sealed, as it were, with her own seal; nay, more, even in Christian marriages this power, productive of so great good, has been weakened by the sinfulness of man. Of what advantage is it if a state can institute nuptials estranged from the Christian religion, which is the mother of all good, cherishing all sublime virtues, quickening and urging us to everything that is the glory of a lofty and generous soul? When the Christian religion is rejected and repudiated, marriage sinks of necessity into the slavery of man's vicious nature and vile passions, and finds but little protection in the help of natural goodness. A very torrent of evil has flowed from this source, not only into private families, but also into States. For, the salutary fear of God being removed, and there being no longer that refreshment in toil which is nowhere more abounding than in the Christian religion, it very often happens, as indeed is natural,[67] that the mutual services and duties of marriage seem almost unbearable; and thus, very many yearn for the loosening of the tie which they believe to be woven by human law and of their own will, whenever incompatibility of temper, or quarrels, or the violation of the marriage vow, or mutual consent, or other reasons induce them to think that it would be well to be set free. Then, if they are hindered by law from carrying out this shameless desire, they contend that the laws are iniquitous, inhuman, and at variance with the rights of free citizens; adding that every effort should be made to repeal such enactments, and to introduce a more humane code sanctioning divorce.

---

65 L. *jus*; see footnote 16, p. 40.
66 L. *matrimoii species ac notio praestantissima*.
67 L. *quod est factu proclive*; that is, which agrees with the inclination of nature.—P. as from facts is evident.—H. as indeed is evident.—The Latin *proclive* can hardly be understood in the sense of "evident."

28. Now, however much the legislators of these our days may wish to guard themselves against the impiety of men such as we have been speaking of, they are unable to do so, seeing that they profess to hold and defend the very same principles of jurisprudence; and hence, they have to go with times, and render divorce easily obtainable. History itself shows this; for, to pass over other instances, we find that, at the close of the last century, divorces were sanctioned by law in that upheaval or, rather, as it might be called, conflagration in France, when society was wholly degraded by the abandoning of God. Many at the present time would fain have those laws re-enacted, because they wish God and His Church to be altogether exiled and excluded from the midst of human society, madly thinking that in such laws a final remedy must be sought for that moral corruption which is advancing with rapid strides.

29. Truly, it is hardly possible to describe how great are the evils that flow from divorce. Matrimonial contracts are by it made variable; mutual kindness is weakened; deplorable inducements to unfaithfulness are supplied; harm is done to the education and training of children; occasion is afforded for the breaking up of homes; the seeds of dissension are sown among families; the dignity of womanhood is lessened and brought low, and women run the risk of being deserted after having ministered to the pleasures of men. Since, then, nothing has such power to lay waste families and destroy the mainstay of kingdoms as the corruption of morals, it is easily seen that divorces are in the highest degree hostile to the prosperity of families and States, springing as they do from the depraved morals of the people, and, as experience shows us, opening out a way to every kind of evil-doing in public and in private life.

30. Further still, if the matter be duly pondered, we shall clearly see these evils to be the more especially dangerous, because, divorce once being tolerated, there will be no restraint powerful enough to keep it within the bounds marked out or presurmised. Great indeed is the force of example, and even greater still the

might of passion. With such incitements, it follows that the eagerness for divorce, daily spreading by devious ways, will seize upon the minds of many like a virulent contagious disease, or like a flood of water bursting through every barrier. These are truths that doubtlessly are all clear in themselves, but they will become clearer yet if we call to mind the teachings of experience. So soon as the road to divorce began to be made smooth by law, at once quarrels, jealousies, and judicial separations largely increased: and such shamelessness of life followed that men who had been in favor of these divorces repented of what they had done, and feared that, if they did not carefully seek a remedy by repealing the law, the State itself might come to ruin. The Romans of old are said to have shrunk with horror from the first example of divorce, but ere long all sense of decency was blunted in their soul; the meager restraint of passion died out, and the marriage vow was so often broken that what some writers have affirmed would seem to be true—namely, women used to reckon years not by the change of consuls, but of their husbands. In like manner, at the beginning, Protestants allowed legalized divorces in certain although but few cases, and yet from the affinity of circumstances of like kind, the number of divorces increased to such extent in Germany, America, and elsewhere that all-wise thinkers deplored the boundless corruption of morals, and judged the recklessness of the laws to be simply intolerable.

31. Even in Catholic States[68] the evil existed. For whenever at any time divorce was introduced, the abundance of misery that followed far exceeded all that the framers of the law could have foreseen. In fact, many lent their minds to contrive all kinds of fraud and device, and by accusations of cruelty, violence, and adultery to feign grounds for the dissolution of the matrimonial bond of which they had grown weary; and all this with so great havoc to morals that an amendment of the laws was deemed to be urgently needed.

32. Can anyone, therefore, doubt that laws in favor of divorce

---

68 L. *In civitatibus catholici nominis*; that is, in Catholic countries.

would have a result equally baneful and calamitous were they to be passed in these our days? There exists not, indeed, in the projects and enactments of men any power to change the character and tendency, which things have received from nature. Those men, therefore, show but little wisdom in the idea they have formed of the well-being of the commonwealth who think that the inherent character of marriage can be perverted with impunity; and who, disregarding the sanctity of religion and of the sacrament, seem to wish to degrade and dishonor marriage more basely than was done even by heathen laws. Indeed, if they do not change their views, not only private families, but all public society, will have unceasing cause to fear lest they should be miserably driven into that general confusion and overthrow of order, which is even now the wicked aim of socialists and communists. Thus, we see most clearly how foolish and senseless it is to expect any public good from divorce, when, on the contrary, it tends to the certain destruction of society.

33. It must consequently be acknowledged that the Church has deserved exceedingly well of all nations by her ever watchful care in guarding the sanctity and the indissolubility of marriage. Again, no small amount of gratitude is owing to her for having, during the last hundred years, openly denounced the wicked laws, which have grievously offended on this particular subject;[69] as well as for her having branded with anathema the baneful heresy obtaining among Protestants touching divorce and separation;[70] also, for having in many ways condemned the habitual dissolution of marriage among the Greeks;[71] for having declared invalid all marriages contracted upon the understanding that they may be at some future time dissolved;[72] and, lastly,

---

69   Pius VI, *Epist. ad episc. Lucion.*, May 20, 1793; Pius VII, encycl. letter, Feb. 17, 1809, and constitution given July 19, 1817; Pius VIII, encycl. letter, May 29, 1829; Gregory XVI, constitution given August 15, 1832; Pius IX. Address, Sept. 22, 1852.
70   Trid., sess. xxiv, can. 5, 7.
71   Council of Florence and instructions of Eugene IV to the Armenians; Benedict XIV, constitution *Etsi Pastoralis*, May 6, 1742.
72   Cap. 7, *De condit. appos.* (*Corpus juris canonici*, ed. cit., Part 2, col. 684).

for having, from the earliest times, repudiated the imperial laws which disastrously favored divorce.[73]

34. As often, indeed, as the supreme pontiffs have resisted the most powerful among rulers, in their threatening demands that divorces carried out by them should be confirmed by the Church, so often must we account them to have been contending for the safety, not only of religion, but also of the human race. For this reason, all generations of men will admire the proofs of unbending courage, which are to be found in the decrees of Nicholas I against Lothair; of Urban II and Paschal II against Philip I of France; of Celestine III and Innocent III against Alphonsus of Leon and Philip II of France; of Clement VII and Paul III against Henry VIII; and, lastly, of Pius VII, that holy and courageous pontiff, against Napoleon I, when at the height of his prosperity and in the fullness of his power. This being so, all rulers and administrators of the State[74] who are desirous of following the dictates of reason and wisdom, and anxious for the good of their people, ought to make up their minds to keep the holy laws of marriage intact, and to make use of the proffered aid of the Church for securing the safety of morals and the happiness of families, rather than suspect her of hostile intention and falsely and wickedly accuse her of violating the civil law.

---

73 Jerome, *Epist. 69, ad Oceanum* (PL 22, 657); Ambrose, Lib. 8 in cap. 16 Lucae, n. 5 (PL 15, 1857); Augustine, *De nuptiis*, 1, 10, 11 (PL 44, 420). Fifty years after the publication of *Arcanum*, Pope Pius XI published his own encyclical *Casti Connubii* (December 31, 1930), which may be found translated, with notes and bibliography, in J. Husslein, S. J., *Social Wellsprings*, Vol. II, pp. 122–173; also in pamphlet form, translated by Canon G. D. Smith, Catholic Truth Society of London; Paulist Press, New York; with a discussion club outline by Gerald C. Treacey, S. J.; National Catholic Welfare Conference, Washington, 1939. These pontifical acts should be completed by two addresses given by Pope Pius XII (October 29, 1951, and November 26, 1951), English translation published in pamphlet form by the National Catholic Welfare Conference under the title, *Moral Questions Affecting Married Life*, with a discussion outline by Edgar Schmiedeler, O. S. B.
74 L. *rerum publicarum*.

35. They should do this all the more readily because the Catholic Church, though powerless in any way to abandon the duties of her office or the defense of her authority, still very greatly inclines to kindness and indulgence whenever they are consistent with the safety of her rights and the sanctity of her duties. Wherefore, she makes no decrees in relation to marriage without having regard to the state of the body politic and the condition of the general public; and has besides more than once mitigated, as far as possible, the enactments of her own laws when there were just and weighty reasons. Moreover, she is not unaware, and never calls in doubt, that the sacrament of marriage, being instituted for the preservation and increase of the human race, has a necessary relation to circumstances of life which, though connected with marriage, belong to the civil order, and about which the State rightly makes strict inquiry and justly promulgates decrees.

36. Yet, no one doubts that Jesus Christ, the Founder of the Church, willed her sacred power to be distinct from the civil power, and each power to be free and unshackled in its own sphere: with this condition, however—a condition good for both, and of advantage to all men—that union and concord should be maintained between them; and that on those questions which are, though in different ways, of common right and authority, the power to which secular matters have been entrusted should happily and becomingly depend on the other power which has in its charge the interests of heaven. In such arrangement and harmony is found not only the best line of action for each power, but also the most opportune and efficacious method of helping men in all that pertains to their life here, and to their hope of salvation hereafter. For, as We have shown in former encyclical letters,[75] the intellect of man is greatly ennobled by the Christian faith, and made better able to shun and banish all error, while faith borrows in turn no little help from the intellect; and in like manner, when the civil power is on friendly terms with the sacred authority of the Church,

---

75 *Aeterni Patris*, Leo XIII, August 4, 1879.

there accrues to both a great increase of usefulness. The dignity of the one is exalted, and so long as religion is its guide it will never rule unjustly, while the other receives help of protection and defense for the public good of the faithful.

37. Being moved, therefore, by these considerations, as We have exhorted rulers at other times, so still more earnestly We exhort them now, to concord and friendly feeling; and we are the first to stretch out Our hand to them with fatherly benevolence, and to offer to them the help of Our supreme authority, a help which is the more necessary at this time when, in public opinion, the authority of rulers is wounded and enfeebled. Now that the minds of so many are inflamed with a reckless spirit of liberty, and men are wickedly endeavoring to get rid of every restraint of authority, however legitimate it may be, the public safety demands that both powers should unite their strength to avert the evils which are hanging, not only over the Church, but also over civil society.

38. But, while earnestly exhorting all to a friendly union of will, and beseeching God, the Prince of peace, to infuse a love of concord into all hearts, We cannot, venerable brothers, refrain from urging you more and more to fresh earnestness, and zeal, and watchfulness, though we know that these are already very great. With every effort and with all authority, strive, as much as you are able, to preserve whole and undefiled among the people committed to your charge the doctrine which Christ our Lord taught us; which the Apostles, the interpreters of the will of God, have handed down; and which the Catholic Church has herself scrupulously guarded, and commanded to be believed in all ages by the faithful of Christ.

39. Let special care be taken that the people be well instructed in the precepts of Christian wisdom, so that they may always remember that marriage was not instituted by the will of man, but, from the very beginning, by the authority and command of God; that it does not admit of plurality of wives or husbands; that Christ, the Author of the New Covenant, raised it from

a rite of nature to be a sacrament, and gave to His Church legislative and judicial power with regard to the bond of union. On this point, the very greatest care must be taken to instruct them, lest their minds should be led into error by the unsound conclusions of adversaries who desire that the Church should be deprived of that power.

40. In like manner, all ought to understand clearly that, if there be any union of a man and a woman among the faithful of Christ which is not a sacrament, such union has not the force and nature of a proper marriage; that, although contracted in accordance with the laws of the State, it cannot be more than a rite or custom introduced by the civil law. Further, the civil law can deal with and decide those matters alone which in the civil order spring from marriage, and which cannot possibly exist, as is evident, unless there be a true and lawful cause of them, that is to say, the nuptial bond. It is of the greatest consequence to husband and wife that all these things should be known and well understood by them, in order that they may conform to the laws of the State, if there be no objection on the part of the Church; for the Church wishes the effects of marriage to be guarded in all possible ways, and that no harm may come to the children.

41. In the great confusion of opinions, however, which day by day is spreading more and more widely, it should further be known that no power can dissolve the bond of Christian marriage whenever this has been ratified and consummated; and that, of a consequence, those husbands and wives are guilty of a manifest crime who plan, for whatever reason, to be united in a second marriage before the first one has been ended by death. When, indeed, matters have come to such a pitch that it seems impossible for them to live together any longer, then the Church allows them to live apart, and strives at the same time to soften the evils of this separation by such remedies and helps as are suited to their condition; yet she never ceases to endeavor to bring about a reconciliation, and never despairs of doing so. But these are extreme cases; and they would seldom

exist if men and women entered into the married state with proper dispositions, not influenced by passion, but entertaining right ideas of the duties of marriage and of its noble purpose; neither would they anticipate their marriage by a series of sins drawing down upon them the wrath of God.

42. To sum up all in a few words, there would be a calm and quiet constancy in marriage if married people would gather strength and life from the virtue of religion alone, which imparts to us resolution and fortitude; for religion would enable them to bear tranquilly and even gladly the trials of their state, such as, for instance, the faults that they discover in one another, the difference of temper and character, the weight of a mother's cares, the wearing anxiety about the education of children, reverses of fortune, and the sorrows of life.

43. Care also must be taken that they do not easily enter into marriage with those who are not Catholics; for, when minds do not agree as to the observances of religion, it is scarcely possible to hope for agreement in other things. Other reasons also proving that persons should turn with dread from such marriages are chiefly these: that they give occasion to forbidden association and communion in religious matters; endanger the faith of the Catholic partner; are a hindrance to the proper education of the children; and often lead to a mixing up of truth and falsehood, and to the belief that all religions are equally good.

44. Lastly, since We well know that none should be excluded from Our charity, We commend, venerable brothers, to your fidelity and piety those unhappy persons who, carried away by the heat of passion, and being utterly indifferent to their salvation, live wickedly together without the bond of lawful marriage. Let your utmost care be exercised in bringing such persons back to their duty; and, both by your own efforts and by those of good men who will consent to help you, strive by every means that they may see how wrongly they have acted; that they may do penance; and that they may be induced to enter into a lawful marriage according to the Catholic rite.

45. You will at once see, venerable brothers, that the doctrine and precepts in relation to Christian marriage, which We have thought good to communicate to you in this letter, tend no less to the preservation of civil society than to the everlasting salvation of souls. May God grant that, by reason of their gravity and importance, minds may everywhere be found docile and ready to obey them! For this end let us all suppliantly, with humble prayer, implore the help of the Blessed and Immaculate Virgin Mary, that, our hearts being quickened to the obedience of faith, she may show herself our mother and our helper. With equal earnestness let us ask the princes of the Apostles, Peter and Paul, the destroyers of heresies, the sowers of the seed of truth, to save the human race by their powerful patronage from the deluge of errors that is surging afresh. In the meantime, as an earnest of heavenly gifts, and a testimony of Our special benevolence, We grant to you all, venerable brothers, and to the people confided to your charge, from the depths of Our heart, the apostolic benediction.

IV

Freemasonry and Naturalism

INTRODUCTION

In his encyclical on *Civil Government* (*Diuturnum*, art. 25), Pope Leo XIII had denounced the peril created by the increasing boldness of political sects and secret societies. The present encyclical, *Humanum Genus* (April 20, 1884) is a complete doctrinal justification of this attitude. Freemasonry is described in it as busy spreading the doctrine which Leo XIII so often condemned as being that of the naturalists. Naturalism consists in placing nature and human reason above the supernatural order, including God and His laws. The naturalists are sound in stressing the existence of the natural order and of its laws, but they are wrong in denying the divine origin of nature and in refusing to subject it to the supernatural order of grace. The effects of their attitude are exactly the reverse of what they are hoping to achieve. In affirming the self-sufficiency of the natural order, they cut it off from the only power that can heal the wounds inflicted upon nature by original sin. The spreading of naturalism does not herald the triumph of nature, it spells its destruction.

The reason Pope Leo XIII wrote this denunciation of Freemasonry is given in art. 8, where this secret society is depicted as one of the major perils that threaten the Church. Italian Freemasonry was well known to the popes. They also had first-hand information concerning the part played by Freemasonry in the cruel persecution of the Church at the time of the French Revolution.

It is sometimes said that what the Pope here has in mind is particularly *European* Freemasonry. He most certainly recognized differences of attitude among the various branches of Freemasonry, but he also knew that, despite these differences due to the fact that all the masonic groups have not reached the same level of development, Freemasonry is fundamentally one. Like all secret societies and revolutionary parties, Freemasonry is swayed by men who only reveal the part of their intentions which they consider advisable to disclose. Their main problem is to recruit followers, and the main method they all apply is to gain control of the school system of a country.

This, of course, is the more easily denied as those who are in charge of applying the method are the first ones to deny it. The description of the tactics used by Freemasonry, as given in art. 9 of this encyclical is precisely intended to dispel current illusions concerning the distinction between a good Freemasonry and a bad one. Another important document on the same subject is the apostolic letter of Pope Leo XIII, *Praeclara Gratulationis* (June 20, 1894), wherein the same collusion between Freemasonry and naturalism is once more denounced. This second document, exceptionally addressed "to all the rulers and to all their peoples," including the non-Christian rulers and their non-Christian peoples, attributes to world Freemasonry the ambition of getting complete political control of each and every State, so as ultimately to become the supreme ruler of the world.

SUMMARY

(1) The kingdom of Satan opposed to the kingdom of God. (2) The two cities defined by St. Augustine. (3–5) Warning to the world of the danger. (6) Especially under the form which this danger assumes in Freemasonry. (7) Freemasonry is still more dangerous for the State than for the Church; experience proves it. (8) This is the reason why, having refuted communism (*Quod Apostolici Muneris*), established the basis for domestic society (*Arcanum*), and defined the notion of a sound political government (*Diuturnum*), it is necessary that the Pope should denounce the evil of Freemasonry. (9) This condemnation applies to the many societies which carry the work of Freemasonry at various levels and under different names. (10) Naturalism provides the foundations for the doctrines of Freemasonry, but all

Humanum Genus

are guilty of having accepted membership in it. (12) Definition of naturalism. (13) Freemasonry implements the conclusions of naturalism. (14) Freemasonry is opposed to the Church. (15) And, consequently, to the authority of the Roman Pontiffs. (16) As well as religion under all its forms. (17) Naturalists do not consider certain the existence of God, the immateriality of a soul and its immortality; Freemasons leave everyone free to think what he pleases in such matters. (18–19) The laws of nature and the principles of morality vanish together with these fundamental truths. (20) Since they deny or ignore original sin, naturalists and Freemasons are bound to exaggerate the natural inclination of man to virtue and to justice; they favor the quest for pleasure and the free enjoyment of passions. (21) Freemasons want to place family and education under the sole sway of the State. (22) Naturalists hold that all men are equal, that no man has any right to rule another man; their State is godless. (23) These doctrines are also held by Freemasons. (24) Freemasons are attempting to restore paganism by taking God out of both homes and States. (25) Now, on the contrary, the true bond of society is God. (26) All men are truly equal so far as regards their common origin, their common nature, and their ultimate end, but they are inequal as regards their physical, intellectual, and moral powers. (27) Freemasons work, in fact, for the revolution intended by the socialists and the communists. (28) They only subtract the State from the authority of the Church in order to submit it to their own authority. (29) Not so with the Church, whose doctrine fully establishes the authority of the civil power. (30) The condemnations of Freemasonry by the Popes are confirmed. (31) No Catholic is permitted to join Freemasonry for any reason whatsoever. (32) The best protection against error is the teaching of Christian philosophy. (33) Both clergy and laity should join in fighting secret societies. (34) The spreading of the Third Order of St. Francis of Assisi should do much to counteract the influence of such societies. (35) The restoration of Catholic guilds, or associations of workmen, would help safeguarding their interests, both material and spiritual. (36) Parents and teachers should warn the young against joining any group without taking counsel from their parents or spiritual directors. (37) Invitation to prayer. (38) Apostolic benediction.

IV

Humanum Genus
ON FREEMASONRY
April 20, 1884

1. The race of man,[1] after its miserable fall from God, the Creator and the Giver of heavenly gifts, "through the envy of the devil," separated into two diverse and opposite parts, of which the one steadfastly contends for truth and virtue, the other of those things which are contrary to virtue and to truth. The one is the kingdom of God on earth, namely, the true Church of Jesus Christ; and those who desire from their heart to be united with it, so as to gain salvation, must of necessity serve God and His only-begotten Son with their whole mind and with an entire will. The other is the kingdom of Satan, in whose possession and control are all whosoever follow the fatal example of their leader and of our first parents, those who refuse to obey the divine and eternal law, and who have many aims of their own in contempt of God, and many aims also against God.

2. This twofold kingdom St. Augustine keenly discerned and described after the manner of two cities, contrary in their laws because striving for contrary objects; and with a subtle brevity he expressed the efficient cause of each in these words: "Two loves formed two cities: the love of self, reaching even to contempt of God, an earthly city; and the love of God, reaching to contempt of self, a heavenly one."[2] At every period of time, each has been in conflict with the other, with a variety and multiplicity of weapons and of warfare, although not always with equal ardor and assault. At this period, however, the partisans of evil seem to be combining together, and to be struggling with united vehemence, led on or assisted by that strongly organized and

---

1 L. *humanum genus*; that is, humankind.
2 *De civ. Dei*, 14, 28 (PL 41, 436).

widespread association called the Freemasons. No longer making any secret of their purposes, they are now boldly rising up against God Himself. They are planning the destruction of holy Church publicly and openly, and this with the set purpose of utterly despoiling the nations of Christendom, if it were possible, of the blessings obtained for us through Jesus Christ our Savior. Lamenting these evils, We are constrained by the charity which urges Our heart to cry out often to God: "For lo, Thy enemies have made a noise; and they that hate Thee have lifted up the head. They have taken a malicious counsel against Thy people, and they have consulted against Thy saints. They have said, 'come, and let us destroy them, so that they be not a nation.'"[3]

3. At so urgent a crisis, when so fierce and so pressing an onslaught is made upon the Christian name, it is Our office to point out the danger, to mark who are the adversaries, and to the best of Our power to make head against their plans and devices, that those may not perish whose salvation is committed to Us, and that the kingdom of Jesus Christ entrusted to Our charge may not stand and remain whole, but may be enlarged by an ever-increasing growth throughout the world.

4. The Roman Pontiffs, Our predecessors, in their incessant watchfulness over the safety of the Christian people, were prompt in detecting the presence and the purpose of this capital enemy; immediately, it sprang into the light instead of hiding as a dark conspiracy; and, moreover, they took occasion with true foresight to give, as it were on their guard, and not allow themselves to be caught by the devices and snares laid out to deceive them.

5. The first warning of the danger was given by Clement XII in the year 1738,[4] and his constitution was confirmed and renewed by Benedict XIV.[5] Pius VII followed the same path;[6] and Leo

---

[3] Ps. 82:24.
[4] Const. *In Eminenti*, April 24, 1738.
[5] Const. *Providas*, May 18, 1751.
[6] Const. *Ecclesiam a Jesu Christo*, Sept. 13, 1821.

XII, by his apostolic constitution, *Quo Graviora*,[7] put together the acts and decrees of former Pontiffs on this subject, and ratified and confirmed them forever. In the same sense spoke Pius VIII,[8] Gregory XVI,[9] and, many times over, Pius IX.[10]

6. For as soon as the constitution and the spirit of the masonic sect were clearly discovered by manifest signs of its actions, by the investigation of its causes,[11] by publication of its laws, and of its rites and commentaries, with the addition often of the personal testimony of those who were in the secret, this apostolic see denounced the sect of the Freemasons, and publicly declared its constitution, as contrary to law and right, to be pernicious no less to Christendom than to the State;[12] and it forbade any one to enter the society, under the penalties which the Church is wont to inflict upon exceptionally guilty persons. The sectaries, indignant at this, thinking to elude or to weaken the force of these decrees, partly by contempt of them, and partly by calumny, accused the sovereign Pontiffs who had passed them, either of exceeding the bounds of moderation in their decrees or of decreeing what was not just. This was the manner in which they endeavored to elude the authority and the weight of the apostolic constitutions of Clement XII and Benedict XIV, as well as of Pius VII and Pius IX.[13] Yet, in the very society itself, there were to be found men who unwillingly acknowledged that the Roman Pontiffs had acted within their right, according to the Catholic doctrine and discipline. The Pontiffs received the same assent, and in strong terms, from many princes and heads of governments, who made it their business either to delate the masonic society to the apostolic

---

7 Const. given March 13, 1825.
8 Encyc. *Traditi*, May 21, 1829.
9 Encyc. *Mirari*, August 15, 1832.
10 Encyc. *Qui Pluribus*, Nov. 9, 1846; address *Multiplices inter*, Sept. 25, 1865. etc.
11 L. *cogitatione causarum*. — P. by cases investigated; probably a simple misprint of cases for causes.
12 L. *civitati*; that is, to the body politic.
13 Clement XII (1730–40); Benedict XIV (1740–58); Pius VII (1800–23); Pius IX (1846–78).

see, or of their own accord by special enactments to brand it as pernicious, as, for example, in Holland, Austria, Switzerland, Spain, Bavaria, Savoy, and other parts of Italy.

7. But, what is of highest importance, the course of events has demonstrated the prudence of Our predecessors. For their provident and paternal solicitude had not always and everywhere the result desired; and this, either because of the simulation and cunning of some who were active agents in the mischief, or else of the thoughtless levity of the rest who ought, in their own interest, to have given to the matter their diligent attention. In consequence, the sect of Freemasons grew with a rapidity beyond conception in the course of a century and a half, until it came to be able, by means of fraud or of audacity, to gain such entrance into every rank of the State as to seem to be almost its ruling power. This swift and formidable advance has brought upon the Church, upon the power of princes, upon the public well-being, precisely that grievous harm, which Our predecessors had long before foreseen. Such a condition has been reached that henceforth there will be grave reason to fear, not indeed for the Church—for her foundation is much too firm to be overturned by the effort of men—but for those States in which prevails the power, either of the sect of which we are speaking or of other sects not dissimilar which lend themselves to it as disciples and subordinates.

8. For these reasons We no sooner came to the helm of the Church than We clearly saw and felt it to be Our duty to use Our authority to the very utmost against so vast an evil. We have several times already, as occasion served, attacked certain chief points of teaching which showed in a special manner the perverse influence of Masonic opinions. Thus, in Our encyclical letter, *Quod Apostolici Muneris*, We endeavored to refute the monstrous doctrines of the socialists and communists; afterwards, in another beginning "*Arcanum*," We took pains to defend and explain the true and genuine idea of domestic life, of which marriage is the spring and origin; and again, in that

which begins "*Diuturnum*,"[14] We described the ideal of political government conformed to the principles of Christian wisdom, which is marvellously in harmony, on the one hand, with the natural order of things, and, in the other, with the well-being of both sovereign princes and of nations. It is now Our intention, following the example of Our predecessors, directly to treat of the masonic society itself, of its whole teaching, of its aims, and of its manner of thinking and acting, in order to bring more and more into the light its power for evil, and to do what We can to arrest the contagion of this fatal plague.

9. There are several organized bodies which, though differing in name, in ceremonial, in form, and origin, are nevertheless so bound together by community of purpose and by the similarity of their main opinions, as to make in fact one thing with the sect of the Freemasons, which is a kind of center whence they all go forth, and whither they all return. Now, these no longer show a desire to remain concealed; for they hold their meetings in the daylight and before the public eye, and publish their own newspapers; and yet, when thoroughly understood, they are found still to retain the nature and the habits of secret societies. There are many things like mysteries, which it is the fixed rule to hide with extreme care, not only from strangers, but from very many members, also; such as their secret and final designs, the names of the chief leaders, and certain secret and inner meetings, as well as their decisions, and the ways and means of carrying them out. This is, no doubt, the object of the manifold difference among the members as to right, office, and privilege, of the received distinction of orders and grades, and of that severe discipline which is maintained.

Candidates are generally commanded to promise — nay, with a special oath, to swear — that they will never, to any person, at any time or in any way, make known the members, the passes,[15] or the subjects discussed. Thus, with a fraudulent external appearance, and with a style of simulation which is always the same, the

---

14   See pp. 63, 109, 175–186.
15   L. *notas*.

Freemasons, like the Manichees of old, strive, as far as possible, to conceal themselves, and to admit no witnesses but their own members. As a convenient manner of concealment, they assume the character of literary men and scholars associated for purposes of learning. They speak of their zeal for a more cultured refinement, and of their love for the poor; and they declare their one wish to be the amelioration of the condition of the masses, and to share with the largest possible number all the benefits of civil life. Were these purposes aimed at in real truth, they are by no means the whole of their object. Moreover, to be enrolled, it is necessary that the candidates promise and undertake to be thenceforward strictly obedient to their leaders and masters with the utmost submission and fidelity, and to be in readiness to do their bidding upon the slightest expression of their will; or, if disobedient, to submit to the direst penalties and death itself. As a fact, if any are judged to have betrayed the doings of the sect or to have resisted commands given, punishment is inflicted on them not infrequently, and with so much audacity and dexterity that the assassin very often escapes the detection and penalty of his crime.

10. But to simulate and wish to lie hid; to bind men like slaves in the very tightest bonds, and without giving any sufficient reason; to make use of men enslaved to the will of another for any arbitrary act; to arm men's right hands for bloodshed after securing impunity for the crime — all this is an enormity from which nature recoils. Wherefore, reason and truth itself make it plain that the society of which we are speaking is in antagonism with justice and natural uprightness. And this becomes still plainer, inasmuch as other arguments, also, and those very manifest, prove that it is essentially opposed to natural virtue. For, no matter how great may be men's cleverness in concealing and their experience in lying, it is impossible to prevent the effects of any cause from showing, in some way, the intrinsic nature of the cause whence they come. "A good tree cannot produce bad fruit, nor a bad tree produce good fruit."[16]

---

16 Matt. 7:18.

Now, the masonic sect produces fruits that are pernicious and of the bitterest savor. For, from what We have above most clearly shown, that which is their ultimate purpose forces itself into view — namely, the utter overthrow of that whole religious and political order of the world which the Christian teaching has produced, and the substitution of a new state of things in accordance with their ideas, of which the foundations and laws shall be drawn from mere naturalism.

11. What We have said, and are about to say, must be understood of the sect of the Freemasons taken generically, and in so far as it comprises the associations kindred to it and confederated with it, but not of the individual members of them. There may be persons amongst these, and not a few who, although not free from the guilt of having entangled themselves in such associations, yet are neither themselves partners in their criminal acts nor aware of the ultimate object which they are endeavoring to attain. In the same way, some of the affiliated societies, perhaps, by no means approve of the extreme conclusions which they would, if consistent, embrace as necessarily following from their common principles, did not their very foulness strike them with horror. Some of these, again, are led by circumstances of times and places either to aim at smaller things than the others usually attempt or than they themselves would wish to attempt. They are not, however, for this reason, to be reckoned as alien to the masonic federation; for the masonic federation is to be judged not so much by the things which it has done, or brought to completion, as by the sum of its pronounced opinions.

12. Now, the fundamental doctrine of the naturalists, which they sufficiently make known by their very name, is that human nature and human reason ought in all things to be mistress and guide. Laying this down, they care little for duties to God, or pervert them by erroneous and vague opinions. For they deny that anything has been taught by God; they allow no dogma of religion or truth which cannot be understood by the human intelligence, nor any teacher who ought to be believed by reason

of his authority. And since it is the special and exclusive duty of the Catholic Church fully to set forth in words truths divinely received, to teach, besides other divine helps to salvation, the authority of its office, and to defend the same with perfect purity, it is against the Church that the rage and attack of the enemies are principally directed.

13. In those matters which regard religion, let it be seen how the sect of the Freemasons acts, especially where it is more free to act without restraint, and then let anyone judge whether in fact it does not wish to carry out the policy of the naturalists. By a long and persevering labor, they endeavor to bring about this result—namely, that the teaching office[17] and authority of the Church may become of no account in the civil State; and for this same reason, they declare to the people and contend that Church and State[18] ought to be altogether disunited. By this means, they reject from the laws and from the commonwealth the wholesome influence of the Catholic religion; and they consequently imagine that States[19] ought to be constituted without any regard for the laws and precepts of the Church.

14. Nor do they think it enough to disregard the Church—the best of guides—unless they also injure it by their hostility. Indeed, with them it is lawful to attack with impunity the very foundations of the Catholic religion, in speech, in writing, and in teaching; and even the rights of the Church are not spared, and the offices with which it is divinely invested are not safe. The least possible liberty to manage affairs is left to the Church; and this is done by laws not apparently very hostile, but in reality, framed and fitted to hinder freedom of action. Moreover, We see exceptional and onerous laws imposed upon the clergy, to the end that they may be continually diminished in number and in necessary means. We see also the remnants of the possessions of the Church fettered by the strictest conditions, and

---

17 L. *magisterium*.
18 L. *rem sacram remque civilem*; that is, religious affairs and political affairs.
19 L. *civitates*.

subjected to the power and arbitrary will of the administrators of the State,[20] and the religious orders rooted up and scattered.

15. But, against the apostolic see and the Roman Pontiff, the contention of these enemies has been for a long time directed. The Pontiff was first, for specious reasons, thrust out from the bulwark of his liberty and of his right, the civil princedom;[21] soon, he was unjustly driven into a condition which was unbearable because of the difficulties raised on all sides; and now, the time has come when the partisans of the sects openly declare, what in secret among themselves they have for a long time plotted, that the sacred power of the Pontiffs must be abolished, and that the papacy itself, founded by divine right, must be utterly destroyed. If other proofs were wanting, this fact would be sufficiently disclosed by the testimony of men well informed, of whom some at other times, and others again recently, have declared it to be true of the Freemasons that they especially desire to assail the Church with irreconcilable hostility, and that they will never rest until they have destroyed whatever the supreme Pontiffs have established for the sake of religion.

16. If those who are admitted as members are not commanded to abjure by any form of words the Catholic doctrines, this omission, so far from being adverse to the designs of the Freemasons is more useful for their purposes. First, in this way, they easily deceive the simple-minded and the heedless, and can induce a far greater number to become members. Again, as all who offer themselves are received whatever may be their form of religion, they thereby teach the great error of this age — that a regard for religion should be held as an indifferent matter, and that all religions are alike. This manner of reasoning is calculated to bring about the ruin of all forms of religion, and especially of the Catholic religion, which, as it is the only one that is true, cannot, without great injustice, be regarded as merely equal to other religions.

---

20   L. *reipublicae*; that is, of the commonwealth.
21   L. *principatu civili*; that is, his temporal power.

17. But the naturalists go much further; for, having, in the highest things, entered upon a wholly erroneous course, they are carried headlong to extremes, either by reason of the weakness of human nature, or because God inflicts upon them the just punishment of their pride. Hence, it happens that they no longer consider as certain and permanent those things which are fully understood by the natural light of reason, such as certainly are — the existence of God, the immaterial nature of the human soul, and its immortality. The sect of the Freemasons, by a similar course of error, is exposed to these same dangers; for, although in a general way they may profess the existence of God, they themselves are witnesses that they do not all maintain this truth with the full assent of the mind or with a firm conviction. Neither do they conceal that this question about God is the greatest source and cause of discords among them; in fact, it is certain that a considerable contention about this same subject has existed among them very lately. But, indeed, the sect allows great liberty to its votaries, so that to each side is given the right to defend its own opinion, either that there is a God, or that there is none; and those who obstinately contend that there is no God are as easily initiated as those who contend that God exists, though, like the pantheists, they have false notions concerning Him: all which is nothing else than taking away the reality, while retaining some absurd representation of the divine nature.

18. When this greatest fundamental truth has been overturned or weakened, it follows that those truths, also, which are known by the teaching of nature must begin to fall — namely, that all things were made by the free will of God the Creator; that the world is governed by Providence; that souls do not die; that to this life of men upon the earth there will succeed another and an everlasting life.

19. When these truths are done away with, which are as the principles of nature and important for knowledge and for practical use, it is easy to see what will become of both public and private morality. We say nothing of those more heavenly virtues,

which no one can exercise or even acquire without a special gift and grace of God; of which necessarily no trace can be found in those who reject as unknown the redemption of mankind, the grace of God, the sacraments, and the happiness to be obtained in heaven. We speak now of the duties which have their origin in natural probity. That God is the Creator of the world and its provident Ruler; that the eternal law commands the natural order to be maintained, and forbids that it be disturbed; that the last end of men is a destiny far above human things and beyond this sojourning upon the earth: these are the sources and these the principles of all justice and morality.

If these be taken away, as the naturalists and Freemasons desire, there will immediately be no knowledge as to what constitutes justice and injustice, or upon what principle morality is founded. And, in truth, the teaching of morality which alone finds favor with the sect of Freemasons,[22] and in which they contend that youth should be instructed, is that which they call "civil,"[23] and "independent," and "free," namely, that which does not contain any religious belief. But, how insufficient such teaching is, how wanting in soundness, and how easily moved by every impulse of passion, is sufficiently proved by its sad fruits, which have already begun to appear. For, wherever, by removing Christian education, this teaching[24] has begun more completely to rule, there goodness and integrity of morals have begun quickly to perish, monstrous and shameful opinions have grown up, and the audacity of evil deeds has risen to a high degree. All this is commonly complained of and deplored; and not a few of those who by no means wish to do so are compelled by abundant evidence to give not infrequently the same testimony.

20. Moreover, human nature was stained by original sin, and is therefore more disposed to vice than to virtue. For a virtuous

---

22   L. *Massonum familiae*; that is, the masonic family (including its many branches).
23   L. *civicam*; that is, civic; in other words, a code of ethics mainly concerned with the duties of man as a citizen.
24   L. *illa*; that is, this free and irreligious code of masonry. — P. understands *illa* as meaning the sect.

life, it is absolutely necessary to restrain the disorderly movements of the soul, and to make the passions obedient to reason. In this conflict, human things must very often be despised, and the greatest labors and hardships must be undergone, in order that reason may always hold its sway. But, the naturalists and Freemasons, having no faith in those things which we have learned by the revelation of God, deny that our first parents sinned, and consequently think that free will is not at all weakened and inclined to evil.[25] On the contrary, exaggerating rather the power and the excellence of nature,[26] and placing therein alone the principle and rule of justice, they cannot even imagine that there is any need at all of a constant struggle and a perfect steadfastness to overcome the violence and rule of our passions.

Wherefore, we see that men are publicly tempted by the many allurements of pleasure; that there are journals and pamphlets with neither moderation nor shame; that stage-plays are remarkable for license; that designs for works of art are shamelessly sought in the laws of a so-called verism;[27] that the contrivances of a soft and delicate life are most carefully devised; and that all the blandishments of pleasure are diligently sought out by which virtue may be lulled to sleep. Wickedly, also, but at the same time quite consistently, do those act who do away with the expectation of the joys of heaven, and bring down all happiness to the level of mortality, and, as it were, sink it in the earth. Of what We have said the following fact, astonishing not so much in itself as in its open expression, may serve as a confirmation. For, since generally no one is accustomed to obey crafty and clever men so submissively as those whose soul is weakened and broken down by the domination of the passions, there have been in the sect of the Freemasons some who have plainly determined

---

25 Trid., sess. vi, *De justif*, c. 1. Text of the Council of Trent: *"tametsi in eis* (sc. Judaeis) *liberum arbitrium minime extinctum esset, viribus licet attenuatum et inclinatum.*
26 L. *exagerantes naturae virtutem et excellentiam.* — P. exaggerating, rather our natural virtue and excellence.
27 L. *verisimi*; that is, verism, a school of art exaggerating the esthetic value of ugliness and vulgarity.

and proposed that, artfully and of set purpose, the multitude should be satiated with a boundless license of vice, as, when this had been done, it would easily come under their power and authority for any acts of daring.

21. What refers to domestic life in the teaching of the naturalists is almost all contained in the following declarations: that marriage belongs to the genus of commercial contracts, which can rightly be revoked by the will of those who made them, and that the civil rulers of the State have power over the matrimonial bond; that in the education of youth nothing is to be taught in the matter of religion as of certain and fixed opinion; and each one must be left at liberty to follow when he comes of age, whatever he may prefer. To these things, the Freemasons fully assent; and not only assent, but have long endeavored to make them into a law and institution. For in many countries, and those nominally Catholic,[28] it is enacted that no marriages shall be considered lawful except those contracted by the civil rite; in other places, the law permits divorce; and in others, every effort is used to make it lawful as soon as may be. Thus, the time is quickly coming when marriages will be turned into another kind of contract—that is into changeable and uncertain unions which fancy may join together, and which the same, when changed, may disunite.

With the greatest unanimity, the sect of the Freemasons also endeavors to take to itself the education of youth. They think that they can easily mold to their opinions that soft and pliant age, and bend it whither they will; and that nothing can be more fitted than this to enable them to bring up the youth of the State after their own plan. Therefore, in the education and instruction of children, they allow no share, either of teaching or of discipline, to the ministers of the Church; and in many places, they have procured that the education of youth shall be exclusively in the hands of laymen, and that nothing which

---

28   L. *iisdemque catholici nominis*; that is, considered and called Catholic; probably without the strong pejorative connotation which can be attributed to "nominally."

treats of the most important and most holy duties of men to God shall be introduced into the instructions on morals.

22. Then come their doctrines of politics, in which the naturalists lay down that all men have the same right, and are in every respect of equal and like condition; that each one is naturally free; that no one has the right to command another; that it is an act of violence to require men to obey any authority other than that which is obtained from themselves. According to this, therefore, all things belong to the free people; power is held by the command or permission of the people, so that, when the popular will changes, rulers may lawfully be deposed and the source of all rights and civil duties is either in the multitude or in the governing authority when this is constituted according to the latest doctrines. It is held also that the State should be without God;[29] that in the various forms of religion there is no reason why one should have precedence of another; and that they are all to occupy the same place.

23. That these doctrines are equally acceptable to the Freemasons, and that they would wish to constitute States according to this example and model, is too well known to require proof. For some time past, they have openly endeavored to bring this about with all their strength and resources; and in this, they prepare the way for not a few bolder men who are hurrying on even to worse things, in their endeavor to obtain equality and community of all goods by the destruction of every distinction of rank and property.[30]

24. What, therefore, sect of the Freemasons is, and what course it pursues, appears sufficiently from the summary We have briefly given. Their chief dogmas are so greatly and manifestly at variance with reason that nothing can be more perverse. To wish to destroy the religion and the Church which God Himself has established, and whose perpetuity He insures by His protection, and to bring back after a lapse of eighteen centuries the

---

29 L. *atheam*; that is, atheistic, godless.
30 L. *fortunarum*; that is, of fortunes.

manners and customs of the pagans, is signal folly and audacious impiety. Neither is it less horrible nor more tolerable that they should repudiate the benefits which Jesus Christ so mercifully obtained, not only for individuals, but also for the family and for civil society, benefits which, even according to the judgment and testimony of enemies of Christianity, are very great. In this insane and wicked endeavor we may almost see the implacable hatred and spirit of revenge with which Satan himself is inflamed against Jesus Christ. — So also the studious endeavor of the Freemasons to destroy the chief foundations of justice and honesty, and to co-operate with those who would wish, as if they were mere animals, to do what they please, tends only to the ignominious and disgraceful ruin of the human race.

The evil, too, is increased by the dangers which threaten both domestic and civil society. As We have elsewhere shown,[31] in marriage, according to the belief of almost every nation, there is something sacred and religious; and the law of God has determined that marriages shall not be dissolved. If they are deprived of their sacred character, and made dissoluble, trouble and confusion in the family will be the result, the wife being deprived of her dignity and the children left without protection as to their interests and well being. — To have in public matters no care for religion, and in the arrangement and administration of civil affairs to have no more regard for God than if He did not exist, is a rashness unknown to the very pagans; for in their heart and soul the notion of a divinity and the need of public religion were so firmly fixed that they would have thought it easier to have a city without foundation than a city without God. Human society, indeed for which by nature we are formed, has been constituted by God the Author of nature; and from Him, as from their principle and source, flow in all their strength and permanence the countless benefits with which society abounds. As we are each of us admonished by the very voice of nature to worship God in piety and holiness, as the Giver unto us of life and of all that is good therein, so also and for the same reason,

---

31 See *Arcanum*, no. 19.

nations and States are bound to worship Him; and therefore, it is clear that those who would absolve society from all religious duty act not only unjustly but also with ignorance and folly.

25. As men are by the will of God born for civil union and society, and as the power to rule is so necessary a bond of society that, if it be taken away, society must at once be broken up, it follows that from Him who is the Author of society has come also the authority to rule; so that whosoever rules, he is the minister of God. Wherefore, as the end and nature of human society so require, it is right to obey the just commands of lawful authority, as it is right to obey God who ruleth all things; and it is most untrue that the people have it in their power to cast aside their obedience whensoever they please.

26. In like manner, no one doubts that all men are equal one to another, so far as regards their common origin and nature, or the last end which each one has to attain, or the rights and duties which are thence derived. But, as the abilities of all are not equal, as one differs from another in the powers of mind or body, and as there are very many dissimilarities of manner, disposition, and character, it is most repugnant to reason to endeavor to confine all within the same measure, and to extend complete equality to the institutions of civil life. Just as a perfect condition of the body results from the conjunction and composition of its various members, which, though differing in form and purpose, make, by their union and the distribution of each one to its proper place, a combination beautiful to behold, firm in strength, and necessary for use; so, in the commonwealth, there is an almost infinite dissimilarity of men, as parts of the whole. If they are to be all equal, and each is to follow his own will, the State will appear most deformed; but if, with a distinction of degrees of dignity, of pursuits and employments, all aptly conspire for the common good, they will present the image of a State both well-constituted and conformable to nature.

27. Now, from the disturbing errors which We have described the greatest dangers to States are to be feared. For, the fear of God

and reverence for divine laws being taken away, the authority of rulers despised, sedition permitted and approved, and the popular passions urged on to lawlessness, with no restraint save that of punishment, a change and overthrow of all things will necessarily follow. Yea, this change and overthrow is deliberately planned and put forward by many associations of communists and socialists; and to their undertakings, the sect of Freemasons is not hostile, but greatly favors their designs, and holds in common with them their chief opinions. And if these men do not at once and everywhere endeavor to carry out their extreme views, it is not to be attributed to their teaching and their will, but to the virtue of that divine religion which cannot be destroyed; and also because the sounder part of men, refusing to be enslaved to secret societies, vigorously resist their insane attempts.

28. Would that all men would judge of the tree by its fruit, and would acknowledge the seed and origin of the evils which press upon us, and of the dangers that are impending! We have to deal with a deceitful and crafty enemy, who, gratifying the ears of people and of princes, has ensnared them by smooth speeches and by adulation. Ingratiating themselves with rulers under a pretense of friendship, the Freemasons have endeavored to make them their allies and powerful helpers for the destruction of the Christian name; and that they might more strongly urge them on, they have, with determined calumny, accused the Church of invidiously contending with rulers in matters that affect their authority and sovereign power. Having, by these artifices, insured their own safety and audacity, they have begun to exercise great weight in the government of States: but nevertheless, they are prepared to shake the foundations of empires, to harass the rulers of the State, to accuse, and to cast them out, as often as they appear to govern otherwise than they themselves could have wished. In like manner, they have by flattery deluded the people. Proclaiming with a loud voice liberty and public prosperity, and saying that it was owing to the Church and to sovereigns that the multitude was not drawn out of their unjust servitude and poverty, they have imposed

upon the people, and, exciting them by a thirst for novelty, they have urged them to assail both the Church and the civil power. Nevertheless, the expectation of the benefits which was hoped for is greater than the reality; indeed, the common people, more oppressed than they were before, are deprived in their misery of that solace which, if things had been arranged in a Christian manner, they would have had with ease and in abundance. But, whoever strive against the order which Divine Providence has constituted pay usually the penalty of their pride, and meet with affliction and misery where they rashly hoped to find all things prosperous and in conformity with their desires.

29. The Church, if she directs men to render obedience chiefly and above all to God the sovereign Lord, is wrongly and falsely believed either to be envious of the civil power or to arrogate to herself something of the rights of sovereigns. On the contrary, she teaches that what is rightly due to the civil power must be rendered to it with a conviction and consciousness of duty. In teaching that from God Himself comes the right of ruling, she adds a great dignity to civil authority, and on small help towards obtaining the obedience and good will of the citizens. The friend of peace and sustainer of concord, she embraces all with maternal love, and, intent only upon giving help to mortal man, she teaches that to justice must be joined clemency, equity to authority, and moderation to lawgiving; that no one's right must be violated; that order and public tranquillity are to be maintained and that the poverty of those are in need is, as far as possible, to be relieved by public and private charity. "But for this reason," to use the words of St. Augustine, "men think, or would have it believed, that Christian teaching is not suited to the good of the State; for they wish the State to be founded not on solid virtue, but on the impunity of vice."[32] Knowing these things, both princes and people would act with political wisdom,[33] and according to the needs of general safety, if, instead

---

32 *Epistola 137, ad Volusianum*, c. v, n. 20 (PL 33, 525).
33 L. *prudentiae*; that is, prudence.

of joining with Freemasons to destroy the Church, they joined with the Church in repelling their attacks.

30. Whatever the future may be, in this grave and widespread evil it is Our duty, venerable brethren, to endeavor to find a remedy. And because We know that Our best and firmest hope of a remedy is in the power of that divine religion which the Freemasons hate in proportion to their fear of it, We think it to be of chief importance to call that most saving power to Our aid against the common enemy. Therefore, whatsoever the Roman Pontiffs Our predecessors have decreed for the purpose of opposing the undertakings and endeavors of the masonic sect, and whatsoever they have enacted to enter or withdraw men from societies of this kind, We ratify and confirm it all by our apostolic authority: and trusting greatly to the good will of Christians, We pray and beseech each one, for the sake of his eternal salvation, to be most conscientiously careful not in the least to depart from what the apostolic see has commanded in this matter.

31. We pray and beseech you, venerable brethren, to join your efforts with Ours, and earnestly to strive for the extirpation of this foul plague, which is creeping through the veins of the body politic. You have to defend the glory of God and the salvation of your neighbor; and with the object of your strife before you, neither courage nor strength will be wanting. It will be for your prudence to judge by what means you can best overcome the difficulties and obstacles you meet with. But, as it befits the authority of Our office that We Ourselves should point out some suitable way of proceeding, We wish it to be your rule, first of all, to tear away the mask from Freemasonry, and to let it be seen as it really is; and by sermons and pastoral letters to instruct the people as to the artifices used by societies of this kind in seducing men and enticing them into their ranks, and as to the depravity of their opinions and the wickedness of their acts. As Our predecessors have many times repeated, let no man think that he may for any reason whatsoever join the masonic sect, if he values his Catholic name and his eternal salvation as he ought to value them. Let no

one be deceived by a pretense of honesty. It may seem to some that Freemasons demand nothing that is openly contrary to religion and morality; but, as the whole principle and object of the sect lies in what is vicious and criminal, to join with these men or in any way to help them cannot be lawful.

32. Further, by assiduous teaching and exhortation, the multitude must be drawn to learn diligently the precepts of religion; for which purpose we earnestly advise that by opportune writings and sermons they be taught the elements of those sacred truths in which Christian philosophy is contained. The result of this will be that the minds of men will be made sound by instruction, and will be protected against many forms of error and inducements to wickedness, especially in the present unbounded freedom of writing and insatiable eagerness for learning.

33. Great, indeed, is the work; but in it, the clergy will share your labors, if, through your care, they are fitted for it by learning and a well-turned life. This good and great work requires to be helped also by the industry of those amongst the laity in whom a love of religion and of country is joined to learning and goodness of life. By uniting the efforts of both clergy and laity, strive, venerable brethren, to make men thoroughly know and love the Church; for, the greater their knowledge and love of the Church, the more will they be turned away from clandestine societies.

34. Wherefore, not without cause do We use this occasion to state again what We have stated elsewhere, namely, that the Third Order of St. Francis, whose discipline We a little while ago prudently mitigated,[34] should be studiously promoted and

---

34 The text here refers to the encyclical letter *Auspicato Concessum* (Sept. 17, 1882), in which Pope Leo XIII had recently glorified St. Francis of Assisi on the occasion of the seventh centenary of his birth. In this encyclical, the Pope had presented the Third Order of St. Francis as a Christian answer to the social problems of the times. The constitution *Misericors Dei filius* (June 23, 1883) expressly recalled that the neglect in which Christian virtues are held is the main cause of the evils that threaten societies. In confirming the rule of the Third Order and adapting it to the needs of modern times, Pope Leo XIII had intended to bring back the largest possible number of souls to the practice of these virtues.

sustained; for the whole object of this Order, as constituted by its founder, is to invite men to an imitation of Jesus Christ, to a love of the Church, and to the observance of all Christian virtues; and therefore it ought to be of great influence in suppressing the contagion of wicked societies. Let, therefore, this holy sodality be strengthened by a daily increase. Amongst the many benefits to be expected from it will be the great benefit of drawing the minds of men to liberty, fraternity, and equality of right; not such as the Freemasons absurdly imagine, but such as Jesus Christ obtained for the human race and St. Francis aspired to: the liberty, We mean, of sons of God, through which we may be free from slavery to Satan or to our passions, both of them most wicked masters; the fraternity whose origin is in God, the common Creator and Father of all; the equality which, founded on justice and charity, does not take away all distinctions among men, but, out of the varieties of life, of duties, and of pursuits, forms that union and that harmony which naturally tend to the benefit and dignity of society.

35. In the third place, there is a matter wisely instituted by our forefathers, but in course of time laid aside, which may now be used as a pattern and form of something similar. We mean the associations of guilds of workmen, for the protection, under the guidance of religion, both of their temporal interests and of their morality. If our ancestors, by long use and experience, felt the benefit of these guilds, our age perhaps will feel it the more by reason of the opportunity which they will give of crushing the power of the sects. Those who support themselves by the labor of their hands, besides being, by their very condition, most worthy above all others of charity and consolation, are also especially exposed to the allurements of men whose ways lie in fraud and deceit. Therefore, they ought to be helped with the greatest possible kindness, and to be invited to join associations that are good, lest they be drawn away to others that are evil. For this reason, We greatly wish, for the salvation of the people, that, under the auspices and patronage of the bishops, and at convenient times, these guilds may be generally restored. To Our great delight,

sodalities of this kind and also associations of masters have in many places already been established, having, each class of them, for their object to help the honest workman, to protect and guard his children and family, and to promote in them piety, Christian knowledge, and a moral life. And in this matter, We cannot omit mentioning that exemplary society, named after its founder, St. Vincent, which has deserved so well of the lower classes.[35] Its acts and its aims are well known. Its whole object is to give relief to the poor and miserable. This it does with singular prudence and modesty; and the less it wishes to be seen, the better is it fitted for the exercise of Christian charity, and for the relief of suffering.

36. In the fourth place, in order more easily to attain what We wish, to your fidelity and watchfulness We commend in a special manner the young, as being the hope of human society. Devote the greatest part of your care to their instruction; and do not think that any precaution can be great enough in keeping them from masters and schools whence the pestilent breath of the sects is to be feared. Under your guidance, let parents, religious instructors, and priests having the cure of souls use every opportunity, in their Christian teaching, of warning their children and pupils of the infamous nature of these societies, so that they may learn in good time to beware of the various and fraudulent artifices by which their promoters are accustomed to ensnare people. And those who instruct the young in religious knowledge will act wisely if they induce all of them to resolve and to undertake never to bind themselves to any society without the knowledge of their parents, or the advice of their parish priest or director.

37. We well know, however, that our united labors will by no means suffice to pluck up these pernicious seeds from the Lord's field, unless the Heavenly Master of the vineyard shall mercifully help us in our endeavors. We must, therefore, with great and anxious care, implore of Him the help which the greatness of the danger and of the need requires. The sect of the Freemasons shows itself insolent and proud of its success, and seems

---

35 L. *de populo inferioris ordinis.* — P. of the people of the lower order.

as if it would put no bounds to its pertinacity. Its followers, joined together by a wicked compact and by secret counsels, give help one to another, and excite one another to an audacity for evil things. So vehement an attack demands an equal defense—namely, that all good men should form the widest possible association of action and of prayer. We beseech them, therefore, with united hearts, to stand together and unmoved against the advancing force of the sects; and in mourning and supplication to stretch out their hands to God, praying that the Christian name may flourish and prosper, that the Church may enjoy its needed liberty, that those who have gone astray may return to a right mind, that error at length may give place to truth, and vice to virtue. Let us take our helper and intercessor the Virgin Mary, Mother of God, so that she, who from the moment of her conception overcame Satan may show her power over these evil sects, in which is revived the contumacious spirit of the demon, together with his unsubdued perfidy and deceit. Let us beseech Michael, the prince of the heavenly angels, who drove out the infernal foe; and Joseph, the spouse of the most holy Virgin, and heavenly patron of the Catholic Church; and the great Apostles, Peter and Paul, the fathers and victorious champions of the Christian faith. By their patronage, and by perseverance in united prayer, we hope that God will mercifully and opportunely succor the human race, which is encompassed by so many dangers.

38. As a pledge of heavenly gifts and of Our benevolence, We lovingly grant in the Lord, to you, venerable brethren, and to the clergy and all the people committed to your watchful care, Our apostolic benediction.

V

On Civil Government

INTRODUCTION

The encyclical *Diuturnum*, dated June 29, 1881, deals with the origin and nature of civil government. This document is dominated by the memory of the recent death of the Russian emperor, Alexander II, murdered by nihilists. This tragedy was for the Pope an occasion to remind temporal rulers of this truth, that no political authority will ever be safe so long as the divine nature and origin of political power will be either denied or forgotten. This is the document in which the Catholic doctrine that elections designate the future political ruler, but do not confer or delegate authority, is formulated in its fullest force. Particular attention should be devoted to the passage where political authority is said to come to rulers from on high because no man has of himself the power of bending the free will of any other man (art. 11). The full loyalty of Christian citizens to the established governments of their countries is no less forcefully stressed, and we should remember that such has been the Christian doctrine ever since the times of Jesus Christ Himself, of St. Paul and of the early apologists, all of whom lived under the authority of non-Christian emperors and often of persecutors of the Church. This justifies the assertion, familiar to Pope Leo XIII, that, did they know their own interests, all rulers would look above themselves for a confirmation of their authority.

SUMMARY

(1–2) The personal safety of political rulers is now being threatened. (3) The Christian doctrine is the only safeguard for political power. (4–5) This doctrine is opposed by the philosophers who teach that authority comes to rulers from the people. (6–7) In truth, the people designates the ruler, it does not confer authority. (8–10) Only God can impart political authority. (11) This, which is taught by Scripture, is also a natural evidence; one cannot understand otherwise how such a being as man can be both free and destined to live a social life. (12) The free consent of men is not the origin of political power. (13–14) Only the obedience of their subjects can ensure the stability of the governments. (15) But political authority must conform with the law of nature and the divine law. (16) Rulers are exposed to the most severe punishments if they do not govern their subjects as God governs the world. (17) This is as necessary for the security of the rulers as it is for the dignity of the citizens. (18–20) That Christian institutions can achieve this twofold end is seen from the loyalty of the early Christians toward their pagan rulers. (21) Hence, in later times, the consecration of the Christian princes by the Church. (22) Hence, also, the constant effort of the Church to mediate for peace between rulers and peoples. (23) The will of the people is a weak foundation for authority. (24) Fear is a still weaker one. (25) The Roman Pontiffs have always favored civil peace and order. (26) But, since the Church also urges the princes to be just, she should be trusted by both peoples and rulers. (27) Therefore, let archbishops and bishops warn the people against joining forbidden sects and invite them to obey their rulers for the sake of God. (28) Invitation to prayer, and apostolic benediction.

V

Diuturnum
ON THE ORIGIN OF CIVIL POWER
June 29, 1881

1. The long-continued and most bitter war waged against the divine authority of the Church has reached the culmination to which it was tending, the common danger, namely, of human society, and especially of the civil power on which the public safety chiefly reposes. In our own times most particularly this result is apparent. For popular passions now reject, with more boldness than formerly, every restraint of authority. So great is the license on all sides, so frequent are seditions and tumults, that not only is obedience often refused to those who rule states, but a sufficiently safe guarantee of security does not seem to have been left to them.

2. For a long time, indeed, pains have been taken to render rulers the object of contempt and hatred to the multitude. The flames of envy thus excited have at last burst forth, and attempts have been several times made, at very short intervals, on the life of sovereign princes, either by secret plots or by open attacks. The whole of Europe was lately filled with horror at the horrible murder of a most powerful emperor.[1] Whilst the minds of men are still filled with astonishment at the magnitude of the crime, abandoned men do not fear publicly to utter threats and intimidations against other European princes.

3. These perils to commonwealth, which are before Our eyes, fill Us with grave anxiety, when We behold the security of rulers and the tranquillity of empires, together with the safety of nations, put in peril almost from hour to hour. Nevertheless,

---

1 An allusion to Alexander II (1818–81), Emperor of Russia, a liberally minded sovereign and a great social reformer, who was murdered March 13, 1881 by a group of nihilists in St. Petersburg.

the divine power of the Christian religion has given birth to excellent principles of stability and order for the State, while at the same time it has penetrated into the customs and institutions of States. And of this power, not the least nor last fruit is a just and wise proportion of mutual rights and duties in both princes and peoples. For in the precepts and example of Christ our Lord there is a wonderful force for restraining in their duty as much those who obey as those who rule; and for keeping between them that agreement which is most according to nature, and that concord of wills, so to speak, from which arises a course of administration tranquil and free from all disturbance. Wherefore, being, by the favor of God, entrusted with the government of the Catholic Church, and made guardian and interpreter of the doctrines of Christ, We judge that it belongs to Our jurisdiction, venerable brethren, publicly to set forth what Catholic truth demands of everyone in this sphere of duty; thus making clear also by what way and by what means measures may be taken for the public safety in so critical a state of affairs.

4. Although man, when excited by a certain arrogance and contumacy, has often striven to cast aside the reins of authority, he has never yet been able to arrive at the state of obeying no one. In every association and community of men, necessity itself compels that some should hold preeminence, lest society, deprived of a prince or head by which it is ruled should come to dissolution and be prevented from attaining the end for which it was created and instituted. But, if it was not possible that political power should be removed from the midst of states, it is certain that men have used every art to take away its influence and to lessen its majesty, as was especially the case in the sixteenth century, when a fatal novelty of opinions infatuated many. Since that epoch, not only has the multitude striven after a liberty greater than is just, but it has seen fit to fashion the origin and construction of the civil society of men in accordance with its own will.

5. Indeed, very many men of more recent times, walking in the footsteps of those who in a former age assumed to themselves

the name of philosophers,² say that all power comes from the people; so that those who exercise it in the State do so not as their own, but as delegated to them by the people, and that, by this rule, it can be revoked by the will of the very people by whom it was delegated. But from these, Catholics dissent, who affirm that the right to rule is from God, as from a natural and necessary principle.

6. It is of importance, however, to remark in this place that those who may be placed over the State may in certain cases be chosen by the will and decision of the multitude, without opposition to or impugning of the Catholic doctrine. And by this choice, in truth, the ruler is designated, but the rights of ruling are not thereby conferred. Nor is the authority delegated to him, but the person by whom it is to be exercised is determined upon.

7. There is no question here respecting forms of government, for there is no reason why the Church should not approve of the chief power being held by one man or by more, provided only it be just, and that it tend to the common advantage. Wherefore, so long as justice be respected, the people are not hindered from choosing for themselves that form of government which suits best either their own disposition, or the institutions and customs of their ancestors.³

8. But, as regards political power, the Church rightly teaches that it comes from God, for it finds this clearly testified in the sacred Scriptures and in the monuments of antiquity; besides, no other doctrine can be conceived which is more agreeable to reason, or more in accord with the safety of both princes and peoples.

9. In truth, that the source of human power is in God the books of the Old Testament in very many places clearly establish. "By me kings reign ... by me princes rule, and the mighty decree

---

2   The name of Philosophers is usually given to a group of eighteenth-century French writers, especially Voltaire, d'Alembert, and Diderot. Their main views are contained in the *Encyclopédie* (1751–72).
3   See Introduction.

justice."[4] And in another place: "Give ear you that rule the people... for power is given you of the Lord and strength by the Most High."[5] The same thing is contained in the Book of Ecclesiasticus: "Over every nation he hath set a ruler."[6] These things, however, which they had learned of God, men were little by little untaught through heathen superstition, which even as it has corrupted the true aspect and often the very concept of things, so also it has corrupted the natural form and beauty of the chief power. Afterwards, when the Christian Gospel shed its light, vanity yielded to truth, and that noble and divine principle whence all authority flows began to shine forth. To the Roman governor, ostentatiously pretending that he had the power of releasing and of condemning, our Lord Jesus Christ answered: "Thou shouldst not have any power against me unless it were given thee from above."[7] And St. Augustine, in explaining this passage, says: "Let us learn what He said, which also He taught by His Apostle, that there is no power but from God."[8] The faithful voice of the Apostles, as an echo, repeats the doctrine and precepts of Jesus Christ. The teaching of Paul to the Romans, when subject to the authority of heathen princes, is lofty and full of gravity: "There is not power but from God," from which, as from its cause, he draws this conclusion: "The prince is the minister of God."[9]

10. The Fathers of the Church have taken great care to proclaim and propagate this very doctrine in which they had been instructed. "We do not attribute," says St. Augustine, "the power of giving government and empires to any but the true God."[10] On the same passage, St. John Chrysostom says: "That there are kingdoms, and that some rule, while others are subject, and that none of these things is brought about by accident or rashly... is,

---

4 Prov. 8:15–16.
5 Wisd. 6:3–4.
6 Ecclus. 7:14.
7 John 19:11.
8 Tract. 116 in Joan., n. 5 (PL 35, 1942).
9 P. and H. from which he draws this seemingly necessary conclusion. Rom. 13:1–4.
10 *De civ., Dei*, 5, 21 (PL 41, 167).

I say, a work of divine wisdom."[11] The same truth is testified by St. Gregory the Great, saying: "We confess that power is given from above to emperors and kings."[12] Verily the holy doctors have undertaken to illustrate also the same precepts by the natural light of reason in such a way that they must appear to be altogether right and true, even to those who follow reason for their sole guide.

11. And, indeed, nature, or rather God who is the Author of nature, wills that man should live in a civil society; and this is clearly shown both by the faculty of language, the greatest medium of intercourse,[13] and by numerous innate desires of the mind, and the many necessary things, and things of great importance, which men isolated cannot procure, but which they can procure when joined and associated with others. But now, a society can neither exist nor be conceived in which there is no one to govern the wills of individuals, in such a way as to make, as it were, one will out of many, and to impel them rightly and orderly to the common good; therefore, God has willed that in a civil society there should be some to rule the multitude. And this also is a powerful argument, that those by whose authority the State is administered must be able so to compel the citizens to obedience that it is clearly a sin in the latter not to obey. But no man has in himself or of himself the power of constraining the free will of others by fetters of authority of this kind. This power resides solely in God, the Creator and Legislator of all things; and it is necessary that those who exercise it should do it as having received it from God. "There is one lawgiver and judge, who is able to destroy and deliver."[14] And this is clearly seen in every kind of power. That that which resides in priests comes from God is so acknowledged that among all nations they are recognized as, and called, the ministers of God. In like

---

11   *In Epist. ad Rom.*, Homil. 23, n. 1 (PG 60, 615).
12   *In Epist. lib. II*, epist. 61.
13   L. *maxima societatis conciliatrix loquendi facultas*; that is, language, the greatest unifying bond of society.
14   James 4:12.

manner, the authority of fathers of families preserves a certain impressed image and form of the authority which is in God, "of whom all paternity in heaven and earth is named."[15] But in this way, different kinds of authority have between them wonderful resemblances, since, whatever there is of government and authority, its origin is derived from one and the same Creator and Lord of the world, who is God.

12. Those who believe civil society to have risen from the free consent of men, looking for the origin of its authority from the same source, say that each individual has given up something of his right,[16] and that voluntarily every person has put himself into the power of the one man in whose person the whole of those rights has been centered. But, it is a great error not to see, what is manifest, that men, as they are not a nomad race, have been created, without their own free will, for a natural community of life. It is plain, moreover, that the pact,[17] which they allege is openly a falsehood and a fiction, and that it has no authority to confer on political power such great force, dignity, and firmness as the safety of the State and the common good of the citizens require. Then only will the government have all those ornaments and guarantees, when it is understood to emanate from God as its august and most sacred source.

13. And, it is impossible that any should be found not only more true but even more advantageous than this opinion. For the authority of the rulers of a State,[18] if it be a certain communication of divine power, will by that very reason immediately acquire a dignity greater than human — not, indeed, that impious and most absurd dignity sometimes desired by heathen emperors when affecting divine honors, but a true and solid one received by a certain divine gift and benefaction. Whence it will

---

15   Eph. 3:15.
16   An allusion to the doctrine of "Social contract," developed by Jean-Jacques Rousseau (1712–78). According to this doctrine, all political power comes to rulers from the people.
17   L. *pactum.* — P. and H. agreement.
18   L. *civitatis*; that is, a body politic.

Diuturnum

behoove citizens to submit themselves and to be obedient to rulers, as to God, not so much through fear of punishment as through respect for their majesty; nor for the sake of pleasing, but through conscience, as doing their duty. And by this means authority will remain far more firmly seated in its place. For the citizens, perceiving the force of this duty[19] would necessarily avoid dishonesty and contumacy, because they must be persuaded that they who resist State authority resist the divine will; that they who refuse honor to rulers refuse it to God Himself.

14. This doctrine the Apostle Paul particularly inculcated on the Romans; to whom he wrote with so great authority and weight on the reverence to be entertained toward the higher powers, that it seems nothing could be prescribed more weightily: "Let every soul be subject to higher powers, for there is no power but from God, and those that are, are ordained of God. Therefore, he that resisteth the power resisteth the ordinance of God, and they that resist purchase to themselves damnation...wherefore be subject of necessity, not only for wrath, but also for conscience' sake."[20] And in agreement with this is the celebrated declaration of Peter, the Prince of the Apostles, on the same subject: "Be ye subject, therefore, to every human creature for God's sake; whether it be to the king as excelling, or to governors, as sent by him for the punishment of evildoers, and for the praise of the good, for so is the will of God."[21]

15. The one only reason which men have for not obeying is when anything is demanded of them which is openly repugnant to the natural or the divine law, for it is equally unlawful to command to do anything in which the law of nature or the will of God is violated. If, therefore, it should happen to anyone to be compelled to prefer one or the other, viz., to disregard either the commands of God or those of rulers, he must obey Jesus Christ, who commands us to "give to Caesar the things

---

19 L. *officii*.
20 Rom. 13:1–2, 5.
21 1 Peter 2:13, 15.

that are Caesar's, and to God the things that are God's,"[22] and must reply courageously after the example of the Apostles: "We ought to obey God rather than men."[23] And, yet there is no reason why those who so behave themselves should be accused of refusing obedience; for, if the will of rulers is opposed to the will and the laws of God, they themselves exceed the bounds of their own power and pervert justice; nor can their authority then be valid, which, when there is no justice, is null.

16. But in order that justice may be retained in government it is of the highest importance that those who rule States[24] should understand that political power was not created for the advantage of any private individual; and that the administration of the State[25] must be carried on to the profit of those who have been committed to their care, not to the profit of those to whom it has been committed. Let princes take example from the Most High God, by whom authority is given to them; and, placing before themselves His model in governing the State, let them rule over the people with equity and faithfulness, and let them add to that severity, which is necessary, a paternal charity. On this account, they are warned in the oracles of the sacred Scriptures, that they will have themselves some day to render an account to the King of kings and Lord of lords; if they shall fail in their duty, that it will not be possible for them in any way to escape the severity of God: "The Most High will examine your work and search out your thoughts: because being ministers of his kingdom you have not judged rightly... Horribly and speedily will he appear to you, for a most severe judgment shall be for them that bear rule... For God will not accept any man's person, neither will he stand in awe of any man's greatness; for he made the little and the great, and he hath equally care of all. But a greater punishment is ready for the more mighty."[26]

---

22   Matt. 22:21.
23   Acts 5:29.
24   L. *civitates*.
25   L. *reipublicae*; that is, the commonwealth.
26   Wisd. 6:4–6, 8–9.

Diuturnum

17. And if these precepts protect the State,[27] all cause or desire for seditions is removed; the honor and security of rulers, the quiet and wellbeing of societies[28] will be secure. The dignity also of the citizen is best provided for; for to them, it has been permitted to retain even in obedience that greatness which conduces to the excellence of man. For they understand that, in the judgment of God, there is neither slave nor free man; that there is one Lord of all, rich "to all that call upon Him,"[29] but that they on this account submit to and obey their rulers, because these in a certain sort bring before them the image of God, "whom to serve is to reign."

18. But the Church has always so acted that the Christian form of civil government may not dwell in the minds of men, but that it may be exhibited also in the life and habits of nations. As long as there were at the helm of the States pagan emperors, who were prevented by superstition from rising to that form of imperial government which We have sketched, she studied how to instill into the minds of subjects, immediately on their embracing the Christian institutions, the teaching that they must be desirous of bringing their lives into conformity with them. Therefore, the pastors of souls, after the example of the Apostle Paul, were accustomed to teach the people with the utmost care and diligence "to be subject to princes and powers, to obey at a word,"[30] and to pray God for all men and particularly "for kings and all that are in a high station: for this is good and acceptable in the sight of God our Savior."[31] And the Christians of old left the most striking proofs of this; for, when they were harassed in a very unjust and cruel way by pagan emperors, they nevertheless at no time omitted to conduct themselves obediently and submissively, so that, in fact, they seemed to vie with each other: those in cruelty, and these in obedience.

---

27   L. *rempublicam*; see footnote 269.
28   L. *civitatum*.—P. and H. of the States.
29   Rom. 10:12.
30   Tit. 3:1.
31   1 Tim. 2:1–3.

19. This great modesty, this fixed determination to obey, was so well known that it could not be obscured by the calumny and malice of enemies. On this account, those who were going to plead in public before the emperors for any persons bearing the Christian name proved by this argument especially that it was unjust to enact laws against the Christians because they were in the sight of all men exemplary in their bearing according to the laws. Athenagoras thus confidently addresses Marcus Aurelius Antoninus and Lucius Aurelius Commodus, his son: "You allow us, who commit no evil, yea, who demean ourselves the most piously and justly of all toward God and likewise toward your government, to be driven about, plundered and exiled."[32] In like manner, Tertullian openly praises the Christians because they were the best and surest friends of all to the Empire: "The Christian is the enemy of no one, much less of the emperor, whom he knows to be appointed by God, and whom he must, therefore, of necessity love, reverence and honor, and wish to be preserved together with the whole Roman Empire."[33] Nor did he hesitate to affirm that, within the limits of the Empire, the number of enemies was wont to diminish just in proportion as the number of Christians increased.[34] There is also a remarkable testimony to the same point in the Epistle to Diognetus, which confirms the statement that the Christians at that period were not only in the habit of obeying the laws, but in every office, they of their own accord did more, and more perfectly, than they were required to do by the laws. "Christians observe these things which have obtained the sanction of the law, and in the character of their lives they even go beyond the law."[35]

20. The case, indeed, was different when they were ordered by the edicts of emperors and the threats of praetors to abandon the Christian faith or in any way fail in their duty. At these times, undoubtedly, they preferred to displease men rather than God.

---

32 *Legatio pro christianis*, 1 (PG 6, 891B–894A).
33 *Apolog.*, 35.
34 *Apolog.*, 37 (PL 1, 526A).
35 *Ad Diogn.*, 10 (*A Diognete*, ed. H. I. Marrou, Paris, 1951, pp. 64–65).

Yet, even under these circumstances, they were so far from doing anything seditious or despising the imperial majesty that they took it on themselves only to profess themselves Christians, and declare that they would not in any way alter their faith. But they had no thought of resistance, calmly and joyfully they went to the torture of the rack, in so much that the magnitude of the torments gave place to their magnitude of mind. During the same period, the force of Christian principles was observed in like manner in the army. For it was a mark of a Christian soldier to combine the greatest fortitude with the greatest attention to military discipline, and to add to nobility of mind immovable fidelity towards his prince. But, if anything dishonorable was required of him, as, for instance, to break the laws of God, or to turn his sword against innocent disciples of Christ, then, indeed, he refused to execute the orders, yet in such wise that he would rather retire from the army and die for his religion than oppose the public authority by means of sedition and tumult.

21. But afterward, when Christian rulers were at the head of States, the Church insisted much more on testifying and preaching how much sanctity was inherent in the authority of rulers. Hence, when people thought of princedom, the image of a certain sacred majesty would present itself to their minds, by which they would be impelled to greater reverence and love of rulers. And on this account, she wisely provides that kings should commence their reign with the celebration of solemn rites; which, in the Old Testament, was appointed by divine authority.[36]

22. But from the time when the civil society of men, raised from the ruins of the Roman Empire, gave hope of its future Christian greatness, the Roman Pontiffs, by the institution of the Holy Empire, consecrated the political power in a wonderful manner. Greatly, indeed, was the authority of rulers ennobled; and it is not to be doubted that what was then instituted would always have been a very great gain, both to ecclesiastical and civil society, if princes and peoples had ever looked to the same object

---

36   1 Kings 9:16; 10:1; 16:13.

as the Church. And, indeed, tranquillity and a sufficient prosperity lasted so long as there was a friendly agreement between these two powers. If the people were turbulent, the Church was at once the mediator for peace. Recalling all to their duty, she subdued the more lawless passions partly by kindness and partly by authority. So, if, in ruling, princes erred in their government, she went to them and, putting before them the rights, needs, and lawful wants of their people, urged them to equity, mercy, and kindness. Whence it was often brought about that the dangers of civil wars and popular tumults were stayed.

23. On the other hand, the doctrines on political power[37] invented by late writers have already produced great ills amongst men, and it is to be feared that they will cause the very greatest disasters to posterity. For an unwillingness to attribute the right of ruling to God, as its Author, is not less than a willingness to blot out the greatest splendor of political power and to destroy its force. And they who say that this power depends on the will of the people err in opinion first of all; then they place authority on too weak and unstable a foundation. For the popular passions, incited and goaded on by these opinions, will break out more insolently; and, with great harm to the common weal, descend headlong by an easy and smooth road to revolts and to open sedition. In truth, sudden uprisings and the boldest rebellions immediately followed in Germany the so-called Reformation,[38] the authors and leaders of which, by their new doctrines, attacked at the very foundation religious and civil authority; and this with so fearful an outburst of civil war and with such slaughter that there was scarcely any place free from tumult and bloodshed. From this heresy there arose in the last century a false philosophy—a new right[39] as it is called, and

---

37 L. *de potestate politica doctrinae.*—P. and H. the theories of the body politic.
38 Especially the Peasant Revolt and its repression by the German princes. Luther himself then had to stress the duty of the citizens to obey the civil power ("On the Civil Power," 1523).
39 L. *et jus quod appellant novum*; that is, the so called new right.

a popular authority, together with an unbridled license which many regard as the only true liberty. Hence, we have reached the limit of horrors, to wit, communism, socialism, nihilism, hideous deformities of the civil society of men and almost its ruin. And yet, too many attempt to enlarge the scope of these evils, and under the pretext of helping the multitude, already have fanned no small flames of misery. The things we thus mention are neither unknown nor very remote from us.

24. This, indeed, is all the graver because rulers, in the midst of such threatening dangers, have no remedies sufficient to restore discipline and tranquillity. They supply themselves with the power of laws, and think to coerce, by the severity of their punishment, those who disturb their governments. They are right to a certain extent, but yet should seriously consider that no power of punishment can be so great that it alone can preserve the State.[40] For fear, as St. Thomas admirably teaches, "is a weak foundation; for those who are subdued by fear would, should an occasion arise in which they might hope for immunity, rise more eagerly against their rulers, in proportion to the previous extent of their restraint through fear." And besides, "from too great fear many fall into despair; and despair drives men to attempt boldly to gain what they desire."[41] That these things are so we see from experience. It is, therefore, necessary to seek a higher and more reliable reason for obedience, and to say explicitly that legal severity cannot be efficacious unless men are led on by duty, and moved by the salutary fear of God. But, this is what religion can best ask of them, religion which by its power enters into the souls and bends the very wills of men causing them not only to render obedience to their rulers, but also to show their affection and good will, which is in every society of men the best guardian of safety.

25. For this reason the Roman Pontiffs are to be regarded as having greatly served the public good, for they have ever endeavored

---

40 L. *respublicas*; see footnote 25.
41 *On the Governance of Rulers*, 1, 10.

to break the turbulent and restless spirit of innovators, and have often warned men of the danger they are to civil society. In this respect, we may worthily recall to mind the declaration of Clement VII to Ferdinand, King of Bohemia and Hungary: "In the cause of faith your own dignity and advantage and that of other rulers are included, since the faith cannot be shaken without your authority being brought down; which has been most clearly shown in several instances." In the same way, the supreme forethought and courage of Our predecessors have been shown, especially of Clement XI, Benedict XIV, and Leo XII,[42] who, when in their day the evil of vicious doctrine was more widely spreading and the boldness of the sects was becoming greater, endeavored by their authority to close the door against them. And We Ourselves have several times declared what great dangers are impending, and have pointed out the best ways of warding them off. To princes and other rulers of the State, we have offered the protection of religion, and we have exhorted the people to make abundant use of the great benefits which the Church supplies. Our present object is to make rulers understand that this protection, which is stronger than any, is again offered to them; and We earnestly exhort them in our Lord to defend religion, and to consult the interest of their Lord to defend religion, and to consult the interest of their States by giving that liberty to the Church which cannot be taken away without injury and ruin to the commonwealth.

26. The Church of Christ, indeed, cannot be an object of suspicion to rulers, nor of hatred to the people; for it urges rulers to follow justice, and in nothing to decline from their duty; while at the same time it strengthens and in many ways supports their authority. All things that are of a civil nature the Church acknowledges and declares to be under the power and authority of the ruler; and in things whereof for different reasons the decision belongs both to the sacred and to the civil power, the Church wishes that there should be harmony

---

42 Clement XI (1700–21); Benedict XIV (1740–58); Leo XII (1823–29).

between the two so that injurious contests may be avoided. As to what regards the people, the Church has been established for the salvation of all men and has ever loved them as a mother. For it is the Church, which by the exercise of her charity, has given gentleness to the minds of men, kindness to their manners, and justice to their laws. Never opposed to honest liberty, the Church has always detested a tyrant's rule. This custom which the Church has ever had of deserving well of mankind is notably expressed by St. Augustine when he says that "the Church teaches kings to study the welfare of their people, and people to submit to their kings, showing what is due to all: and that to all is due charity and to no one injustice."[43]

27. For these reasons, venerable brethren, your work will be most useful and salutary if you employ with us every industry and effort which God has given you in order to avert the dangers and evils of human society. Strive with all possible care to make men understand and show forth in their lives what the Catholic Church teaches on government and the duty of obedience. Let the people be frequently urged by your authority and teaching to fly from the forbidden sects, to abhor all conspiracy, to have nothing to do with sedition, and let them understand that they who for God's sake obey their rulers render a reasonable service and a generous obedience. And as it is God "who gives safety to kings,"[44] and grants to the people "to rest in the beauty of peace and in the tabernacles of confidence and in wealthy repose,"[45] it is to Him that we must pray, beseeching Him to incline all minds to uprightness and truth, to calm angry passions, to restore the long-wished-for tranquillity to the world.

28. That we may pray with greater hope, let us take as our intercessors and protectors of our welfare the Virgin Mary, the great Mother of God, the Help of Christians, and protector

---

43 *De mor. eccl.*, 1, 30, 53 (PL 32, 1236).
44 Ps. 152:11.
45 Isa. 37:18.

of the human race; St. Joseph, her chaste spouse, in whose patronage the whole Church greatly trusts; and the Princes of the Apostles, Peter and Paul, the guardians and protectors of the Christian name.

VI

The Christian Constitution of States

INTRODUCTION

The encyclical *Immortale Dei*, dated November 1, 1885, can be considered the most perfect exposition and clarification of the problem of Church and State contained in the letters of Pope Leo XIII. It presupposes a conception of the State conformable to the principles of Christian philosophy, that is, to the principles of St. Thomas Aquinas. The foundation for such a doctrine is provided by the teachings of the Gospel. The State holds authority from God. From this fact, Leo XIII deduces two series of consequences. First, this divine origin of the temporal power confers upon it a sacred character, which is the most powerful guarantee such a power can be given in the sight of men. This is why Leo XIII ceaselessly repeats that all States should consider the Church the safest of their allies. Secondly, for the very same reason, the State must recognize its indebtedness to the source of its power by making public profession of religion (art. 6), or, more precisely still, of the true religion (art. 7).

The traditional doctrine of the distinction of "the two powers," that of the Church and that of the State, is restated with perfect clarity, as well as the reasons why, when their respective objects are correctly understood, no conflict can arise between these two distinct jurisdictions (art. 13).

A particularly important feature of this encyclical is also one of those which, especially if misinterpreted, is likely to create difficulties in the minds of many modern readers. Leo XIII traces the cause of modern errors concerning the true nature of the State to the false notion that all men are naturally equal (art. 24),

The Christian Constitution of States

whence it follows that political authority is not a fact of nature, but, rather, the effect of some convention. This doctrine does not need to be toned down, but it must be correctly understood. Pope Leo XIII is simply calling to our attention this elementary evidence that, in point of fact, men are unequal. Identical in nature, men can imagine themselves as theoretically equal, but they cannot deny the fact that even in the most democratic of States, the only use they can make of this abstract equality is to express an opinion as to who should be their rulers. There is no society without a political power, a police, and some judges; consequently, it is simply not true that men are equal; it would be much more true to say that the notion of society implies that of hierarchy and therefore of inequality.

The consequences of the error denounced by Pope Leo XIII are particularly serious with respect to the rights of the true religion. If all power comes to the sovereigns from the will of the citizens, it follows that no power comes to them from God and, consequently, that there should be complete separation of Church and State. The reasons why this doctrine should be rejected are developed at great length (arts. 29–35). In short, the distinction of the two powers does not preclude their collaboration; their free collaboration does not prevent them from forming a hierarchy; the fact that Christians belong in the spiritual society of the Church does not entail the consequences that they should not share in the conduct of political affairs (arts. 44–45). The distinction of the two powers is intended to ensure their union and their friendly collaboration, not their separation.

The study of this encyclical should be complemented by that of other papal documents, such as the encyclical of Pope Pius XII, *Summi Pontificatus* (*On the Function of the State in the Modern World*, October 20, 1939), official English translation with discussion club outline published by the National Catholic Welfare Conference, Washington; the allocution of Pope Pius XII to the Sacred College on June 1, 1946, *Ancora Una Volta* (*Catholics and World Reconstruction*), translated by Canon G. D. Smith and published by the Catholic Truth Society of London;

Immortale Dei

the Christmas message of Pope Pius XII, December 24, 1944, translated by John B. Harney, C. S. P., with a discussion club outline by Gerald C. Treacy, S. J., and published as *Pius XII and Democracy* by the Paulist Press; and his letter on *Woman's Duties in Social and Political Life*, with a discussion club outline by Fr. Treacy, S. J., also published by the Paulist Press. On the problem of the relations of Church and State, see the encyclical of Pope Pius XI, *Mit brennender Sorge* (*The Church in Germany*, March 14, 1937), published by the National Catholic Welfare Conference.

SUMMARY

(1) The Church is the source of many and great temporal benefits. (2) The contrary reproach has already been refuted by St. Augustine, but its recent revival under a new form invites a restatement of the Christian doctrine of the State. (3) According to the principles of Christian philosophy, there is no power but from God. (4) Any mode of government is legitimate provided only that it strives to govern the State in the same way that God governs the world. (5) Rulers should therefore behave as fathers rather than as masters; they must govern with justice and for the common good of all. (6) Since it holds its power from God, the State is bound to make public profession of the true religion, to favor it, and to help it in leading to the enjoyment of their supreme good the citizens over whom they rule. (7) It is easy to ascertain which is the true religion. (8–9) The Church has been established for the eternal salvation of souls under the leadership of an infallible teacher of truth. (10) The Church is a true society, but it is a supernatural and spiritual one. (11) The Church, not the State, is in charge of legislating for all that concerns religion. (12) The Church has never ceased to claim for herself and to exercise this authority. (13) God, therefore, has established two powers: the ecclesiastical power set over divine things, and the civil power set over human things. (14) Distinction of the two powers according to the distinction of their respective objects. (15–16) Special agreements between

Church and State can be made on special occasions. (17) The State always benefits by such an understanding with the Church. (18) For, indeed, the ruling powers are then invested with a more than human sacredness. (19) And all the social and moral virtues contribute to the common good of each and all. (20) Testimony of St. Augustine on this point. (21) Glorious history of the Christian States. (22–23) This history was interrupted by the harmful spirit of innovation, which prevailed in all domains ever since the sixteenth century. (24) The new conception of law laid down the principle that all men are equal in right and in no way submitted to any authority. (25) Even the authority of God is passed over in silence. (26) Religion is then considered a matter of private judgment. (27) The rights of the Church are no longer respected. (28–30) Hence, the doctrine which favors the separation of the matters affecting the Church from those of the State; an absurd doctrine indeed since both powers come from God. (31) The two doctrines of the sovereignty of the people and of indifference in matters of religion ultimately lead to atheism. (32) The same remarks apply to the unrestricted liberty of thinking and of publishing; the Church of Christ is the true and sole teacher of virtue and guardian of morals. (33) Freedom is necessary to the Church for the fulfillment of her mission. (34) The aforementioned sophisms have been repeatedly denounced by the Church. (35) Doctrine of the Church in these matters. (36) No particular form of government is condemned so long as it does not contradict Catholic doctrine, but the Church refuses to place the various forms of religion on the same footing. (37) The Church does not oppose true liberty, which is the power not to be enslaved to error and to passion. (38) This true liberty has always been approved and protected by the Church. (39) The Church favors scientific research and scientific discoveries for the simple reason that all truth proceeds from God. (40) Catholics have a duty, not only to hold this doctrine, but openly to profess it. (42) A State indifferent in matters of religion is less bad than a State actively hostile to religion, yet, as has been said, its principles cannot be approved of. (43) Catholics must conform their

Immortale Dei

private lives to the teaching of the Gospel; they also must take part in public affairs in order to Christianize the legislation of the country; special provision should be made for the religious instruction of youth. (44) Generally speaking, Catholics should actively interest themselves in the conduct of public affairs. (45) To do so does not make them responsible for what is wrong in the actual methods of government; it gives them an opportunity to improve the situation. (46) To endeavor to bring back all civil society to the form of Christianity is the goal to be pursued by Catholics. (47) Naturalism and rationalism must be absolutely rejected. (48) But differences of opinion are free concerning purely political or administrative problems. (49) Publicists and journalists must not let dissensions divide men whose common aim and purpose it is to insure the maintenance of religion and the State. (50) Prayer and apostolic benediction.

VI

Immortale Dei
ON THE CHRISTIAN CONSTITUTION OF STATES
November 1, 1885

1. The Catholic Church, that imperishable handiwork of our all-merciful God, has for her immediate and natural purpose the saving of souls and securing our happiness in heaven. Yet, in regard to things temporal, she is the source of benefits as manifold and great as if the chief end of her existence were to ensure the prospering of our earthly life. And, indeed, wherever the Church has set her foot she has straightway changed the face of things, and has attempered the moral tone of the people[1] with a new civilization and with virtues before unknown. All nations, which have yielded to her sway, have become eminent by their gentleness,[2] their sense of justice, and the glory of their high deeds.

2. And yet a hackneyed reproach of old date is leveled against her, that the Church is opposed to the rightful aims of the civil government,[3] and is wholly unable to afford help in spreading that welfare and progress which justly and naturally are sought after by every well-regulated State.[4] From the very beginning Christians were harassed by slanderous accusations of this nature, and on that account were held up to hatred and execration, for being (so they were called) enemies of the Empire. The Christian religion was moreover commonly charged with being the cause of the calamities that so frequently befell the State,[5] whereas, in very truth, just punishment was being awarded to guilty nations

---

1 L. *popularesque mores.*—the manners of the people."
2 L. *mansuetudine.*—E. gentleness.—P. and H. culture.
3 L. *reipublicae.*—E. the aspirations of society.
4 L. *civitas*; that is, the body politic, or polity.
5 L. *respublica*; that is, the commonwealth.

by an avenging God. This odious calumny, with most valid reason, nerved the genius and sharpened the pen of St. Augustine, who, notably in his treatise, *The City of God*, set forth in so bright a light the worth of Christian wisdom in its relation to the public weal[6] that he seems not merely to have pleaded the cause of the Christians of his day, but to have refuted for all future times impeachments so grossly contrary to truth. The wicked proneness, however, to levy like charges and accusations has not been lulled to rest. Many, indeed, are they who have tried to work out a plan of civil society based on doctrines other than those approved by the Catholic Church. Nay, in these latter days, a novel conception of law[7] has begun here and there to gain increase and influence, the outcome, as it is maintained, of an age arrived at full stature, and the result of progressive liberty. But, though endeavors of various kinds have been ventured on, it is clear that no better mode has been devised for the building up and ruling the State than that which is the necessary growth of the teachings of the Gospel. We deem it, therefore, of the highest moment, and a strict duty of Our apostolic office, to contrast with the lessons taught by Christ the novel theories now advanced touching the State.[8] By this means, We cherish a hope that the bright shining of the truth may scatter the mists of error and doubt, so that one and all may see clearly the imperious law of life[9] which they are bound to follow and obey.

3. It is not difficult to determine what would be the form and character of the State were it governed according to the principles of Christian philosophy. Man's natural instinct moves him to live in civil society, for he cannot, if dwelling apart, provide

---

6 L. *cum re publica.* — E. in connection with the public weal.
7 L. *novum, ut appellant, jus.* The Latin word *jus* (as in English just, justice, etc.) points out the body of laws and juridical dispositions that exercise sway over the relations between persons and goods in a given society; in a more recondite sense, it points out the general conception of right and wrong dominating these laws and regulations. — E. a novel form of jurisprudence.
8 L. *de re publica*; that is concerning the nature of the public weal.
9 L. *summa illa praecepta vivendi.* — E. the supreme rules of life.

himself with the necessary requirements of life, nor procure the means of developing his mental and moral faculties. Hence, it is divinely ordained that he should lead his life — be it family,[10] or civil — with his fellow men, amongst whom alone his several wants can be adequately supplied. But, as no society can hold together unless someone be over all, directing all to strive earnestly for the common good, every body politic[11] must have a ruling authority, and this authority, no less than society itself, has its source in nature, and has, consequently, God for its Author. Hence, it follows that all public power must proceed from God. For God alone is the true and supreme Lord of the world. Everything, without exception, must be subject to Him, and must serve him, so that whosoever holds the right to govern holds it from one sole and single source, namely, God, the sovereign Ruler of all. "There is no power but from God."[12]

4. The right to rule is not necessarily, however, bound up with any special mode of government. It may take this or that form, provided only that it be of a nature of the government, rulers must ever bear in mind that God is the paramount ruler of the world, and must set Him before themselves as their exemplar and law in the administration of the State. For, in things visible God has fashioned secondary causes, in which His divine action can in some wise be discerned, leading up to the end to which the course of the world is ever tending. In like manner, in civil society, God has always willed that there should be a ruling authority, and that they who are invested with it should reflect the divine power and providence in some measure over the human race.

5. They, therefore, who rule should rule with even-handed justice, not as masters, but rather as fathers, for the rule of God over man is most just, and is tempered always with a father's kindness. Government should, moreover, be administered for the well-being of the citizens, because they who govern others possess

---

10 P. and H. add: social.
11 L. *civili hominum communitati.* — P. and H. every civilized community.
12 Rom. 13:1.

authority solely for the welfare of the State. Furthermore, the civil power must not be subservient to the advantage of any one individual or of some few persons, inasmuch as it was established for the common good of all. But, if those who are in authority rule unjustly, if they govern overbearingly or arrogantly, and if their measures prove hurtful to the people, they must remember that the Almighty will one day bring them to account, the more strictly in proportion to the sacredness of their office and pre-eminence of their dignity. "The mighty shall be mightily tormented."[13] Then, truly, will the majesty of the law[14] meet with the dutiful and willing homage of the people, when they are convinced that their rulers hold authority from God, and feel that it is a matter of justice and duty to obey them, and to show them reverence and fealty, united to a love not unlike that which children show their parents. "Let every soul be subject to higher powers."[15] To despise legitimate authority, in whomsoever vested, is unlawful, as a rebellion against the divine will, and whoever resists that, rushes willfully to destruction. "He that resisteth the power resisteth the ordinance of God, and they that resist, purchase to themselves damnation."[16] To cast aside obedience, and by popular violence to incite to revolt, is therefore treason, not against man only, but against God.

6. As a consequence, the State,[17] constituted as it is, is clearly bound to act up to the manifold and weighty duties linking it to God, by the public profession of religion. Nature and reason, which command every individual devoutly to worship God in holiness, because we belong to Him and must return to Him, since from Him we came, bind also the civil community by a like law. For, men living together in society are under the power of God no less than individuals are, and society, no less than individuals, owes gratitude to God who gave it being and

---

[13] Wisd. 6:7.
[14] L. *majestatem imperii*; that is, the majesty of the government.
[15] Rom. 13:1.
[16] Rom. 13:2.
[17] L. *civitatem*; that is, the body politic.

maintains it and whose ever-bounteous goodness enriches it with countless blessings. Since, then, no one is allowed to be remiss in the service due to God, and since the chief duty of all men is to cling to religion in both its teaching and practice-not such religion as they may have a preference for, but the religion which God enjoins, and which certain and most clear marks show to be the only one true religion — it is a public crime to act as though there were no God. So, too, is it a sin for the State not to have care for religion as a something beyond its scope, or as of no practical benefit; or out of many forms of religion to adopt that one which chimes in with the fancy; for we are bound absolutely to worship God in that way which He has shown to be His will.[18] All who rule, therefore, would hold in honor the holy name of God, and one of their chief duties must be to favor religion, to protect it, to shield it under the credit and sanction of the laws, and neither to organize nor enact any measure that may compromise its safety. This is the bounden duty of rulers to the people over whom they rule. For one and all are we destined by our birth and adoption to enjoy, when this frail and fleeting life is ended, a supreme and final good in heaven, and to the attainment of this, every endeavor should be directed. Since, then, upon this depends the full and perfect happiness of mankind, the securing of this end should be of all imaginable interests the most urgent. Hence, civil society, established for the common welfare, should not only safeguard the wellbeing of the community, but have also at heart the interests of its individual members, in such mode as not in any way to hinder, but in every manner to render as easy as may be, the possession of that highest and unchangeable good for which all should seek. Wherefore, for this purpose, care must especially be taken to preserve unharmed and unimpeded the religion whereof the practice is the link connecting man with God.

---

18 E. In like manner societies (*civitates*) cannot, without crime, act as though God did not exist, or cast off the care of religion as alien to them or useless, or out of several kinds of religion adopt whichever they prefer. On the contrary, societies are absolutely bound to the worship of God in the way which He has shown to be His will.

7. Now, it cannot be difficult to find out which is the true religion, if only it be sought with an earnest and unbiased mind; for proofs are abundant and striking. We have, for example, the fulfillment of prophecies, miracles in great numbers, the rapid spread of the faith in the midst of enemies and in face of overwhelming obstacles, the witness of the martyrs, and the like. From all these, it is evident that the only true religion is the one established by Jesus Christ Himself, and which He committed to His Church to protect and to propagate.

8. For the only-begotten Son of God established on earth a society which is called the Church, and to it He handed over the exalted and divine office which He had received from His Father, to be continued through the ages to come. "As the Father hath sent Me, I also send you."[19] "Behold I am with you all days, even to the consummation of the world."[20] Consequently, as Jesus Christ came into the world that men "might have life and have it more abundantly,"[21] so also has the Church for its aim and end the eternal salvation of souls, and hence it is so constituted as to open wide its arms to all mankind, unhampered by any limit of either time or place. "Preach ye the Gospel to every creature."[22]

9. Over this mighty multitude God has Himself set rulers with power to govern, and He has willed that one should be the head of all, and the chief and unerring teacher of truth, to whom He has given "the keys of the kingdom of heaven."[23] "Feed My lambs, feed My sheep."[24] "I have prayed for thee that thy faith fail not."[25]

10. This society is made up of men, just as civil society is, and yet is supernatural and spiritual, on account of the end for which it was founded, and of the means by which it aims at attaining that end. Hence, it is distinguished and differs from civil society, and,

---

19   John 20:21.
20   Matt. 28:20.
21   John 10:10.
22   Mark 16:15.
23   Matt. 16:19.
24   John 21: 16–17.
25   Luke 22:32.

On the Christian Constitution of States

what is of highest moment, it is a society chartered as of right divine, perfect in its nature and in its title, to possess in itself and by itself, through the will and loving kindness of its Founder, all needful provision for its maintenance and action. And just as the end at which the Church aims is by far the noblest of ends, so is its authority the most exalted of all authority, nor can it be looked upon as inferior to the civil power, or in any manner dependent upon it.

11. In very truth, Jesus Christ gave to His Apostles unrestrained authority in regard to things sacred, together with the genuine and most true power of making laws, as also with the twofold right of judging and of punishing, which flows from that power. "All power is given to Me in heaven and on earth: going therefore teach all nations... teaching them to observe all things whatsoever I have commanded you."[26] And in another place: "If he will not hear them, tell the Church."[27] And again: "In readiness to revenge all disobedience."[28] And once more: "That... I may not deal more severely according to the power which the Lord hath given me, unto edification and not unto destruction."[29] Hence, it is the Church, and not the State,[30] that is to be man's guide to heaven. It is to the Church that God has assigned the charge of seeing to, and legislating for, all that concerns religion; of teaching all nations; of spreading the Christian faith as widely as possible; in short, of administering freely and without hindrance, in accordance with her own judgment, all matters that fall within its competence.[31]

12. Now, this authority, perfect in itself, and plainly meant to be unfettered, so long assailed by a philosophy that truckles to the State,[32] the Church, has never ceased to claim for herself

---

26   Matt. 28:18–20.
27   Matt. 18:12.
28   2 Cor. 10:6.
29   2 Cor. 13:10.
30   L. *civitas*.
31   L. *rem christianam*. — E. of administering its affairs freely and without hindrance according to its own judgment.
32   L. *principum assentatrice*. — E. by a philosophy subservient to princes.

and openly to exercise. The Apostles themselves were the first to uphold it, when, being forbidden by the rulers of the synagogue to preach the Gospel, they courageously answered: "We must obey God rather than men."[33] This same authority the holy Fathers of the Church were always careful to maintain by weighty arguments, according as occasion arose, and the Roman Pontiffs have never shrunk from defending it with unbending constancy. Nay, more, princes and all invested with power to rule have themselves approved it, in theory alike and in practice. It cannot be called in question that in the making of treaties, in the transaction of business matters, in the sending and receiving ambassadors, and in the interchange of other kinds of official dealings they have been wont to treat with the Church as with a supreme and legitimate power. And, assuredly, all ought to hold that it was not without a singular disposition of God's providence that this power of the Church was provided with a civil sovereignty as the surest safeguard of her independence.

13. The Almighty, therefore, has given the charge of the human race to two powers, the ecclesiastical and the civil, the one being set over divine, and the other over human, things. Each in its kind is supreme, each has fixed limits within which it is contained, limits which are defined by the nature and special object of the province of each, so that there is, we may say, an orbit traced out within which the action of each is brought into play by its own native right. But, inasmuch as each of these two powers has authority over the same subjects, and as it might come to pass that one and the same thing—related differently, but still remaining one and the same thing—might belong to the jurisdiction and determination of both, therefore God, who foresees all things, and who is the author of these two powers, has marked out the course of each in right correlation to the other. "For the powers that are, are ordained of God."[34] Were this not so, deplorable contentions and conflicts would often arise, and, not infrequently, men, like travelers at the meeting of two roads,

33 Acts 5:29.
34 Rom. 13:1.

would hesitate in anxiety and doubt, not knowing what course to follow. Two powers would be commanding contrary things, and it would be a dereliction of duty to disobey either of the two.

14. But it would be most repugnant to them to think thus of the wisdom and goodness of God. Even in physical things, albeit of a lower order, the Almighty has so combined the forces and springs of nature with tempered action and wondrous harmony that no one of them clashes with any other, and all of them most fitly and aptly work together for the great purpose of the universe. There must, accordingly, exist between these two powers a certain orderly connection, which may be compared to the union of the soul and body in man. The nature and scope of that connection can be determined only, as We have laid down, by having regard to the nature of each power, and by taking account of the relative excellence and nobleness of their purpose. One of the two has for its proximate and chief object the well-being of this mortal life; the other, the everlasting joys of heaven. Whatever, therefore in things human is of a sacred character, whatever belongs either of its own nature or by reason of the end to which it is referred, to the salvation of souls, or to the worship of God, is subject to the power and judgment of the Church. Whatever is to be ranged under the civil and political order is rightly subject to the civil authority. Jesus Christ has Himself given command that what is Caesar's is to be rendered to Caesar, and that what belongs to God is to be rendered to God.

15. There are, nevertheless, occasions when another method of concord[35] is available for the sake of peace and liberty: We mean when rulers of the State and the Roman Pontiff come to an understanding touching some special matter. At such times the Church gives signal proof of her motherly love by showing the greatest possible kindliness and indulgence.

---

35 L. *alius quoque concordiae modus*; that is, a concordat, or agreement, between the Pope and secular government for the regulation of ecclesiastical affairs in a certain country.

16. Such, then, as We have briefly pointed out, is the Christian organization of civil society; not rashly or fancifully shaped out, but educed from the highest and truest principles, confirmed by natural reason itself.

17. In such organization[36] of the State there is nothing that can be thought to infringe upon the dignity of rulers, and nothing unbecoming them; nay, so far from degrading the sovereign power in its due rights, it adds to it permanence and luster. Indeed, when more fully pondered, this mutual coordination has a perfection in which all other forms of government are lacking, and from which excellent results would flow, were the several component parts to keep their place and duly discharge the office and work appointed respectively for each. And, doubtless, in the constitution of the State such as We have described, divine and human things are equitably shared;[37] the rights of citizens assured to them, and fenced round by divine, by natural, and by human law; the duties incumbent on each one being wisely marked out, and their fulfillment fittingly insured. In their uncertain and toilsome journey to the everlasting city[38] all see that they have safe guides and helpers on their way,[39] and are conscious that others have charge to protect their persons alike and their possessions, and to obtain or preserve for them everything essential for their present life. Furthermore, domestic society acquires that firmness and solidity so needful to it from the holiness of marriage, one and indissoluble, wherein the rights and duties of husband and wife are controlled with wise justice and equity; due honor is assured to the woman; the authority of the husband is conformed to the pattern afforded by the authority of God; the power of the father is tempered by a due regard for the dignity of the mother and her offspring; and the best possible provision is made for the guardianship, welfare, and education of the children.

---

36 L. *reipublicae*; that is, the constitution of a country.
37 L. *partita*.—E. divided.
38 L. *ad sempiternam illam civitatem*.—P. and H. the city made without hands.
39 L. *ad ingrediendum duces, ad perveniendum adjutores*; that is, guides to find their way, helpers to reach their goal.

18. In political affairs, and all matters civil, the laws aim at securing the common good, and are not framed according to the delusive caprices and opinions of the mass of the people, but by truth and by justice; the ruling powers are invested with a sacredness more than human, and are withheld from deviating from the path of duty, and from overstepping the bounds of rightful authority; and the obedience is not the servitude of man to man, but submission to the will of God, exercising His sovereignty through the medium of men. Now, this being recognized as undeniable, it is felt that the high office of rulers should be held in respect; that public authority should be constantly and faithfully obeyed; that no act of sedition should be committed; and that the civic order of the commonwealth should be maintained as sacred.

19. So, also, as to the duties of each one toward his fellow men, mutual forbearance, kindliness, generosity are placed in the ascendant; the man who is at once a citizen and a Christian is not drawn aside by conflicting obligations; and, lastly, the abundant benefits with which the Christian religion, of its very nature, endows even the mortal life of man are acquired for the community and civil society. And this to such an extent that it may be said in sober truth: "The condition of the commonwealth depends on the religion with which God is worshipped; and between one and the other there exists an intimate and abiding connection."[40]

20. Admirably, according to his wont, does St. Augustine, in many passages, enlarge upon the nature[41] of these advantages; but nowhere more markedly and to the point than when he addresses the Catholic Church in the following words: "Thou dost teach and train children with much tenderness, young men with much vigor, old men with much gentleness; as the age not of the body alone, but of the mind of each requires. Women thou dost subject to their husbands in chaste and faithful obedience, not for the

---

40 Sacr. Imp. ad Cyrillum Alexand. et Episcopos metrop.; See Labbeus, *Collect. Conc.*, Vol. 3.
41 L. *vim*. — E. the force. — P. and H. the potency. — Beware of the often weak, but classical, acceptation of *vis*, in the sense of "meaning," "import," "nature."

gratifying of their lust, but for bringing forth children, and for having a share in the family concerns. Thou dost set husbands over their wives, not that they may play false to the weaker sex, but according to the requirements of sincere affection. Thou dost subject children to their parents in a kind of free service, and dost establish parents over their children with a benign rule... Thou joinest together, not in society only, but in a sort of brotherhood, citizen with citizen, nation with nation, and the whole race of men, by reminding them of their common parentage. Thou teachest kings to look to the interests of their people, and dost admonish the people to be submissive to their kings. With all care dost thou teach all to whom honor is due, and affection, and reverence, and fear, consolation, and admonition and exhortation, and discipline, and reproach, and punishment. Thou showest that all these are not equally incumbent on all, but that charity is owing to all, and wrongdoing to none."[42] And in another place, blaming the false wisdom of certain time-serving philosophers, he observes: "Let those who say that the teaching of Christ is hurtful to the State produce such armies as the maxims of Jesus have enjoined soldiers to bring into being; such governors of provinces; such husbands and wives; such parents and children; such masters and servants; such kings; such judges, and such payers and collectors of tribute, as the Christian teaching instructs them to become, and then let them dare to say that such teaching is hurtful to the State. Nay, rather will they hesitate to own that this discipline, if duly acted up to, is the very mainstay of the commonwealth."[43]

21. There was once a time when States were governed by the philosophy of the Gospel.[44] Then it was that the power and divine virtue of Christian wisdom had diffused itself throughout the laws, institutions, and morals of the people, permeating all ranks and relations of civil society. Then, too, the religion instituted by Jesus Christ, established firmly in befitting dignity, flourished

---

42 *De moribus ecclesiae*, 1, cap. 30, n. 63 (PL 32, 1336).
43 *Epist. 138 ad Marcellinum*, cap. 2, n. 15 (PL 33, 532).
44 L. *evangelica philosophia*. — P. and H. the principles of Gospel teaching. — E. the philosophy of the Gospel.

everywhere, by the favor of princes and the legitimate protection of magistrates; and Church and State[45] were happily united in concord and friendly interchange of good offices. The State,[46] constituted in this wise, bore fruits important beyond all expectation, whose remembrance is still, and always will be, in renown, witnessed to as they are by countless proofs which can never be blotted out or ever obscured by any craft of any enemies. Christian Europe has subdued barbarous nations, and changed them from a savage to a civilized condition, from superstition to true worship. It victoriously rolled back the tide of Mohammedan conquest; retained the headship of civilization; stood forth in the front rank as the leader and teacher of all, in every branch of national culture; bestowed on the world the gift of true and many-sided liberty; and most wisely founded very numerous institutions for the solace of human suffering. And if we inquire how it was able to bring about so altered a condition of things, the answer is—beyond all question, in large measure, through religion, under whose auspices so many great undertakings were set on foot, through whose aid they were brought to completion.

22. A similar state of things would certainly have continued had the agreement of the two powers been lasting. More important results even might have been justly looked for, had obedience waited upon the authority, teaching, and counsels of the Church, and had this submission been specially marked by greater and more unswerving loyalty. For that should be regarded in the light of an ever-changeless law which Ivo of Chartres wrote to Pope Paschal II: "When kingdom and priesthood are at one, in complete accord, the world is well ruled, and the Church flourishes, and brings forth abundant fruit. But when they are at variance, not only smaller interests prosper not, but even things of greatest moment fall into deplorable decay."[47]

---

45 L. *sacerdotium atque imperium*; that is, in the language of the Middle Ages, to which the Pope is here alluding, the papacy and the Holy Roman Empire.
46 L. *civitas*.
47 *Epist. 238*, to Pope Paschal II (PL 162, 246B).

Immortale Dei

23. But that harmful and deplorable passion for innovation which was aroused in the sixteenth century threw first of all into confusion the Christian religion, and next, by natural sequence, invaded the precincts of philosophy, whence it spread amongst all classes of society. From this source, as from a fountain-head, burst forth all those later tenets of unbridled license which, in the midst of the terrible upheavals of the last century, were wildly conceived and boldly proclaimed as the principles and foundation of that new conception of law[48] which was not merely previously unknown, but was at variance on many points with not only the Christian, but even the natural law.[49]

24. Amongst these principles the main one lays down that as all men are alike by race and nature, so in like manner all are equal in the control of their life; that each one is so far his own master as to be in no sense under the rule of any other individual; that each is free to think on every subject just as he may choose, and to do whatever he may like to do; that no man has any right to rule over other men. In a society grounded upon such maxims all government is nothing more nor less than the will of the people, and the people, being under the power of itself alone, is alone its own ruler. It does choose, nevertheless, some to whose charge it may commit itself, but in such wise that it makes over to them not the right so much as the business of governing, to be exercised, however, in its name.

25. The authority of God is passed over in silence, just as if there were no God; or as if He cared nothing for human society; or as if men, whether in their individual capacity or bound together in social relations, owed nothing to God; or as if there could be a government of which the whole origin and power and authority did not reside in God Himself. Thus, as is evident, a State[50] becomes nothing but a multitude which is its own master and ruler. And since the people is declared to contain within itself

---

48 L. *novi juris*; see previous note on the Latin word "jus."
49 L. *a jure non solum christiano, sed etiam naturali*; see previous note on the Latin word "jus."
50 L. *respublica*.—E. the State thus composed.

the spring-head of all rights and of all power, it follows that the State[51] does not consider itself bound by any kind of duty toward God. Moreover, it believes that it is not obliged to make public profession of any religion; or to inquire which of the very many religions is the only one true; or to prefer one religion to all the rest; or to show to any form of religion special favor; but, on the contrary, is bound to grant equal rights to every creed, so that public order may not be disturbed by any particular form of religious belief.

26. And it is a part of this theory that all questions that concern religion are to be referred to private judgment; that everyone is to be free to follow whatever religion he prefers, or none at all if he disapprove of all. From this, the following consequences logically flow: that the judgment of each one's conscience is independent of all law; that the most unrestrained opinions may be openly expressed as to the practice or omission of divine worship; and that everyone has unbounded license to think whatever he chooses and to publish abroad whatever he thinks.

27. Now, when the State[52] rests on foundations like those just named—and for the time being they are greatly in favor—it readily appears into what and how unrightful a position the Church is driven. For, when the management of public business is in harmony with doctrines of such a kind, the Catholic religion is allowed a standing in civil society equal only, or inferior, to societies alien from it; no regard is paid to the laws of the Church, and she who, by the order and commission of Jesus Christ, has the duty of teaching all nations, finds herself forbidden to take any part in the instruction of the people. With reference to matters that are of twofold jurisdiction, they who administer the civil power lay down the law at their own will, and in matters that appertain to religion defiantly put aside the most sacred decrees of the Church. They claim jurisdiction over the marriages of Catholics, even over the bond as well as

---

51 L. *civitas*.
52 L. *reipublicae*.

Immortale Dei

the unity and the indissolubility of matrimony. They lay hands on the goods of the clergy, contending that the Church cannot possess property. Lastly, they treat the Church with such arrogance that, rejecting entirely her title to the nature and rights of a perfect society, they hold that she differs in no respect from other societies in the State,[53] and for this reason possesses no right nor any legal power of action, save that which she holds by the concession and favor of the government. If in any State the Church retains her own agreement[54] publicly entered into by the two powers, men forthwith begin to cry out that matters affecting the Church must be separated from those of the State.[55]

28. Their object in uttering this cry is to be able to violate unpunished their plighted faith, and in all things to have unchecked control. And as the Church, unable to abandon her chiefest and most sacred duties, cannot patiently put up with this, and asks that the pledge given to her be fully and scrupulously acted up to, contentions frequently arise between the ecclesiastical and the civil power, of which the issue commonly is that the weaker power yields to the one which is stronger in human resources.

29. Accordingly, it has become the practice and determination under this condition of public polity (now so much admired by many) either to forbid the action of the Church altogether, or to keep her in check and bondage to the State. Public enactments are in great measure framed with this design. The drawing up of laws, the administration of State affairs, the godless education of youth, the spoliation and suppression of religious orders, the overthrow of the temporal power of the Roman Pontiff, all alike aim to this one end — to paralyze the action of Christian institutions, to cramp to the utmost the freedom of the Catholic Church, and to curtail her ever single prerogative.

30. Now, natural reason itself proves convincingly that such concepts of the government of a State are wholly at variance

---

[53] L. *respublica*.
[54] That is, a concordat, as defined in the previous note.
[55] L. *reipublicae*. — E. the affairs (*rationes*) of...the State.

with the truth. Nature itself bears witness that all power, of every kind, has its origin from God, who is its chief and most august source.

31. The sovereignty of the people, however, and this without any reference to God, is held to reside in the multitude; which is doubtless a doctrine exceedingly well calculated to flatter and to inflame many passions, but which lacks all reasonable proof, and all power of insuring public safety and preserving order. Indeed, from the prevalence of this teaching, things have come to such a pass that may hold as an axiom of civil jurisprudence that seditions may be rightfully fostered. For the opinion prevails that princes are nothing more than delegates chosen to carry out the will of the people; whence, it necessarily follows that all things are as changeable as the will of the people, so that risk of public disturbance is ever hanging over our heads.

To hold, therefore, that there is no difference in matters of religion between forms that are unlike each other, and even contrary to each other, most clearly leads in the end to the rejection of all religion in both theory and practice. And this is the same thing as atheism; however, it may differ from it in name. Men who really believe in the existence of God must, in order to be consistent with themselves and to avoid absurd conclusions, understand that differing modes of divine worship involving dissimilarity and conflict even on most important points cannot all be equally probable, equally good, and equally acceptable to God.

32. So, too, the liberty of thinking, and of publishing, whatsoever each one likes, without any hindrance, is not in itself an advantage over which society can wisely rejoice. On the contrary, it is the fountainhead and origin of many evils. Liberty is a power perfecting man, and hence, should have truth and goodness for its object. But the character of goodness and truth cannot be changed at option. These remain ever one and the same, and are no less unchangeable than nature itself. If the mind assents to false opinions, and the will chooses and follows after what is wrong, neither can attain its native fullness, but both must fall

from their native dignity into an abyss of corruption. Whatever, therefore, is opposed to virtue and truth may not rightly be brought temptingly before the eye of man, much less sanctioned by the favor and protection of the law. A well-spent life is the only way to heaven, whither all are bound, and on this account, the State[56] is acting against the laws and dictates of nature whenever it permits the license of opinion and of action to lead minds astray from truth and souls away from the practice of virtue. To exclude the Church, founded by God Himself, from life, from laws, from the education of youth, from domestic society is a grave and fatal error. A State from which religion is banished can never be well regulated; and already perhaps more than is desirable is known of the nature and tendency of the so-called civil philosophy of life and morals. The Church of Christ is the true and sole teacher of virtue and guardian of morals. She it is who preserves in their purity the principles from which duties flow, and, by setting forth most urgent reasons for virtuous life, bids us not only to turn away from wicked deeds, but even to curb all movements of the mind that are opposed to reason, even though they be not carried out in action.

33. To wish the Church to be subject to the civil power in the exercise of her duty is a great folly and a sheer injustice. Whenever this is the case, order is disturbed, for things natural are put above things supernatural; the many benefits which the Church, if free to act, would confer on society are either prevented or at least lessened in number; and a way is prepared for enmities and contentions between the two powers,[57] with how evil result to both the issue of events has taught us only too frequently.

34. Doctrines such as these, which cannot be approved by human reason, and most seriously affect the whole civil order, Our predecessors the Roman Pontiffs (well aware of what their apostolic office required of them) have never allowed to pass uncondemned.

---

56 L. *civitas*.
57 L. *utrique reipublicae*; that is, to the two societies, the temporal one and the religious one. — E. conflicts between the two powers, with an evil result to both, of which we have a too frequent experience.

On the Christian Constitution of States

Thus, Gregory XVI in his encyclical letter *Mirari Vos*, dated August 15, 1832, inveighed with weighty words against the sophisms which even at his time were being publicly inculcated-namely, that no preference should be shown for any particular form of worship; that it is right for individuals to form their own personal judgments about religion; that each man's conscience is his sole and allsufficing guide; and that it is lawful for every man to publish his own views, whatever they may be, and even to conspire against the State.[58] On the question of the separation of Church and State the same Pontiff writes as follows: "Nor can We hope for happier results either for religion or for the civil government from the wishes of those who desire that the Church be separated from the State,[59] and the concord between the secular and ecclesiastical authority be dissolved. It is clear that these men, who yearn for a shameless liberty, live in dread of an agreement which has always been fraught with good, and advantageous alike to sacred and civil interests." To the like effect, also, as occasion presented itself, did Pius IX brand publicly many false opinions which were gaining ground, and afterwards ordered them to be condensed in summary form in order that in this sea of error Catholics might have a light which they might safely follow.[60]

---

58 L. *De rationibus rei sacrae reique civilis distrahendis*; that is, On the question of separating political affairs from religious affairs.
59 L. *Ecclesiam a regno*; that is, the Church from government. — E. those who desire that the Church be separated from the State and the agreement between the secular power and the sacerdotal authority be broken up.
60 Pope Pius IX, encyclical *Quanta Cura* (Dec. 8, 1864): *Syllabus*. It will suffice to indicate a few of them:
Prop. 19. The Church is not a true, perfect, and wholly independent society, possessing in its own unchanging rights conferred upon it by its divine Founder; but it is for the civil power to determine what are the rights of the Church, and the limits within which it may use them.
Prop. 29. The State, as the origin and source of all rights, enjoys a right that is unlimited.
Prop. 55. The Church must be separated from the State and the State from the Church.
Prop. 79. It is untrue that the civil liberty of every form of worship, and the full power given to all of openly and publicly manifesting whatsoever opinions and thoughts, lead to the more ready corruption of the minds and morals of the people, and to the spread of the plague of religious indifference.

35. From these pronouncements of the Popes it is evident that the origin of public power is to be sought for in God Himself, and not in the multitude, and that it is repugnant to reason to allow free scope for sedition. Again, that it is not lawful for the State, any more than for the individual, either to disregard all religious duties or to hold in equal favor different kinds of religion; that the unrestrained freedom of thinking and of openly making known one's thoughts is not inherent in the rights of citizens, and is by no means to be reckoned worthy of favor and support. In like manner, it is to be understood that the Church no less than the State itself is a society perfect in its own nature and its own right, and that those who exercise sovereignty ought not so to act as to compel the Church to become subservient or subject to them, or to hamper her liberty in the management of her own affairs, or to despoil her in any way of the other privileges conferred upon her by Jesus Christ. In matters, however, of mixed jurisdiction, it is in the highest degree consonant to nature, as also to the designs of God, that so far from one of the powers separating itself from the other, or still less coming into conflict with it, complete harmony, such as is suited to the end for which each power exists,[61] should be preserved between them.

36. This, then, is the teaching of the Catholic Church concerning the constitution and government of the State. By the words and decrees just cited, if judged dispassionately, no one of the several forms of government is in itself condemned, inasmuch as none of them contains anything contrary to Catholic doctrine, and all of them are capable, if wisely and justly managed, to insure the welfare of the State. Neither is it blameworthy in itself, in any manner, for the people to have a share greater or less, in the government: for at certain times, and under certain laws,

---

61 L. *concordiam, eamque cum causis proximis congruentem, quae causae utramque societatem genuerunt*; that is, harmony, such as is suited to the proximate causes that have brought about the rise of the two societies.—E. concord should be preserved between them as suited the end for which each power exists.

such participation may not only be of benefit to the citizens, but may even be of obligation. Nor is there any reason why anyone should accuse the Church of being wanting in gentleness of action or largeness of view, or of being opposed to real and lawful liberty. The Church, indeed, deems it unlawful to place the various forms of divine worship on the same footing as the true religion, but does not, on that account, condemn those rulers who, for the sake of securing some great good or of hindering some great evil, allow patiently custom or usage to be a kind of sanction for each kind of religion having its place in the State. And, in fact, the Church is wont to take earnest heed that no one shall be forced to embrace the Catholic faith against his will, for, as St. Augustine wisely reminds us, "Man cannot believe otherwise than of his own will."

37. In the same way, the Church cannot approve of that liberty which begets a contempt of the most sacred laws of God, and casts off the obedience due to lawful authority, for this is not liberty so much as license, and is most correctly styled by St. Augustine the "liberty of self-ruin," and by the Apostle St. Peter the "cloak of malice."[62] Indeed, since it is opposed to reason, it is a true slavery, "for whosoever committeth sin is the slave of sin."[63] On the other hand, that liberty is truly genuine, and to be sought after, which in regard to the individual does not allow men to be the slaves of error and of passion, the worst of all masters; which, too, in public administration guides the citizens in wisdom and provides for them increased means of well-being; and which, further, protects the State from foreign interference.

38. This honorable liberty, alone worthy of human beings, the Church approves most highly and has never slackened her endeavor to preserve, strong and unchanged, among nations. And, in truth, whatever in the State is of chief avail for the common welfare; whatever has been usefully established to curb the license of rulers who are opposed to the true interests of

---

62   1 Peter 2:16.
63   John 8:34.

Immortale Dei

the people, or to keep in check the leading authorities from unwarrantably interfering in municipal or family affairs; whatever tends to uphold the honor, manhood, and equal rights of individual citizens—of all these things, as the monuments of past ages bear witness, the Catholic Church has always been the originator, the promoter, or the guardian. Ever, therefore, consistent with herself, while on the one hand, she rejects that exorbitant liberty which in individuals and in nations ends in license or in thraldom, on the other hand, she willingly and most gladly welcomes whatever improvements the age brings forth, if these really secure the prosperity of life here below, which is, as it were, a stage in the journey to the life that will know no ending.

39. Therefore, when it is said that the Church is hostile to modern political regimes and that she repudiates the discoveries of modern research, the charge is a ridiculous and groundless calumny. Wild opinions she does repudiate, wicked and seditious projects she does condemn, together with that attitude of mind which points to the beginning of a willful departure from God. But, as all truth must necessarily proceed from God, the Church recognizes in all truth that is reached by research a trace of the divine intelligence. And as all truth in the natural order is powerless to destroy belief in the teachings of revelation, but can do much to confirm it, and as every newly discovered truth may serve to further the knowledge or the praise of God, it follows that whatsoever spreads the range of knowledge will always be willingly and even joyfully welcomed by the Church. She will always encourage and promote, as she does in other branches of knowledge, all study occupied with the investigation of nature. In these pursuits, should the human intellect discover anything not known before, the Church makes no opposition. She never objects to search being made for things that minister to the refinements and comforts of life. So far, indeed, from opposing these she is now, as she ever has been, hostile alone to indolence and sloth, and earnestly wishes that the talents of men may bear more and more abundant fruit by cultivation and exercise. Moreover, she gives encouragement to every kind of art and handicraft, and through her influence,

directing all strivings after progress toward virtue and salvation, she labors to prevent man's intellect and industry from turning him away from God and from heavenly things.

40. All this, though so reasonable and full of counsel, finds little favor nowadays when States[64] not only refuse to conform to the rules of Christian wisdom, but seem even anxious to recede from them further and further on each successive day. Nevertheless, since truth when brought to light is wont, of its own nature, to spread itself far and wide, and gradually take possession of the minds of men, We, moved by the great and holy duty of Our apostolic mission to all nations, speak, as We are bound to do, with freedom. Our eyes are not closed to the spirit of the times. We repudiate not the assured and useful improvements of our age, but devoutly wish affairs of State to take a safer course than they are now taking, and to rest on a more firm foundation without injury to the true freedom of the people; for the best parent and guardian of liberty amongst men is truth. "The truth shall make you free."[65]

41. If in the difficult times in which Our lot is cast, Catholics will give ear to Us, as it behooves them to do, they will readily see what are the duties of each one in matters of opinion as well as action. As regards opinion, whatever the Roman Pontiffs have hitherto taught, or shall hereafter teach, must be held with a firm grasp of mind, and, so often as occasion requires, must be openly professed.

42. Especially with reference to the so-called "liberties" which are so greatly coveted in these days, all must stand by the judgment of the apostolic see, and have the same mind. Let no man be deceived by the honest outward appearance of these liberties, but let each one reflect whence these have had their origin, and by what efforts they are everywhere upheld and promoted. Experience has made Us well acquainted with their results to the State, since everywhere they have borne fruits which the good and wise bitterly deplore. If there really exist anywhere, or if we

---

64 L. *civitates*; that is, societies.
65 John 8:32.

in imagination conceive, a State, waging wanton and tyrannical war against Christianity, and if we compare with it the modern form of government just described, this latter may seem the more endurable of the two. Yet, undoubtedly, the principles on which such a government is grounded are, as We have said, of a nature which no one can approve.

43. Secondly, action may relate to private and domestic matters, or to matters public. As to private affairs, the first duty is to conform life and conduct to the gospel precepts, and to refuse to shrink from this duty when Christian virtue demands some sacrifice slightly more difficult to make. All, moreover, are bound to love the Church as their common mother, to obey her laws, promote her honor, defend her rights, and to endeavor to make her respected and loved by those over whom they have authority. It is also of great moment to the public welfare to take a prudent part in the business of municipal administration, and to endeavor above all to introduce effectual measures, so that, as becomes a Christian people, public provision may be made for the instruction of youth in religion and true morality. Upon these things the well-being of every State greatly depends.

44. Furthermore, it is in general fitting and salutary that Catholics should extend their efforts beyond this restricted sphere, and give their attention to national politics. We say "in general" because these Our precepts are addressed to all nations. However, it may in some places be true that, for most urgent and just reasons, it is by no means expedient for Catholics to engage in public affairs or to take an active part in politics. Nevertheless, as We have laid down, to take no share in public matters would be as wrong as to have no concern for, or to bestow no labor upon, the common good, and the more so because Catholics are admonished, by the very doctrines which they profess, to be upright and faithful in the discharge of duty, while, if they hold aloof, men whose principles offer but small guarantee for the welfare of the State will the more readily seize the reins of government. This would tend also to the injury of the Christian

On the Christian Constitution of States

religion, forasmuch as those would come into power who are badly disposed toward the Church, and those who are willing to befriend her would be deprived of all influence.

45. It follows clearly, therefore, that Catholics have just reasons for taking part in the conduct of public affairs. For in so doing, they assume not nor should they assume the responsibility of approving what is blameworthy in the actual methods of government,[66] but seek to turn these very methods, so far as is possible, to the genuine and true public good, and to use their best endeavors at the same time to infuse, as it were, into all the veins of the State[67] the healthy sap and blood of Christian wisdom and virtue. The morals and ambitions of the heathens differed widely from those of the Gospel, yet Christians were to be seen living undefiled everywhere in the midst of pagan superstition, and, while always true to themselves, coming to the front boldly wherever an opening was presented. Models of loyalty to their rulers, submissive, so far as was permitted, to the sovereign power,[68] they shed around them on every side a halo of sanctity; they strove to be helpful to their brethren, and to attract others to the wisdom of Jesus Christ, yet were bravely ready to withdraw from public life, nay, even to lay down their life, if they could not without loss of virtue retain honors, dignities, and offices. For this reason, Christian ways and manners speedily found their way not only into private houses but into the camp, the senate, and even into the imperial palaces. "We are but of yesterday," wrote Tertullian, "yet we swarm in all your institutions, we crowd your cities, islands, villages, towns, assemblies, the army itself. your wards and corporations, the palace, the senate, and the law courts."[69] So that the Christian faith, when once it became lawful to make public profession of

---

66 L. *rerum publicarum rationibus.* — E. for they do not assume these responsibilities in approval of what is unlawful in the methods of government at this time.
67 L. *reipublicae*; that is, of the commonwealth.
68 L. *imperio legume*; that is, to the authority of laws. — E. models of fidelity to their princes, obedient, as far as was lawful, to the sovereign power.
69 Apologet, 27 (P4 1, 525).

the Gospel, appeared in most of the cities of Europe, not like an infant crying in its cradle, but already grown up and full of vigor.

46. In these Our days it is well to revive these examples of Our forefathers. First and foremost, it is the duty of all Catholics worthy of the name and wishful to be known as most loving children of the Church, to reject without swerving whatever is inconsistent with so fair a title; to make use of popular institutions, so far as can honestly be done, for the advancement of truth and righteousness; to strive that liberty of action shall not transgress the bounds marked out by nature and the law of God; to endeavor to bring back all civil society to the pattern and form of Christianity which We have described. It is barely possible to lay down any fixed method by which such purposes are to be attained, because the means adopted must suit places and times widely differing from one another. Nevertheless, above all things, unity of aim must be preserved, and similarity must be sought after in all plans of action. Both these objects will be carried into effect without fail if all will follow the guidance of the apostolic see as their rule of life and obey the bishops whom the Holy Spirit has placed to rule the Church of God.[70] The defense of Catholicism, indeed, necessarily demands that in the profession of doctrines taught by the Church all shall be of one mind and all steadfast in believing; and care must be taken never to connive, in any way, at false opinions, never to withstand them less strenuously than truth allows. In mere matters of opinion, it is permissible to discuss things with moderation, with a desire of searching into the truth, without unjust suspicion or angry recriminations.

47. Hence, lest concord be broken by rash charges, let this be understood by all, that the integrity of Catholic faith cannot be reconciled with opinions verging on naturalism or rationalism, the essence of which is utterly to do away with Christian institutions and to install in society the supremacy of man to the exclusion of God. Further, it is unlawful to follow one line of conduct in private life and another in public, respecting privately

---

70 Acts 20:28.

the authority of the Church, but publicly rejecting it; for this would amount to joining together good and evil, and to putting man in conflict with himself; whereas he ought always to be consistent, and never in the least point nor in any condition of life to swerve from Christian virtue.

48. But in matters merely political, as, for instance, the best form of government, and this or that system of administration, a difference of opinion is lawful. Those, therefore, whose piety is in other respects known, and whose minds are ready to accept in all obedience the decrees of the apostolic see, cannot in justice be accounted as bad men because they disagree as to subjects We have mentioned; and still graver wrong will be done them, if — as We have more than once perceived with regret — they are accused of violating, or of wavering in, the Catholic faith.

49. Let this be well borne in mind by all who are in the habit of publishing their opinions, and above all by journalists. In the endeavor to secure interests of the highest order, there is no room for intestine strife or party rivalries; since all should aim with one mind and purpose to make safe that which is the common object of all — the maintenance of religion and of the State.[71] If, therefore, they have hitherto been dissensions, let them henceforth be gladly buried in oblivion. If rash or injurious acts have been committed, whoever may have been at fault, let mutual charity make amends, and let the past be redeemed by a special submission of all to the apostolic see. In this way, Catholics will attain two most excellent results: they will become helpers to the Church in preserving and propagating Christian wisdom, and they will confer the greatest benefit on civil society, the safety of which is exceedingly imperiled by evil teachings and bad passions.

50. This, venerable brethren, is what We have thought it Our duty to expound to all nations of the Catholic world touching the Christian constitution of States[72] and the duties of

---

71 L. *remque publicam*; that is, the commonwealth.
72 L. *civitatum*; that is, the Christian constitution of States.

individual citizens. It behooves Us now with earnest prayer to implore the protection of heaven, beseeching God, who alone can enlighten the minds of men and move their will, to bring about those happy ends for which We yearn and strive, for His greater glory and the general salvation of mankind. As a happy augury of the divine benefits, and in token of Our paternal benevolence, to you, venerable brothers, and to the clergy and to the whole people committed to your charge and vigilance, We grant lovingly in the Lord the apostolic benediction.

VII

On Socialism

INTRODUCTION

This encyclical letter of Pope Leo XIII, *Quod Apostolici Muneris*, was published December 28, 1878. It is expressly directed against "the sect of the socialists," or, in other words, "against the plague of socialism." The word "socialism" here designates a body of interrelated doctrinal positions held in common by several different political groups, organizations, or parties. Whatever their names — socialists, communists, or even nihilists — they fall under the same principles. These principles are: denial of all authority; equality of all men in both duties and rights; dissolubility of the bond of marriage and, consequently, of all family ties; in fine, socialists oppose the right of property despite the fact that this right is guaranteed by natural law. All these doctrines are supported and spread by means of an intense propaganda which more and more frequently incites to violence.

The study of this encyclical should be complemented by that of the letter *Divini Redemptoris (Atheistic Communism)*, issued by Pope Pius XI on March 19, 1937. English translation with notes and bibliography in J. Husslein, S. J., *Social Wellsprings*, vol. II, pp. 339–374. Also published in pamphlet form by the Catholic Truth Society, London, 1952; new translation by Canon G. D. Smith, with an analysis of the encyclical; National Catholic Welfare Conference, Washington, 1937; Vatican Press translation; Paulist Press, New York, with discussion club outline by Rev. Gerald C. Treacy, S. J.; no date.

SUMMARY

(1) Who the socialists are. (2) Their main errors. (3) Similar doctrines already condemned by several different popes. (4) The Church is the best guarantee of social peace. (5) The inequality of rights and of power proceeds from the very Author of nature, that is, God. (6) There is no power but from God. (7) The power of rulers is limited by the divine and the natural law. (8) Indissolubility and sanctity of the bond of marriage. (9) Why the Church maintains the right of property. (10) The freedom of the Church should be insured in order that her healing force may be felt. (11) Christian doctrine as the remedy to these evils. (12) Christmas message.

VII

Quod Apostolici Muneris
ON SOCIALISM
December 28, 1878

1. At the very beginning of Our pontificate, as the nature of Our apostolic office demanded, we hastened to point out in an encyclical letter addressed to you, venerable brethren, the deadly plague that is creeping into the very fibers of human society and leading[1] it on to the verge of destruction; at the same time, We pointed out also the most effectual remedies by which society might be restored[2] and might escape from the very serious dangers which threaten it. But the evils which We then deplored have so rapidly increased that We are again compelled to address you, as though we heard the voice of the prophet ringing in Our ears: "Cry, cease not, lift up thy voice like a trumpet."[3] You understand,[4] venerable brethren, that We speak of that sect of men who, under various and almost barbarous names, are called socialists, communists, or nihilists, and who, spread over all the world, and bound together by the closest ties in a wicked confederacy, no longer seek the shelter of secret meetings, but, openly and boldly marching forth in the light of day, strive to bring to a head what they have long been planning—the overthrow of all civil society whatsoever.

Surely these are they who, as the sacred Scriptures testify, "Defile the flesh, despise dominion and blaspheme majesty."[5] They leave nothing untouched or whole which by both human and divine laws has been wisely decreed for the health and beauty of life. They refuse obedience to the higher powers, to whom,

---

1 H. driving it. W. bringing it.
2 W. renewed unto salvation.
3 Isa. 58:1.
4 L. *Nullo autem negotio intelligitis.* W. You understand as a matter of course.
5 Jude 8.

according to the admonition of the Apostle, every soul ought to be subject, and who derive the right of governing from God; and they proclaim the absolute equality of all men in rights and duties. They debase the natural union of man and woman, which is held sacred even among barbarous peoples; and its bond, by which the family is chiefly held together, they weaken, or even deliver up to lust. Lured, in fine, by the greed of present goods, which is "the root of all evils which some coveting have erred from the faith,"[6] they assail the right of property sanctioned by natural law; and by a scheme of horrible wickedness, while they seem desirous of caring for the needs and satisfying the desires of all men, they strive to seize and hold in common whatever has been acquired[7] either by title of lawful inheritance, or by labor of brain and hands, or by thrift in one's mode of life. These are the startling theories they utter in their meetings, set forth in their pamphlets, and scatter abroad in a cloud of journals and tracts. Wherefore, the revered majesty and power of kings have won such fierce hatred from their seditious people that disloyal traitors, impatient of all restraint, have more than once within a short period raised their arms in impious attempt against the lives of their own sovereigns.

2. But the boldness of these bad men, which day by day more and more threatens civil society[8] with destruction, and strikes the souls of all with anxiety and fear, finds its cause and origin in those poisonous doctrines which, spread abroad in former times among the people,[9] like evil seed bore in due time such fatal fruit. For you know, venerable brethren, that that most deadly war which from the sixteenth century down has been waged by innovators against the Catholic faith, and which has grown in intensity up to today, had for its object to subvert all revelation, and overthrow the supernatural order, that thus the way might be opened for the discoveries, or rather the hallucinations,[10] of

---

6   1 Tim. 6:10.
7   W. individually acquired; individually is a gloss.
8   L. *civili consortio*. W. the civilized community.
9   L. *inter populos diffusae*. W. scattered far and wide among the nations.
10 L. *solius rationis inventis seu potius deliramentis*. W. of unaided reason, with its vagaries or rather ravings.

reason alone. This kind of error, which falsely usurps to itself the name of reason, as it lures and whets the natural appetite[11] that is in man of excelling, and gives loose rein to unlawful desires of every kind, has easily penetrated not only the minds of a great multitude of men but to a wide extent civil society, also. Hence, by a new species of impiety, unheard of even among the heathen nations, states have been constituted without any count at all of God or of the order established by him; it has been given out that public authority neither derives its principles, nor its majesty, nor its power of governing from God, but rather from the multitude,[12] which, thinking itself absolved from all divine sanction, bows only to such laws as it shall have made at its own will. The supernatural truths of faith having been assailed and cast out as though hostile to reason, the very Author and Redeemer of the human race has been slowly and little by little banished from the universities, the lyceums and gymnasia[13]—in a word, from every public institution. In fine, the rewards and punishments of a future and eternal life having been handed over to oblivion, the ardent desire of happiness has been limited to the bounds of the present. Such doctrines as these having been scattered far and wide, so great a license of thought and action having sprung up on all sides, it is no matter for surprise that men of the lowest class, weary of their wretched home or workshop, are eager to attack the homes and fortunes of the rich; it is no matter for surprise that already there exists no sense of security[14] either in public or private life, and that the human race should have advanced to the very verge of final dissolution.

3. But the supreme pastors of the Church, on whom the duty falls of guarding the Lord's flock from the snares of the enemy, have striven in time to ward off the danger and provide for the

---

11 L. *appetentiam natuarliter homini insertam*. W. the eagerness to outstrip others which is interwoven with man's nature.
12 L. *a populi multitudine*. W. from the mass of the people.
13 L. *a studiorum Universitatibus, Lyceis, et Gymnasiis*. H. from the universities, the high schools, and junior colleges. W. from the scheme of studies at universities, colleges, and high schools.
14 L. *tranquilitas*. W. tranquility.

On Socialism

safety of the faithful. For, as soon as the secret societies began to be formed, in whose bosom the seeds of the errors which we have already mentioned were even then being nourished, the Roman Pontiffs Clement XII and Benedict XIV did not fail to unmask the evil counsels of the sects, and to warn the faithful of the whole globe against the ruin which would be wrought. Later on again, when a licentious sort of liberty was attributed to man by a set of men who gloried in the name of philosophers,[15] and a new right,[16] as they call it, against the natural and divine law began to be framed and sanctioned, Pope Pius VI, of happy memory, at once exposed in public documents the guile and falsehood of their doctrines, and at the same time foretold with apostolic foresight the ruin into which the people[17] so miserably deceived would be dragged. But, as no adequate precaution was taken to prevent their evil teachings from leading the people more and more astray, and lest they should be allowed to escape in[18] the public statutes of States, Popes Pius VII and Leo XII condemned by anathema the secret sects,[19] and again warned society of the danger which threatened them. Finally, all have witnessed with what solemn words and great firmness and constancy of soul our glorious predecessor, Pius IX, of happy memory, both in his allocutions and in his encyclical letters addressed to the bishops of all the world, fought now against the wicked attempts of the sects, now openly by name against the pest of socialism, which was already making headway.

4. But it is to be lamented that those to whom has been committed the guardianship of the public weal,[20] deceived by the wiles of wicked men and terrified by their threats, have looked upon the Church with a suspicious and even hostile eye, not perceiving

---

15 See footnote 246.
16 L. *novum jus*. W. a new law.
17 L. *plebs*. H. men. W. the deluded multitudes.
18 L. *neve in publica regnorum scita evaderent*. H. lest they be allowed to find their place in the public statutes of states. W. and of obtaining ascendency even in public decisions of government.
19 On Freemasonry, *Humanum genus*.
20 L. *communis boni cura*. W. the care of the common welfare.

that the attempts of the sects would be vain if the doctrine of the Catholic Church and the authority of the Roman Pontiffs had always survived, with the honor that belongs to them, among princes and peoples. For, "the church of the living God, which is the pillar and ground of truth,"[21] hands down those doctrines and precepts whose special object is the safety and peace of society and the uprooting of the evil growth of socialism.

5. For, indeed, although the socialists, stealing[22] the very Gospel itself with a view to deceive more easily the unwary, have been accustomed to distort it so as to suit their own purposes, nevertheless so great is the difference between their depraved teachings and the most pure doctrine of Christ that none greater could exist: "for what participation hath justice with injustice or what fellowship hath light with darkness?"[23] Their habit, as we have intimated, is always to maintain that nature has made all men equal, and that, therefore, neither honor nor respect is due to majesty, nor obedience to laws, unless, perhaps, to those sanctioned by their own good pleasure. But, on the contrary, in accordance with the teachings of the Gospel, the equality of men consists in this: that all, having inherited the same nature, are called to the same most high dignity of the sons of God, and that, as one and the same end is set before all, each one is to be judged by the same law and will receive punishment or reward according to his deserts. The inequality of rights and of power proceeds from the very Author of nature, "from whom all paternity in heaven and earth is named."[24] But the minds of princes and their subjects are, according to Catholic doctrine and precepts, bound up one with the other in such a manner, by mutual duties and rights, that the thirst for power is restrained and the rational ground of obedience made easy, firm, and noble.

6. Assuredly, the Church wisely inculcates the apostolic precept on the mass of men: "There is no power but from God; and

---

21 1 Tim. 3:15.
22 L. *ipso Evangelio abutentes*. W. turning to evil use the Gospel itself.
23 2 Cor. 6:14.
24 Eph. 3:15.

those that are, are ordained of God. Therefore, he that resisteth the power resisteth the ordinance of God. And they that resist purchase to themselves damnation." And again she admonishes those "subject by necessity" to be so "not only for wrath but also for conscience' sake," and to render "to all men their dues; tribute to whom tribute is due, custom to whom custom, fear to whom fear, honor to whom honor."[25] For, He who created and governs all things has, in His wise providence, appointed that the things which are lowest should attain their ends by those which are intermediate, and these again by the highest. Thus, as even in the kingdom of heaven He hath willed that the choirs of angels be distinct and some subject to others, and also in the Church has instituted various orders and a diversity of offices, so that all are not apostles or doctors or pastors,[26] so also has He appointed that there should be various orders in civil society, differing indignity, rights, and power, whereby the State,[27] like the Church, should be one body, consisting of many members, some nobler than others, but all necessary to each other and solicitous for the common good.

7. But, that rulers may use the power conceded to them to save and not to destroy, the Church of Christ seasonably warns even princes that the sentence of the Supreme Judge overhangs them, and, adopting the words of divine wisdom, calls upon all in the name of God: "Give ear, you that rule the people, and that please yourselves in multitudes of nations; for power is given you by the Lord, and strength by the Most High, who will examine your works, and search out your thoughts.... For a most severe judgment shall be for them that bear rule.... For God will not except any man's person, neither will he stand in awe of any man's greatness, for he hath made the little and the great; and he hath equally care of all. But, a greater punishment is ready for the more mighty."[28] And if at any time it happen that the power

---

25 Rom. 13:5,7.
26 1 Cor. 12:28.
27 L. *civitas*, that is: the body politic.
28 Wisd. 6:3–4, 8–9.

of the State²⁹ is rashly and tyrannically wielded by princes, the teaching of the Catholic Church does not allow an insurrection on private authority against them, lest public order be only the more disturbed, and lest society take greater hurt therefrom. And when affairs come to such a pass that there is no other hope of safety, she teaches that relief may be hastened by the merits of Christian patience and by earnest prayers to God. But, if the will of legislators and princes shall have sanctioned or commanded anything repugnant to the divine or natural law, the dignity and duty of the Christian name, as well as the judgment³⁰ of the Apostle, urge that "God is to be obeyed rather than man."³¹

8. Even family life itself, which is the cornerstone of all society and government, necessarily feels and experiences the salutary power of the Church, which redounds to the right ordering and preservation of every State³² and kingdom. For you know, venerable brethren, that the foundation of this society rests first of all in the indissoluble union of man and wife according to the necessity of natural law, and is completed in the mutual rights and duties of parents and children, masters and servants. You know also that the doctrines of socialism strive almost completely to dissolve this union; since, that stability which is imparted to it by religious wedlock being lost, it follows that the power of the father over his own children, and the duties of the children toward their parents, must be greatly weakened. But the Church, on the contrary, teaches that "marriage, honorable in all,"³³ which God himself instituted in the very beginning of the world, and made indissoluble for the propagation and preservation of the human species, has become still more binding and more holy through Christ, who raised it to the dignity of a sacrament, and chose to use it as the figure of His own union with the Church.³⁴

---

29 L. *publicam... potestatem.* W. the public exercise of authority.
30 L. *Apostolica sententia.* W. the Apostolic injunction, that is: the precept of St. Paul.
31 Acts 5:29.
32 L. *omnis civitatis et regni.* W. of every city and every State.
33 Heb. 13:4.
34 L. *respublicas.* W. over the State at large.

Wherefore, as the Apostle has it,[35] as Christ is the head of the Church, so is the man the head of the woman; and as the Church is subject to Christ, who embraces her with a most chaste and undying love, so also should wives be subject to their husbands, and be loved by them in turn with a faithful and constant affection. In like manner does the Church temper the use of parental and domestic authority, that it may tend to hold children and servants to their duty, without going beyond bounds. For, according to Catholic teaching, the authority of our heavenly Father and Lord is imparted to parents and masters, whose authority, therefore, not only takes its origin and force from Him, but also borrows its nature and character. Hence, the Apostle exhorts children to "obey their parents in the Lord, and honor their father and mother, which is the first commandment with promise";[36] and he admonishes parents: "And you, fathers, provoke not your children to anger, but bring them up in the discipline and correction of the Lord."[37] Again, the apostle enjoins the divine precept on servants and masters, exhorting the former to be "obedient to their lords according to the flesh of Christ... with a good will serving, as to the Lord"; and the latter, to "forbear threatenings, knowing that the Lord of all is in heaven, and there is no respect of persons with God."[38] If only all these matters were faithfully observed according to the divine will by all on whom they are enjoined, most assuredly every family would be a figure of the heavenly home, and the wonderful blessings there begotten would not confine themselves to the households alone, but would scatter their riches abroad through the nations.

9. But Catholic wisdom, sustained by the precepts of natural and divine law, provides with especial care for public and private tranquillity in its doctrines and teachings regarding the duty of government and the distribution of the goods which are

---

35   Eph. 5:23.
36   Eph. 6:1–2.
37   Eph. 6:4.
38   Eph. 6:5–9.

Quod Apostolici Muneris

necessary for life and use. For, while the socialists would destroy the "right" of property, alleging it to be a human invention altogether opposed to the inborn equality of man, and, claiming a community of goods, argue that poverty should not be peaceably endured, and that the property and privileges of the rich may be rightly invaded, the Church, with much greater wisdom and good sense, recognizes the inequality among men, who are born with different powers of body and mind, inequality in actual possession, also, and holds that the right of property and of ownership, which springs from nature itself, must not be touched and stands inviolate. For she knows that stealing and robbery were forbidden in so special a manner by God, the Author and Defender of right,[39] that He would not allow man even to desire what belonged to another, and that thieves and despoilers, no less than adulterers and idolaters, are shut out from the Kingdom of Heaven. But not the less on this account does our holy Mother not neglect the care of the poor or omit to provide for their necessities; but, rather, drawing them to her with a mother's embrace, and knowing that they bear the person of Christ Himself, who regards the smallest gift to the poor[40] as a benefit conferred on Himself, holds them in great honor. She does all she can to help them; she provides homes and hospitals where they may be received, nourished, and cared for all the world over and watches over these. She is constantly pressing on the rich that most grave precept to give what remains[41] to the poor; and she holds over their heads the divine sentence that unless they succor the needy they will be repaid by eternal torments. In fine, she does all she can to relieve and comfort the poor, either by holding up to them the example of Christ, "who being rich became poor for our sake,[42] or by reminding them of his own words, wherein he pronounced the poor blessed and bade them hope for the reward of eternal bliss. But who

---

39 L. *omnis juris*. W. of every right.
40 L. *vel in minimum pauperem*. W. upon the lowliest among the poor.
41 L. *ut quod superest pauperibus tribuant*. W. to give of their superfluity to the poor.
42 2 Cor. 8:9.

does not see that this is the best method of arranging[43] the old struggle between the rich and poor? For, as the very evidence of facts and events shows, if this method is rejected or disregarded, one of two things must occur: either the greater portion of the human race will fall back into the vile condition of slavery which so long prevailed among the pagan nations, or human society must continue to be disturbed by constant eruptions, to be disgraced by rapine and strife, as we have had sad witness even in recent times.

10. These things being so, then, venerable brethren, as at the beginning of Our pontificate We, on whom the guidance of the whole Church now lies, pointed out a place of refuge[44] to the peoples and the princes tossed about by the fury of the tempest, so now, moved by the extreme peril that is on them, We again lift up Our voice, and beseech them again and again for their own safety's sake as well as that of their people to welcome and give ear to the Church which has had such wonderful influence on the public prosperity of kingdoms, and to recognize that political and religious affairs[45] are so closely united that what is taken from the spiritual weakens the loyalty of subjects and the majesty of the government. And, since they know that the Church of Christ has such power to ward off the plague of socialism as cannot be found in human laws, in the mandates of magistrates, or in the force of armies, let them restore that Church to the condition and liberty in which she may exert her healing force for the benefit of all society.[46]

11. But you, venerable brethren, who know the origin and the drift of these gathering evils, strive with all your force of soul to implant the Catholic teaching deep in the minds of all. Strive

---

43 L. *dissidii componendi*. W. of appeasing the undying conflict. H. of harmonizing the old struggle.
44 L. *portum*. W. the port.
45 L. *rationes*. W. the relations. — The meaning is: that the interests of religion and those of political authority are so united...
46 L. *in totius humanae societatis commodum*. W. for the good of society in general. — The meaning is: for the benefit of the whole society of human beings.

that all may have the habit of clinging to God with filial love and revering His divinity from their tenderest years; that they may respect the majesty of princes and of laws; that they may restrain their passions and stand fast by the order which God has established in civil and domestic society. Moreover, labor hard[47] that the children of the Catholic Church neither join nor favor in any way whatsoever this abominable sect; let them show, on the contrary, by noble deeds and right dealing in all things, how well and happily human society would hold together were each member to shine as an example of right-doing and of virtue. In fine, as the recruits of socialism are especially sought among artisans and workmen, who, tired, perhaps, of labor, are more easily allured by the hope of riches and the promise of wealth, it is well to encourage societies of artisans and workmen which, constituted under the guardianship of religion, may tend to make all associates contented with their lot and move them to a quiet and peaceful life.

12. Venerable brethren, may He who is the beginning and end of every good work inspire your and Our endeavors. And, indeed, the very thought of these days, in which the anniversary of our Lord's birth is solemnly observed, moves us to hope for speedy help. For the new life which Christ at His birth brought to a world already aging and steeped in the very depths of wickedness He bids us also to hope for, and the peace which He then announced by the angels to men He has promised to us also. For the Lord's "hand is not shortened that he cannot save, neither is his ear heavy that he cannot hear."[48] In these most auspicious days, then, venerable brethren, wishing all joy and happiness to you and to the faithful of your churches, We earnestly pray the Giver of all good that again "there may appear unto men the goodness and kindness of God our Saviour,"[49] who brought us out of the power of our most deadly enemy into the most

---

47 L. *insuper adlaboretis oportet*. W. moreover, it behooves you to strive earnestly.
48 Isa. 59:1.
49 Titus 3:4.

noble dignity of the sons of God. And that We may the sooner and more fully gain our wish, do you, venerable brethren, join with Us in lifting up your fervent prayers to God and beg the intercession of the Blessed and Immaculate Virgin Mary, and of Joseph her spouse, and of the blessed Apostles Peter and Paul, in whose prayers We have the greatest confidence. And in the meanwhile, We impart to you, with the inmost affection of the heart, and to your clergy and faithful people, the apostolic benediction as an augury of the divine gifts.

VIII

Rights and Duties of Capital and Labor

INTRODUCTION

The encyclical letter *Rerum Novarum*, published on May 15, 1891, has been given various titles, all stressing the importance attributed by Pope Leo XIII to a bettering of the social condition of the working class. Indeed, this is an essential part of its object, but the Pope himself has defined it in wider terms as dealing with the rights and duties by which rich and poor, or capital and labor, are bound together in the body politic. This is clearly stated in *Rerum Novarum* (art. 1), and no less clearly restated in the encyclical *Graves De Communi* (art. 2). Accordingly, the emphasis should not be placed on either side of the problem, but on both.

This justly famous encyclical contains a particularly striking sentence, in that it perfectly describes the spirit in which all the teachings of Pope Leo XIII concerning social problems have been conceived and should be understood. This golden rule will be found in art. 18: "Nothing is more useful than to look upon the world as it really is—and at the same time to seek elsewhere for the solace to its troubles." Only those who do not take a realistic view of the world can fail to see that religion alone has an answer to its problems.

In many respects, *Rerum Novarum* is a general review of the fundamental positions stated by Pope Leo XIII in his other encyclicals, yet there are in it certain things which he has never said elsewhere or, at least, not with such a forceful clarity. To look upon the world as it really is means to see it as inhabited by men whose natural inequalities necessarily beget social inequalities; it is to accept the fact that, ever since original sin, work has ceased to be a freely chosen delight; it is to become reconciled to the idea that, for the same reason, hardships, sufferings, and death will have no cessation or end so long as the world and mankind continue to exist; in short, it is not to turn the world into the fool's paradise imagined by so many social reformers.

This lack of realism is denounced by the Pope in the doctrine of class war and of a natural antagonism between capital and labor, whereas, in objective reality, there is between social classes a natural solidarity which should bind them in friendliness and good feeling. But it must be denounced for a deeper and higher reason. Nature is best judged from the point of view of religion and of the supernatural order. For the Christian who looks at it under this supernatural light, wealth appears as being *in reality* an obstacle to eternal happiness (art. 22), whereas poverty and manual work appear as truly and really most noble since the Son of God, that is, God Himself, has chosen to spend the better part of his life as a poor carpenter (art. 23). The true remedy to the evils of society presupposes the recognition of the brotherly bond that unites all men as children of the same common Father. God alone can give to men the perfect happiness for which they vainly crave in this world.

What is proper to *Rerum Novarum* is the exceptional importance it attributes to the applications of the doctrine, first with regard to particular problems, next with regard to concrete social institutions. An outstanding example of the first case is found in art. 33, where the Pope establishes that, from the point of view of the State, "the interests of all, whether high or low, are equal." The recognition of social inequalities does not justify any inequality of interest, love, and care on the part of public powers. The doctrine taught by Christian philosophy, that to the extent that they are "parts of a whole" the parts are identical to the whole provides a metaphysical justification for the conclusion that the State has no right to neglect a portion of the citizens and to favor another. With respect to the problems raised by concrete social institutions, let us note the discussions devoted by Pope Leo XIII to unionized labor, to the right to strike and to the proper use to be made of it (arts. 36–38); his remarks on the condition of mine workers; on the employment of women and children in factories; on the widely debated notion of the "living wage" (arts. 43–44); on the sanitary precautions to be observed in work shops, etc. These developments, and similar ones, justify the subtitle of *The Worker's Charter* sometimes given to this encyclical. Indeed, it does contain such a charter, together with a charter for the employer, and, as will be seen, many other things.

Later documents provide confirmations and precisions concerning the exact meaning of the doctrine: the letter *Nihil Nobis*, to Gaspard Decurtins, August 6, 1893, and the letter *Permoti Nos*, to Peter-Lambert Cardinal Goossens, July 10, 1895, on the social question in Belgium.

The teaching of Pope Leo XIII has been taken up and developed in the encyclical of Pope Pius XI, *Quadragesimo Anno* (*Reconstructing the Social Order*, May 15, 1931), translated in J. Husslein, S.J., *Social Wellsprings*, Vol. 2, pp. 174–234; also published by the Catholic Truth Society of London; by the National Catholic Welfare Conference; and, with a discussion club outline by Gerald C. Treacy, S.J., by the Paulist Press.

On the United States and the problem of social reconstruction, see the encyclical of Pope Pius XII to the American hierarchy, *Sertum Laetitiae* (November 1, 1939), published in translation both by the National Catholic Welfare Conference and by the Paulist Press.

SUMMARY

(1) The revolutionary spirit has invaded all departments of human life. (2) The responsibility of the apostolic office urges the Pope to speak on the condition of the working classes and to define the relative rights and mutual duties of rich and poor, of capital and of labor. (3) Workers are no longer protected by the ancient guilds or by the moral authority of the Church,

and the practice of usury has reduced the masses to a condition little better than that of slavery. (4) The remedy imagined by socialism consists in doing away with private property and transferring it to the State. (5) Yet, since men work in view of acquiring property, socialism harms the interests of every worker. (6) Moreover, socialism is against justice because the right to own private property is a natural right. (7) As a provident rational being, man is particularly entitled to own the very soil whose produce he must store in view of the future. (8) The fact that God has given the earth to the human race in general is no obstacle to the right to private property. (9) On the contrary, man appropriates to himself by his labor the portion of the soil which he cultivates. (10) This is the reason why he should own the soil itself and not only its fruits. (11) This natural law has always been confirmed by the human laws. (12) Its necessity is still better seen from the point of view of the domestic society and its needs. (13) Without the right to property, the parents cannot provide for their children; the family precedes the State in existence and its rights are at least equal to those of the body politic. (14) The State has a duty to help families and to insure in them the observance of mutual rights, but paternal authority cannot be abolished nor absorbed by that of the State. (15) In violating natural justice, therefore, socialism would open the door to class war and submit many citizens to a new kind of slavery. (16) No workable solution of the social problem will be found if men leave out religion and the Church. (17) Inequalities in capacity, skill, health, and strength are facts of nature; inequalities in fortune necessarily follow from these natural inequalities. (18) Since they are consequences of sin, the pains and hardships of life will last as long as the human race. (19) Against the false notion of class war, the Church maintains the ideal of a harmonious agreement between capital and labor. (20) Mutual duties of rich and poor, or of employers and workers. (21) Above all, let us remember that the things of earth cannot be correctly valued without taking into consideration the life to come. (22) Riches are an obstacle to eternal happiness; charity removes this obstacle. (23) Poverty is no disgrace, for God Himself chose to be a carpenter. (24) The true worth of man lies in his virtues, not in his wealth. (25) This Christian teaching substitutes the bond of brotherly love for the separation caused by pride. (26) The social action exercised by the Church. (27) History shows that civil society was renovated in all its parts by the teachings of Christianity. (28) The Church does not neglect the temporal and earthly interests of her children. (29) Constant interventions of the Church in behalf of the poor. (30) Hence the justification for the patrimony of the poor progressively constituted by the Church; no State-organized system of relief will ever make up for Christian charity. (31) Necessity for co-operation between Church and State. (32) How the State can contribute to the welfare of the body politic. (33) From the point of view of the State the interests of all the members of the body politic are equal. (34) Justice demands that the interests of workers should be protected. (35) The State should anxiously safeguard the community and all its members; their welfare is the object of the government of the State. (36) The State must step in every time the general interest, or that of any particular class, is in jeopardy; the settling of strikes harmful to the community, the fight against inhuman conditions of labor, are duties of the State. (37) The poor are entitled to special protection from the State. (38) But to help them does not consist in violating private property. (39) The laws should rather aim at preventing social troubles by removing their causes. (40) The highest interests of the worker are those of his soul; in this respect, all men are equal and have an equal right to be protected by the State. (41) The obligation of the cessation from work on Sundays and certain holy days should be enforced by the State. (42) The State is also qualified to supervise labor regulations and conditions, especially with regard to the working of women and children. (43) Views commonly received concerning just wages. (44) These views overlook two characters essential to human labor, namely, that it is both personal and necessary. (45) Wages should not be insufficient to support a frugal wage-earner. (46) The law should

Rights and Duties of Capital and Labor

favor the owning of private property for as many citizens as possible. (47) Private ownership will make property more equitably distributed, it will increase production, it will strengthen the love of the citizens for their country. (48) Societies for mutual help, private foundations to provide for workers, and other types of associations can do much to draw together employers and employees. (49) Trade unions are the most important of these associations. (50) Trade unions answer a natural need. (51) Consequently, they exist in their own right. (52) Nevertheless, the State has a duty to prevent association whose purposes are dangerous to the body politic. (53) This right of association exists even within the Church. (54) But all Christian workers should keep away from such associations, or societies, as are in the hands of secret leaders. (55) Those Catholics deserve to be praised who, in union with their bishops, are striving to better the condition of the working class by all possible rightful means. (56) Associations must be firmly and wisely conducted in order to achieve unity of purpose and harmony of action. (57) The aim and purpose of such associations is to help their members to better their condition to the utmost in body, soul, and property. (58) Rules for the sound administration of such associations. (59) The example of the early Christians illustrates the social benefits brought about by a Christian way of life. (60) The State also will benefit by it. (61) Many workers made bitter by empty promises would then gladly come back to the Christian ideal of charity and brotherly love. (62) Religion alone can destroy at its root the evil now threatening societies with ruin. (63) The co-operation of the Church will never be found lacking; she will never cease to preach the Gospel doctrines of Christian life. (64) Apostolic benediction.

VIII

Rerum Novarum

ON CAPITAL AND LABOR

May 15, 1891

1. That the spirit of revolutionary change, which has long been disturbing the nations of the world, should have passed beyond the sphere of politics and made its influence felt in the cognate sphere of practical economics is not surprising. The elements of the conflict now raging are unmistakable, in the vast expansion of industrial pursuits and the marvelous discoveries of science; in the changed relations between masters and workmen; in the enormous fortunes of some few individuals, and the utter poverty of the masses; in the increased self-reliance and closer mutual combination of the working classes;[1] as also, finally, in the prevailing moral degeneracy. The momentous gravity of the state of things now obtaining fills every mind with painful apprehension; wise men are discussing it; practical men are proposing schemes; popular meetings, legislatures, and rulers of nations are all busied with it — actually, there is no question which has taken a deeper hold on the public mind.

2. Therefore, venerable brethren, as on former occasions when it seemed opportune to refute false teaching, We have addressed you in the interests of the Church and of the common weal, and have issued letters bearing on political power, human liberty, the Christian constitution of the State, and like matters, so have We thought it expedient now to speak on the condition of the working classes.[2] It is a subject on which We have already

---

1 NC. Increased self-reliance on the part of workers as well as a closer bond of union with one another; that is, the labor unions.
2 The title sometimes given to this encyclical, *On the Condition of the Working Classes*, is therefore perfectly justified. A few lines after this sentence, the Pope gives a more comprehensive definition of the subject of *Rerum novarum*. We are using it as a title.

touched more than once, incidentally. But, in the present letter, the responsibility of the apostolic office urges Us to treat the question of set purpose and in detail, in order that no misapprehension may exist as to the principles which truth and justice dictate for its settlement. The discussion is not easy, nor is it void of danger. It is no easy matter to define the relative rights and mutual duties of the rich and of the poor,[3] of capital and of labor. And the danger lies in this, that crafty agitators are intent on making use of these differences of opinion to pervert men's judgments and to stir up the people to revolt.

3. In any case we clearly see, and on this, there is general agreement, that some opportune remedy must be found quickly for the misery and wretchedness pressing so unjustly on the majority of the working class: for the ancient workingmen's guilds were abolished in the last century, and no other protective organization took their place. Public institutions and the laws set aside the ancient religion. Hence, by degrees it has come to pass that working men have been surrendered, isolated and helpless, to the hardheartedness of employers and the greed of unchecked competition. The mischief has been increased by rapacious usury, which, although more than once condemned by the Church, is nevertheless, under a different guise, but with like injustice, still practiced by covetous and grasping men. To this must be added that the hiring of labor and the conduct of trade are concentrated in the hands of comparatively few; so that a small number of very rich men have been able to lay upon the teeming masses of the laboring poor[4] a yoke little better than that of slavery itself.

4. To remedy these wrongs the socialists, working on the poor man's envy of the rich, are striving to do away with private property, and contend that individual possessions should become the

---

3   L. *locupletes et proletarios.* — NC (rightly) the rich and the proletariat. — P. the wealthy and the poor.
4   L. *infinitae proletariorum multitudini*; that is the infinite multitude of the proletarians. — P. upon the masses of the poor. — NC. On the unnumbered masses of non-owning workers.

common property of all, to be administered by the State or by municipal bodies. They hold that by thus transferring property from private individuals to the community, the present mischievous state of things will be set to rights, inasmuch as each citizen will then get his fair share of whatever there is to enjoy. But their contentions are so clearly powerless to end the controversy that were they carried into effect the working man himself would be among the first to suffer. They are, moreover, emphatically unjust, for they would rob the lawful possessor, distort the functions of the State,[5] and create utter confusion in the community.

5. It is surely undeniable that, when a man engages in remunerative labor, the impelling reason and motive of his work is to obtain property, and thereafter to hold it as his very own. If one man hires out to another his strength or skill, he does so for the purpose of receiving in return what is necessary for the satisfaction of his needs; he therefore expressly intends to acquire a right full and real, not only to the remuneration, but also to the disposal of such remuneration, just as he pleases. Thus, if he lives sparingly, saves money, and, for greater security, invests his savings in land, the land, in such case, is only his wages under another form; and, consequently, a working man's little estate thus purchased should be as completely at his full disposal as are the wages he receives for his labor. But it is precisely in such power of disposal that ownership obtains, whether the property consists of land or chattels. Socialists, therefore, by endeavoring to transfer the possessions of individuals to the community at large, strike at the interests of every wage-earner, since they would deprive him of the liberty of disposing of his wages, and thereby of all hope and possibility of increasing his resources and of bettering his condition in life.

6. What is of far greater moment, however, is the fact that the remedy they propose is manifestly against justice. For, every man has by nature the right to possess property as his own. This

---

5 L. *pervertit officia rei publicae.* — P. bring the State into a sphere that is not its own. — NC. perverts the functions of the State.

is one of the chief points of distinction between man and the animal creation,[6] for the brute has no power of self-direction, but is governed by two main instincts, which keep his powers on the alert, impel him to develop them in a fitting manner, and stimulate and determine him to action without any power of choice. One of these instincts is self-preservation, the other the propagation of the species. Both can attain their purpose by means of things which lie within range; beyond their verge, the brute creation cannot go, for they are moved to action by their senses only, and in the special direction which these suggest. But with man, it is wholly different. He possesses, on the one hand, the full perfection of the animal being, and hence enjoys at least as much as the rest of the animal kind, the fruition of things material. But animal nature, however perfect, is far from representing the human being in its completeness, and is in truth but humanity's humble handmaid, made to serve and to obey. It is the mind, or reason, which is the predominant element in us who are human creatures; it is this which renders a human being human, and distinguishes him essentially from the brute. And on this very account—that man alone among the animal creation is endowed with reason—it must be within his right to possess things not merely for temporary and momentary use, as other living things do, but to have and to hold them in stable and permanent possession; he must have not only things that perish in the use, but those also which, though they have been reduced into use, continue for further use in after time.

7. This becomes still more clearly evident if man's nature be considered a little more deeply. For man, fathoming by his faculty of reason matters without number, linking the future with the present, and being master of his own acts, guides his ways under the eternal law and the power of God, whose providence governs all things. Wherefore, it is in his power to exercise his choice not only as to matters that regard his present welfare, but also about those which he deems may be for his advantage in time

---

6 L. *et genus... animantium... ceterarum.*—NC. and other living things.

yet to come. Hence, man not only should possess the fruits of the earth, but also the very soil, inasmuch as from the produce of the earth he has to lay by provision for the future. Man's needs do not die out, but forever recur; although satisfied today, they demand fresh supplies for tomorrow. Nature accordingly must have given to man a source that is stable and remaining always with him, from which he might look to draw continual supplies. And this stable condition of things he finds solely in the earth and its fruits. There is no need to bring in the State.[7] Man precedes the State,[8] and possesses, prior to the formation of any State,[9] the right of providing for the substance of his body.

8. The fact that God has given the earth for the use and enjoyment of the whole human race can in no way be a bar to the owning of private property. For God has granted the earth to mankind in general, not in the sense that all without distinction can deal with it as they like, but rather that no part of it was assigned to anyone in particular, and that the limits of private possession have been left to be fixed by man's own industry, and by the laws of individual races.[10] Moreover, the earth, even though apportioned among private owners, ceases not thereby to minister to the needs of all, inasmuch as there is not one who does not sustain life from what the land produces. Those who do not possess the soil contribute their labor; hence, it may truly be said that all human subsistence is derived either from labor on one's own land, or from some toil, some calling, which is paid for either in the produce of the land itself, or in that which is exchanged for what the land brings forth.[11]

---

7 L. *reipublicae*.
8 L. *respublica*.
9 L. *civitas*. — NC. (rightly) polity; that is, a politically organized community, a body politic.
10 L. *institutis populorum*. — P. the laws of individual people. — NC. the institutions of peoples.
11 L. *cujus merces tandem non aliunde quam a multiplici terrae fetu ducitur, cum eoque permutatur*. — NC. the compensation for which is drawn ultimately from no other source than from the varied products of the earth and is exchanged for them.

On Capital and Labor

9. Here, again, we have further proof that private ownership is in accordance with the law of nature. Truly, that which is required for the preservation of life, and for life's well-being, is produced in great abundance from the soil, but not until man has brought it into cultivation and expended upon it his solicitude and skill. Now, when man thus turns the activity of his mind and the strength of his body toward procuring the fruits of nature, by such act he makes his own that portion of nature's field which he cultivates — that portion on which he leaves, as it were, the impress of his personality;[12] and it cannot but be just that he should possess that portion as his very own, and have a right to hold it without any one being justified in violating that right.

10. So strong and convincing are these arguments that it seems amazing that some should now be setting up anew certain obsolete opinions in opposition to what is here laid down. They assert that it is right for private persons to have the use of the soil and its various fruits, but that it is unjust for anyone to possess outright either the land on which he has built or the estate which he has brought under cultivation. But those who deny these rights do not perceive that they are defrauding man of what his own labor has produced. For the soil which is tilled and cultivated with toil and skill utterly changes its condition; it was wild before, now it is fruitful; was barren, but now brings forth in abundance. That which has thus altered and improved the land becomes so truly part of itself as to be in great measure indistinguishable and inseparable from it. Is it just that the fruit of a man's own sweat and labor should be possessed and enjoyed by anyone else? As effects follow their cause, so is it just and right that the results of labor should belong to those who have bestowed their labor.

11. With reason, then, the common opinion of mankind, little affected by the few dissentients who have contended for the opposite view, has found in the careful study of nature, and

---

12 L. *formam quamdam personae suae impressam*; that is, as a form of his own personality. — Our text gives "individuality" instead of "personality." — P. (rightly) personality.

in the laws of nature, the foundations of the division of property, and the practice of all ages has consecrated the principle of private ownership, as being pre-eminently in conformity with human nature, and as conducing in the most unmistakable manner to the peace and tranquility of human existence. The same principle is confirmed and enforced by the civil laws—laws which, so long as they are just, derive from the law of nature their binding force. The authority of the divine law adds its sanction, forbidding us in severest terms even to covet that which is another's: "Thou shalt not covet thy neighbor's wife; nor his house, nor his field, nor his man-servant,[13] nor his maid-servant, nor his ox, nor his ass, nor anything that is his."[14]

12. The rights here spoken of, belonging to each individual man, are seen in much stronger light when considered in relation to man's social and domestic obligations. In choosing a state of life, it is indisputable that all are at full liberty to follow the counsel of Jesus Christ as to observing virginity, or to bind themselves by the marriage tie. No human law can abolish the natural and original right of marriage, nor in any way limit the chief and principal purpose of marriage ordained by God's authority from the beginning: "Increase and multiply."[15] Hence, we have the family, the "society" of a man's house—a society very small, one must admit, but nonetheless a true society, and one older than any State.[16] Consequently, it has rights and duties peculiar to itself which are quite independent of the State.

13. That right to property, therefore, which has been proved to belong naturally to individual persons, must in like wise belong to a man in his capacity of head of a family; nay, that right is all the stronger in proportion as the human person receives a wider extension in the family group. It is a most sacred law of

---

13   L. *non ancillam* (only). — NC. nor his maid-servant. — Deut. 5:21: "nor his manservant, nor his maidservant."
14   Deut. 5:21.
15   Gen. 1:28.
16   L. *omni civitate*. — P. anterior to every kind of State or nation. — NC. older than any polity.

nature that a father should provide food and all necessaries for those whom he has begotten; and, similarly, it is natural that he should wish that his children, who carry on, so to speak, and continue his personality, should be by him provided with all that is needful to enable them to keep themselves decently from want and misery amid the uncertainties of this mortal life. Now, in no other way can a father effect this except by the ownership of productive property, which he can transmit to his children by inheritance. A family, no less than a State, is, as We have said, a true society, governed by an authority peculiar to itself, that is to say, by the authority of the father. Provided, therefore, the limits which are prescribed by the very purposes for which it exists be not transgressed, the family has at least equal rights with the State in the choice and pursuit of the things needful to its preservation and its just liberty.[17] We say, "at least equal rights"; for, inasmuch as the domestic household is antecedent, as well in idea as in fact, to the gathering of men into a community, the family must necessarily have rights and duties which are prior to those of the community, and founded more immediately in nature. If the citizens, if the families on entering into association and fellowship, were to experience hindrance in a commonwealth instead of help, and were to find their rights attacked instead of being upheld, society would rightly be an object of detestation rather than of desire.[18]

14. The contention, then, that the civil government should at its option intrude into and exercise intimate control over the family and the household is a great and pernicious error. True, if a family finds itself in exceeding distress, utterly deprived of the counsel of friends, and without any prospect of extricating itself, it is right that extreme necessity be met by public aid,

---

17   L. *cum societate civili.* — P. with the State. — NC. with those of civil society.
18   The London text translates as follows: If the citizens of the State, if the families, on entering into association and fellowship, were to experience at the hands of the State hindrance instead of help, and were to find their rights attacked instead of being upheld, that association [vis., the State] would rightly be an object of detestation, rather than of desire.

since each family is a part of the commonwealth. In like manner, if within the precincts of the household there occur grave disturbance of mutual rights, public authority should intervene to force each party to yield to the other its proper due; for this is not to deprive citizens of their rights, but justly and properly to safeguard and strengthen them.

But, the rulers of the commonwealth must go no further;[19] here, nature bids them stop. Paternal authority can be neither abolished nor absorbed by the State;[20] for it has the same source as human life itself. "The child belongs to the father," and is, as it were, the continuation of the father's personality; and speaking strictly, the child takes its place in civil society, not of its own right, but in its quality as member of the family in which it is born. And for the very reason that "the child belongs to the father"[21] it is, as St. Thomas Aquinas says, "before it attains the use of free will, under the power and the charge of its parents."[22] The socialists, therefore, in setting aside the parent and setting up a State supervision,[23] act against natural justice, and destroy the structure of the home.[24]

15. And in addition to injustice, it is only too evident what an upset and disturbance there would be in all classes, and to how intolerable and hateful a slavery citizens would be subjected. The door would be thrown open to envy, to mutual invective, and to discord; the sources of wealth themselves would run dry, for no one would have any interest in exerting his talents or his industry; and that ideal equality about which they entertain

---

19   L. *qui praesint rebus publicis.*
20   L. *a republica.*
21   L. *filii sunt aliquid patris.* — P. the child belongs to the father. — H. children are in some way part of the father. — NC. children are a part of their father.
22   *Summa theologiae,* IIa-IIae, q. x, art. 12, Answer.
23   L. *quod igitur Socialistae, posthabita providentia parentum, introducunt providentiam reipublicae*; that is, that the socialists substitute care by the commonwealth for care by the parents.
24   L. *ac domorum compaginem dissolvunt.* — The London translation says: and break into pieces the stability of all family life. — P. and threaten the very existence of family life.

pleasant dreams would be in reality the leveling down of all to a like condition of misery and degradation.

Hence, it is clear that the main tenet of socialism, community of goods, must be utterly rejected, since it only injures those whom it would seem meant to benefit, is directly contrary to the natural rights of mankind, and would introduce confusion and disorder into the commonweal. The first and most fundamental principle, therefore, if one would undertake to alleviate the condition of the masses, must be the inviolability of private property. This being established, we proceed to show where the remedy sought for must be found.

16. We approach the subject with confidence, and in the exercise of the rights which manifestly appertain to Us, for no practical solution of this question will be found apart from the intervention of religion and of the Church. It is We who are the chief guardian of religion and the chief dispenser of what pertains to the Church; and by keeping silence, we would seem to neglect the duty incumbent on us. Doubtless, this most serious question demands the attention and the efforts of others besides ourselves—to wit, of the rulers of States,[25] of employers of labor, of the wealthy, aye, of the working classes themselves, for whom We are pleading. But We affirm without hesitation that all the striving of men will be vain if they leave out the Church. It is the Church that insists, on the authority of the Gospel, upon those teachings whereby the conflict can be brought to an end, or rendered, at least, far less bitter; the Church uses her efforts not only to enlighten the mind, but to direct by her precepts the life and conduct of each and all; the Church improves and betters the condition of the working man by means of numerous organizations; does her best to enlist the services of all classes in discussing and endeavoring to further in the most practical way, the interests of the working classes; and considers that for this purpose recourse should be had, in due measure and degree, to the intervention of the law and of State authority.[26]

---

25 L. *principum reipublicae.*
26 L. *auctoritatemque reipublicae*; that is, and the authority of the commonwealth.

17. It must be first of all recognized that the condition of things inherent in human affairs must be borne with, for it is impossible to reduce civil society to one dead level. Socialists may in that intent do their utmost, but all striving against nature is in vain. There naturally exist among mankind manifold differences of the most important kind; people differ in capacity, skill, health, strength; and unequal fortune is a necessary result of unequal condition. Such inequality is far from being disadvantageous either to individuals or to the community. Social and public life can only be maintained by means of various kinds of capacity for business and the playing of many parts; and each man, as a rule, chooses the part which suits his own peculiar domestic condition. As regards bodily labor, even had man never fallen from the state of innocence, he would not have remained wholly idle; but that which would then have been his free choice and his delight became afterwards compulsory, and the painful expiation for his disobedience. "Cursed be the earth in thy work; in thy labor thou shalt eat of it all the days of thy life."[27]

18. In like manner, the other pains and hardships of life will have no end or cessation on earth; for the consequences of sin are bitter and hard to bear, and they must accompany man so long as life lasts. To suffer and to endure, therefore, is the lot of humanity; let them strive as they may, no strength and no artifice will ever succeed in banishing from human life the ills and troubles which beset it. If any there are who pretend differently — who hold out to a hard-pressed people the boon of freedom from pain and trouble, an undisturbed repose, and constant enjoyment — they delude the people and impose upon them, and their lying promises will only one day bring forth evils worse than the present. Nothing is more useful than to look upon the world as it really is, and at the same time to seek elsewhere, as We have said, for the solace to its troubles.

19. The great mistake made in regard to the matter now under consideration is to take up with the notion that class is naturally

---

27 Gen. 3:17.

On Capital and Labor

hostile to class, and that the wealthy and the working men[28] are intended by nature to live in mutual conflict. So irrational and so false is this view that the direct contrary is the truth. Just as the symmetry of the human frame is the result of the suitable arrangement of the different parts of the body, so in a State[29] is it ordained by nature that these two classes should dwell in harmony and agreement, so as to maintain the balance of the body politic. Each needs the other: capital cannot do without labor, nor labor without capital.[30] Mutual agreement results in the beauty of good order,[31] while perpetual conflict necessarily produces confusion and savage barbarity. Now, in preventing such strife as this, and in uprooting it, the efficacy of Christian institutions is marvelous and manifold. First of all, there is no intermediary more powerful than religion (whereof the Church is the interpreter and guardian) in drawing the rich and the working class[32] together, by reminding each of its duties to the other, and especially of the obligations of justice.

20. Of these duties, the following bind the proletarian and the worker: fully and faithfully to perform the work which has been freely and equitably agreed upon; never to injure the property, nor to outrage the person, of an employer; never to resort to violence in defending their own cause, nor to engage in riot or disorder; and to have nothing to do with men of evil principles, who work upon the people with artful promises of great results, and excite foolish hopes, which usually end in useless regrets and grievous loss. The following duties bind the wealthy owner and the employer: not to look upon their workers as their bondsmen, but to respect in every man his dignity as a person ennobled by Christian character.[33] They are reminded that, according to

---

28 L. *proletarios*; that is, the proletariat.
29 L. *in civitate*; that is, in a body politic.
30 L. *non res sine opera, nec sine re potest opera consistere.*—Note that the Latin word res has a wider meaning than the modern word *capital*.
31 NC. concord begets beauty and order in things.
32 L. *proletarios*; that is, the proletarians.
33 L. *dignitatem personae utique nobilitatam ab eo, character christianus qui dicitur.*—P. and H. to respect in every man his dignity as a man and

natural reason and Christian philosophy, working for gain is creditable, not shameful, to a man, since it enables him to earn an honorable livelihood; but to misuse men as though they were things in the pursuit of gain, or to value them solely for their physical powers—that is truly shameful and inhuman. Again, justice demands that, in dealing with the working man, religion and the good of his soul must be kept in mind. Hence, the employer is bound to see that the worker has time for his religious duties; that he be not exposed to corrupting influences and dangerous occasions; and that he be not led away to neglect his home and family, or to squander his earnings.[34] Furthermore, the employer must never tax his workers beyond their strength, or employ them in work unsuited to their sex and age. His great and principal duty is to give everyone what is just. Doubtless, before deciding whether wages are fair, many things have to be considered; but wealthy owners and all masters of labor should be mindful of this—that to exercise pressure upon the indigent and the destitute for the sake of gain, and to gather one's profit out of the need of another, is condemned by all laws, human and divine. To defraud any one of wages that are his due is a great crime which cries to the avenging anger of Heaven. "Behold, the hire of the laborers...which by fraud has been kept back by you, crieth; and the cry of them hath entered into the ears of the Lord of Sabbath."[35] Lastly, the rich must religiously refrain from cutting down the workmen's[36] earnings, whether by force, by fraud, or by usurious dealing; and with all the greater reason because the laboring man is, as a rule, weak and unprotected, and because his slender means should in proportion to their scantiness be accounted sacred.

Were these precepts carefully obeyed and followed out, would they not be sufficient of themselves to keep under all strife and all its causes?

---

as a Christian.—NC. the dignity of human personality...ennobled as it has been through what we call the Christian character.
34   L. *parcimoniaeaque studio.*—NC. the practice of thrift.
35   James 5:4.
36   L. *proletariorum*; that is, of the proletarians.

21. But the Church, with Jesus Christ as her Master and Guide, aims higher still. She lays down precepts yet more perfect, and tries to bind class to class in friendliness and good feeling. The things of earth cannot be understood or valued aright without taking into consideration the life to come, the life that will know no death. Exclude the idea of futurity, and forthwith the very notion of what is good and right would perish; nay, the whole scheme of the universe would become a dark and unfathomable mystery. The great truth which we learn from nature herself is also the grand Christian dogma on which religion rests as on its foundation—that, when we have given up this present life, then shall we really begin to live. God has not created us for the perishable and transitory things of earth, but for things heavenly and everlasting; He has given us this world as a place of exile, and not as our abiding place. As for riches and the other things which men call good and desirable, whether we have them in abundance, or are lacking in them—so far as eternal happiness is concerned—it makes no difference; the only important thing is to use them aright. Jesus Christ, when He redeemed us with plentiful redemption, took not away the pains and sorrows which in such large proportion are woven together in the web of our mortal life. He transformed them into motives of virtue and occasions of merit; and no man can hope for eternal reward unless he follow in the blood-stained footprints of his Savior. "If we suffer with Him, we shall also reign with Him."[37] Christ's labors and sufferings, accepted of His own free will, have marvellously sweetened all suffering and all labor. And not only by His example, but by His grace and by the hope held forth of everlasting recompense, has He made pain and grief more easy to endure; "for that which is at present momentary and light of our tribulation, worketh for us above measure exceedingly an eternal weight of glory."[38]

22. Therefore, those whom fortune favors are warned that riches do not bring freedom from sorrow and are of no avail

---

37 2 Tim. 2:12.
38 2 Cor. 4:17.

for eternal happiness, but rather are obstacles;[39] that the rich should tremble at the threatenings of Jesus Christ—threatenings so unwonted in the mouth of our Lord[40]—and that a most strict account must be given to the Supreme Judge for all we possess. The chief and most excellent rule for the right use of money is one the heathen philosophers hinted at, but which the Church has traced out clearly, and has not only made known to men's minds, but has impressed upon their lives. It rests on the principle that it is one thing to have a right to the possession of money and another to have a right to use money as one wills. Private ownership, as we have seen, is the natural right of man, and to exercise that right, especially as members of society, is not only lawful, but absolutely necessary. "It is lawful," says St. Thomas Aquinas, "for a man to hold private property; and it is also necessary for the carrying on of human existence."[41] But if the question be asked: How must one's possessions be used?—the Church replies without hesitation in the words of the same holy Doctor: "Man should not consider his material possessions as his own, but as common to all, so as to share them without hesitation when others are in need. Whence the apostle saith, 'Command the rich of this world to offer with no stint, to apportion largely.'"[42] True, no one is commanded to distribute to others that which is required for his own needs and those of his household; nor even to give away what is reasonably required to keep up becomingly his condition in life, "for no one ought to live other than becomingly."[43] But, when what necessity demands has been supplied, and one's standing fairly taken thought for, it becomes a duty to give to the indigent out of what remains over. "Of that which remaineth, give alms."[44] It is a duty, not of justice (save in extreme cases), but of Christian charity—a duty not enforced by human law. But

---

39 Matt. 19:23–24.
40 Luke 6:24–25.
41 *Summa theologiae*, IIa-IIae, q. lxvi, art. 2, answer.
42 Ibid.
43 Ibid., q. xxxii, a. 6, answer.
44 Luke 11:41.

the laws and judgments of men must yield place to the laws and judgments of Christ the true God, who in many ways urges on His followers the practice of almsgiving—"It is more blessed to give than to receive";[45] and who will count a kindness done or refused to the poor as done or refused to Himself—"As long as you did it to one of My least brethren you did it to Me."[46] To sum up, then, what has been said: Whoever has received from the divine bounty a large share of temporal blessings, whether they be external and material, or gifts of the mind, has received them for the purpose of using them for the perfecting of his own nature, and, at the same time, that he may employ them, as the steward of God's providence, for the benefit of others. "He that hath a talent," said St. Gregory the Great, "let him see that he hide it not; he that hath abundance, let him quicken himself to mercy and generosity; he that hath art and skill, let him do his best to share the use and the utility hereof with his neighbor."[47]

23. As for those who possess not the gifts of fortune, they are taught by the Church that in God's sight poverty is no disgrace, and that there is nothing to be ashamed of in earning their bread by labor. This is enforced by what we see in Christ Himself, who, "whereas He was rich, for our sakes became poor;"[48] and who, being the Son of God, and God Himself, chose to seem and to be considered the son of a carpenter—nay, did not disdain to spend a great part of His life as a carpenter Himself. "Is not this the carpenter, the son of Mary?"[49]

24. From contemplation of this divine Model, it is more easy to understand that the true worth and nobility of man lie in his moral qualities, that is, in virtue; that virtue is, moreover, the common inheritance of men, equally within the reach of high and low, rich and poor;[50] and that virtue, and virtue alone,

---

45 Acts 20:35.
46 Matt. 25:40.
47 *Hom. in Evang.*, 9, n. 7 (PL 76, 1109B).
48 2 Cor. 8:9.
49 Mark 6:3.
50 L. *divitibus et proletariis*; that is, the rich and the proletarians.

wherever found, will be followed by the rewards of everlasting happiness. Nay, God Himself seems to incline rather to those who suffer misfortune; for Jesus Christ calls the poor "blessed;"[51] He lovingly invites those in labor and grief to come to Him for solace;[52] and He displays the tenderest charity toward the lowly and the oppressed. These reflections cannot fail to keep down the pride of the well-to-do, and to give heart to the unfortunate; to move the former to be generous and the latter to be moderate in their desires. Thus, the separation which pride would set up tends to disappear, nor will it be difficult to make rich and poor[53] join hands in friendly concord.

25. But, if Christian precepts prevail, the respective classes will not only be united in the bonds of friendship, but also in those of brotherly love. For they will understand and feel that all men are children of the same common Father, who is God; that all have alike the same last end, which is God Himself, who alone can make either men or angels absolutely and perfectly happy; that each and all are redeemed and made sons of God, by Jesus Christ, "the first-born among many brethren"; that the blessings of nature and the gifts of grace belong to the whole human race in common, and that from none except the unworthy is withheld the inheritance of the kingdom of Heaven. "If sons, heirs also; heirs indeed of God, and co-heirs with Christ."[54]

Such is the scheme of duties and of rights which is shown forth to the world by the Gospel. Would it not seem that, were society penetrated with ideas like these, strife must quickly cease?

26. But the Church, not content with pointing out the remedy, also applies it. For the Church does her utmost to teach and to train men, and to educate them and by the intermediary of her bishops and clergy diffuses her salutary teachings far and

---

51   Matt. 5:3.
52   Matt. 11:28.
53   L. *ut ordinis utriusque, junctis amice dextris, copulentur voluntates.* — NC. that the two classes, with hands clasped in friendship, will be united in heart.
54   Rom. 8:17.

wide. She strives to influence the mind and the heart so that all may willingly yield themselves to be formed and guided by the commandments of God. It is precisely in this fundamental and momentous matter, on which everything depends that the Church possesses a power peculiarly her own. The instruments[55] which she employs are given to her by Jesus Christ Himself for the very purpose of reaching the hearts of men, and drive their efficiency from God. They alone can reach the innermost heart and conscience, and bring men to act from a motive of duty, to control their passions and appetites, to love God and their fellow men with a love that is outstanding and of the highest degree and to break down courageously every barrier which blocks the way to virtue.

27. On this subject we need but recall for one moment the examples recorded in history. Of these facts, there cannot be any shadow of doubt: for instance, that civil society was renovated in every part by Christian institutions;[56] that in the strength of that renewal the human race was lifted up to better things—nay, that it was brought back from death to life, and to so excellent a life that nothing more perfect had been known before, or will come to be known in the ages that have yet to be. Of this beneficent transformation, Jesus Christ was at once the first cause and the final end; as from Him all came, so to Him was all to be brought back. For, when the human race, by the light of the Gospel message, came to know the grand mystery of the Incarnation of the Word and the redemption of man, at once the life of Jesus Christ, God and Man, pervaded every race and nation, and interpenetrated them with His faith, His precepts, and His laws. And if human society[57] is to be healed now, in no other way can it be healed save by a return to Christian life and Christian institutions. When a society is perishing, the

---

55   L. *instrumentis.*—P. agencies.
56   L. *institutis christianis.*—P. by the teachings of Christianity.—NC. (rightly) by Christian institutions.
57   L. *quare si societati generis humani*; that is, the society made up by all those who belong in the human race.

wholesome advice to give to those who would restore it is to call it to the principles from which it sprang; for the purpose and perfection of an association is to aim at and to attain that for which it is formed, and its efforts should be put in motion and inspired by the end and object which originally gave it being. Hence, to fall away from its primal constitution implies disease; to go back to it, recovery. And this may be asserted with utmost truth both of the whole body of the commonwealth and of that class of its citizens[58]—by far the great majority—who get their living by their labor.

28. Neither must it be supposed that the solicitude of the Church is so preoccupied with the spiritual concerns of her children as to neglect their temporal and earthly interests. Her desire is that the poor,[59] for example, should rise above poverty and wretchedness, and better their condition in life; and for this, she makes a strong endeavor. By the fact that she calls men to virtue and forms them to its practice, she promotes this in no slight degree. Christian morality, when adequately and completely practiced, leads of itself to temporal prosperity, for it merits the blessing of that God who is the source of all blessings; it powerfully restrains the greed of possession and the thirst for pleasure—twin plagues, which too often make a man who is void of self-restraint miserable in the midst of abundance;[60] it makes men supply for the lack of means through economy, teaching them to be content with frugal living, and further, keeping them out of the reach of those vices which devour not small incomes merely, but large fortunes, and dissipate many a goodly inheritance.

---

58 L. *quemadmodum de toto reipublicae corpore, eodem modo de illo ordine civium.*—NC. translates *ordine* by "order" rather than by "class," which may be a useful precaution in view of avoiding some modern connotations of the word "class." An "order" is nothing else than the economic and social level at which each one of us happens to find himself placed.
59 L. *de proletaries nominatim vult et contendit*; that is, concerning the proletarians, in particular, the Church desires and strives, etc.
60 1 Tim. 6:10.

29. The Church, moreover, intervenes directly on behalf of the poor,[61] by setting on foot and maintaining many associations which she knows to be efficient for the relief of poverty. Herein, again, she has always succeeded so well as to have even extorted the praise of her enemies. Such was the ardor of brotherly love among the earliest Christians that numbers of those who were in better circumstances despoiled themselves of their possessions in order to relieve their brethren; whence, "neither was there any one needy among them."[62] To the order of deacons, instituted in that very intent, was committed by the Apostles the charge of the daily doles; and the Apostle Paul, though burdened with the solicitude of all the churches, hesitated not to undertake laborious journeys in order to carry the alms of the faithful to the poorer Christians. Tertullian calls these contributions, given voluntarily by Christians in their assemblies, deposits of piety,[63] because, to cite his own words, they were employed "in feeding the needy, in burying them, in support of youths and maidens destitute of means and deprived of their parents, in the care of the aged, and the relief of the shipwrecked."[64]

30. Thus, by degrees, came into existence the patrimony which the Church has guarded with religious care as the inheritance of the poor.[65] Nay, in order to spare them the shame of begging, the Church has provided aid for the needy. The common Mother of rich and poor has aroused everywhere the heroism of charity, and has established congregations of religious and many other useful institutions for help and mercy, so that hardly any kind of suffering could exist which was not afforded relief. At the present day many there are who, like the heathen of old, seek to blame and condemn the Church for such eminent charity. They would substitute in its stead a system of relief organized by the State. But no human expedients will ever make up for the

---

61   L. *ut bene habeant proletarii*; that is, for the well-being of the proletarians.—P. the poor.—NC. the non-owning workers.
62   Acts 4:34.
63   L. *deposita pietatis*.—NC. piety's deposit fund.
64   *Apologia secunda*, 39, (*Apologeticus*, cap. 39; PLI, 533A).
65   L. *indigentium*; that is, the needy ones.

devotedness and self-sacrifice of Christian charity. Charity, as a virtue, pertains to the Church; for virtue, it is not, unless it be drawn from the Most Sacred Heart of Jesus Christ; and whosoever turns his back on the Church cannot be near to Christ.[66]

31. It cannot, however, be doubted that to attain the purpose we are treating of, not only the Church, but all human agencies, must concur. All who are concerned in the matter should be of one mind and according to their ability act together. It is with this, as with providence that governs the world; the results of causes do not usually take place save where all the causes cooperate.

It is sufficient, therefore, to inquire what part the State[67] should play in the work of remedy and relief.

32. By the State[68] we here understand, not the particular form of government prevailing in this or that nation, but the State as rightly apprehended; that is to say, any government conformable in its institutions to right reason and natural law, and to those dictates of the divine wisdom which we have expounded in the encyclical *On the Christian Constitution of the State*.[69] The foremost duty, therefore, of the rulers of the State[70] should be to make sure that the laws and institutions, the general character and administration of the commonwealth, shall be such as of themselves to realize public well-being and private prosperity. This is the proper scope of wise statesmanship[71] and is the work of the rulers. Now a State[72] chiefly prospers and thrives through

---

66 L. *vagatur autem a Christo longius, quicumque ab Ecclesia discesserit.* — NC. and whosoever departs from the Church wanders far from Christ.
67 L. *rempublicam hoc loco intelligimus non quali populus utitur unus et alter.* — In this passage, *respublica* means "form of government"; literally: by *respublica* we here understand, not the particular form of government, etc.
68 L. *a republica.*
69 L. *de civitatum constitutione christiana*; that is, on the Christian constitution of body politics.
70 L. *civitas.*
71 L. *Id est enim civilis prudentiae munus*; that is, This is the function of the virtue of political prudence.
72 L. *civitates.*

moral rule, well-regulated family life, respect for religion and justice, the moderation and fair imposing of public taxes, the progress of the arts and of trade, the abundant yield of the land—through everything, in fact, which makes the citizens better and happier. Hereby, then, it lies in the power of a ruler to benefit every class in the State, and amongst the rest to promote to the utmost the interests of the poor;[73] and this in virtue of his office, and without being open to suspicion of undue interference—since it is the province of the commonwealth to serve the common good. And the more that is done for the benefit of the working classes by the general laws of the country, the less need will there be to seek for special means to relieve them.

33. There is another and deeper consideration that must not be lost sight of. As regards the State,[74] the interests of all, whether high or low, are equal. The members of the working classes[75] are citizens by nature and by the same right as the rich; they are real parts, living the life which makes up, through the family, the body of the commonwealth;[76] and it need hardly be said that they are in every city[77] very largely in the majority. It would be irrational to neglect one portion of the citizens and favor another, and therefore, the public administration must duly and solicitously provide for the welfare and the comfort of the working classes;[78] otherwise, that law of justice will be violated which ordains that each man shall have his due. To cite the wise words of St. Thomas Aquinas: "As the part and the whole are in a certain sense identical, so that which belongs to the whole in a sense belongs to the part."[79] Among the many and grave duties of rulers who would do their best for the people, the first

---

73 L. *proletariorum*; that is, of the proletarians.
74 L. *civitatis*.
75 L. *proletarii*; that is, the proletarians.
76 L. *Sunt nimirum proletarii pari jure cum locupletibus natura cives, hoc est partes verae vitamque viventes, unde constat, interjectis familiis, corpus reipublicae.*
77 L. *in omni urbe.*
78 L. *ordinis proletariorum*; that is, of the proletariat.
79 *Summa theologiae*, IIa-IIae, q. lxi, art. 1, ad 2m.

and chief is to act with strict justice—with that justice which is called distributive—toward each and every class alike.

34. But although all citizens, without exception, can and ought to contribute to that common good in which individuals share so advantageously to themselves, yet it should not be supposed that all can contribute in the like way and to the same extent. No matter what changes may occur in forms of government, there will ever be differences and inequalities of condition in the State. Society cannot exist or be conceived of without them. Some there must be who devote themselves to the work of the commonwealth, who make the laws or administer justice, or whose advice and authority govern the nation in times of peace, and defend it in war. Such men clearly occupy the foremost place in the State, and should be held in highest estimation, for their work concerns most nearly and effectively the general interests of the community. Those who labor at a trade or calling do not promote the general welfare in such measure as this, but they benefit the nation, if less directly, in a most important manner. We have insisted, it is true, that, since the end of society is to make men better, the chief good that society can possess is virtue. Nevertheless, it is the business of a well-constituted body politic to see to the provision of those material and external helps "the use of which is necessary to virtuous action."[80] Now, for the provision of such commodities, the labor of the working class[81]—the exercise of their skill, and the employment of their strength, in the cultivation of the land, and in the workshops of trade—is especially responsible and quite indispensable. Indeed, their co-operation is in this respect so important that it may be truly said that it is only by the labor of working men that States grow rich. Justice, therefore, demands that the interests of the working classes should be carefully watched over by the administration, so that they who contribute so largely to the advantage of the community may themselves share in the benefits which

---

80 Thomas Aquinas, *On the Governance of Rulers*, I, 15 (*Opera omnia*, ed. Vives, Vol. 27, p. 356).
81 L. *ordinis proletariorum*; that is, of the proletariat.

they create—that being housed, clothed, and bodily fit, they may find their life less hard and more endurable. It follows that whatever shall appear to prove conducive to the well-being of those who work should obtain favorable consideration. There is no fear that solicitude of this kind will be harmful to any interest; on the contrary, it will be to the advantage of all, for it cannot but be good for the commonwealth to shield from misery those on whom it so largely depends for the things that it needs.

35. We have said that the State must not absorb the individual or the family; both should be allowed free and untrammeled action so far as is consistent with the common good and the interest of others. Rulers should, nevertheless, anxiously safeguard the community and all its members; the community, because the conservation thereof is so emphatically the business of the supreme power, that the safety of the commonwealth is not only the first law, but it is a government's whole reason of existence; and the members, because both philosophy and the Gospel concur in laying down that the object of the government of the State[82] should be, not the advantage of the ruler, but the benefit of those over whom he is placed. As the power to rule comes from God, and is, as it were, a participation in His, the highest of all sovereignties, it should be exercised as the power of God is exercised—with a fatherly solicitude which not only guides the whole, but reaches also individuals.

36. Whenever the general interest or any particular class suffers, or is threatened with harm, which can in no other way be met or prevented, the public authority must step in to deal with it. Now, it is to the interest of the community, as well as of the individual, that peace and good order should be maintained; that all things should be carried on in accordance with God's laws and those of nature; that the discipline of family life should be observed and that religion should be obeyed;[83] that a high standard of

---

82 L. *procurationem reipublicae*; that is, the administration of the commonwealth.
83 L. *omnem convictus domestici disciplinam observari et coli religionem.*

morality should prevail, both in public and private life; that justice should be held sacred and that no one should injure another with impunity; that the members of the commonwealth should grow up to man's estate strong and robust, and capable, if need be, of guarding and defending their country. If by a strike of workers or concerted interruption of work there should be imminent danger of disturbance to the public peace; or if circumstances were such as that among the working class the ties of family life were relaxed; if religion were found to suffer through the workers not having time and opportunity afforded them to practice its duties; if in workshops and factories there was danger to morals through the mixing of the sexes or from other harmful occasions of evil; or if employers laid burdens upon their workmen[84] which were unjust, or degraded them with conditions repugnant to their dignity as human beings; finally, if health were endangered by excessive labor, or by work unsuited to sex or age — in such cases, there can be no question but that, within certain limits, it would be right to invoke the aid and authority of the law. The limits must be determined by the nature of the occasion which calls for the law's interference — the principle being that the law must not undertake more, nor proceed further, than is required for the remedy of the evil or the removal of the mischief.

37. Rights must be religiously respected wherever they exist, and it is the duty of the public authority to prevent and to punish injury, and to protect every one in the possession of his own. Still, when there is question of defending the rights of individuals, the poor and badly off have a claim to especial consideration. The richer class have many ways of shielding themselves, and stand less in need of help from the State;[85] whereas the mass of the poor have no resources of their own to fall back upon, and must chiefly depend upon the assistance of the State. And it is for this reason that wage-earners, since they mostly belong in the mass of the needy, should be specially cared for and protected by the government.

---

84 L. *aut opificum ordinem herilis ordo iniquis premat oneribus.*
85 L. *minus eget tutela publica.* — NC. is in less need of governmental protection.

38. Here, however, it is expedient to bring under special notice certain matters of moment. First of all, there is the duty of safeguarding private property by legal enactment and protection. Most of all it is essential, where the passion of greed is so strong, to keep the populace[86] within the line of duty; for, if all may justly strive to better their condition, neither justice nor the common good allows any individual to seize upon that which belongs to another, or, under the futile and shallow pretext of equality, to lay violent hands on other people's possessions. Most true it is that by far the larger part of the workers prefers to better themselves by honest labor rather than by doing any wrong to others. But, there are not a few who are imbued with evil principles and eager for revolutionary change,[87] whose main purpose is to stir up disorder and incite their fellows to acts of violence. The authority of the law should intervene to put restraint upon such firebrands, to save the working classes from being led astray by their maneuvers, and to protect lawful owners from spoliation.

39. When workers have recourse to a strike and become voluntarily idle, it is frequently because the hours of labor are too long, or the work too hard, or because they consider their wages insufficient. The grave inconvenience of this not uncommon occurrence should be obviated by public remedial measures; for such paralyzing of labor not only affects the masters and their workers alike, but is extremely injurious to trade and to the general interests of the public; moreover, on such occasions, violence and disorder are generally not far distant; and thus, it frequently happens that the public peace is imperiled. The laws should forestall and prevent such troubles from arising; they should lend their influence and authority to the removal in good time of the causes, which lead to conflicts between employers and employed.

40. The working man, too, has interests in which he should be protected by the State; and first of all, there are the interests

---

86   L. *plebs.*—London text: the people.—NC. the masses.
87   L. *rerumque novarum cupidi.*—NC. eager for revolution.

of his soul. Life on earth, however good and desirable in itself, is not the final purpose for which man is created; it is only the way and the means to that attainment of truth and that love of goodness in which the full life of the soul consists. It is the soul which is made after the image and likeness of God; it is in the soul that the sovereignty resides in virtue whereof man is commanded to rule the creatures below him and to use all the earth and the ocean for his profit and advantage. "Fill the earth and subdue it; and rule over the fishes of the sea, and the fowls of the air, and all living creatures that move upon the earth."[88] In this respect, all men are equal; there is here no difference between rich and poor, master and servant, ruler and ruled, "for the same is Lord over all."[89] No man may with impunity outrage that human dignity which God Himself treats with great reverence, nor stand in the way of that higher life which is the preparation of the eternal life of heaven. Nay, more; no man has in this matter power over himself. To consent to any treatment which is calculated to defeat the end and purpose of his being is beyond his right; he cannot give up his soul to servitude, for it is not man's own rights which are here in question, but the rights of God, the most sacred and inviolable of rights.

41. From this follows the obligation of the cessation from work and labor on Sundays and certain holy days. The rest from labor is not to be understood as mere giving way to idleness; much less must it be an occasion for spending money and for vicious indulgence, as many would have it to be; but it should be rest from labor, hallowed by religion. Rest (combined with religious observances) disposes man to forget for a while the business of his everyday life, to turn his thoughts to things heavenly, and to the worship which he so strictly owes to the eternal Godhead. It is this, above all, which is the reason and motive of Sunday rest; a rest sanctioned by God's great law of the Ancient Covenant—"Remember thou keep holy the Sabbath day,"[90] and

---

88 Gen. 1:28.
89 Rom. 10:12.
90 Exod. 20:8.

taught to the world by His own mysterious "rest" after the creation of man: "He rested on the seventh day from all His work which He had done."[91]

42. If we turn not to things external and material, the first thing of all to secure is to save unfortunate working people from the cruelty of men of greed, who use human beings as mere instruments for money-making. It is neither just nor human so to grind men down with excessive labor as to stupefy their minds and wear out their bodies. Man's powers, like his general nature, are limited, and beyond these limits, he cannot go. His strength is developed and increased by use and exercise, but only on condition of due intermission and proper rest. Daily labor, therefore, should be so regulated as not to be protracted over longer hours than strength admits. How many and how long the intervals of rest should be must depend on the nature of the work, on circumstances of time and place, and on the health and strength of the workman. Those who work in mines and quarries, and extract coal, stone and metals from the bowels of the earth, should have shorter hours in proportion as their labor is more severe and trying to health. Then, again, the season of the year should be taken into account; for not infrequently a kind of labor is easy at one time, which at another is intolerable or exceedingly difficult. Finally, work which is quite suitable for a strong man cannot rightly be required from a woman or a child. And, in regard to children, great care should be taken not to place them in workshops and factories until their bodies and minds are sufficiently developed. For, just as very rough weather destroys the buds of spring, so does too early an experience of life's hard toil blight the young promise of a child's faculties, and render any true education impossible. Women, again, are not suited for certain occupations; a woman is by nature fitted for home-work, and it is that which is best adapted at once to preserve her modesty and to promote the good bringing up of children and the well-being of the family. As a general principle, it may be laid down that a workman ought to have leisure

---

91 Gen. 2:2.

and rest proportionate to the wear and tear of his strength, for waste of strength must be repaired by cessation from hard work.

In all agreements between masters and workers, there is always the condition expressed or understood that there should be allowed proper rest for soul and body. To agree in any other sense would be against what is right and just; for it can never be just or right to require on the one side, or to promise on the other, the giving up of those duties which a man owes to his God and to himself.

43. We now approach a subject of great importance, and one in respect of which, if extremes are to be avoided, right notions are absolutely necessary. Wages, as we are told, are regulated by free consent, and therefore the employer, when he pays what was agreed upon, has done his part and seemingly is not called upon to do anything beyond. The only way, it is said, in which injustice might occur would be if the master refused to pay the whole of the wages, or if the workman should not complete the work undertaken; in such cases, the public authority should intervene, to see that each obtains his due, but not under any other circumstances.

44. To this kind of argument, a fair-minded man will not easily or entirely assent; it is not complete, for there are important considerations which it leaves out of account altogether. To labor is to exert oneself for the sake of procuring what is necessary for the various purposes of life, and chief of all for self-preservation. "In the sweat of thy face thou shalt eat bread."[92] Hence, a man's labor necessarily bears two notes or characters. First of all, it is personal, inasmuch as the force which acts is bound up with the personality and is the exclusive property of him who acts, and, further, was given to him for his advantage. Secondly, man's labor is necessary; for without the result of labor a man cannot live, and self-preservation is a law of nature, which it is wrong to disobey. Now, were we to consider labor merely in so far as it is personal, doubtless it would be within the workman's right

---

92 Gen. 3:19.

to accept any rate of wages whatsoever; for in the same way as he is free to work or not, so is he free to accept a small wage or even none at all. But our conclusion must be very different if, together with the personal element in a man's work, we consider the fact that work is also necessary for him to live: these two aspects of his work are separable in thought, but not in reality. The preservation of life is the bounden duty of one and all, and to be wanting therein is a crime. It necessarily follows that each one has a natural right to procure what is required in order to live, and the poor can procure that in no other way than by what they can earn through their work.

45. Let the working man and the employer make free agreements, and in particular, let them agree freely as to the wages; nevertheless, there underlies a dictate of natural justice more imperious and ancient[93] than any bargain between man and man, namely, that wages ought not to be insufficient to support a frugal and well-behaved wage-earner. If through necessity or fear of a worse evil the workman accepts harder conditions because an employer or contractor will afford him no better, he is made the victim of force and injustice. In these and similar questions, however — such as, for example, the hours of labor in different trades, the sanitary precautions to be observed in factories and workshops, etc. — in order to supersede undue interference on the part of the State,[94] especially as circumstances, times, and localities differ so widely, it is advisable that recourse be had to societies or boards[95] such as We shall mention presently, or to some other mode of safeguarding the interests of the wage-earners; the State[96] being appealed to, should circumstances require, for its sanction and protection.

---

93 L. *antiquius.* — Probably in the classical meaning of: more respectable, or venerable.
94 L. *ne magistratus inferat se importunius.* — NC. in order to avoid unwarranted governmental intervention.
95 L. *collegiorum.* — P. societies or boards. — NC. organizations.
96 L. *tutela presidioque reipublicae*; that is, the sanction and protection of public authority.

46. If a workman's wages be sufficient to enable him comfortably to support himself, his wife, and his children, he will find it easy, if he be a sensible man, to practice thrift, and he will not fail, by cutting down expenses, to put by some little savings and thus secure a modest source of income. Nature itself would urge him to this. We have seen that this great labor question cannot be solved save by assuming as a principle that private ownership must be held sacred and inviolable. The law, therefore, should favor ownership, and its policy should be to induce as many as possible of the people to become owners.

47. Many excellent results will follow from this; and, first of all, property will certainly become more equitably divided. For, the result of civil change and revolution has been to divide cities into two classes separated by a wide chasm. On the one side, there is the party which holds power because it holds wealth; which has in its grasp the whole of labor and trade; which manipulates for its own benefit and its own purposes all the sources of supply, and which is not without influence even in the administration of the commonwealth. On the other side, there is the needy and powerless multitude, sick and sore in spirit and ever ready for disturbance. If working people can be encouraged to look forward to obtaining a share in the land, the consequence will be that the gulf between vast wealth and sheer poverty will be bridged over, and the respective classes will be brought nearer to one another. A further consequence will result in the great abundance of the fruits of the earth. Men always work harder and more readily when they work on that which belongs to them; nay, they learn to love the very soil that yields in response to the labor of their hands, not only food to eat, but an abundance of good things for themselves and those that are dear to them. That such a spirit of willing labor would add to the produce of the earth and to the wealth of the community is self-evident. And a third advantage would spring from this: men would cling to the country in which they were born, for no one would exchange his country for a foreign land if his own afforded him the means of living a decent and happy life.

These three important benefits, however, can be reckoned on only provided that a man's means be not drained and exhausted by excessive taxation. The right to possess private property is derived from nature, not from man; and the State has the right to control its use in the interests of the public good alone, but by no means to absorb it altogether. The State would therefore be unjust and cruel if under the name of taxation it were to deprive the private owner of more than is fair.

48. In the last place, employers and workmen may of themselves effect much, in the matter We are treating, by means of such associations and organizations as afford opportune aid to those who are in distress, and which draw the two classes more closely together. Among these may be enumerated societies for mutual help; various benevolent foundations established by private persons to provide for the workman, and for his widow or his orphans, in case of sudden calamity, in sickness, and in the event of death; and institutions for the welfare of boys and girls, young people, and those more advanced in years.

49. The most important of all are workingmen's unions, for these virtually include all the rest. History attests to what excellent results were brought about by the artificers' guilds of olden times. They were the means of affording not only many advantages to the workmen, but in no small degree of promoting the advancement of art, as numerous monuments remain to bear witness. Such unions should be suited to the requirements of this our age—an age of wider education, of different habits, and of far more numerous requirements in daily life. It is gratifying to know that there are actually in existence not a few associations of this nature, consisting either of workmen alone, or of workmen and employers together, but it were greatly to be desired that they should become more numerous and more efficient. We have spoken of them more than once, yet it will be well to explain here how notably they are needed, to show that they exist of their own right, and what should be their organization and their mode of action.

50. The consciousness of his own weakness urges man to call in aid from without. We read in the pages of Holy Writ: "It is better that two should be together than one; for they have the advantage of their society. If one falls, he shall be supported by the other. Woe to him that is alone, for when he falleth he hath none to lift him up."[97] And further: "A brother that is helped by his brother is like a strong city."[98] It is this natural impulse which binds men together in civil society; and it is likewise this which leads them to join together in associations which are, it is true, lesser and not independent societies, but, nevertheless, real societies.

51. These lesser societies and the larger society[99] differ in many respects, because their immediate purpose and aim are different. Civil society exists for the common good, and hence is concerned with the interests of all in general, albeit with individual interests also in their due place and degree. It is therefore called a public society, because by its agency, as St. Thomas of Aquinas says, "Men establish relations in common with one another in the setting up of a commonwealth."[100] But, societies which are formed in the bosom of the commonwealth are styled private, and rightly so, since their immediate purpose is the private advantage of the associates. "Now, a private society," says St. Thomas again, "is one which is formed for the purpose of carrying out private objects; as when two or three enter into partnership with the view of trading in common."[101] Private societies, then, although they exist within the body politic, and are severally part of the commonwealth, cannot nevertheless be absolutely, and as such, prohibited by public authority. For, to enter into a "society" of this kind is the natural right of man; and the State has for its office to protect natural rights, not to destroy them; and, if it forbid its citizens to form associations, it

---

97 Eccle. 4:9–10.
98 Prov. 18:19.
99 That is, the commonwealth.
100 *Contra impugnantes Dei cultum et religionem*, Part 2, ch. 8 (*Opera omnia*, ed. Vives, Vol. 29, p. 16).
101 Ibid.

contradicts the very principle of its own existence, for both they and it exist in virtue of the like principle, namely, the natural tendency of man to dwell in society.

52. There are occasions, doubtless, when it is fitting that the law should intervene to prevent certain associations, as when men join together for purposes which are evidently bad, unlawful, or dangerous to the State. In such cases, public authority may justly forbid the formation of such associations, and may dissolve them if they already exist. But every precaution should be taken not to violate the rights of individuals and not to impose unreasonable regulations under pretense of public benefit. For laws only bind when they are in accordance with right reason, and, hence, with the eternal law of God.[102]

53. And here we are reminded of the confraternities, societies, and religious orders which have arisen by the Church's authority and the piety of Christian men. The annals of every nation down to our own days bear witness to what they have accomplished for the human race. It is indisputable that on grounds of reason alone such associations, being perfectly blameless in their objects, possess the sanction of the law of nature. In their religious aspect, they claim rightly to be responsible to the Church alone. The rulers of the State accordingly have no rights over them, nor can they claim any share in their control; on the contrary, it is the duty of the State to respect and cherish them, and, if need be, to defend them from attack. It is notorious that a very different course has been followed, more especially in our own times. In many places the State authorities[103] have laid violent hands on these communities, and committed manifold injustice against them; it has placed them under control of the civil law, taken away their rights as corporate bodies, and despoiled them of

---

102 "Human law is law only by virtue of its accordance with right reason; and thus it is manifest that it flows from the eternal law. And in so far as it deviates from right reason it is called an unjust law; in such case it is no law at all, but rather a species of violence." Thomas Aquinas, *Summa theologiae*, Ia-IIae, q. xciii, art. 3, ad. 2.
103 L. respublica.

their property, in such property the Church had her rights, each member of the body had his or her rights, and there were also the rights of those who had founded or endowed these communities for a definite purpose, and, furthermore, of those for whose benefit and assistance they had their being. Therefore, We cannot refrain from complaining of such spoliation as unjust and fraught with evil results; and with all the more reason do We complain because, at the very time when the law proclaims that association is free to all, We see that Catholic societies, however peaceful and useful, are hampered in every way, whereas the utmost liberty is conceded to individuals whose purposes are at once hurtful to religion and dangerous to the commonwealth.

54. Associations of every kind, and especially those of working men, are now far more common than heretofore. As regards many of these there is no need at present to inquire whence they spring, what are their objects, or what the means they imply. Now, there is a good deal of evidence in favor of the opinion that many of these societies are in the hands of secret leaders, and are managed on principles ill-according with Christianity and the public well-being; and that they do their utmost to get within their grasp the whole field of labor, and force working men either to join them or to starve. Under these circumstances, Christian working men must do one of two things: either join associations in which their religion will be exposed to peril, or form associations among themselves and unite their forces so as to shake off courageously the yoke of so unrighteous and intolerable an oppression. No one who does not wish to expose man's chief good to extreme risk will for a moment hesitate to say that the second alternative should, by all means, be adopted.

55. Those Catholics are worthy of all praise — and they are not a few — who, understanding what the times require, have striven, by various undertakings and endeavors, to better the condition of the working class[104] by rightful means. They have taken up the

---

104 L. proletarios. — P. the working people. — NC. the non-owning working class.

cause of the working man, and have spared no efforts to better the condition both of families and individuals; to infuse a spirit of equity into the mutual relations of employers and employed; to keep before the eyes of both classes the precepts of duty and the laws of the Gospel—that Gospel which, by inculcating self-restraint, keeps men within the bounds of moderation, and tends to establish harmony among the divergent interests and the various classes which compose the body politic. It is with such ends in view that we see men of eminence, meeting together for discussion, for the promotion of concerted action, and for practical work. Others, again, strive to unite working men of various grades into associations, help them with their advice and means, and enable them to obtain fitting and profitable employment. The bishops, on their part, bestow their ready goodwill and support; and with their approval and guidance many members of the clergy, both secular and regular, labor assiduously on behalf of the spiritual interest of the members of such associations. And there are not wanting Catholics blessed with affluence, who have, as it were, cast in their lot with the wage-earners, and who have spent large sums in founding and widely spreading benefit and insurance societies, by means of which the working man may without difficulty acquire through his labor not only many present advantages, but also the certainty of honorable support in days to come. How greatly such manifold and earnest activity has benefited the community at large is too well known to require Us to dwell upon it. We find therein grounds for most cheering hope in the future, provided always that the associations We have described continue to grow and spread, and are well and wisely administered. The State should watch over these societies of citizens banded together in accordance with their rights, but it should not thrust itself into their peculiar concerns and their organization, for things move and live by the spirit inspiring them, and may be killed by the rough grasp of a hand from without.

56. In order that an association may be carried on with unity of purpose and harmony of action, its administration and government should be firm and wise. All such societies, being free to

exist, have the further right to adopt such rules and organization as may best conduce to the attainment of their respective objects. We do not judge it possible to enter into minute particulars touching the subject of organization; this must depend on national character, on practice and experience, on the nature and aim of the work to be done, on the scope of the various trades and employments, and on other circumstances of fact and of time—all of which should be carefully considered.

57. To sum up, then, We may lay it down as a general and lasting law that working men's associations should be so organized and governed as to furnish the best and most suitable means for attaining what is aimed at, that is to say, for helping each individual member to better his condition to the utmost in body, soul, and property. It is clear that they must pay special and chief attention to the duties of religion and morality, and that social betterment should have this chiefly in view; otherwise, they would lose wholly their special character, and end by becoming little better than those societies which take no account whatever of religion. What advantage can it be to a working man to obtain by means of a society material well-being, if he endangers his soul for lack of spiritual food? "What doth it profit a man, if he gain the whole world and suffer the loss of his soul?"[105] This, as our Lord teaches, is the mark or character that distinguishes the Christian from the heathen. "After all these things do the heathen seek... Seek ye first the Kingdom of God and His justice: and all these things shall be added unto you."[106] Let our associations, then, look first and before all things to God; let religious instruction[107] have therein the foremost place, each one being carefully taught what is his duty to God, what he has to believe, what to hope for, and how he is to work out his salvation; and let all be warned and strengthened with special care against wrong principles and false

---

105 Matt. 16:26.
106 Matt. 6:32–33.
107 L. *eruditioni religiosae*; that is, religious education. The Latin root *eruditio* points out a teaching intended for beginners, while *instructio* designates advanced studies.

teaching. Let the working man be urged and led to the worship of God, to the earnest practice of religion, and, among other things, to the keeping holy of Sundays and holy days. Let him learn to reverence and love holy Church, the common Mother of us all; and hence, to obey the precepts of the Church, and to frequent the sacraments, since they are the means ordained by God for obtaining forgiveness of sin and for leading a holy life.

58. The foundations of the organization being thus laid in religion, We next proceed to make clear the relations of the members one to another, in order that they may live together in concord and go forward prosperously and with good results. The offices and charges of the society should be apportioned for the good of the society itself, and in such mode, that difference in degree or standing should not interfere with unanimity and goodwill. It is most important that office bearers be appointed with due prudence and discretion, and each one's charge carefully mapped out, in order that no members may suffer harm. The common funds must be administered with strict honesty, in such a way that a member may receive assistance in proportion to his necessities. The rights and duties of the employers, as compared with the rights and duties of the employed, ought to be the subject of careful consideration. Should it happen that either a master or a workman believes himself injured, nothing would be more desirable than that a committee should be appointed, composed of reliable and capable members of the association, whose duty would be, conformably with the rules of the association, to settle the dispute. Among the several purposes of a society, one should be to try to arrange for a continuous supply of work at all times and seasons; as well as to create a fund out of which the members may be effectually helped in their needs, not only in the cases of accident, but also in sickness, old age, and distress.

59. Such rules and regulations, if willingly obeyed by all, will sufficiently ensure the well-being of the less well-to-do;[108] whilst such mutual associations among Catholics are certain to be

---

108 L. *tenuiorum*. — P. of poor people. — NC. of the poor.

productive in no small degree of prosperity to the State.[109] Is it not rash to conjecture the future from the past? Age gives way to age, but the events of one century are wonderfully like those of another, for they are directed by the providence of God, who overrules the course of history in accordance with His purposes in creating the race of man. We are told that it was cast as a reproach on the Christians in the early ages of the Church that the greater number among them had to live by begging or by labor. Yet, destitute though they were of wealth and influence, they ended by winning over to their side the favor of the rich and the goodwill of the powerful. They showed themselves industrious, hard-working, assiduous, and peaceful, ruled by justice, and, above all, bound together in brotherly love. In presence of such mode of life and such example, prejudice gave way, the tongue of malevolence was silenced, and the lying legends of ancient superstition little by little yielded to Christian truth.

60. At the time being, the condition of the working classes is the pressing question of the hour, and nothing can be of higher interest to all classes of the State than that it should be rightly and reasonably settled. But, it will be easy for Christian working men to solve it aright if they will form associations, choose wise guides, and follow on the path which with so much advantage to themselves and the common weal was trodden by their fathers before them. Prejudice, it is true, is mighty, and so is the greed of money; but if the sense of what is just and rightful be not deliberately stifled, their fellow citizens are sure to be won over to a kindly feeling towards men whom they see to be in earnest as regards their work and who prefer so unmistakably right dealing to mere lucre, and the sacredness of duty to every other consideration.

61. And further great advantage would result from the state of things We are describing; there would exist so much more ground for hope, and likelihood, even, of recalling to a sense of their duty those working men who have either given up their faith altogether, or whose lives are at variance with its precepts. Such men feel

---

109 L. *in civitate*.

in most cases that they have been fooled by empty promises and deceived by false pretexts. They cannot but perceive that their grasping employers too often treat them with great inhumanity and hardly care for them outside the profit their labor brings; and if they belong to any union, it is probably one in which there exists, instead of charity and love, that intestine strife which ever accompanies poverty when unresigned and unsustained by religion.[110] Broken in spirit and worn down in body, how many of them would gladly free themselves from such galling bondage![111] But human respect, or the dread of starvation, makes them tremble to take the step. To such as these, Catholic associations are of incalculable service, by helping them out of their difficulties, inviting them to companionship, and receiving the returning wanderers to a haven where they may securely find repose.

62. We have now laid before you, venerable brethren, both who are the persons and what are the means whereby this most arduous question must be solved. Everyone should put his hand to the work which falls to his share, and that at once and straightway, lest the evil which is already so great become through delay absolutely beyond remedy. Those who rule the commonwealths[112] should avail themselves of the laws and institutions of the country; masters and wealthy owners must be mindful of their duty; the working class,[113] whose interests are at stake, should make every lawful and proper effort; and since religion alone, as We said at the beginning, can avail to destroy the evil at its root, all men should rest persuaded that that main thing needful is to re-establish Christian morals,[114] apart from which all the plans and devices of the wisest will prove of little avail.

---

110   P. *petulantis atque incredulae paupertatis.*—P. unresigned and irreligious poverty.—NC. of aggravating and irreligious poverty.
111   L. *e servitude tam humili.*—P. from this galling slavery.—NC. from a servitude so degrading.
112   L. *qui gerunt respublicas.*—P. those who rule the State.—NC. those in charge of states.
113   L. *proletarii*; that is, the proletarians.
114   L. *instaurare mores christianos.*—P. to return to real Christianity.—NC. Christian morals must be re-established.

63. In regard to the Church, her cooperation will never be found lacking, be the time or the occasion what it may; and she will intervene with all the greater effect in proportion as her liberty of action is the more unfettered. Let this be carefully taken to heart by those whose office it is to safeguard the public welfare. Every minister of holy religion must bring to the struggle the full energy of his mind and all his power of endurance. Moved by your authority, venerable brethren, and quickened by your example, they should never cease to urge upon men of every class, upon the high-placed as well as the lowly, the Gospel doctrines of Christian life; by every means in their power they must strive to secure the good of the people; and above all must earnestly cherish in themselves, and try to arouse in others, charity, the mistress and the queen of virtues. For, the happy results we all long for must be chiefly brought about by the plenteous outpouring of charity; of that true Christian charity which is the fulfilling of the whole Gospel law, which is always ready to sacrifice itself for others' sake, and is man's surest antidote against worldly pride and immoderate love of self; that charity whose office is described and whose Godlike features are outlined by the Apostle St. Paul in these words: "Charity is patient, is kind, . . . seeketh not her own, . . . suffereth all things, . . . endureth all things."[115]

64. On each of you, venerable brethren, and on your clergy and people, as an earnest of God's mercy and a mark of Our affection, we lovingly in the Lord bestow the apostolic benediction.

---

115 1 Cor. 13:4–7.

IX

On Christian Citizenship

INTRODUCTION

The encyclical *Sapientiae Christianae,* dated January 10, 1890, differs from most of the other ones by its object. Instead of primarily dealing with problems arising from the relations of Church and State, or with difficulties encountered by Catholics in consequence of these relations, this encyclical considers Catholics as citizens of the perfect society called the Church, and defines the nature of this particular kind of citizenship. Without excluding the consideration of other problems, the center of interest is here provided by the problem of describing the duties of Catholics as citizens of the holy City of God (as in the encyclical *Sancta Dei Civitas,* December 3, 1880).

Catholics should feel for their Church the same love and devotion they feel for their country, or, rather, a still deeper love, since the good of the soul, for which they are indebted to the Church, is far superior to the well-being of the body (art. 5). The whole effort of Pope Leo XIII in this letter is devoted to making clear that, although there can be no better citizens than the Catholics so long as there are no conflicts between Church and State, they must obey God rather than man in case there are such conflicts.

In this demonstration, the stress is placed on two points: (1) since the natural love of our country and the supernatural love for the Church proceed from God as from their common cause, these should be no conflict between these two loyalties nor between the duties arising thereof; (2) if, however, the State happens to overlook that its citizens have duties toward the Church, conflicts of jurisdiction may arise and, in such cases,

Catholics cannot withdraw their allegiance from God in order to please men (art. 7). There is no sedition in doing so, for commands contrary to the divine law are themselves no laws; there is therefore no sedition in refusing to obey them (art. 10). The same notion can be expressed in saying that it is the essential duty of Christians never to set human laws above the divine law (art. 11).

After reminding Catholics that they have a duty to stand by their Church, the Pope defines the chief elements of this duty. These are two in number: to profess openly and unflinchingly the Catholic doctrine, and to propagate it to the utmost of their power (art. 15). In connection with the first of these two duties, the all-important statement made by the Pope, that "so soon as Catholic truth is apprehended by a simple and unprejudiced soul, reason yields assent" (art. 15) must be stressed. This which is a fact of experience, makes it a duty, even for laymen, to preach the Christian truth by deed and word (art. 16).

Let us remember, however, that Christ has not trained isolated champions of the saving truth; He has founded a Church, that is, a united body of such fighters, bound together by their common acceptance of one and the same faith as well as by their unanimous obedience to one and the same chief: one Christ, one Church, one Christian doctrine, one and the same will, and one and the same mode of action in all Christians throughout the whole Christian world (art. 21). This perfect unity of obedience should extend from the Pontiff up to the Bishops and from the solemn pronouncements of the Church in matters of faith up to the directives issued by the hierarchy (art. 24). In all such problems, the final decision as to what are the commands of God as expressed in holy Scripture belongs to the Pontiff. Were it not so, there would be no authorized interpreter of the commands of God.

This leads the Pope to a fuller explanation of the nature of the Church as a divinely established and constituted society whose proximate purpose it is "to lead the world to peace and holiness" (art. 25). The exclusive authority that belongs to the Church in all spiritual matters follows from this definition. The State has authority over its own temporal jurisdiction, but it is not to Caesar that Jesus Christ has entrusted the keys of the heavenly kingdom (art. 27). This distinction between the two powers does not entail their separation (art. 30). On the contrary, it is the duty of the Church to do her utmost in order to let the spirit of the gospel pervade the law and institution of the nations (art. 31). The proper attitude recommended to Catholics in performing this task is then defined as equally remote from false prudence and from false zeal. The firm resolve to accept discipline and to obey authority, coupled with courage and constancy, are the dispositions required from any Catholic anxious to do his duty and to behave as a true citizen of the Church (art. 36). The root of these virtues lies in a life itself regulated by the discipline of Christian virtues (art. 38), that is, in a life careful to avoid sin (art. 39) and quickened by charity (art. 40). Since family is the cradle of society, Christian discipline should begin with family life and extend from there to the life of Christian schools, thus preparing the future welfare of the State (art. 42). These duties are imperative, since not to fight for Jesus Christ amounts to fighting against Him (art. 43).

SUMMARY

(1–2) There is no true society where there is no respect for natural law and for divine law. (3) The doctrines and practices of the Christian religion should be restored in the family circle and through the whole range of society. (4) Every man who is baptized becomes thereby a subject of the Church. (5). (4) Every man who is baptized becomes thereby a subject of the Church. (5) He must love this holy City of which he is a citizen. (6) There should be no conflict between his duties as a citizen of the State and his duties as a citizen of the Church. (7) Should such conflicts arise, Catholics must adhere to the laws of Christ. (8–10) There is no sedition in refusing obedience to that which is not truly a law. (11) While we should love both countries, the love of our heavenly country must surpass the love of our earthly home. (12) Those who deny revelation and attribute to human nature the power which belongs to God make it more and more difficult for Catholics publicly to profess Christian truth. (13–14) This

On Christian Citizenship

is one more reason why every Catholic should increase his own faith and why he should not hesitate to preach it. (15) This can be done in both word and deed. (16) No private individual is exempted from this duty. (17) But no faithful should act as an isolated champion of the faith. (18–19) Unanimity of opinions is required for uniformity of action. (20–21) Unlike those who profess to follow reason alone, Christians achieve this unanimity owing to the unity of their faith. (22) This unity should be perfect. (23) It only can be so through submission to the sole authority of the Pope. (24) Without this infallible authority, there would be no sure interpreter of the word of God. (25) The purpose of the Church is to lead the world to peace and holiness. (26) Distinction of the two powers. (27–28) The Church is in charge of governing the souls and, being in itself a perfect society, she cannot link herself to any political party or subject herself to the exigencies of any politics. (29) Differences of political opinion are legitimate among Catholics, so long as these do not prevent them from joining their efforts when the higher interests of the Church are at stake. (30) The fact that Church and State both possess individual sovereignty does not mean that they are separated, and still less antagonistic. (31) The Church has a duty to oppose any antireligious move on the part of the State. (32) Let us avoid the past dissensions among Catholics which have contributed to the present condition of things. (33–35) Those who take part in public affairs should avoid two opposite excesses: false prudence and false courage. (36) Courage combined with the love of obedience are the marks of a true Catholic spirit. (37) The Pope and the bishops united with the apostolic see have authority "to regulate the actions of Christian citizens." (38) Christian virtues should precede all endeavors. (39) Sin cannot destroy the Church, but it does make nations miserable. (40–41) Charity is the bond of Christian life, and no real union of men is possible without it. (42) No restoration of society without a restoration of Christian discipline in families. (43) Appeal to the bishops for unrestricted co-operation. (44) Apostolic benediction.

IX

Sapientiae Christianae
ON CHRISTIANS AS CITIZENS
January 10, 1890

1. From day to day it becomes more and more evident how needful it is that the principles of Christian wisdom should ever be borne in mind, and that the life, the morals, and the institutions of nations should be wholly conformed to them. For, when these principles have been disregarded, evils so vast have accrued that no right-minded man can face the trials of the time being without grave anxiety or consider the future without alarm. Progress, not inconsiderable indeed, has been made towards securing the well-being of the body and of material things, but the material world, with the possession of wealth, power, and resources, although it may well procure comforts and increase the enjoyment of life, is incapable of satisfying our soul created for higher and more glorious things.[1] To contemplate God, and to tend to Him, is the supreme law of the life of man. For we were created in the divine image and likeness, and are impelled, by our very nature, to the enjoyment of our Creator. But not by bodily motion or effort do we make advance toward God, but through acts of the soul, that is, through knowledge and love. For, indeed, God is the first and supreme truth, and the mind alone feeds on truth. God is perfect holiness and the sovereign good, to which only the will can desire and attain, when virtue is its guide.

---

1 L. *sed omnis natura, quae hominis percellit sensus… non potest.*—H. But all nature which appeals to the senses of man and all possession of wealth, and power, and abundance, even though it confer advantages and increase the enjoyments of life, is unable to satisfy the soul which is born for things greater and grander.—P. But all natural advantages that administer to the senses of man, while bringing in their train the possession of wealth, power, and limitless resources, may indeed greatly avail to procure the comforts and increase the enjoyments of life, but are incapable of satisfying the soul created for higher and more glorious benefits.

2. But what applies to individual men applies equally to society — domestic alike and civil.[2] Nature did not form society in order that man should seek in it his last end, but in order that in it and through it he should find suitable aids whereby to attain to his own perfection. If, then, a political government strives after external advantages only, and the achievement of a cultured and prosperous life; if, in administering public affairs, it is wont to put God aside, and show no solicitude for the upholding of moral law, it deflects woefully from its right course and from the injunctions of nature; nor should it be accounted as a society or a community of men, but only as the deceitful imitation or appearance of a society.

3. As to what We have called the goods of the soul, which consist chiefly in the practice of the true religion and in the unswerving observance of the Christian precepts, We see them daily losing esteem among men, either by reason of forgetfulness or disregard, in such wise that all that is gained for the well-being of the body seems to be lost for that of the soul. A striking proof of the lessening and weakening of the Christian faith is seen in the insults too often done to the Catholic Church, openly and publicly — insults, indeed, which an age cherishing religion would not have tolerated. For these reasons, an incredible multitude of men is in danger of not achieving salvation; and even nations and empires themselves cannot long remain unharmed, since, when Christian institutions and morality decline, the main foundation of human society goes together with them. Force alone will remain to preserve public tranquillity and order. But force is very feeble when the bulwark of religion has been removed, and, being more apt to beget slavery than obedience, it bears within itself the germs of ever-increasing troubles. The present century has encountered memorable disasters, and it is not certain that some equally terrible are not impending.

The very times in which we live are warning us to seek remedies there where alone they are to be found — namely, by

---

2 H. both in the family and in the State.

re-establishing in the family circle and throughout the whole range of society the doctrines and practices of the Christian religion. In this lies the sole means of freeing us from the ills now weighing us down, of forestalling the dangers now threatening the world. For the accomplishment of this end, venerable brethren, We must bring to bear all the activity and diligence that lie within Our power. Although we have already, under other circumstances, and whenever occasion required, treated of these matters, We deem it expedient in this letter to define more in detail the duties of the Catholics, inasmuch as these would, if strictly observed, wonderfully contribute to the good of the commonwealth. We have fallen upon times when a violent and well-nigh daily battle is being fought about matters of highest moment, a battle in which it is hard not to be sometimes deceived, not to go astray and, for many, not to lose heart. It behooves us, venerable brethren, to warn, instruct, and exhort each of the faithful with an earnestness befitting the occasion: that none may abandon the way of truth.[3]

4. It cannot be doubted that duties more numerous and of greater moment devolve on Catholics than upon such as are either not sufficiently enlightened in relation to the Catholic faith, or who are entirely unacquainted with its doctrines. Considering that forthwith upon salvation being brought out for mankind, Jesus Christ laid upon His Apostles the injunction to "preach the Gospel to every creature," He imposed, it is evident, upon all men the duty of learning thoroughly and believing what they were taught. This duty is intimately bound up with the gaining of eternal salvation: "He that believeth and is baptized shall be saved; but he that believeth not, shall be condemned."[4] But the man who has embraced the Christian faith, as in duty bound, is by that very fact a subject of the Church as one of the children born of her, and becomes a member of that greatest and holiest body, which it is the special charge of the Roman Pontiff to rule with supreme power, under its invisible head, Jesus Christ.

---

3   Tobias 1:2.
4   Mark 16:16.

5. Now, if the natural law enjoins us to love devotedly and to defend the country in which we had birth, and in which we were brought up, so that every good citizen hesitates not to face death for his native land, very much more is it the urgent duty of Christians to be ever quickened by like feelings toward the Church. For the Church is the holy City of the living God, born of God Himself, and by Him built up and established. Upon this earth, indeed, she accomplishes her pilgrimage, but by instructing and guiding men she summons them to eternal happiness. We are bound, then, to love dearly the country whence we have received the means of enjoyment this mortal life affords, but we have a much more urgent obligation to love, with ardent love, the Church to which we owe the life of the soul, a life that will endure forever. For fitting it is to prefer the good of the soul to the well-being of the body, inasmuch as duties toward God are of a far more hallowed character than those toward men.

6. Moreover, if we would judge aright, the supernatural love for the Church and the natural love of our own country proceed from the same eternal principle, since God Himself is their Author and originating Cause. Consequently, it follows that between the duties they respectively enjoin, neither can come into collision with the other. We can, certainly, and should love ourselves, bear ourselves kindly toward our fellow men, nourish affection for the State and the governing powers; but at the same time, we can and must cherish toward the Church a feeling of filial piety, and love God with the deepest love of which we are capable. The order of precedence of these duties is, however, at times, either under stress of public calamities, or through the perverse will of men, inverted. For, instances occur where the State seems to require from men as subjects one thing, and religion, from men as Christians, quite another; and this in reality without any other ground, than that the rulers of the State either hold the sacred power of the Church of no account, or endeavor to subject it to their own will. Hence, arises a conflict, and an occasion, through such conflict, of virtue being put to the proof. The two powers are confronted and urge their

behests in a contrary sense; to obey both is wholly impossible. No man can serve two masters,[5] for to please the one amounts to contemning the other.

7. As to which should be preferred no one ought to balance for an instant. It is a high crime indeed to withdraw allegiance from God in order to please men, an act of consummate wickedness to break the laws of Jesus Christ, in order to yield obedience to earthly rulers, or, under pretext of keeping the civil law, to ignore the rights of the Church; "we ought to obey God rather than men."[6] This answer, which of old Peter and the other Apostles were used to give the civil authorities who enjoined unrighteous things, we must, in like circumstances, give always and without hesitation. No better citizen is there, whether in time of peace or war, than the Christian who is mindful of his duty; but such a one should be ready to suffer all things, even death itself, rather than abandon the cause of God or of the Church.

8. Hence, they who blame, and call by the name of sedition, this steadfastness of attitude in the choice of duty have not rightly apprehended the force and nature of true law. We are speaking of matters widely known, and which We have before now more than once fully explained. Law is of its very essence a mandate of right reason, proclaimed by a properly constituted authority, for the common good. But true and legitimate authority is void of sanction, unless it proceeds from God, the supreme Ruler and Lord of all. The Almighty alone can commit power to a man over his fellow men;[7] nor may that be accounted as right reason, which is in disaccord with truth and with divine reason; nor that held to be true good, which is repugnant to the supreme and unchangeable good, or that wrests aside and draws away the wills of men from the charity of God.

---

5 Matt. 6:24.
6 Acts 5:29.
7 Note the extreme importance of this principle; it justifies the doctrine according to which the only conceivable foundation of political authority must be divine in origin.

9. Hallowed, therefore, in the minds of Christians is the very idea of public authority, in which they recognize some likeness and symbol as it were of the Divine Majesty, even when it is exercised by one unworthy. A just and due reverence to the laws abides in them, not from force and threats, but from a consciousness of duty; "for God hath not given us the spirit of fear."[8]

10. But, if the laws of the State are manifestly at variance with the divine law, containing enactments hurtful to the Church, or conveying injunctions adverse to the duties imposed by religion, or if they violate in the person of the supreme Pontiff the authority of Jesus Christ, then, truly, to resist becomes a positive duty, to obey, a crime; a crime, moreover, combined with misdemeanor against the State itself, inasmuch as every offense leveled against religion is also a sin against the State. Here, anew it becomes evident how unjust is the reproach of sedition; for the obedience due to rulers and legislators is not refused, but there is a deviation from their will in those precepts only which they have no power to enjoin. Commands that are issued adversely to the honor due to God, and hence are beyond the scope of justice, must be looked upon as anything rather than laws. You are fully aware, venerable brothers, that this is the very contention of the Apostle St. Paul, who, in writing to Titus, after reminding Christians that they are "to be subject to princes and powers, and to obey at a word," at once adds: "And to be ready to every good work."[9] Thereby he openly declares that, if laws of men contain injunctions contrary to the eternal law of God, it is right not to obey them. In like manner, the Prince of the Apostles gave this courageous and sublime answer to those who would have deprived him of the liberty of preaching the Gospel: "If it be just in the sight of God to hear you rather than God, judge ye, for we cannot but speak the things which we have seen and heard."[10]

---

8   2 Tim. 1:7.
9   Titus 3:1.
10 Acts 4:19–20.

11. Wherefore, to love both countries, that of earth below and that of heaven above, yet in such mode that the love of our heavenly surpass the love of our earthly home, and that human laws be never set above the divine law, is the essential duty of Christians, and the fountainhead, so to say, from which all other duties spring. The Redeemer of mankind of Himself has said: "For this was I born, and for this came I into the world, that I should give testimony to the truth."[11] In like manner: "I am come to cast fire upon earth, and what will I but that it be kindled?"[12] In the knowledge of this truth, which constitutes the highest perfection of the mind; in divine charity which, in like manner, completes the will, all Christian life and liberty abide. This noble patrimony of truth and charity entrusted by Jesus Christ to the Church she defends and maintains ever with untiring endeavor and watchfulness.

12. But, with what bitterness and in how many guises war has been waged against the Church it would be ill-timed now to urge. From the fact that it has been vouchsafed to human reason to snatch from nature, through the investigations of science, many of her treasured secrets and to apply them befittingly to the diverse requirements of life, men have become possessed with so arrogant a sense of their own powers as already to consider themselves able to banish from social life the authority and empire of God. Led away by this delusion, they make over to human nature the dominion of which they think God has been despoiled; from nature, they maintain, we must seek the principle and rule of all truth; from nature, they aver, alone spring, and to it should be referred, all the duties that religious feeling prompts.[13] Hence, they deny all revelation from on high, and all fealty due to the Christian teaching of morals as well as all obedience to the Church, and they go so far as to deny her power of making laws and exercising every other kind of right, even

---

11   John 18:37.
12   Luke 12:49.
13   H. They proclaim that nature alone is the foundation of all truth; and that all the duties of religion proceed from and are to be derived from it.

disallowing the Church any place among the civil institutions of the commonweal.[14] These men aspire unjustly, and with their might strive, to gain control over public affairs and lay hands on the rudder of the State, in order that the legislation may the more easily be adapted to these principles, and the morals of the people influenced in accordance with them. Whence it comes to pass that in many countries Catholicism is either openly assailed or else secretly interfered with, full impunity being granted to the most pernicious doctrines, while the public profession of Christian truth is shackled oftentimes with manifold constraints.

13. Under such evil circumstances, therefore, each one is bound in conscience to watch over himself, taking all means possible to preserve the faith inviolate in the depths of his soul, avoiding all risks,[15] and arming himself on all occasions, especially against the various specious sophisms rife among non-believers. In order to safeguard this virtue of faith in its integrity, We declare it to be very profitable and consistent with the requirements of the time, that each one, according to the measure of his capacity and intelligence, should make a deep study of Christian doctrine, and imbue his mind with as perfect a knowledge as may be of those matters that are interwoven with religion and lie within the range of reason.[16] And as it is necessary that faith should not only abide untarnished in the soul, but should grow with ever painstaking increase, the suppliant and humble entreaty of the apostles ought constantly to be addressed to God: "Increase our faith."[17]

14. But in this same matter, touching Christian faith, there are other duties whose exact and religious observance, necessary at all times in the interests of eternal salvation, become more especially so in these our days. Amid such reckless and widespread

---

14 L. *reipublicae.*—P. the State.—H. even there can be no place for the Church in the commonwealth.
15 L. *cavendo pericula.*—H. guarding against danger.
16 H. and to imbue the mind as far as possible with those things of religion which can be obtained by human reason.
17 Luke 17:5.

folly of opinion, it is, as We have said, the office of the Church to undertake the defense of truth and uproot errors from the mind, and this charge has to be at all times sacredly observed by her, seeing that the honor of God and the salvation of men are confided to her keeping. But, when necessity compels, not those only who are invested with the power of rule are bound to safeguard the integrity of faith, but, as St. Thomas maintains: "Each one is under obligation to show forth his faith, either to instruct and encourage others of the faithful, or to repel the attacks of unbelievers."[18] To recoil before an enemy, or to keep silence when from all sides such clamors are raised against truth, is the part of a man either devoid of character or who entertains doubt as to the truth of what he professes to believe. In both cases, such mode of behaving is base and is insulting to God, and both are incompatible with the salvation of mankind. This kind of conduct is profitable only to the enemies of the faith, for nothing emboldens the wicked so greatly as the lack of courage on the part of the good. Moreover, want of vigor on the part of Christians is so much the more blameworthy, as not seldom little would be needed on their part to bring to naught false charges and refute erroneous opinions, and by always exerting themselves more strenuously they might reckon upon being successful. After all, no one can be prevented from putting forth that strength of soul which is the characteristic of true Christians, and very frequently by such display of courage our enemies lose heart and their designs are thwarted. Christians are, moreover, born for combat, whereof the greater the vehemence, the more assured, God aiding, the triumph: "Have confidence; I have overcome the world."[19] Nor is there any ground for alleging that Jesus Christ, the Guardian and Champion of the Church, needs not in any manner the help of men. Power certainly is not wanting to Him, but in His loving kindness, He would assign to us a share in obtaining and applying the fruits of salvation procured through His grace.

---

18 *Summa theologiae*, IIa-IIae, qu. iii, art. 2, ad 2m.
19 John 16:33.

15. The chief elements[20] of this duty consist in professing openly and unflinchingly the Catholic doctrine, and in propagating it to the utmost of our power. For, as is often said, with the greatest truth, there is nothing so hurtful to Christian wisdom as that it should not be known, since it possesses, when loyally received, inherent power to drive away error. So soon as Catholic truth is apprehended by a simple and unprejudiced soul, reason yields assent. Now, faith, as a virtue, is a great boon of divine grace and goodness; nevertheless, the objects themselves to which faith is to be applied are scarcely known in any other way than through the hearing. "How shall they believe Him of whom they have not heard? and how shall they hear without a preacher? Faith then cometh by hearing, and hearing by the word of Christ."[21] Since, then, faith is necessary for salvation, it follows that the word of Christ must be preached. The office, indeed, of preaching, that is, of teaching, lies by divine right in the province of the pastors, namely, of the bishops whom "the Holy Spirit has placed to rule the Church of God."[22] It belongs, above all, to the Roman Pontiff, vicar of Jesus Christ, established as head of the universal Church, teacher of all that pertains to morals and faith.

16. No one, however, must entertain the notion that private individuals are prevented from taking some active part in this duty of teaching, especially those on whom God has bestowed gifts of mind with the strong wish of rendering themselves useful. These, so often as circumstances demand, may take upon themselves, not, indeed, the office of the pastor, but the task of communicating to others what they have themselves received, becoming, as it were, living echoes of their masters in the faith. Such cooperation on the part of the laity has seemed to the Fathers of the Vatican Council so opportune and fruitful of good that they thought well to invite it. "All faithful Christians, but those chiefly who are in a prominent position, or engaged in teaching,

---

20 L. *Hujusce partes oficii primae sunt…* —H. the chief demands…
21 Rom. 10:14, 17.
22 Acts 20:28.

we entreat, by the compassion of Jesus Christ, and enjoin by the authority of the same God and Savior, that they bring aid to ward off and eliminate these errors from holy Church, and contribute their zealous help in spreading abroad the light of undefiled faith."[23] Let each one, therefore, bear in mind that he both can and should, so far as may be, preach the Catholic faith by the authority of his example, and by open and constant profession of the obligations it imposes. In respect, consequently, to the duties that bind us to God and the Church, it should be borne earnestly in mind that in propagating Christian truth and warding off errors the zeal of the laity should, as far as possible, be brought actively into play.

17. The faithful would not, however, so completely and advantageously satisfy these duties as is fitting they should were they to enter the field as isolated champions of the faith. Jesus Christ, indeed, has clearly intimated that the hostility and hatred of men, which He first and foremost experienced, would be shown in like degree toward the work founded by Him, so that many would be barred from profiting by the salvation for which all are indebted to His loving kindness. Wherefore, He willed not only to train disciples in His doctrine, but to unite them into one society, and closely conjoin them in one body, "which is the Church,"[24] whereof He would be the head. The life of Jesus Christ pervades, therefore, the entire framework of this body, cherishes and nourishes its every member, uniting each with each, and making all work together to the same end, albeit the action of each be not the same.[25] Hence, it follows that not only is the Church a perfect society far excelling every other, but it is enjoined by her Founder that for the salvation of mankind she is to contend "as an army drawn up in battle array."[26] The organization and constitution of Christian society can in no

---

23 Constitution *Dei Filius*, at end.
24 Col. 1:24.
25 L. *quamvis non eadem sit actio singulorum.* — H. though individual acts are separately accomplished. Cf. Rom. 12:4–5.
26 Cant. 6:9.

wise be changed, neither can any one of its members live as he may choose, nor elect that mode of fighting which best pleases him. For, in effect, he scatters and gathers not who gathers not with the Church and with Jesus Christ, and all who fight not jointly with him and with the Church are in very truth contending against God.[27]

18. To bring about such a union of minds and uniformity of action — not without reason so greatly feared by the enemies of Catholicism — the main point is that a perfect harmony of opinion should prevail; in which intent we find Paul the Apostle exhorting the Corinthians with earnest zeal and solemn weight of words: "Now I beseech you, brethren, by the name of our Lord Jesus Christ, that you all speak the same thing, and that there be no schisms among you: but that you be perfectly in the same mind, and in the same judgment."[28]

19. The wisdom of this precept is readily apprehended. In truth, thought is the principle of action, and hence there cannot exist agreement of will, or similarity of action, if people all think differently one from the other.

20. In the case of those who profess to take reason as their sole guide, there would hardly be found, if, indeed, there ever could be found, unity of doctrine. Indeed, the art of knowing things as they really are is exceedingly difficult; moreover, the mind of man is by nature feeble and drawn this way and that by a variety of opinions, and not seldom led astray by impressions coming from without; and, furthermore, the influence of the passions oftentimes takes away, or certainly at least diminishes, the capacity for grasping the truth. On this account, in controlling State affairs means are often used to keep those together by force who cannot agree in their way of thinking.[29]

---

27 Cf. Luke 11:22.
28 1 Cor. 1:10.
29 H. For this reason in the government of States [*civitatibus*] care is often taken that they who differ in opinion and view should be bound in unity by constraint.

21. It happens far otherwise with Christians; they receive their rule of faith from the Church, by whose authority and under whose guidance they are conscious that they have beyond question attained to truth. Consequently, as the Church is one, because Jesus Christ is one, so throughout the whole Christian world there is, and ought to be, but one doctrine: "One Lord, one faith;"[30] "but having the same spirit of faith,"[31] they possess the saving principle whence proceed spontaneously one and the same will in all, and one and the same tenor of action.

22. Now, as the Apostle Paul urges, this unanimity ought to be perfect. Christian faith reposes not on human but on divine authority, for what God has revealed: "we believe not on account of the intrinsic evidence of the truth perceived by the natural light of our reason, but on account of the authority of God revealing, who cannot be deceived nor Himself deceive."[32] It follows as a consequence that whatever things are manifestly revealed by God we must receive with a similar and equal assent. To refuse to believe any one of them is equivalent to rejecting them all, for those at once destroy the very groundwork of faith who deny that God has spoken to men, or who bring into doubt His infinite truth and wisdom. To determine, however, which are the doctrines divinely revealed belongs to the teaching Church, to whom God has entrusted the safekeeping and interpretation of His utterances. But, the supreme teacher in the Church is the Roman Pontiff. Union of minds, therefore, requires, together with a perfect accord in the one faith, complete submission and obedience of will to the Church and to the Roman Pontiff, as to God Himself. This obedience should, however, be perfect, because it is enjoined by faith itself, and has this in common with faith, that it cannot be given in shreds; nay, were it not absolute and perfect in every particular, it might wear the name of obedience, but its essence would disappear. Christian usage attaches such value to this perfection of obedience that it has

---

30 Eph. 4:5.
31 2 Cor. 4:13.
32 Constitution *Dei Filius*, cap. 3.

been, and will ever be, accounted the distinguishing mark by which we are able to recognize Catholics. Admirably does the following passage from St. Thomas Aquinas set before us the right view: "The formal object of faith is primary truth, as it is shown forth in the Holy Scriptures, and in the teaching of the Church, which proceeds from the fountainhead of truth. It follows, therefore, that he who does not adhere, as to an infallible divine rule, to the teaching of the Church, which proceeds from the primary truth manifested in the holy Scriptures, possesses not the habit of faith; but matters of faith he holds otherwise than true faith.[33] Now, it is evident that he who clings to the doctrines of the Church as to an infallible rule yields his assent to everything the Church teaches; but otherwise, if with reference to what the Church teaches he holds what he likes but does not hold what he does not like, he adheres not to the teaching of the Church as to an infallible rule, but to his own will."[34]

23. "The faith of the whole Church should be one, according to the precept (1 Cor. 1:10): "Let all speak the same thing, and let there be no schisms among you"; and this cannot be observed save on condition that questions which arise touching faith should be determined by him who presides over the whole Church, whose sentence must consequently be accepted without wavering. And hence, to the sole authority of the supreme Pontiff does it pertain to publish a new revision of the symbol, as also to decree all other matters that concern the universal Church."[35]

24. In defining the limits of the obedience owed to the pastors of souls, but most of all to the authority of the Roman Pontiff, it must not be supposed that it is only to be yielded in relation to dogmas of which the obstinate denial cannot be disjoined from

---

33 H. but he holds that which is of faith [*fidei*] in a manner different from that which is by faith. — L. is clearer: *ea quae sunt fidei alio modo tenet quam per fidem*; that is, he holds that which is of faith, but he does not hold it by faith.
34 *Summa theologiae*, IIa-IIae, q. v, art. 3.
35 Ibid., q. i, art. 10.

the crime of heresy. Nay, further, it is not enough sincerely and firmly to assent to doctrines which, though not defined by any solemn pronouncement of the Church, are by her proposed to belief, as divinely revealed, in her common and universal teaching, and which the Vatican Council declared are to be believed "with Catholic and divine faith."[36] But, this likewise must be reckoned amongst the duties of Christians, that they allow themselves to be ruled and directed by the authority and leadership of bishops, and, above all, of the apostolic see. And how fitting it is that this should be so anyone can easily perceive. For the things contained in the divine oracles have reference to God in part, and in part to man, and to whatever is necessary for the attainment of his eternal salvation. Now, both these, that is to say, what we are bound to believe and what we are obliged to do, are laid down, as we have stated, by the Church using her divine right, and in the Church by the supreme Pontiff. Wherefore, it belongs to the Pope to judge authoritatively what things the sacred oracles contain, as well as what doctrines are in harmony, and what in disagreement, with them; and also, for the same reason, to show forth what things are to be accepted as right, and what to be rejected as worthless; what it is necessary to do and what to avoid doing, in order to attain eternal salvation. For, otherwise, there would be no sure interpreter of the commands of God, nor would there be any safe guide showing man the way he should live.

25. In addition to what has been laid down, it is necessary to enter more fully into the nature of the Church. She is not an association of Christians brought together by chance, but is a divinely established and admirably constituted society, having for its direct and proximate purpose to lead the world to peace and holiness. And since the Church alone has, through the grace of God, received the means necessary to realize such end, she has her fixed laws, special spheres of action,[37] and a certain method,

---

36 Vatican Council, *Constit. de fide catholica*, cap. 3, *De fide*. Cf. H. Denziger, *Enchiridion Symbolorum* 11 ed., Freiburg i. Br., 1911), p. 476.
37 L. *certa officia.*—H. definite functions.

fixed and conformable to her nature, of governing Christian peoples. But, the exercise of such governing power is difficult, and leaves room for numberless conflicts, inasmuch as the Church rules peoples scattered through every portion of the earth, differing in race and customs, who, living under the sway of the laws of their respective countries, owe obedience alike to the civil and religious authorities. The duties enjoined are incumbent on the same persons, as already stated, and between them there exists neither contradiction nor confusion; for some of these duties have relation to the prosperity of the State, others refer to the general good of the Church, and both have as their object to train men to perfection.

26. The tracing out of these rights and duties being thus set forth, it is plainly evident that the governing powers are wholly free to carry out the business of the State; and this not only not against the wish of the Church, but manifestly with her co-operation, inasmuch as she strongly urges to the practice of piety, which implies right feeling towards God, and by that very fact inspires a right-mindedness toward the rulers in the State.[38] The spiritual power, however, has a far loftier purpose, the Church directing her aim to govern the minds of men in the defending of the "kingdom of God, and His justice,"[39] a task she is wholly bent upon accomplishing.

27. No one can, however, without risk to faith, foster any doubt as to the Church alone having been invested with such power of governing souls as to exclude altogether the civil authority. In truth, it was not to Caesar but to Peter that Jesus Christ entrusted the keys of the kingdom of Heaven. From this doctrine touching the relations of politics and religion originate important consequences, which we cannot pass over in silence.

28. A notable difference exists between every kind of civil rule and that of the kingdom of Christ. If this latter bear a certain

---

38 H. the practice of piety, which is justice towards God, in the same way she urges men to act with justice towards their rulers.
39 Matt. 6:33.

likeness and character to a civil kingdom, it is distinguished from it by its origin, principle, and essence. The Church, therefore, possesses the right to exist and to protect herself by institutions and laws in accordance with her nature. And since she not only is a perfect society in herself, but superior to every other society of human growth, she resolutely refuses, promoted alike by right and by duty, to link herself to any mere party and to subject herself to the fleeting exigencies of politics. On like grounds, the Church, the guardian always of her own right and most observant of that of others, holds that it is not her province to decide which is the best amongst many diverse forms of government and the civil institutions of Christian States, and amid the various kinds of State rule she does not disapprove of any, provided the respect due to religion and the observance of good morals be upheld. By such standard of conduct should the thoughts and mode of acting of every Catholic be directed.

29. There is no doubt that in the sphere of politics ample matter may exist for legitimate difference of opinion, and that, the single reserve being made of the rights of justice and truth, all may strive to bring into actual working the ideas believed likely to be more conducive than others to the general welfare. But to attempt to involve the Church in party strife, and seek to bring her support to bear against those who take opposite views is only worthy of partisans. Religion should, on the contrary, be accounted by everyone as holy and inviolate; nay, in the public order itself of States—which cannot be severed from the laws influencing morals and from religious duties—it is always urgent, and indeed, the main preoccupation, to take thought how best to consult the interests of Catholicism. Wherever these appear by reason of the efforts of adversaries to be in danger, all differences of opinion among Catholics should forthwith cease, so that, like thoughts and counsels prevailing, they may hasten to the aid of religion, the general and supreme good, to which all else should be referred. We think it well to treat this matter somewhat more in detail.

On Christians as Citizens

30. The Church alike and the State, doubtless, both possess individual sovereignty; hence, in the carrying out of public affairs, neither obeys the other within the limits to which each is restricted by its constitution. It does not hence follow, however, that Church and State are in any manner severed, and still less antagonistic; Nature, in fact, has given us not only physical existence, but moral life likewise. Hence, from the tranquillity of public order, which is the immediate purpose of civil society, man expects to derive his well-being, and still more the sheltering care necessary to his moral life, which consists exclusively in the knowledge and practice of virtue.[40] He wishes, moreover, at the same time, as in duty bound, to find in the Church the aids necessary to his religious perfection, in the knowledge and practice of the true religion; of that religion which is the queen of virtues, because in binding these to God it completes them all and perfects them. Therefore, they who are engaged in framing constitutions and in the religious nature of man, and take care to help him, but in a right and orderly way, to gain perfection, neither enjoining nor forbidding anything save what is reasonably consistent with civil as well as with religious requirements. On this very account, the Church cannot stand by, indifferent as to the import and significance of laws enacted by the State; not insofar, indeed, as they refer to the State, but in so far as, passing beyond their due limits, they trench upon the rights of the Church.

31. From God has the duty been assigned to the Church not only to interpose resistance, if at any time the State rule should run counter to religion, but, further, to make a strong endeavor that the power of the Gospel may pervade the law and institutions of the nations. And inasmuch as the destiny of the State depends

---

40 L. *Quare a tranquillitate ordinis publici, quam proximi habet civilis conjunctio propositam, hoc petit homo, ut bene sibi esse liceat, ac multo magis ut satis praesidii ad perficiendos mores suppeditet: quae perfecctio nusquam nisi in cognitione consistit atque exercitatione virtutis.*—P. Hence from the tranquility of public order, whose immediate purpose is civil society, man expects that this may be able to fulfill his needful well-being, and still more supply the sheltering care which perfects his moral life, which consists mainly in the knowledge and practice of virtue.

mainly on the disposition of those who are at the head of affairs, it follows that the Church cannot give countenance or favor to those whom she knows to be imbued with a spirit of hostility to her; who refuse openly to respect her rights; who make it their aim and purpose to tear asunder the alliance that should, by the very nature of things, connect the interests of religion with those of the State. On the contrary, she is (as she is bound to be) the upholder of those who are themselves imbued with the right way of thinking as to the relations between Church and State, and who strive to make them work in perfect accord for the common good. These precepts contain the abiding principle by which every Catholic should shape his conduct in regard to public life. In short, where the Church does not forbid taking part in public affairs, it is fit and proper to give support to men of acknowledged worth, and who pledge themselves to deserve well in the Catholic cause, and on no account may it be allowed to prefer to them any such individuals as are hostile to religion.

32. Whence, it appears how urgent is the duty to maintain perfect union of minds, especially at these our times, when the Christian name is assailed with designs so concerted and subtle. All who have it at heart to attach themselves earnestly to the Church, which is "the pillar and ground of the truth,"[41] will easily steer clear of masters who are "lying and promising them liberty, when they themselves are slaves of corruption."[42] Nay, more, having made themselves sharers in the divine virtue which resides in the Church, they will triumph over the craft of their adversaries by wisdom, and over their violence by courage. This is not now the time and place to inquire whether and how far the inertness and internal dissensions of Catholics have contributed to the present condition of things; but it is certain at least that the perverse-minded would exhibit less boldness, and would not have brought about such an accumulation of ills, if the faith "which worketh by charity"[43] had been generally more

---

41   1 Tim. 3:15.
42   2 Peter 2:1, 19.
43   Gal. 5:6.

energetic and lively in the souls of men, and had there not been so universal a drifting away from the divinely established rule of morality[44] throughout Christianity. May at least the lessons afforded by the memory of the past have the good result of leading to a wiser mode of acting in the future.

33. As to those who mean to take part in public affairs, they should avoid with the very utmost care two criminal excesses: so-called prudence and false courage. Some there are, indeed, who maintain that it is not opportune boldly to attack evil-doing in its might and when in the ascendant, lest, as they say, opposition should exasperate minds already hostile. These make it a matter of guesswork as to whether they are for the Church or against her, since on the one hand they give themselves out as professing the Catholic faith, and yet wish that the Church should allow certain opinions, at variance with her teaching, to be spread abroad with impunity. They moan over the loss of faith and the perversion of morals, yet trouble themselves not to bring any remedy; nay, not seldom, even add to the intensity of the mischief through too much forbearance or harmful dissembling. These same individuals would not have anyone entertain a doubt as to their good will towards the Holy See; yet they have always a something by way of reproach against the supreme Pontiff.

34. The prudence of men of this cast is of that kind which is termed by the Apostle Paul "wisdom of the flesh" and "death" of the soul, "because it is not subject to the law of God, neither can it be."[45] Nothing is less calculated to amend such ills than prudence of this kind. For the enemies of the Church have for their object—and they hesitate not to proclaim it, and many among them boast of it—to destroy outright, if possible, the Catholic religion, which is alone the true religion. With such a purpose in hand, they shrink from nothing, for they are fully conscious that the more faint-hearted those who withstand them become,

---

44   L. *tradita nobic divinitus disciplina...* —H. the discipline of Christianity entrusted to us from on high...
45   Cf. Rom. 8:6–7.

the more easy will it be to work out their wicked will. Therefore, they who cherish the "prudence of the flesh" and who pretend to be unaware that every Christian ought to be a valiant soldier of Christ; they who would fain obtain the rewards owing to conquerors, while they are leading the lives of cowards, untouched in the fight,[46] are so far from thwarting the onward march of the evil-disposed that, on the contrary, they even help it forward.

35. On the other hand, not a few, impelled by a false zeal, or — what is more blameworthy still — affecting sentiments which their conduct belies, take upon themselves to act a part which does not belong to them. They would fain see the Church's mode of action influenced by their ideas and their judgment to such an extent that everything done otherwise they take ill or accept with repugnance. Some, yet again, expend their energies in fruitless contention, being worthy of blame equally with the former.[47] To act in such manner is not to follow lawful authority but to forestall it, and, unauthorized, assume the duties of the spiritual rulers, to the great detriment of the order which God established in His Church to be observed forever, and which He does not permit to be violated with impunity by any one, whoever he may be.

36. Honor, then, to those who shrink not from entering the arena as often as need calls, believing and being convinced that the violence of injustice will be brought to an end and finally give way to the sanctity of right and religion! They truly seem invested with the dignity of time-honored virtue, since they are struggling to defend religion, and chiefly against the faction banded together to attack Christianity with extreme daring and without tiring, and to pursue with incessant hostility the sovereign Pontiff, fallen into their power. But men of this high character maintain, without wavering, the love of obedience, nor are they wont to undertake anything upon their own authority. Now, since a like resolve to obey, combined with constancy and sturdy courage, is needful,

---

46   L. *intacti a certamine.* — H. and take no part in the battle.
47   H. Such men as these spend their strength vainly and are not less blameworthy.

so that whatever trials the pressure of events may bring about, they may be "deficient in nothing,"[48] We greatly desire to fix deep in the minds of each one that which Paul calls the "wisdom of the spirit,"[49] for in controlling human actions this wisdom follows the excellent rule of moderation, with the happy result that no one either timidly despairs through lack of courage or presumes overmuch from want to prudence. There is, however, a difference between the political prudence that relates to the general good and that which concerns the good of individuals. This latter is shown forth in the case of private persons who obey the prompting of right reason in the direction of their own conduct; while the former is the characteristic of those who are set over others, and chiefly of rulers of the State, whose duty it is to exercise the power of command, so that the political prudence of private individuals would seem to consist wholly in carrying out faithfully the orders issued by lawful authority.[50]

37. The like disposition and the same order should prevail in the Christian society[51] by so much the more that the political prudence of the Pontiff embraces diverse and multiform things, for it is his charge not only to rule the Church, but

---

48 James 1:4.
49 Rom. 8:6.
50 "Prudence proceeds from reason, and to reason it specially pertains to guide and govern. Whence it follows that, in so much as any one takes part in the control and government of affairs, in so far ought he to be gifted with reason and prudence. But it is evident that the subject, so far as subject, and the servant ought neither to control nor govern, but rather to be controlled and governed. Prudence, then, is not the special virtue of the servant, so far as servant, nor of the subject, so far as subject. But because any man, on account of his character of a reasonable being, may have some share in the government on account of the rational choice which he exercises, it is fitting that in such proportion he should possess the virtue of prudence. Whence it manifestly results that prudence exists in the ruler as the art of building exists in the architect, whereas prudence exists in the subject as the art of building exists in the hand of the workman employed in the construction." *Summa theologiae*, IIa-IIae, q. xlvii, art. 12, answer. St. Thomas Aquinas refers to Aristotle, *Ethic. Nic.*, Bk. VI, 8, 1141b 21–29.
51 L. *in christiana republica*; that is, in the Christian commonwealth.—H. These dispositions and this order should be found in the heart of Christian society—the Church.

generally so to regulate the actions of Christian citizens that these may be in apt conformity to their hope of gaining eternal salvation. Whence, it is clear that, in addition to the complete accordance of thought and deed, the faithful should follow the practical political wisdom of the ecclesiastical authority.[52] Now, the administration of Christian affairs immediately under the Roman Pontiff appertains to the bishops, who, although they attain not to the summit of pontifical power, are nevertheless truly princes in the ecclesiastical hierarchy; and as each one of them administers a particular church, they are "as master-workers... in the spiritual edifice,"[53] and they have members of the clergy to share their duties and carry out their decisions. Everyone has to regulate his mode of conduct according to this constitution of the Church, which it is not in the power of any man to change. Consequently, just as in the exercise of their episcopal authority the bishops ought to be united with the apostolic see so should the members of the clergy and the laity live in close union with their bishops. Among the prelates, indeed, one or other there may be affording scope to criticism either in regard to personal conduct or in reference to opinions by him entertained about points of doctrine; but no private person may arrogate to himself the office of judge which Christ our Lord has bestowed on that one alone whom He placed in charge of His lambs and of His sheep. Let everyone bear in mind that most wise teaching of Gregory the Great: "Subjects should be admonished not rashly to judge their prelates, even if they chance to see them acting in a blameworthy manner, lest, justly reproving what is wrong, they be led by pride into greater wrong. They are to be warned against the danger of setting themselves up in audacious opposition to the superiors whose shortcomings they may notice. Should, therefore, the superiors really have committed grievous sins, their inferiors, penetrated

---

52   L. *necesse esse politicam potestatis ecclesiasticae observare in agendo sapientiam.* — P. the faithful should imitate the practical wisdom of the ecclesiastical authority. — H. the faithful should accept religiously as their rule of conduct the political wisdom of ecclesiastical authority.

53   Thomas Aquinas, *Quaest Quodl.*, 1, G. 7, art. 2, answer.

with the fear of God, ought not to refuse them respectful submission. The actions of superiors should not be smitten by the sword of the word, even when they are rightly judged to have deserved censure."[54]

38. However, all endeavors will avail but little unless our life be regulated conformably with the discipline of the Christian virtues. Let us call to mind what holy Scripture records concerning the Jewish nation: "As long as they sinned not in the sight of their God, it was well with them: for their God hateth iniquity. And even … when they had revolted from the way that God had given them to walk therein, they were destroyed in battles by many nations."[55] Now, the nation of the Jews bore an inchoate semblance to the Christian people, and the vicissitudes of their history in olden times have often foreshadowed the truth that was to come, saving that God in His goodness has enriched and loaded us with far greater benefits, and on this account, the sins of Christians are much greater, and bear the stamp of more shameful and criminal ingratitude.

39. The Church, it is certain, at no time and in no particular is deserted by God; hence, there is no reason why she should be alarmed at the wickedness of men; but in the case of nations falling away from Christian virtue there is not a like ground of assurance, "for sin maketh nations miserable."[56] If every bygone age has experienced the force of this truth, wherefore should not our own? There are, in truth, very many signs which proclaim that just punishments are already menacing, and the condition of modern States tends to confirm this belief, since we perceive many of them in sad plight from intestine disorders, and not one entirely exempt. But, should those leagued together in wickedness hurry onward in the road they have boldly chosen, should they increase in influence and power in proportion as they make headway in their evil purposes and crafty schemes, there will be

---

54   *Regula pastoralis*, Part 3, cap. 4 (PL 77, 55).
55   Judith 5:21–22.
56   Prov. 14:34.

ground to fear lest the very foundations nature has laid for States to rest upon be utterly destroyed. Nor can such misgivings be removed by any mere human effort, especially as a vast number of men, having rejected the Christian faith, are on that account justly incurring the penalty of their pride, since blinded by their passions they search in vain for truth, laying hold on the false for the true, and thinking themselves wise when they call "evil good, and good evil," and "put darkness in the place of light, and light in the place of darkness."[57] It is therefore necessary that God come to the rescue, and that, mindful of His mercy, He turn an eye of compassion on human society.

40. Hence, We renew the urgent entreaty We have already made, to redouble zeal and perseverance, when addressing humble supplications to our merciful God, so that the virtues whereby a Christian life is perfected may be reawakened. It is, however, urgent before all, that charity, which is the main foundation of the Christian life, and apart from which the other virtues exist not or remain barren, should be quickened and maintained. Therefore, it is that the Apostle Paul, after having exhorted the Colossians to flee all vice and cultivate all virtue, adds: "Above all things, have charity, which is the bond of perfection."[58] Yea, truly, charity is the bond of perfection, for it binds intimately to God those whom it has embraced and with loving tenderness, causes them to draw their life from God, to act with God, to refer all to God. Howbeit, the love of God should not be severed from the love of our neighbor, since men have a share in the infinite goodness of God and bear in themselves the impress of His image and likeness. "This commandment we have from God, that he who loveth God, love also his brother."[59] "If any man say I love God, and he hateth his brother, he is a liar."[60] And, this commandment concerning charity, its divine proclaimer styled new, not in the sense that a previous law, or even nature

---

57 Isa. 5:20.
58 Col. 3: 14.
59 1 John 4:21.
60 1 John 4:20.

itself, had not enjoined that men should love one another, but because the Christian precept of loving each other in that manner was truly new, and quite unheard of in the memory of man. For, that love with which Jesus Christ is beloved by His Father and with which He Himself loves men, He obtained for His disciples and followers that they might be of one heart and of one mind in Him by charity, as He Himself and His Father are one by their nature.

41. No one is unaware how deeply and from the very beginning the import of that precept[61] has been implanted in the breast of Christians, and what abundant fruits of concord, mutual benevolence, piety, patience, and fortitude it has produced. Why, then, should we not devote ourselves to imitate the examples set by our fathers? The very times in which we live should afford sufficient motives for the practice of charity.[62] Since impious men are bent on giving fresh impulse to their hatred against Jesus Christ, Christians should be quickened anew in piety; and charity, which is the inspirer of lofty deeds, should be imbued with new life. Let dissensions, therefore, if there be any, wholly cease; let those strifes which waste the strength of those engaged in the fight, without any advantage resulting to religion, be scattered to the winds; let all minds be united in faith and all hearts in charity, so that, as it behooves, life may be spent in the practice of the love of God and the love of men.

42. This is a suitable moment for us to exhort especially heads of families to govern their households according to these precepts, and to be solicitous without failing for the right training of their children. The family may be regarded as the cradle of civil society, and it is in great measure within the circle of family life that the destiny of the States[63] is fostered. Whence it is that they

---

61 L. *Hujus vis praecepti nemo ignorat.*—P. omits *vis.*—H. No one is ignorant of the force of this commandment.—Note that although the first meaning of the word *vis* is "force," it is often used in the encyclicals in one of the classical senses of notion, meaning, sense, import, nature.
62 H. should incite us not a little to practice charity.
63 L. *fortuna civitatum*; that is, the destiny of the nations.

who would break away from Christian discipline are working to corrupt family life, and to destroy it utterly, root and branch. From such an unholy purpose they allow not themselves to be turned aside by the reflection that it cannot, even in any degree, be carried out without inflicting cruel outrage on the parents. These hold from nature their right of training the children to whom they have given birth, with the obligation super-added of shaping and directing the education of their little ones to the end for which God vouchsafed the privilege of transmitting the gift of life. It is, then, incumbent on parents to strain every nerve to ward off such an outrage, and to strive manfully to have and to hold exclusive authority to direct the education of their offspring, as is fitting, in a Christian manner, and first and foremost to keep them away from schools where there is risk of their drinking in the poison of impiety. Where the right education of youth is concerned, no amount of trouble or labor can be undertaken, how great soever, but that even greater still may not be called for. In this regard, indeed, there are to be found in many countries Catholics worthy of general admiration, who incur considerable outlay and bestow much zeal in founding schools for the education of youth. It is highly desirable that such noble example may be generously followed, where time and circumstances demand, yet all should be intimately persuaded that the minds of children are most influenced by the training they receive at home. If in their early years they find within the walls of their homes the rule of an upright life and the discipline of Christian virtues, the future welfare of society will in great measure be guaranteed.

43. And now We seem to have touched upon those matters which Catholics ought chiefly nowadays to follow, or mainly to avoid. It rests with you, venerable brothers, to take measures that Our voice may reach everywhere, and that one and all may understand how urgent it is to reduce to practice the teachings set forth in this Our letter. The observance of these duties cannot be troublesome or onerous, for the yoke of Jesus Christ is sweet, and His burden is light. If anything, however,

appear too difficult of accomplishment, you will afford aid by the authority of your example, so that each one of the faithful may make more strenuous endeavor, and display a soul unconquered by difficulties. Bring it home to their minds, as We have Ourselves oftentimes conveyed the warning, that matters of the highest moment and worthy of all honor are at stake, for the safeguarding of which every most toilsome effort should be readily endured; and that a sublime reward is in store for the labors of a Christian life. On the other hand, to refrain from doing battle for Jesus Christ amounts to fighting against Him; He Himself assures us "He will deny before His Father in heaven those who shall have refused to confess Him on earth."[64] As for Ourselves and you all, never assuredly, so long as life lasts, shall We allow Our authority, Our counsels, and Our solicitude to be in any wise lacking in the conflict. Nor is it to be doubted but that especial aid of the great God will be vouchsafed, so long as the struggle endures, to the flock alike and to the pastors.

Sustained by this confidence, as a pledge of heavenly gifts, and of Our loving kindness in the Lord to you, venerable brothers, to your clergy and to all your people, We accord the apostolic benediction.

---

64 Luke 9:26.

Appendix

I

On the Evils Affecting Modern Society

INTRODUCTION

This first encyclical letter of Leo XIII, *Inscrutabili*, (April 21, 1878) deals with the evils which overwhelm society. It can be used as an introduction to the reading of those following. This encyclical is dominated by the still recent memory of the harmful consequences, to both the Church and Italy, of the revolution of 1870. Pope Pius IX, Leo's predecessor, had vigorously protested against the violence done to the Church. Her ancient temporal possessions had been seized by the Piedmontese army and the situation created by this act of violence was not to be until the time, when, during the reign of Pius XI, the Lateran Treaty established by the Vatican City State in the fullness of its independence (February 11, 1929). For these reasons, a large section of this encyclical was mainly directed to the Italian nation, but, as is always the case with pontifical documents, its teaching was not confined within the limits of any particular historical occasion.

SUMMARY

(1–2) Description of the evils which overwhelm societies. (3) Their main source is the rejection of the authority of the Church. (4) Invitation to fight this evil. (5–6) The Church as the source of civilization. (7) Achievements of the papacy in promoting civilization. (8) If the authority of the Church had been respected, many misfortunes would have been avoided. (9) This should particularly be felt in Italy. (10) What the Popes have done for Italy. (11–12) In order to safeguard this civilizing authority, the temporal independence of the papacy should be restored. (13) It is no less necessary that all teaching contrary to that of the Church be rejected and that true philosophy be taught to youth. (14) This presupposes a reformation of modern family life. (15) The activities of Catholic associations should be directed toward this end. (16) These evils will be brought to an end by the submission of men to the authority of the Church. (17) The union of the hierarchy with the apostolic see is both a protection and a promise of better times for the Church.

I

Inscrutabili Dei Consilio
ON THE EVILS OF SOCIETY
April 21, 1878

1. When by God's unsearchable design, We, though all unworthy, were raised to the height of apostolic dignity, at once We felt Ourselves moved by an urgent desire and, as it were, necessity, to address you by letter, not merely to express to you Our very deep feeling of love, but further, in accordance with the task entrusted to Us from heaven, to strengthen you who are called to share Our solicitude, that you may help Us to carry on the battle now being waged on behalf of the Church of God and the salvation of souls.

2. For, from the very beginning of Our pontificate, the sad sight has presented itself to Us of the evils by which the human race is oppressed on every side: the widespread subversion of the primary truths on which, as on its foundations, human society is based; the obstinacy of mind that will not brook any authority however lawful; the endless sources of disagreement,[1] whence arrive civil strife, and ruthless war and bloodshed; the contempt of law which molds characters and is the shield of righteousness; the insatiable craving for things perishable, with complete forgetfulness of things eternal, leading up to the desperate madness whereby so many wretched beings, in all directions, scruple not to lay violent hands upon themselves;[2] the reckless mismanagement, waste, and misappropriation of the public funds; the shamelessness of those who, full of treachery, make semblance of being champions of country, of freedom, and every kind of right; in fine, the deadly kind of plague which infects in its inmost recesses, allowing it no respite and foreboding ever fresh disturbances and final disaster.[3]

---

1 H. the perpetual desire of dissension.
2 H. that wretched beings dare to lay violent hands even on themselves.
3 This description of what is usually called a "corrupt government" or the government of a "corrupt party" is, in fact, the description of what

3. Now, the source of these evils lies chiefly, We are convinced, in this, that the holy and venerable authority of the Church, which in God's name rules mankind, upholding and defending all lawful authority, has been despised and set aside. The enemies of public order, being fully aware of this, have thought nothing better suited to destroy the foundations of society than to make an unflagging attack upon the Church of God, to bring her into discredit and odium[4] by spreading infamous calumnies and accusing her of being opposed to genuine progress. They labor to weaken her influence and power by wounds daily inflicted, and to overthrow the authority of the Bishop of Rome, in whom the abiding and unchangeable principles of right and good find their earthly guardian and champion. From these causes have originated laws that shake the structure of the Catholic Church, the enacting whereof we have to deplore in so many lands; hence, too, have flowed forth contempt of episcopal authority; the obstacles thrown in the way of the discharge of ecclesiastical duties; the dissolution of religious bodies; and the confiscation of property that was once the support of the Church's ministers and of the poor. Thereby, public institutions, vowed to charity and benevolence, have been withdrawn from the wholesome control of the Church; thence, also, has arisen that unchecked freedom to teach and spread abroad all mischievous principles, while the Church's claim to train and educate youth is in every way outraged and baffled. Such, too, is the purpose of the seizing of the temporal power, conferred many centuries ago by Divine Providence on the Bishop of Rome, that he might without let or hindrance use the authority conferred by Christ for the eternal welfare of the nations.[5]

4. We have recalled to your minds, venerable brothers, this deathly mass of ills, not to increase the sorrow naturally caused

---

necessarily happens to any government, or ruling party, when it rejects the moral rules taught by the Church. A religious error is the main root of all social and political evils.

4 H. to render her odious and hateful.

5 An allusion to the capture of the Papal States by the Piedmontese army (1860) and to the usurpation of the temporal power of the Popes by King Victor Emmanuel II, in 1870.

by this most sad state of things, but because we believe that from its consideration you will most plainly see how serious are the matters claiming our attention as well as devotedness, and with what energy We should work and, more than ever, under the present adverse conditions, protect, so far as in Us lies, the Church of Christ and the honor of the apostolic see—the objects of so many slanders—and assert their claims.

5. It is perfectly clear and evident, venerable brothers, that the very notion of civilization is a fiction of the brain if it rest not on the abiding principles of truth and the unchanging laws of virtue[6] and justice, and if unfeigned love knit not together the wills of men, and gently control the interchange and the character of their mutual service. Now, who would make bold to deny that the Church, by spreading the Gospel throughout the nations, has brought the light of truth amongst people utterly savage and steeped in foul superstition, and has quickened them alike to recognize the Divine Author of nature and duly to respect themselves? Further, who will deny that the Church has done away with the curse of slavery and restored men to the original dignity of their noble nature; and—by uplifting the standard of redemption in all quarters of the globe, by introducing, or shielding under her protection, the sciences and arts, by founding and taking into her keeping excellent charitable institutions which provide relief for ills of every kind—has throughout the world, in private or in public life, civilized the human race, freed it from degradation, and with all care trained it to a way of living such as befits the dignity and the hopes of man? And if any one of sound mind compare the age in which We live, so hostile to religion and to the Church of Christ, with those happy times when the Church was revered as a mother by the nations, beyond all question he will see that our epoch is rushing wildly along the straight road to destruction; while in those times which most abounded in excellent institutions, peaceful life, wealth, and prosperity the people showed themselves most obedient to the Church's rule and laws. Therefore, if the many blessings We

---

6 H. of right.

have mentioned, due to the agency and saving help of the Church, are the true and worthy outcome of civilization, the Church of Christ, far from being alien to or neglectful of progress, has a just claim to all men's praise as its nurse, its mistress,[7] and its mother.

6. Furthermore, that kind of civilization that conflicts with the doctrines and laws of holy Church is nothing but a worthless imitation and meaningless name.[8] Of this, those peoples on whom the Gospel light has never shown afford ample proof, since in their mode of life a shadowy semblance only of civilization is discoverable, while its true and solid blessings have never been possessed. Undoubtedly, that cannot by any means be accounted the perfection of civilized life, which sets all legitimate authority boldly at defiance;[9] nor can that be regarded as liberty which, shamefully and by the vilest means, spreading false principles, and freely indulging the sensual gratification of lustful desires, claims impunity for all crime and misdemeanor, and thwarts the goodly influence of the worthiest citizens of whatsoever class. Delusive, perverse, and misleading as are these principles, they cannot possibly have any inherent power to perfect the human race[10] and fill it with blessing, for "sin maketh nations miserable."[11] Such principles, as a matter of course, must hurry nations, corrupted in mind and heart, into every kind of infamy, weaken all right order, and thus, sooner or later, bring the standing and peace of the State to the very brink of ruin.

7. Again, if We consider the achievements of the see of Rome, what can be more wicked than to deny how much and how well the Roman bishops have served civilized society at large? For Our predecessors, to provide for the peoples' good, encountered struggles of every kind, endured to the utmost burdensome toils, and never

---

7   H. its patroness.
8   H. is a civilization in appearance only, a mere name without the substance.
9   H. We cannot look on an audacious disdain of all legitimate power as a perfection of civil life.
10 L. *familiam*.—H. nature.
11 Prov. 14:34.

hesitated to expose themselves to most dangerous trials.[12] With eyes fixed on heaven, they neither bowed down their head before the threats of the wicked, nor allowed themselves to be led by flattery or bribes into unworthy compliance. This apostolic chair it was that gathered and held together the crumbling remains of the old order of things; this was the kindly light by whose help the culture of Christian times shone far and wide; this was an anchor or safety in the fierce storms by which the human race has been convulsed; this was the sacred bond of union that linked together nations distant in region and differing in character;[13] in short, this was a common center from which was sought instruction in faith and religion, no less than guidance and advice for the maintenance of peace and the functions of practical life. In very truth, it is the glory of the supreme Pontiffs that they steadfastly set themselves up as a wall and a bulwark to save human society from falling back into its former superstition and barbarism.

8. Would that this healing authority had never been slighted or set aside! Assuredly, neither would the civil power have lost that venerable and sacred glory, the lustrous gift of religion, which alone renders the state of subjection noble and worthy of man;[14] nor would so many revolutions and wars have been fomented to ravage the world with desolation and bloodshed; nor would kingdoms, once so flourishing, but now fallen from the height of prosperity, lie crushed beneath the weight of every kind of calamity. Of this, the peoples of the East also furnish an example, who, by breaking the most sweet yoke that bound them to this apostolic see, forfeited the splendor of their former greatness, their renown in science and art, and the dignity of their sway.[15]

9. Of these remarkable benefits, however, which illustrious monuments of all ages prove to have flowed upon every quarter of

---

12   H. to the most arduous difficulties.
13   L. *moribus*; that is, the ways of life.—H. cultures.
14   H. the civil power in that case would assuredly not have lost the august and holy repute which it formerly derived from religion, and which alone renders the state of obedience noble and worthy of man.
15   H. of their empire.

the world from the apostolic see, this land of Italy has had the most abounding experience. For it has derived advantages from the see of Rome proportionate to the greater nearness of its natural situation. Unquestionably, to the Roman Pontiffs, it is that Italy must own herself indebted for the substantial glory and majesty by which she has been preeminent amongst nations. The influence and fatherly care of the Popes have upon many occasions shielded her from hostile attack and brought her relief and aid, the effect of which is that the Catholic faith has been ever maintained inviolate in the hearts of Italians.

10. These services of Our predecessors, to omit mention of many others, have been witnessed to in a special manner by the records of the times of St. Leo the Great, Alexander III, Innocent III, St. Pius V, Leo X, and other Pontiffs,[16] by whose exertions or protection Italy has escaped unscathed from the utter destruction threatened by barbarians; has kept unimpaired her old faith, and, amid the darkness and defilement of the ruder age, has cultivated and preserved in vigor the luster of science and the splendor of art. To this, furthermore, bears witness Our own fostering city, the home of the Popes, which, under their rule, reaped this special benefit, that it not only was the strong citadel of the faith, but also became the refuge of the liberal arts and the very abode of wisdom [17] winning for itself the admiration and respect of the whole world. As these facts in all their amplitude have been handed down in historical records for the perpetual remembrance of posterity, it is easy to understand that it is only with hostile design and shameless calumny — meant to mislead men — that anyone can venture in speech and in writing to

---

16   Pope St. Leo I, Leo the Great (440–61), caused Attila, King of the Huns, to retreat without having attacked Rome. Pope Alexander III (1159–81) fought against the German Emperor Friedrick Barbarossa, to whom he opposed the Lombard League. Pope Innocent III (1198–1216) strongly resisted the French King Philip Augustus. St. Pius V was Pope from 1566 to 1572 and during his reign occurred the naval victory over the Turks at Lepanto in 1571. Leo X (John of Medici), Pope from 1513 to 1521, presided over one of the most brilliant epochs in history: the "century of Leo X."
17   L. *sapientiam*; that is, wisdom. — H. sciences.

accuse the apostolic see of being an obstacle to the civil progress of nations and to the prosperity of Italy.

11. Seeing, therefore, that all the hopes of Italy and of the whole world lie in the power, so beneficent to the common good and profit, wherewith the authority of the apostolic see is endowed, and in the close union which binds all the faithful of Christ to the Roman Pontiff, We recognize that nothing should be nearer Our heart than how to preserve safe and sound the dignity of the Roman see, and to strengthen ever more and more the union of members with the head, of the children with their father.

12. Wherefore, that We may above all things, and in every possible way, maintain the rights and freedom of this holy see, We shall never cease to strive that Our authority may meet with due deference; that obstacles may be removed which hamper the free exercise of Our ministry and that We may be restored to that condition of things in which the design of God's wisdom had long ago placed the Roman Pontiffs. We are moved to demand this restoration, venerable brethren, not by any feeling of ambition or desire of supremacy, but by the nature of Our office and by Our sacred promise confirmed on oath; and further, not only because this sovereignty is essential to protect and preserve the full liberty of the spiritual power, but also because it is an ascertained fact that, when the temporal sovereignty of the apostolic see is in question, the cause of the public good and the well-being of all human society in general are also at stake. Hence, We cannot omit, in the discharge of Our duty, which obliges Us to guard the rights of Holy Church, to renew and confirm in every particular by this Our letter those declarations and protests which Pius IX,[18] of sacred memory, Our predecessor, on many and repeated occasions published against the seizing of the civil sovereignty and the infringement of rights belonging

---

18   Pope Pius IX (1846–78) proclaimed the dogmas of the Immaculate Conception and of the infallibility of the Popes in all matters related to faith and morals; published the "Syllabus," or conspectus of modern errors; witnessed the usurpation by Victor Emmanuel II of the temporal power of the Popes, but never acknowledged it.

to the Catholic Church. At the same time, We address ourselves to princes and chief rulers of the nations, and earnestly beseech them in the august name of the Most High God, not to refuse the Church's aid, proffered them in a season of such need, but with united and friendly aims, to join themselves to her as the source of authority and salvation, and to attach themselves to her more and more in the bonds of hearty love and devotedness. God grant that—seeing the truth of Our words and considering within themselves that the teaching of Christ is, as Augustine used to say, "a great blessing to the State, if obeyed,"[19] and that their own peace and safety, as well as that of their people, is bound up with the safety of the Church and the reverence due to her—they may give their whole thought and care to mitigating the evils by which the Church and its visible head are harassed, and so it may, at last, come to pass that the peoples whom they govern may enter on the way of justice and peace, and rejoice in a happy era of prosperity and glory.

13. In the next place, in order that the union of hearts between their chief Pastor and the whole Catholic flock may daily be strengthened, We here call upon you, venerable brothers, with particular earnestness, and strongly urge you to kindle, with priestly zeal and pastoral care, the fire of the love of religion among the faithful entrusted to you, that their attachment to this chair of truth and justice may become closer and firmer, that they may welcome all its teachings with thorough assent of mind and will, wholly rejecting such opinion, even when most widely received, as they know to be contrary to the Church's doctrine. In this matter, the Roman Pontiffs, Our predecessors, and the last of all, Pius IX, of sacred memory, especially in the General Council of the Vatican, have not neglected, so often as there was need, to condemn wide-spreading errors and to smite them with the apostolic condemnation. This they did, keeping before their eyes the words of St. Paul: "Beware lest any man cheat you by philosophy and vain deceit, according to the tradition of men, according to the elements of the world and not according to

---

19 *Letter 138*, to Marcellinus, 15 (PL 33, 532).

Christ."[20] All such censures, We, following in the steps of Our predecessors, do confirm and renew from this apostolic seat of truth, whilst We earnestly ask of the Father of lights[21] that all the faithful, brought to thorough agreement in the like feeling and the same belief, may think and speak even as Ourselves. It is your duty, venerable brothers, sedulously to strive that the seed of heavenly doctrine be sown broadcast in the field of God, and that the teachings of the Catholic faith may be implanted early in the souls of the faithful, may strike deep root in them, and be kept free from the ruinous blight of error. The more the enemies of religion exert themselves to offer the uninformed, especially the young, such instruction as darkens the mind and corrupts morals, the more actively should we endeavor that not only a suitable and solid method of education may flourish but above all that this education be wholly in harmony with the Catholic faith in its literature and system of training,[22] and chiefly in philosophy, upon which the direction of other sciences in great measure depends.[23] Philosophy seeks not the overthrow of divine revelation, but delights rather to prepare its way, and defend it against assailants, both by example and in written works, as the great Augustine and the Angelic Doctor, with all other teachers of Christian wisdom, have proved to Us.

14. Now, the training of youth most conducive to the defense of true faith and religion and to the preservation of morality must find its beginning from an early stage within the circle of home life; and this family Christian training sadly undermined in these our times, cannot possibly be restored to its due dignity, save by those laws under which it was established in the Church by her Divine Founder Himself. Our Lord Jesus Christ, by raising to the dignity of a sacrament the contract of matrimony, in which He would have His own union with the Church typified, not

---

20 Col. 2:8.
21 James 1:17.
22 H. to make the teaching itself conformable in science and in discipline to the Catholic faith.
23 This point is developed in the encyclical *Aeterni Patris*.

only made the marriage tie more holy, but, in addition, provided efficacious sources of aid for parents and children alike, so that, by the discharge of their duties one to another, they might with greater ease attain to happiness both in time and in eternity. But, when impious laws, setting at naught the sanctity of this great sacrament, put it on the same footing of mere civil contracts, the lamentable result followed, that, outraging the dignity of Christian matrimony, citizens made use of legalized concubinage in place of marriage; husband and wife neglected their bounden duty to each other; children refused obedience and reverence to their parents; the bonds of domestic love were loosened; and alas! the worst scandal and of all the most ruinous to public morality, very frequently an unholy passion opened the door to disastrous and fatal separations. These most unhappy and painful consequences, venerable brothers, cannot fail to arouse your zeal and move you constantly and earnestly to warn the faithful committed to your charge to listen with docility to your teaching regarding the holiness of Christian marriage, and to obey laws by which the Church controls the duties of married people and of their offspring.[24]

15. Then, indeed, will that most desirable result come about, that the character and conduct of individuals also will be reformed; for, just as from a rotten stock are produced healthless branches or worthless fruits, so do the ravages of a pestilence which ruins the household spread wide their cruel infection to the hurt and injury of individual citizens. On the other hand, when domestic society is fashioned in the mold of Christian life, each member will gradually grow accustomed to the love of religion and piety, to the abhorrence of false and harmful teaching,[25] to the pursuit of virtue, to obedience to elders, and to the restraint of the insatiable seeking after self-interest alone, which so spoils and weakens the character of men. To this end, it will certainly help not a little to encourage and promote those pious associations

---

24 This point is developed in the encyclical *Arcanum*. See also the encyclical letter of Pope Pius XI, *Divini Illius Magistri* (December 31, 1929, *On the Christian Education of Youth*.)
25 H. to reject with horror all false and pernicious doctrines.

which have been established, in our own times especially, with so great profit to the cause of the Catholic religion.

16. Great indeed and beyond the strength of man are these objects of our hopes and prayers, venerable brothers; but, since God has "made the nations of the earth for health,"[26] when He founded the Church for the welfare of the peoples,[27] and promised that He will abide with her by His assistance to the end of the world, We firmly trust that, through your endeavors, the human race, taking warning from so many evils and visitations, will submit themselves at length to the Church, and turn for health and prosperity to the infallible guidance of this apostolic see.

17. Meanwhile, venerable brothers, before bringing this letter to a close, We must express Our congratulations on the striking harmony and concord which unites your minds among yourselves and with this apostolic see. This perfect union We regard as not merely an impregnable bulwark against hostile attacks, but also as an auspicious and happy omen, presaging better times for the Church; and, while it yields great relief to Our weakness, it seasonably encourages Us to endure with readiness all labors and all struggles on behalf of God's Church in the arduous task which We have undertaken.

18. Moreover, from the causes of hope and rejoicing which We have made known to you We cannot separate those tokens of love and obedience which you, venerable brethren, in these first days of Our pontificate, have shown Our lowliness, and with you so many of the clergy and the faithful, who by letters sent, by offerings given, by pilgrimages undertaken, and by other works of love, have made it clear that the devotion and charity which they manifested to Our most worthy predecessor still lasts, so strong and steadfast and unchanged as not to slacken toward the person of a successor so much inferior. For these splendid tokens of Catholic piety, We

---

26 Wisd. 1:14: "For he created all things that they might be: and he made the nations of the earth for health: and there is no poison of destruction in them, nor kingdom of hell upon the earth."
27 H. but as God has founded His Church for the salvation of the people.

On the Evils of Society

humbly confess to the Lord that He is good and gracious, while to you, venerable brothers, and to all Our beloved children from whom We have received them, We publicly, from the bottom of Our heart, avow the grateful feelings of Our soul, cherishing the fullest confidence that, in the present critical state of things and in the difficulties of the times, this your devotion and love and the devotion and love of the faithful will never fail Us. Nor have We any doubt that these conspicuous examples of filial piety and Christian virtue will be of such avail as to make Our most merciful God, moved by these dutiful deeds, look with favor on His flock and grant the Church peace and victory. But as We are sure that this peace and victory will more quickly and more readily be given Us, if the faithful are unremitting in their prayers and supplications to obtain it, We earnestly exhort you, venerable brothers, to stir up for this end the zeal and ardor of the faithful, taking the Immaculate Queen of Heaven as their intercessor with God, and having recourse as their advocates to St. Joseph, the heavenly patron of the Church, and to Sts. Peter and Paul, the Princes of the Apostles. To the powerful patronage of all these, We humbly commit Our lowliness, all ranks of the ecclesiastical hierarchy, and all the flock of Christ our Lord.

19. For the rest, We trust that these days, on which We renew the memory of Jesus Christ, risen from the dead, may be to you, venerable brothers, and to all the fold of God, a source of blessing and salvation and fullness of holy joy, praying our most gracious God that by the blood of the Lamb without spot, which blotted out the handwriting that was against Us, the sins We have committed may be washed away, and the judgment We are suffering for them may mercifully be mitigated.

"The grace of our Lord Jesus Christ, and the charity of God, and the communication of the Holy Spirit be with you all,"[28] venerable brothers; to each and all of whom, as well as to Our beloved children, the clergy and faithful of your churches, as a pledge of Our special good-will and as an earnest of the protection of heaven, We lovingly impart the apostolic benediction.

---

28   2 Cor. 13:13.

II

On Slavery

INTRODUCTION

The letter *In Plurimis,* addressed to the bishops of Brazil on May 5, 1888, is not an encyclical properly so called. Moreover, it seems to deal with a question which many would now consider a settled one. Officially speaking, slavery has now become an extinct institution in all civilized countries. Yet, apart from the fact that there still is slavery in some parts of the world, this letter remains a most instructive document because, in showing how the Church has brought about an important social reform in the past, it enables us to understand how her present action is preparing another one in the future.

Among so many accusations leveled at the Church in our own days, one of the most common ones is that, by her conservative attitude in social, economic, and political matters, she slows down the revolution of modern societies towards more social justice. Religion, communists often say, is the opium of the people. Against this reproach, two answers at least can be rightly directed. First, in point of fact, violence and revolution have never effectively suppressed the evils they were supposed to abolish; most of the time they have multiplied the sufferings they were trying to alleviate. Secondly, it is the constant doctrine of the Church that error and moral evil are the true roots of social injustices, from which it follows that nothing can be done for temporal societies until a spiritual and religious reformation has taken place in the hearts of men. The Church does not approve of social injustices, but she does not believe that violence be an appropriate method to cure the ailments of nature. The standing lesson we can learn from this letter is that, because the Church has steadily disapproved of slavery during the course of nineteen centuries, slavery has finally disappeared as a legally recognized institution. Yet, during this long space of time, the Church has never invited any slaves to rebel against their masters. In so doing, the Church has spared countless slaves the cruelties which inevitably attend the repression of such revolts, but, at the same time, she has effectively achieved, in the hearts of men, a change that has brought about the abolition of slavery in all civilized countries.

The present attitude of the Church with respect to the problem of social justice should be understood in the light of what precedes. It is simply not true that she condones social injustices. Anyone reading the encyclical *Rerum Novarum* will clearly see that, if men were to follow its teaching, a complete transformation of the present condition of countless workers would necessarily follow. Only this transformation would be effective precisely because it would result, without any bloodshed, from a conversion of many human hearts to the teachings of the Gospel. In other words, the Church is the only institution effectively preparing a long-range social reformation. What benefits can be gained by means of revolutions is there for everybody to see in communist-dominated countries. Violence is more spectacular, but it only multiplies the very injustices it intends to redress; the patient, slow but effective action of the Church through centuries remains the only effective remedy to such evils.

The letter *Catholicae Ecclesiae* (November 10, 1890) re-stated the condemnation of slavery and prescribed practical measures to remedy to the distress of too many human beings still victims of this barbarous institution. The "destruction of slavery" was then assigned by the Pope to certain Catholic missions as their proper end.

SUMMARY

(1) Rejoicing that large numbers of slaves have just been liberated in Brazil. (2) This contributes to the universal restoration of things intended by Jesus Christ in the work of redemption. (3) Slavery never was a natural condition; it was a consequence

of sin. (4) How the division into masters and slaves actually took place. (5) Spreading of slavery among the Greeks and the Romans. (6) Restoration of human brotherhood by Christian charity. (7) Christianity has completely changed the social conditions of slaves. (8) The Christian relations between slaves and masters defined by St. Paul. (9) While condemning the recourse to violence and sedition, the Church has given to the Christian slaves a dignity which placed them above their pagan masters. (10-12) Testimony of the Fathers of the Church. (13-14) Action of the Roman Pontiffs in view of bettering the condition of slaves. (15-17) Opposition of the Church to the fifteenth-century revival of slavery in the newly discovered regions of Africa, Asia, and America. (18-20) The same action extended up to our own days. (21) Good tidings from Brazil. (22) How the newly liberated slaves should make use of their freedom. (23) Apostolic benediction.

11

In Plurimis
ON THE ABOLITION OF SLAVERY
May 5, 1888

TO THE BISHOPS OF BRAZIL,

1. Amid the many and great demonstrations of affection which from almost all the peoples of the earth have come to Us, and are still coming to Us, in congratulation upon the happy attainment of the fiftieth anniversary of Our priesthood, there is one which moves Us in a quite special way. We mean one which comes from Brazil, where, upon the occasion of this happy event, large numbers of those who in that vast empire groan beneath the yoke of slavery, have been legally set free. And this work, so full of the spirit of Christian mercy, has been offered up in cooperation with the clergy, by charitable members of the laity of both sexes, to God, the Author and Giver of all good things, in testimony of their gratitude for the favor of the health and the years which have been granted to Us. But, this was specially acceptable and sweet to Us because it lent confirmation to the belief, which is so welcome to Us, that the great majority of the people of Brazil desire to see the cruelty of slavery ended, and rooted out from the land. This popular feeling has been strongly seconded by the emperor and his august daughter, and also by the ministers, by means of various laws which, with this end in view have been introduced and sanctioned. We told the Brazilian ambassador last January what a consolation these things were to Us, and We also assured him that We would address letters to the bishops of Brazil on behalf of these unhappy slaves.

2. We, indeed, to all men are the Vicar of Christ, the Son of God, who so loved the human race that not only did He not refuse, taking our nature to Himself, to live among men, but delighted in bearing the name of the Son of Man, openly proclaiming that

In Plurimis

He had come upon earth "to preach deliverance to the captives"[1] in order that, rescuing mankind from the worst slavery, which is the slavery of sin, "he might re-establish all things that are in heaven and on earth,"[2] and so bring back all the children of Adam from the depths of the ruin of the common fall to their original dignity. The words of St. Gregory the Great are very applicable here: "Since our Redeemer, the Author of all life, deigned to take human flesh, that by the power of His Godhood the chains by which we were held in bondage being broken, He might restore us to our first state of liberty, it is most fitting that men by the concession of manumission should restore to the freedom in which they were born those whom nature sent free into the world, but who have been condemned to the yoke of slavery by the law of nations."[3] It is right, therefore, and obviously in keeping with Our apostolic office, that We should favor and advance by every means in Our power whatever helps to secure for men, whether as individuals or as communities, safeguards against the many miseries, which, like the fruits of an evil tree, have sprung from the sin of our first parents; and such safeguards, of whatever kind they may be, help not only to promote civilization and the amenities of life, but lead on to that universal restitution of all things which our Redeemer Jesus Christ contemplated and desired.

3. In the presence of so much suffering, the condition of slavery, in which a considerable part of the great human family has been sunk in squalor and affliction now for many centuries, is deeply to be deplored; for the system[4] is one which is wholly opposed to that which was originally ordained by God and by nature. The Supreme Author of all things so decreed that man should exercise a sort of royal dominion over beasts and cattle and fish and fowl, but never that men should exercise a like dominion over their fellow men. As St. Augustine puts it: "Having created man a reasonable being, and after His own likeness, God wished

---

1 Isa. 61:1; Luke 4:19.
2 Eph. 1:10.
3 *Epist.*, lib. 6, ep. 12 (PL 77, 803C–804A).
4 L. *idque*; that is, slavery.

that he should rule only over the brute creation; that he should be the master, not of men, but of beasts." From this, it follows that "the state of slavery is rightly regarded as a penalty upon the sinner; thus, the word slave does not occur in the Bible until the just man Noe branded with it the sin of his son. It was sin, therefore, which deserved this name; it was not natural."[5]

4. From the first sin[6] came all evils, and specially this perversity that there were men who, forgetful of the original brotherhood of the race, instead of seeking, as they should naturally have done, to promote mutual kindness and mutual respect, following their evil desires began to think of other men as their inferiors, and to hold them as cattle born for the yoke. In this way, through an absolute forgetfulness of our common nature, and of human dignity, and the likeness of God stamped upon us all, it came to pass that in the contentions and wars which then broke out, those who were the stronger reduced the conquered into slavery; so that mankind, though of the same race,[7] became divided into two sections, the conquered slaves and their victorious masters. The history of the ancient world presents us with this miserable spectacle down to the time of the coming of our Lord, when the calamity of slavery had fallen heavily upon all the peoples, and the number of freemen had become so reduced that the poet was able to put this atrocious phrase into the mouth of Caesar: "The human race exists for the sake of a few."[8]

5. The system flourished[9] even among the most civilized peoples, among the Greeks and among the Romans, with whom the few imposed their will upon the many; and this power was exercised so unjustly and with such haughtiness that a crowd of slaves[10] was regarded merely as so many chattels—not as persons, but

---

5 *De civ. Dei*, 19, 15 (PL 41, 643).
6 L. *ex primi contagione peccati*; that is, from the contagion of original sin.
7 L. *atque ita multitudo ejusdem generis individua*; that is, and thus a multitude whose members all belonged in one and the same genus.
8 Lucan, *Phars.* 5, 343.
9 L. *Idque apud eas etiam nations viguit*; that is, And this situation obtained even among nations.
10 L. *servorum turbae*; that is, the crowds of slaves.

In Plurimis

as things. They were held to be outside the sphere of law,[11] and without even the claim to retain and enjoy life. "Slaves are in the power of their masters, and this power is derived from the law of nations; for we find that among all nations masters have the power of life and death over their slaves, and whatever a slave earns belongs to his master."[12] Owing to this state of moral confusion it became lawful for men to sell their slaves, to give them in exchange, to dispose of them by will, to beat them, to kill them, to abuse them by forcing them to serve for the gratification of evil passions and cruel superstitions; these things could be done, legally, with impunity, and in the light of heaven. Even those who were wisest in the pagan world, illustrious philosophers and learned jurisconsults, outraging the common feeling of mankind, succeeded in persuading themselves and others that slavery was simply a necessary condition of nature. Nor did they hesitate to assert that the slave class was very inferior to the freemen both in intelligence and perfection of bodily development, and therefore, that slaves, as things wanting in reason and sense, ought in all things to be the instruments of the will, however rash and unworthy, of their masters. Such inhuman and wicked doctrines are to be specially detested; for, when once they are accepted, there is no form of oppression so wicked but that it will defend itself beneath some color of legality and justice. History is full of examples showing what a seedbed of crime, what a pest and calamity, this system has been for states.[13] Hatreds are excited in the breasts of the slaves, and the masters are kept in a state of suspicion and perpetual dread; the slaves prepare to avenge themselves with the torches of the incendiary, and the masters continue the task of oppression with greater cruelty. States[14] are disturbed alternately by the number of the slaves and by the violence of the masters, and so are easily overthrown; hence, in a word, come riots and seditions, pillage and fire.

---

11 L. *omnis expertes juris*; that is, deprived of all legal protection.
12 Justinian, *Inst.*, lib. I, tit. 8, n. I; in *Corpus jurs civilis* (4th ed., Berlin, Weidmann, 1886) Vol. 1, p. 3.
13 L. *in civitates*; that is, for societies.
14 L. *civitates*; that is, for societies.

6. The greater part of humanity was toiling in this abyss of misery, and were the more to be pitied because they were sunk in the darkness of superstition, when in the fullness of time and by the designs of God, light shone down upon the world, and the merits of Christ the Redeemer were poured out upon mankind. By that means they were lifted out of the slough and the distress of slavery, and recalled and brought back from the terrible bondage of sin to their high dignity as the sons of God. Thus, the Apostles, in the early days of the Church, among other precepts for a devout life taught and laid down the doctrine which more than once occurs in the Epistles of St. Paul addressed to those newly baptized: "For you are all the children of God by faith, in Jesus Christ. For as many of you as have been baptized in Christ, have put on Christ. There is neither Jew, nor Greek; there is neither bond, nor free; there is neither male nor female. For you are all one in Christ Jesus."[15] "Where there is neither Gentile nor Jew, circumcision nor uncircumcision, barbarian nor Scythian, bond nor free. But, Christ is all and in all."[16] "For in one Spirit were we all baptized into one body, whether Jews or Gentiles, whether bond or free; and in one Spirit we have all been made to drink."[17] Golden words, indeed, noble and wholesome lessons, whereby its old dignity is given back and with increase to the human race, and men of whatever land or tongue of class are bound together and joined in the strong bonds of brotherly kinship. Those things St. Paul, with that Christian charity with which he was filled, learned from the very heart of Him who, with much surpassing goodness, gave Himself to be the brother of us all, and in His own person, without omitting or excepting any one, so ennobled men that they might become participators[18] in the divine nature. Through this Christian charity, the various races of men were drawn together under the divine guidance in such a wonderful way that they blossomed into a new state of hope

15   Gal. 3:26–28.
16   Col. 3:11.
17   1 Cor. 12:13.
18   L. *consortes*.

In Plurimis

and public happiness; as with the progress of time and events and the constant labor of the Church the various nations were able to gather together, Christian and free, organized anew after the manner of a family.

7. From the beginning the Church spared no pains to make the Christian people,[19] in a matter of such high importance, accept and firmly hold the true teachings of Christ and the Apostles. And, now through the new Adam, who is Christ, there is established a brotherly union between man and man, and people and people; just as in the order of nature they all have a common origin, so in the order which is above nature, they all have one and the same origin in salvation and faith; all alike are called to be the adopted sons of God and the Father, who has paid the self-same ransom for us all; we are all members of the same body, all are allowed to partake of the same divine banquet, and offered to us all are the blessings of divine grace and of eternal life. Having established these principles as beginnings and foundations, the Church, like a tender mother, went on to try to find some alleviation for the sorrows and the disgrace of the life of the slave; with this end in view, she clearly defined and strongly enforced the rights and mutual duties of masters and slaves as they are laid down in the letters of the Apostles. It was in these words that the Princes of the Apostles admonished the slaves they had admitted to the fold of Christ. "Servants, be subject to your masters with all fear, not only to the good and gentle, but also to the froward."[20] "Servants, be obedient to them that are your lords according to the flesh, with fear and trembling in the simplicity of your heart, as to Christ. Not serving to the eye, but as the servants of Christ, doing the will of God from the heart. With a good will serving as to the Lord, and not to men. Knowing that whatsoever good thing any man shall do, the same shall he receive from the Lord, whether he be bond or free."[21] St. Paul says the same to Timothy: "Whosoever are servants under

---

19 L. *populus christianus* (*not* peoples).
20 1 Peter 2:18.
21 Eph. 6:5–8.

the yoke, let them count their masters worthy of all honor; lest the name of the Lord and his doctrine be blasphemed. But they that have believing masters, let them not despise them because they are brethren, but serve them the rather, because they are faithful and beloved, who are partakers of the benefit. These things teach and exhort."[22] In like manner, he commanded Titus to teach servants "to be obedient to their masters, in all things pleasing, not gainsaying. Not defrauding, but in all things showing good fidelity, that they may adorn the doctrine of God our Savior in all things.[23]

8. Those first disciples of the Christian faith very well understood that this brotherly equality of all men in Christ ought in no way to diminish or detract from the respect, honor, faithfulness, and other duties due to those placed above them. From this many good results followed, so that duties became at once more certain of being performed, and lighter and pleasanter to do, and at the same time more fruitful in obtaining the glory of heaven. Thus, they treated their masters with reverence and honor as men clothed in the authority of Him from whom comes all power. Among these disciples, the motive of action was not the fear of punishment or any enlightened prudence or the promptings of utility, but a consciousness of duty and the force of charity. On the other hand, masters were wisely counseled by the Apostle to treat their slaves with consideration in return for their services: "And you, masters, do the same things unto them, forbearing threatenings; knowing that the Lord both of them and you is in heaven, and there is not respect of persons with Him."[24] They were also told to remember that the slave had no reason to regret his lot, seeing that he is "the freeman of the Lord," nor the freeman, seeing that he is "the bondman of Christ,"[25] to feel proud, and to give his commands with haughtiness. It was impressed upon masters that they ought

---

22 1 Tim. 6: 1–2.
23 Titus 2:9–10.
24 Eph. 6:9.
25 1 Cor. 7:22.

to recognize in their slaves their fellow men, and respect them accordingly, recognizing that by nature they were not different from themselves, that by religion and in relation to the majesty of their common Lord all were equal. These precepts, so well calculated to introduce harmony among the various parts of domestic society, were practiced by the Apostles themselves. Specially remarkable is the case of St. Paul when he exerted himself in behalf of Onesimus, the fugitive of Philemon, with whom, when he returned him to his master, he sent this loving recommendation: "And do thou receive him as my own bowels, not now as a servant, but instead of a servant a most dear brother... And if he have wronged thee in anything, or is in thy debt, put that to my account."[26]

9. Whoever compares the pagan and the Christian attitude toward slavery will easily come to the conclusion that the one was marked by great cruelty and wickedness, and the other by great gentleness and humanity, nor will it be possible to deprive the Church of the credit due to her as the instrument of this happy change. And this becomes still more apparent when we consider carefully how tenderly and with what prudence the Church has cut out and destroyed this dreadful curse of slavery. She has deprecated any precipitate action in securing the manumission and liberation of the slaves, because that would have entailed tumults and wrought injury, as well to the slaves themselves as to the commonwealth, but with singular wisdom she has seen that the minds of the slaves should be instructed through her discipline in the Christian faith, and with baptism should acquire habits suitable to the Christian life. Therefore, when, amid the slave multitude whom she has numbered among her children, some, led astray by some hope of liberty, have had recourse to violence and sedition, the Church has always condemned these unlawful efforts and opposed them, and through her ministers has applied the remedy of patience. She taught the slaves to feel that, by virtue of the light of holy faith, and the character they received

---

26 Philemon 12, 18.

from Christ, they enjoyed a dignity which placed them above their heathen lords, but that they were bound the more strictly by the Author and Founder of their faith Himself never to set themselves against these, or even to be wanting in the reverence and obedience due to them. Knowing themselves as the chosen ones of the Kingdom of God, and endowed with the freedom of His children, and called to the good things that are not of this life, they were able to work on without being cast down by the sorrows and troubles of this passing world, but with eyes and hearts turned to heaven were consoled and strengthened in their holy resolutions. St. Peter was addressing himself specially to slaves when he wrote: "For this is thanksworthy, if for conscience towards God a man endure sorrows, suffering wrongfully. For unto this you are called; because Christ also suffered for us, leaving you an example that you should follow his steps."[27]

10. The credit for this solicitude joined with moderation, which in such a wonderful way adorns[28] the divine powers of the Church, is increased by the marvelous and unconquerable courage with which she was able to inspire and sustain so many poor slaves. It was a wonderful sight to behold those who, in their obedience and the patience with which they submitted to every task, were such an example to their masters, refusing to let themselves be persuaded to prefer the wicked commands of those above them to the holy law of God, and even giving up their lives in the most cruel tortures with unconquered hearts and unclouded brows. The pages of Eusebius keep alive for us the memory of the unshaken constancy of the virgin Potamiana, who, rather than consent to gratify the lusts of her master, fearlessly accepted death, and sealed her faithfulness to Jesus Christ with her blood. Many other admirable examples abound of slaves, who, for their souls' sake and to keep their faith with God, have resisted their masters to the death. History has no case to show of Christian slaves for any other cause setting themselves in opposition to their masters of joining in conspiracies against the State.

---

27   1 Peter 2:19–21.
28   L. *exornat*.

In Plurimis

Thence, peace and quiet times having been restored to the Church, the holy Fathers made a wise and admirable exposition of the apostolic precepts concerning the fraternal unanimity which should exist between Christians, and with a like charity extended it to the advantage of slaves, striving to point out that the rights of masters extended lawfully indeed over the works of their slaves, but that their power did not extend to using horrible cruelties against their persons. St. Chrysostom stands pre-eminent among the Greeks, who often treats of this subject, and affirms with exulting mind and tongue that slavery, in the old meaning of the word, had at that time disappeared through the beneficence of the Christian faith, so that it both seemed, and was, a word without any meaning among the disciples of the Lord. For Christ indeed (so he sums up his argument), when in His great mercy to us He wiped away the sin contracted by our birth, at the same time, healed the manifold corruptions of human society; so that, as death itself by His means has laid aside its terrors and become a peaceful passing away to a happy life, so also has slavery been banished. Do not, then, call any Christian man a slave, unless, indeed, he is in bondage again to sin; they are altogether brethren who are born again and received in Christ Jesus. Our advantages flow from the new birth and adoption into the household of God, not from the eminence of our race; our dignity arises from the praise of our truth, not of our blood. But, in order that that kind of evangelical brotherhood may have more fruit, it is necessary that in the actions of our ordinary life there should appear a willing interchange of kindnesses and good offices, so that slaves should be esteemed of nearly equal account with the rest of our household and friends, and that the master of the house should supply them, not only with what is necessary for their life and food, but also all necessary safeguards of religious training. Finally, from the marked address of Paul to Philemon, bidding grace and peace "to the church which is in thy house,"[29] the precept should be held in respect equally by Christian masters and servants, that

---

29   Philemon 2.

On the Abolition of Slavery

they who have an intercommunion of faith should also have an intercommunion of charity.[30]

11. Of the Latin authors, we worthily and justly call to mind St. Ambrose, who so earnestly inquired into all that was necessary for this cause, and so clearly ascribes what is due to each kind of man according to the laws of Christianity, that no one has ever achieved it better, whose sentiments, it is unnecessary to say, fully and perfectly coincide with those of St. Chrysostom.[31] These things were, as is evident, most justly and usefully laid down; but more, the chief point is that they have been observed wholly and religiously from the earliest times wherever the profession of the Christian faith has flourished. Unless this had been the case, that excellent defender of religion, Lactantius, could not have maintained it so confidently, as though a witness of it. "Should anyone say: Are there not among you some poor, some rich, some slaves, some who are masters; is there no difference between different persons? I answer: There is none, nor is there any other cause why we call each other by the name of brother than that we consider ourselves to be equals; first, when we measure all human things, not by the body but by the spirit, although their corporal condition may be different from ours, yet in spirit, they are not slaves to us, but we esteem and call them brethren, fellow workers in religion."[32]

12. The care of the Church extended to the protection of slaves, and without interruption tended carefully to one object, that they should finally be restored to freedom, which would greatly conduce to their eternal welfare. That the event happily responded to these efforts, the annals of sacred antiquity afford abundant proof. Noble matrons, rendered illustrious by the praises of St. Jerome, themselves afforded great aid in carrying

---

30   John Chrysostom, *Hom. in Lazar.* (PG 58, 1039); *Hom. xix in ep. 1 ad Cor.* (PG 61,157–158); *Hom. l in ep. ad Phil.* (PG 62, 705).
31   20. *De Jacob et de vita beata*, cap. 3 (PL 14, 633A–636A); *De patr. Joseph*, cap. 4 (PL 16, 680C–682B); "Exhort. Virgin.," cap. 1. (PL 16, 351A–352B).
32   *Divin. Instit.*, lib. 5, cap. 16 (PL 6, 599A–600A).

In Plurimis

this matter into effect; so that as Salvian relates, in Christian families, even though not very rich, it often happened that the slaves were freed by a generous manumission. But, also, St. Clement long before praised that excellent work of charity by which some Christians became slaves, by an exchange of persons, because they could in no other way liberate those who were in bondage. Wherefore, in addition to the fact that the act of manumission began to take place in churches as an act of piety, the Church ordered it to be proposed to the faithful when about to make their wills, as a work very pleasing to God and of great merit and value with Him. Therefore, those precepts of manumission to the heir were introduced with the words, "for the love of God, for the welfare or benefit of my soul."[33] Neither was anything grudged as the price of the captives, gifts dedicated to God were sold, consecrated gold and silver melted down, the ornaments and gifts of the basilicas alienated, as, indeed, was done more than once by Ambrose, Augustine, Hilary, Eligius, Patrick, and many other holy men.

13. Moreover, the Roman Pontiffs, who have always acted, as history truly relates, as the protectors of the weak and helpers of the oppressed, have done their best for slaves. St. Gregory himself set at liberty as many as possible, and in the Roman Council of 597 desired those to receive their freedom who were anxious to enter the monastic state. Hadrian I maintained that slaves could freely enter into matrimony even without their masters' consent. It was clearly ordered by Alexander III in the year 1167 to the Moorish King of Valencia that he should not make a slave of any Christian, because no one was a slave by the law of nature, all men having been made free by God. Innocent III, in the year 1190, at the prayer of its founders, John de Matha and Felix of Valois, approved and established the Order of the Most Holy Trinity for Redeeming Christians who had fallen into the power of the Turks. At a later date, Honorius III, and, afterwards, Gregory IX, duly approved the Order of St. Mary

---

33 Clement of Rome, I *Ep. ad Cor.*, cap. 55 (PG 1, 319A).

of Help,[34] founded for a similar purpose, which Peter Nolasco had established, and which included the severe rule that its religious should give themselves up as slaves in the place of Christians taken captive by tyrants, if it should be necessary in order to redeem them. The same St. Gregory passed a decree, which was a far greater support of liberty, that it was unlawful to sell slaves to the Church, and he further added an exhortation to the faithful that, as a punishment for their faults, they should give their slaves to God and His saints as an act of expiation.

14. There are also many other good deeds of the Church on the same behalf. For she, indeed, was accustomed by severe penalties to defend slaves from the savage anger and cruel injuries of their masters. To those upon whom the hand of violence had rested, she was accustomed to open her sacred temples as places of refuge to receive the free men into her good faith, and to restrain those by censure who dared by evil inducements to lead a man back again into slavery. In the same way, she was still more favorable to the freedom of the slaves whom, by any means, she held as her own, according to times and places; when she laid down either that those should be released by the bishops from every bond of slavery who had shown themselves during a certain time of trial of praiseworthy honesty of life, or when she easily permitted the bishops of their own will to declare those belonging to them free. It must also be ascribed to the compassion and virtue of the Church that somewhat of the pressure of civil law upon slaves was remitted, and, as far as it was brought about, that the milder alleviations of Gregory the Great, having been incorporated in the written law of nations, became of force. That, however, was done principally by the agency of Charlemagne, who included them in his *Capitularia*, as Gratian afterwards did in his *Decretum*.[35] Finally, monuments, laws, institutions, through a continuous series of ages, teach and splendidly demonstrate the great love of the Church

---

34   L. *Ordinem Mariae Sanctae a Mercede*.
35   Gratian, *Decretum*, Part 1, dist. 54; ed. E. Friedberg, Vol. 1, cols. 206–214.

toward slaves, whose miserable condition she never left destitute of protection, and always to the best of her power alleviated. Therefore, sufficient praise or thanks can never be returned to the Catholic Church, the banisher of slavery and causer of true liberty, fraternity, and equality among men, since she has merited it by the prosperity of nations, through the very great beneficence of Christ our Redeemer.

15. Toward the end of the fifteenth century, at which time the base stain of slavery having been nearly blotted out from among Christian nations, States were anxious to stand firmly in evangelical liberty,[36] and also to increase their empire, this apostolic see took the greatest care that the evil germs of such depravity should nowhere revive. She therefore directed her provident vigilance to the newly discovered regions of Africa, Asia, and America; for a report had reached her that the leaders of those expeditions, Christians though they were, were wickedly making use of their arms and ingenuity for establishing and imposing slavery on these innocent nations. Indeed, since the crude nature of the soil which they had to overcome, nor less the wealth of metals which had to be extracted by digging, required very hard work, unjust and inhuman plans were entered into. For a certain traffic was begun, slaves being transported for that purpose from Ethiopia, which, at that time, under the name of "La tratta dei Negri,"[37] too much occupied those colonies. An oppression of the indigenous inhabitants (who are collectively[38] called Indians), much the same as slavery, followed with a like maltreatment.

16. When Pius II had become assured of these matters without delay, on October 7, 1462, he gave a letter to the bishop of the place in which he reproved and condemned such wickedness. Some time afterwards, Leo X lent, as far as he could, his good offices and authority to the kings of both Portugal and Spain, who took care to radically extirpate that abuse, opposed alike

---

36   L. *civitates*; that is, when societies were anxious to establish themselves more firmly on the basis of evangelical liberty.
37   That is, the trading of slaves.
38   L. *universe*.—H. universally.

to religion, humanity, and justice. Nevertheless, that evil having grown strong, remained there, its impure cause, the unquenchable desire of gain, remaining. Then Paul III, anxious with a fatherly love as to the condition of the Indians and of the Moorish slaves, came to this last determination, that in open day, and, as it were, in the sight of all nations, he declared that they all had a just and natural right of a threefold character, namely, that each one of them was master of his own person, that they could live together under their own laws, and that they could acquire and hold property for themselves. More than this, having sent letters to the Cardinal Archbishop of Toledo, he pronounced an interdict and deprival of sacraments[39] against those who acted contrary to the aforesaid decree, reserving to the Roman Pontiff the power[40] of absolving them.[41]

17. With the same forethought and constancy, other Pontiffs at a later period, as Urban VIII, Benedict XIV, and Pius VII, showed themselves strong asserters of liberty for the Indians and Moors and those who were even as yet not instructed in the Christian faith. The last, moreover, at the Council of the confederated Princes of Europe, held at Vienna, called their attention in common to this point, that that traffic in Negroes, of which We have spoken before, and which had now ceased in many places, should be thoroughly rooted out. Gregory XVI also severely censured those neglecting the duties of humanity and the laws, and restored the decrees and statutory penalties of the apostolic see, and left no means untried that foreign nations, also, following the kindliness of the Europeans, should cease from and abhor the disgrace and brutality of slavery.[42] But, it has turned out most fortunately for Us that We have received the congratulations of the chief princes and rulers of public affairs for having obtained, thanks to Our constant pleadings, some satisfaction for the long-continued and most just complaints of nature and religion.

---

39 L. *interdictionem sacrorum.*—H. deprived of sacred rites.
40 L. *facultatem.*—H. the faculty.
41 Paul III (1534–49), *Veritas ipsa* (June 2, 1559).
42 Gregory XVI (1831–46), *In Supremo Apostolatus Fastigio* (Dec. 3, 1837).

18. We have, however, in Our mind, in a matter of the same kind, another care which gives Us no light anxiety and presses upon Our solicitude. This shameful trading in men has, indeed, ceased to take place by sea, but on land is carried on to too great an extent and too barbarously, and that especially in some parts of Africa. For, it having been perversely laid down by the Mohammedans that Ethiopians and men of similar nations are very little superior to brute beasts, it is easy to see and shudder at the perfidy and cruelty of man. Suddenly, like plunderers making an attack, they invade the tribes of Ethiopians, fearing no such thing; they rush into their villages, houses, and huts; they lay waste, destroy, and seize everything; they lead away from thence the men, women, and children, easily captured and bound, so that they may drag them away by force for their shameful traffic. These hateful expeditions are made into Egypt, Zanzibar, and partly also into the Sudan, as though so many stations. Men, bound with chains are forced to take long journeys, ill supplied with food, under the frequent use of the lash; those who are too weak to undergo this are killed; those who are strong enough go like a flock with a crowd of others to be sold and to be passed over to a brutal and shameless purchaser. But whoever is thus sold and given up is exposed to what is a miserable rending asunder of wives, children, and parents, and is driven by him into whose power he falls into a hard and indescribable slavery; nor can he refuse to conform to the religious rites of Mahomet. These things We have received not long since with the greatest bitterness of feeling from some who have been eyewitnesses, though tearful ones, of that kind of infamy and misery; with these, moreover, what has been related lately by the explorers in equatorial Africa entirely coincides. It is indeed manifest, by their testimony and word, that each year 400,000 Africans are usually thus sold like cattle, about half of whom, wearied out by the roughness of the tracks, fall down and perish there, so that, sad to relate, those traveling through such places see the pathway strewn with the remains of bones.

19. Who would not be moved by the thought of such miseries. We, indeed, who are holding the place[43] of Christ, the loving Liberator and Redeemer of all mankind, and who so rejoice in the many and glorious good deeds of the Church to all who are afflicted, can scarcely express how great is Our commiseration for those unhappy nations, with what fullness of charity We open Our arms to them, how ardently We desire to be able to afford them every alleviation and support, with the hope, that, having cast off the slavery of superstition as well as the slavery of man, they may at length serve the one true God under the gentle yoke of Christ, partakers with Us of the divine inheritance. Would that all who hold high positions in authority and power,[44] or who desire the rights of nations and of humanity to be held sacred, or who earnestly devote themselves to the interests of the Catholic religion, would all, everywhere acting on Our exhortations and wishes, strive together to repress, forbid, and put an end to that kind of traffic, than which nothing is more base and wicked.

20. In the meantime, while by a more strenuous application of ingenuity and labor new roads are being made, and new commercial enterprises undertaken in the lands of Africa, let apostolic men endeavor to find out how they can best secure the safety and liberty of slaves. They will obtain success in this matter in no other way than if, strengthened by divine grace, they give themselves up to spreading our most holy faith and daily caring for it, whose distinguishing fruit is that it wonderfully flavors and develops the liberty "with which Christ made us free."[45] We therefore advise them to look, as if into a mirror of apostolic virtue, at the life and works of St. Peter Claver, to whom We have lately added a crown of glory.[46] Let them look at him who

---

43   L. *qui personam gerimus Christi.* — H. who bear the person of Christ.
44   L. *imperio et potestate.* — H. in empires of states [perhaps misprint for: or states].
45   Gal. 4:31.
46   St. Peter Claver (1581–1654), joined the Society of Jesus in 1602; in 1610, he went to Cartagena, then the main slave market of the New World, and for forty-four years devoted himself to missionary work. He had declared

In Plurimis

for fully forty years gave himself up to minister with the greatest constancy in his labors, to a most miserable assembly of Moorish slaves; truly, he ought to be called the apostle of those whose constant servant he professed himself and gave himself up to be. If they endeavor to take to themselves and reflect the charity and patience of such a man, they will shine indeed as worthy ministers of salvation, authors of consolation, messengers of peace, who, by God's help, may turn solicitude, desolation, and fierceness into the most joyful fertility of religion and civilization.

21. And now, venerable brethren, Our thoughts and letters desire to turn to you that We may again announce to you and again share with you the exceeding joy which We feel on account of the determinations which have been publicly entered into in that empire[47] with regard to slavery. If, indeed, it seemed to Us a good, happy, and propitious event, that it was provided and insisted upon by law that whoever were still in the condition of slaves ought to be admitted to the status and rights of free men, so also it conforms and increases Our hope of future acts which will be the cause of joy, both in civil and religious matters. Thus the name of the Empire of Brazil will be justly held in honor and praise among the most civilized nations, and the name of its august emperor will likewise be esteemed, whose excellent speech is on record, that he desired nothing more ardently than that every vestige of slavery should be speedily obliterated from his territories. But, truly, until those precepts of the laws are carried into effect, earnestly endeavor, We beseech you, by all means, and press on as much as possible the accomplishment of this affair, which no light difficulties hinder. Through your means let it be brought to pass that masters and slaves may mutually agree with the highest goodwill and best good faith, nor let there be any transgression of clemency or justice, but, whatever things have to be carried out, let all be done lawfully, temperately, and

---

his intention to remain "the slave of the Negroes" for his entire life and, in point of fact, is said to have baptized over 300,000 of them. He was canonized by Pope Leo XIII on January 15, 1888.

47 L. *istud... imperium*; that is, Brazil.

in a Christian manner. It is, however, chiefly to be wished that this may be prosperously accomplished, which all desire, that slavery may be banished and blotted out without any injury to divine or human rights, with no political agitation,[48] and so with the solid benefit of the slaves themselves, for whose sake it is undertaken.

22. To each one of these, whether they have already been made free or are about to become so, We address with a pastoral intention and fatherly mind a few salutary cautions culled from the words of the great Apostle of the Gentiles. Let them, then, endeavor piously and constantly to retain grateful memory and feeling towards those by whose council and exertion they were set at liberty. Let them never show themselves unworthy of so great a gift nor ever confound liberty with license; but let them use it as becomes well-ordered citizens for the industry of an active life, for the benefit and advantage both of their family and of the State.[49] To respect and increase the dignity of their princes, to obey the magistrates, to be obedient to the laws, these and similar duties let them diligently fulfill, under the influence, not so much of fear as of religion; let them also restrain and keep in subjection envy of another's wealth or position, which unfortunately daily distresses so many of those in inferior positions, and present so many incitements of rebellion against security of order and peace. Content with their state and lot, let them think nothing dearer, let them desire nothing more ardently than the good things of the heavenly kingdom by whose grace they have been brought to the light and redeemed by Christ; let them feel piously towards God who is their Lord and Liberator; let them love Him, with all their power; let them keep His commandments with all their might; let them rejoice in being sons of His spouse, the Holy Church; let them labor to be as good as possible, and as much as they can let them carefully return His love.

---

48 L. *nulla civitatis perturbatione*.—H. with no agitation in the State.
49 L. *civitas*; that is, of the body politic.

In Plurimis

Do you also, Venerable Brethren, be constant in showing and urging on the freedmen these same doctrines; that, that which is Our chief prayer, and at the same time ought to be yours and that of all good people, religion, amongst the first, may ever feel that she has gained the most ample fruits of that liberty which have been obtained wherever that empire extends.

23. But so that may happily take place, We beg and implore the full grace of God and motherly aid of the Immaculate Virgin. As a foretaste of heavenly gifts and witness of Our fatherly good will towards you, Venerable Brethren, your clergy, and all your people, We lovingly impart the apostolic blessing.

III

Christian Democracy

INTRODUCTION

One of the consequences of the encyclical *Rerum Novarum* was an intense movement in favor of a social reformation conducted in the light of the teachings of the Gospel. Such was particularly the case in Italy, in Germany, and in France, where groups of Christian Democrats and of Christian Socialists began to form and sometimes to oppose other political parties, allegedly on the strength of the directives issued by the Pope in his encyclicals. The letter *Graves de Communi* (January 18, 1901), represent an effort of Pope Leo XIII to clear up certain aspects of his social doctrine.

One of the most interesting aspects of this encyclical is that it shows the Pontiff at grips with such contingent problems as the title which it is advisable to give, or to refuse, to a political party. Behind this question of words a much more important problem is at stake, namely, the determination of the character which a movement must exhibit as a consequence of the fact that it calls itself "Christian."

The first consequence of this decision is that, since this movement calls itself Christian, its basic principle must be Christian faith. As Christian, even democracy ceases to be a *political* form of government. It can mean only a movement directed by a Christian feeling of love for the people. It is important to realize that, from the transcendent point of view of the Papacy, if there is something true in the ideal of a Christian Democracy, it must be true universally and irrespective of the particular form of political government prevailing at a particular time in a particular place, "for the laws of nature and of the Gospel, which by right are superior to all human contingencies, are necessarily independent of all particular forms of civil government, while, at the same time, they are in harmony with all that is not repugnant to morality and justice" (art. 7). This, which happens to be the perfect definition of a genuinely "catholic" truth, also determines the limits within which the remarks of this encyclical apply.

Although certain names should be rejected as decidedly misleading, the main point is not to know what a Christian movement should call itself, but rather to make sure that, whatever its name, it fully agrees with the teaching of the Church in matters of social charity and of social justice. The last words of the Pope on these matters are to remind us of the examples of St. Francis of Assisi and of St. Vincent de Paul. One could not say more clearly that the sanctification of human societies is the only way in which the Church ultimately hopes to achieve their reformation.

SUMMARY

(1) Philosophic and economic factors have embittered the struggle between capital and labor. (2) Two encyclicals have already been devoted to the problem. (3) Some results have already been achieved. (4) There are hesitations concerning the proper name to be given Catholic social movements. (5) Social democracy means socialism. (6) Christian democracy differs from it as much as the profession of Christianity differs from socialism. (7) This name of Christian Democracy should not be distorted to politics. (8) Nor should it be directed against the upper classes of society, for these, too, contribute much to the welfare of the commonwealth. (9) There is no question of using this name to foster in the people a spirit of rebellion against its rulers. (10) Thus understood, the name of Christian Democracy should raise no difficulties. (11) The more so as the word "Christian" recalls that religion is required in order to settle the social question. (12) Catholics should enter associations for bettering the condition of the laboring classes. (13) In

In Plurimis

doing so, Catholics are simply adapting the traditional practice of charity to the new exigencies of the times. (14) Charity has been specially commended by Jesus Christ. (15) To His teachings Christ has added His own example. (16) This new form of charity is not intended to eliminate the ancient ones. (17) Not only temporary help, but also permanent institutions, should be considered in order to encourage thrift and foresight in the minds of the workers. (18) Provided Catholics be of one mind on the nature of the task, the name is secondary in importance. (19) Men of eminence in the community should consider it their duty to help in this work. (20) The older charitable institutions are not threatened by this new form of charity. (21) On the contrary, the growth of socialism is equally dangerous to religion and to the State. (22) Unnecessary dissensions should therefore be avoided in newspapers and in public speeches. (23) All associations should unite in view of Catholic action. (24) Priests also should go out and move among the people, not, however, without great prudence and after the fashion of the saints. (25) It is, at any rate, easy to recommend to the people the respect of law and order, the obedience to authorities, the courageous acceptance of their professional and familial duties and, last not the least, the fidelity to the Church; the example of the Holy Family of Nazareth will remind the people that sanctity can shine in the midst of poverty. (26) Whatever may be done should be done under episcopal guidance. (27) The bishops are exhorted to encourage, guide, and control this movement. (28) This exhortation is confirmed by the words of St. Paul. (29) Apostolic benediction.

III

Graves De Communi Re
ON CHRISTIAN DEMOCRACY
January 18, 1901

1. The grave discussions on economical questions which for some time past have disturbed the peace of several countries of the world are growing in frequency and intensity to such a degree that the minds of thoughtful men are filled, and rightly so, with worry and alarm. These discussions take their rise in the bad philosophical and ethical teaching which is now widespread among the people. The changes, also, which the mechanical inventions of the age have introduced, the rapidity of communication between places, and the devices of every kind for diminishing labor and increasing gain, all add bitterness to the strife; and, lastly, matters have been brought to such a pass by the struggle between capital and labor,[1] fomented as it is by professional agitators, that the countries where these disturbances most frequently occur find themselves confronted with ruin and disaster.

2. At the very beginning of Our pontificate, We clearly pointed out what the peril was which confronted society on this head, and We deemed it Our duty to warn Catholics, in unmistakable language,[2] how great the error was which was lurking in the utterances of socialism, and how great the danger was that threatened not only their temporal possessions, but also their morality and religion. That was the purpose of Our encyclical letter *Quod Apostolici Muneris*, which We published on the 28th of December in the year 1878; but, as these dangers day by day threatened still greater disaster, both to individuals and the commonwealth, We strove with all the more energy to avert

---

1 L. *proletarios*; that is, the proletarians. — H. rich and poor.
2 See, *Quod Apostolici Muneris*, pp. 175–186: *Rerum novarum*, pp. 193–233.

them. This was the object of Our encyclical, *Rerum Novarum*, of the 15th of May, 1891, in which we dwelt at length on the rights and duties, which both classes of society—those, namely, who control capital, and those who contribute labor[3]—are bound in relation to each other; and at the same time, We made it evident that the remedies which are most useful to protect the cause of religion, and to terminate the contest between the different classes of society, were to be found in the precepts of the Gospel.

3. Nor, with God's grace, were Our hopes entirely frustrated. Even those who are not Catholics, moved by the power of truth, avowed that the Church must be credited with a watchful care over all classes of society, and especially those whom fortune had least favored.[4] Catholics, of course, profited abundantly by these letters, for they not only received encouragement and strength for the excellent undertakings in which they were engaged, but also obtained the light which they needed in order to study this order of problems with great sureness and success.[5] Hence, it happened that the differences of opinion which prevailed among them were either removed or lessened. In the order of action, much has been done in favor of the proletariat, especially in those places where poverty was at its worst. Many new institutions were set on foot, those which were already established were increased, and all reaped the benefit of a greater stability. Such are, for instance, the popular bureaus that supply information to the uneducated; the rural banks which make loans to small farmers; the societies for mutual help or relief;[6] the unions of working men and other associations or institutions of the same kind. Thus, under the auspices of the Church, a measure of united action among Catholics was secured, as well as some planning in the setting up of agencies for the protection

---

3 L. *eorum qui rem et eorum qui operam confuerunt*; that is, the class of those who contribute money and the class of those who contribute labor.
4 L. *illos praecipue qui misera in fortuna versantur*; that is, the destitute.—H. the very poor.
5 L. *hujusmodi disciplinae studia*.
6 L. *aliae ad necessitates ob infortunia levandas*; that is, other societies for relief in case of misfortunes.

of the masses[7] which, in fact, are as often oppressed by guile and exploitation of their necessities as by their own indigence and toil.

4. This work of popular aid had, at first, no name of its own. The name of Christian Socialism, with its derivatives, which was adopted by some was very properly allowed to fall into disuse. Afterwards, some asked to have it called the Popular Christian Movement.[8] In the countries most concerned with this matter, there are some who are known as Social Christians.[9] Elsewhere, the movement is described as Christian Democracy and its partisans as Christian Democrats,[10] in opposition to what the socialists call Social Democracy. Not much exception is taken to the first of these two names, i.e., Social Christians, but many excellent men find the term Christian Democracy objectionable. They hold it to be very ambiguous and for this reason open to two objections. It seems by implication covertly to favor popular government and to disparage other methods of political administration. Secondly, it appears to belittle religion by restricting its scope to the care of the poor,[11] as if the other sections of society were not of its concern. More than that, under the shadow of its name there might easily lurk a design to attack all legitimate power, either civil or sacred. Wherefore, since this discussion is now so widespread, and so bitter, the consciousness of duty warns Us to put a check on this controversy and to define what Catholics are to think on this matter. We also propose to describe how the movement may extend its scope and be made more useful to the commonwealth.

5. What Social Democracy is and what Christian Democracy ought to be, assuredly no one can doubt. The first, with due

---

7 L. *plebis*; that is, the masses.
8 L. *actionem Christianam popularem*; that is, Christian popular action.—H. Christian Action for the People.
9 L. *sociales christiani*; that is, not Christian Socialists, but rather, socially minded Christians.
10 L. *democratici Christiani*.
11 L. *plebis*, see footnote 7.

consideration to the greater or less intemperance of its utterance, is carried to such an excess by many as to maintain that there is really nothing existing above the natural order of things, and that the acquirement and enjoyment of corporal and external goods constitute man's happiness. It aims at putting all government in the hands of the masses, reducing all ranks to the same level, abolishing all distinction of class, and finally introducing community of goods. Hence, the right to own private property is to be abrogated, and whatever property a man possesses, or whatever means of livelihood he has, is to be common to all.

6. As against this, Christian Democracy, by the fact that it is Christian, is built, and necessarily so, on the basic principles of divine faith, and it must provide better conditions for the masses, with the ulterior object of promoting the perfection of souls made for things eternal. Hence, for Christian Democracy, justice is sacred; it must maintain that the right of acquiring and possessing property cannot be impugned, and it must safeguard the various distinctions and degrees which are indispensable in every well-ordered commonwealth. Finally, it must endeavor to preserve in every human society the form and the character which God ever impresses on it. It is clear, therefore, that there is nothing in common between Social and Christian Democracy. They differ from each other as much as the sect of socialism[12] differs from the profession of Christianity.

7. Moreover, it would be a crime to distort this name of Christian Democracy to politics, for, although democracy, both in its philological and philosophical significations, implies popular government, yet in its present application it must be employed without any political significance, so as to mean nothing else than this beneficent Christian action in behalf of the people. For, the laws of nature and of the Gospel, which by right are superior to all human contingencies, are necessarily independent of all particular forms of civil government, while at the same time they are in harmony with everything that is not repugnant to

---

12 L. *quantum Socialismi secta.* — H. the sectarianism of Socialism.

morality and justice. They are, therefore, and they must remain absolutely free from the passions and the vicissitudes of parties, so that, under whatever political constitution, the citizens may and ought to abide by those laws, which command them to love God above all things, and their neighbors as themselves. This has always been the policy of the Church.[13] The Roman Pontiffs acted upon this principle, whenever they dealt with different countries,[14] no matter what might be the character of their governments. Hence, the mind and the action of Catholics devoted to promoting the welfare of the working classes can never be actuated with the purpose of favoring and introducing one government in place of another.

8. In the same manner, we must remove from Christian Democracy another possible subject of reproach, namely, that while looking after the advantage of the working people it should seem to overlook the upper classes of society, for they also are of the greatest use in preserving and perfecting the commonwealth. The Christian law of charity, which has just been mentioned, will prevent us from so doing. For it embraces all men, irrespective of ranks, as members of one and the same family, children of the same most beneficent Father, redeemed by the same Saviour, and called to the same eternal heritage. Hence, the doctrine of the Apostle, who warns us that "We are one body and one spirit called to the one hope in our vocation; one Lord, one faith and one baptism; one God and the Father of all who is above all, and through all, and in us all."[15] Wherefore, on account of the union established by nature between the common people[16] and the other classes of society, and which Christian brotherhood makes still closer, whatever diligence we devote to assisting the people will certainly profit also the other classes, the more so since, as will be thereafter shown, their co-operation is proper and necessary for the success of this undertaking.

---

13 L. *disciplina*.—H. the morality.
14 L. *cum civitatibus*; that is, with various body politics.
15 Eph. 4:4–6.
16 L. *plebis*; see footnote 7.

9. Let there be no question of fostering under this name of Christian Democracy any intention of diminishing the spirit of obedience, or of withdrawing people from their lawful rulers. Both the natural and the Christian law command us to revere those who in their various grades are shown above us in the State,[17] and to submit ourselves to their just commands. It is quite in keeping with our dignity as men and Christians to obey, not only exteriorly, but from the heart, as the Apostle expresses it, "for conscience' sake," when he commands us to keep our soul subject to the higher powers.[18] It is abhorrent to the profession of Christianity that anyone should feel unwilling to be subject and obedient to those who rule in the Church, and first of all to the bishops whom (without prejudice to the universal power of the Roman Pontiff) "the Holy Spirit has placed to rule the Church of God, which Christ has purchased by His Blood."[19] He who thinks or acts otherwise is guilty of ignoring the grave precept of the Apostle who bids us to obey our rulers and to be subject to them, for they watch as having to give an account of our souls.[20] Let the faithful everywhere implant these principles deep in their souls, and put them in practice in their daily life, and let the ministers of the Gospel meditate them profoundly, and incessantly labor, not merely by exhortation but especially by example, to teach them to others.

10. We have recalled these principles, which on other occasions We had already elucidated, in the hope that all dispute about the name of Christian Democracy will cease and that all suspicion of any danger coming from what the name signifies will be put at rest. And with reason do We hope so; for, neglecting the opinions of certain men whose views on the nature[21] and efficacy of this kind of Christian Democracy are not free from exaggeration[22] and from error, let no one condemn that zeal

17 L. *in civitate*; that is, in the body politic.
18 Rom. 13:1, 5.
19 Acts 20:28.
20 Heb. 13:11.
21 L. *vi*; that is, the nature.—See footnote 61, p. 264.
22 L. *immoderatione*; that is, excess.

which, in accordance with the natural and divine laws, aims to make the condition of those who toil more tolerable; to enable them to obtain, little by little, those means by which they may provide for the future; to help them to practice in public and in private the duties which morality and religion inculcate; to aid them to feel that they are not animals but men, not heathens but Christians, and so to enable them to strive more zealously and more eagerly for the one thing which is necessary; viz., that ultimate good for which we are born into this world. This is the intention; this is the work of those who wish that the people should be animated by Christian sentiments and should be protected from the contamination of socialism which threatens them.

11. We have designedly made mention here of virtue and religion. For, it is the opinion of some, and the error is already very common, that the social question is merely an *economic* one, whereas in point of fact it is, above all, a moral and religious matter, and for that reason must be settled by the principles of morality and according to the dictates of religion. For, even though wages are doubled[23] and the hours of labor are shortened and food is cheapened, yet, if the working man hearkens to the doctrines that are taught on this subject, as he is prone to do, and is prompted by the examples set before him to throw off respect for God and to enter upon a life of immorality, his labors and his gain will avail him naught.

12. Trial and experience have made it abundantly clear that many a workman lives in cramped and miserable quarters, in spite of his shorter hours and larger wages, simply because he has cast aside the restraints of morality and religion. Take away the instinct which Christian wisdom has planted and nurtured in men's hearts, take away foresight, temperance, frugality, patience, and other rightful, natural habits, no matter how much he may strive, he will never achieve prosperity. That is the reason why We have incessantly exhorted Catholics to enter these associations for bettering the condition of the laboring classes, and to

---

23 L. *ut operam locantibus geminetur merces.*

organize other undertakings with the same object in view; but We have likewise warned them that all this should be done under the auspices of religion, with its help and under its guidance.

13. The zeal of Catholics on behalf of the masses[24] is especially praiseworthy because it is engaged in the very same field in which, under the benign inspiration of the Church the active industry of charity has always labored, adapting itself in all cases to the varying exigencies of the times. For the law of mutual charity perfects, as it were, the law of justice, not merely by giving each man his due and in not impeding him in the exercise of his rights, but also by befriending him, "not with the word alone, or the lips, but in deed and in truth;"[25] being mindful of what Christ so lovingly said to His own: "A new commandment I give unto you, that you love one another, as I have loved you, that you love also one another. By this shall all men know that you are My disciples, if you have love one for the other."[26] This zeal in coming to the rescue of our fellow men should, of course, be solicitous, first for the eternal good of souls, but it must not neglect what is good and helpful for this life.

14. We should remember what Christ said to the disciple of the Baptist who asked him: "Art thou he that art to come or look we for another?"[27] He invoked, as proof of the mission given to Him among men, His exercise of charity, quoting for them the text of Isaias: "The blind see, the lame walk, the lepers are cleansed, the deaf hear, the dead rise again, the poor have the Gospel preached to them."[28] And speaking also of the last judgment and of the rewards and punishments He will assign, He declared that He would take special account of the charity men exercised toward each other. And in that discourse there is one thing that especially excites our surprise, viz., that Christ omits those works of mercy which comfort the soul and referring

---

24 L. *in proletarios*; that is, the proletarians.
25 1 John 3:18.
26 John 13:34–35.
27 Matt. 11:3.
28 Matt. 11:4 5.

only to those which comfort the body, He regards them as being done to Himself: "For I was hungry and you gave Me to eat; I was thirsty and you gave Me to drink; I was a stranger and you took Me in; naked and you covered Me; sick and you visited Me; I was in prison and you came to Me."[29]

15. To the teachings which enjoin the twofold charity of spiritual and corporal works Christ adds His own example, so that no one may fail to recognize the importance which He attaches to it. In the present instance, we recall the sweet words that came from His paternal heart: "I have pity on the multitude,"[30] as well as the desire He had to assist them even if it were necessary to invoke His miraculous power. Of His tender compassion, we have the proclamation made in holy Writ, viz., that "He went about doing good and healing all that were oppressed by the devil."[31] This law of charity which He imposed upon His Apostles, they in the most holy and zealous way put into practice; and after them, those who embraced Christianity originated that wonderful variety of institutions for alleviating all the miseries by which mankind is afflicted. And these institutions carried on and continually increased their powers of relief and were the especial glories of Christianity and of the civilization of which it was the source, so that right-minded men[32] never fail to admire those foundations, aware as they are of the proneness of men to concern themselves about their own and neglect the needs of others.

16. Nor are we to eliminate from the list of good works the giving of money for charity, in pursuance of what Christ has said: "But yet that which remaineth, give alms."[33] Against this, the socialist cries out and demands its abolition as injurious to the native dignity of man. But, if it is done in the manner which the Scripture enjoins,[34] and in conformity with the true Christian

---

29 Matt. 25:35–36.
30 Mark 8:2.
31 Acts 10:38.
32 L. *integri judicii.*—H. of sound intelligence.
33 Luke 11:41.
34 Matt. 6:2–4.

spirit, it neither connotes pride in the giver nor inflicts shame upon the one who receives. Far from being dishonorable for man, it draws closer the bonds of human society of augmenting the force of the obligation of the duties which men are under with regard to each other. No one is so rich that he does not need another's help; no one so poor as not to be useful in some way to his fellow man; and the disposition to ask assistance from others with confidence and to grant it with kindness is part of our very nature. Thus, justice and charity are so linked with each other, under the equable and sweet law of Christ, as to form an admirable cohesive power in human society and to lead all of its members to exercise a sort of providence in looking after their own and in seeking the common good as well.

17. As regards not merely the temporary aid given to the laboring classes, but the establishment of permanent institutions on their behalf, it is most commendable for charity to undertake them. It will thus see that more certain and more reliable means of assistance will be afforded to the necessitous. That kind of help is especially worthy of recognition, which forms the minds of mechanics and laborers to thrift and foresight, so that in course of time they may be able, in part at least, to look out for themselves. To aim at that is not only to dignify the duty of the rich toward the poor,[35] but to elevate the poor themselves, for, while it urges them to work in order to improve their condition, it preserves them meantime from danger, it refrains immoderation in their desires, and acts as a spur in the practice of virtue. Since, therefore, this is of such great avail and so much in keeping with the spirit of the times, it is a worthy object for the charity of righteous men to undertake with prudence and zeal.

18. Let it be understood, therefore, that this devotion of Catholics to comfort and elevate the mass of the people is in keeping with the spirit of the Church and is most conformable to the examples which the Church has always held up for imitation. It matters very little whether it goes under the name of the Popular

---

35 L. *proletarios*, see footnote 24.

Christian Movement or Christian Democracy, if the instructions that have been given by Us be fully carried out with fitting obedience. But, it is of the greatest importance that Catholics should be one in mind, will, and action in a matter of such great moment. And it is also of importance that the influence of these undertakings should be extended by the multiplication of men and means devoted to the same object.

19. Especially must there be appeals to the kindly assistance of those whose rank, wealth, and intellectual as well as spiritual culture[36] give them a certain standing in the community. If their help is not extended, scarcely anything can be done which will help in promoting the wellbeing of the people. Assuredly, the more earnestly many of those who are prominent citizens conspire effectively to attain that object, the quicker and surer will the end be reached. We would, however, have them understand that they are not at all free to look after or neglect those who happen to be beneath them, but that it is a strict duty that binds them. For, no one lives only for his personal advantage in a community; he lives for the common good as well, so that, when others cannot contribute their share for the general good, those who can do so are obliged to make up the deficiency. The very extent of the benefits they have received increases the burden of their responsibility, and a stricter account will have to be rendered to God who bestowed those blessings upon them. What should also urge all to the fulfillment of their duty in this regard is the widespread disaster, which will eventually fall upon all classes of society if his assistance does not arrive in time; and therefore, is it that he who neglects the cause of the distressed masses is disregarding his own interest as well as that of the community.

20. If this action, which is social in the Christian sense of the term[37] develops and grows in accordance with its own nature,

---

36 L. *ingenii animique cultura*.—H. superior culture.
37 H. if such social enterprise, which is, at the same time, Christian enterprise.

there will be no danger, as is feared, that those other institutions, which the piety of our ancestors have established and which are now flourishing, will decline or be absorbed by new foundations. Both of them spring from the same root of charity and religion, and not only do not conflict with each other, but can easily be made to coalesce and combine so perfectly as to provide, all the better by the pooling of their beneficent efforts, for the needs of the masses and for the daily increasing perils to which they are exposed.

21. The condition of things at present proclaims, and proclaims vehemently, that there is need for a union of brave minds with all the resources they can command. The harvest of misery is before our eyes, and the dreadful projects of the most disastrous national upheavals are threatening us from the growing power of the socialistic movement. They have insidiously worked their way into the very heart of the community, and in the darkness of their secret gatherings, and in the open light of day, in their writings and their harangues, they are urging the masses onward to sedition; they fling aside religious discipline; they scorn duties; they clamor only for rights; they are working incessantly on the multitudes of the needy which daily grow greater, and which, because of their poverty are easily deluded and led into error. It is equally the concern of the State and of religion, and all good men should deem it a sacred duty to preserve and guard both in the honor which is their due.

22. That this most desirable agreement of wills should be maintained, it is essential that all refrain from giving any cause of dissension which hurt and divide minds. Hence, in newspapers and in speeches to the people, let them avoid subtle and practically useless questions which are neither easy to solve nor easy to understand except by minds of unusual ability and after the most serious study. It is quite natural for people to hesitate on doubtful subjects, and that different men should hold different opinions, but those who sincerely seek after truth will preserve equanimity, modesty, and courtesy in matters of dispute. They

will not let differences of opinion deteriorate into conflicts of wills. Besides, to whatever opinion a man's judgment may incline, if the matter is yet open to discussion, let him keep it, provided he be always disposed to listen with religious obedience to what the Holy See may decide on the question.

23. The action of Catholics, of whatever description it may be, will work with greater effect if all of the various associations, while preserving their individual rights, move together under one primary and directive force. In Italy, We desire that this directive force should emanate from the Institute of Catholic Congresses and Reunions so often praised by Us, to which Our predecessor and We Ourselves have committed the charge of controlling the common action of Catholics under the authority and direction of the bishops of the country. So let it be for other nations, in case there be any leading organization of this description to which this matter has been legitimately entrusted.

24. Now, in all questions of this sort where the interests of the Church and the Christian people[38] are so closely allied, it is evident what they who are in the sacred ministry should do, and it is clear how industrious they should be in inculcating right doctrine and in teaching the duties of prudence and charity. To go out and move among the people, to exert a healthy influence on them by adapting themselves to the present condition of things, is what more than once in addressing the clergy We have advised. More frequently, also, in writing to the bishops and other dignitaries of the Church, and especially of late,[39] We have lauded this affectionate solicitude for the people and

---

38 L. *plebis christianae.*
39 Letter to the Minister General of the Minorites, November 25, 1898. In this letter, the Pope recalled the instructions given in *Aeterni Patris* concerning the way to be followed in higher studies; the doctrine of Thomas Aquinas should be followed by all the religious who wish truly to philosophize (*qui vere philosophari volunt*); paramount importance of the study of holy Scripture; how to preach the word of God; forceful exhortation addressed to the Franciscans to go out of their monasteries and, following the example of St. Francis, devote themselves to the salvation of the masses; importance of the Third Order of St. Francis with regard to this work.

declared it to be the special duty of both the secular and regular clergy. But, in the fulfillment of this obligation let there be the greatest caution and prudence exerted, and let it be done after the fashion of the saints. Francis, who was poor and humble, Vincent of Paul, the father of the afflicted classes, and very many others whom the Church keeps ever in her memory were wont to lavish their care upon the people, but in such wise as not to be engrossed overmuch or to be unmindful of themselves or to let it prevent them from laboring with the same assiduity in the perfection of their own soul and the cultivation of virtue.

25. There remains one thing upon which We desire to insist very strongly, in which not only the ministers of the Gospel, but also all those who are devoting themselves to the cause of the people, can with very little difficulty bring about a most commendable result. That is to inculcate in the minds of the people, in a brotherly way and whenever the opportunity presents itself, the following principles; viz.: to keep aloof on all occasions from seditious acts and seditious men; to hold inviolate the rights of others; to show a proper respect to superiors; to willingly perform the work in which they are employed; not to grow weary of the restraint of family life which in many ways is so advantageous; to keep to their religious practices above all, and in their hardships and trials to have recourse to the Church for consolation. In the furtherance of all this, it is of great help to propose the splendid example of the Holy Family of Nazareth, and to advise the invocation of its protection, and it also helps to remind the people of the examples of sanctity which have shone in the midst of poverty, and to hold up before them the reward that awaits them in the better life to come.

26. Finally, We recur again to what We have already declared and We insist upon it most solemnly; viz., that whatever projects individuals or associations form in this matter should be formed under episcopal authority. Let them not be led astray by an excessive zeal in the cause of charity. If it leads them to be wanting in proper submission, it is not a sincere zeal;

it will not have any useful result and cannot be acceptable to God. God delights in the souls of those who put aside their own designs and obey the rulers of His Church as if they were obeying Him; He assists them even when they attempt difficult things and benignly leads them to their desired end. Let them show, also, examples of virtue, so as to prove that a Christian is a hater of idleness and self-indulgence, that he stands firm and unconquered in the midst of adversity. Examples of that kind have a power of moving people to dispositions of soul that make for salvation, and have all the greater force as the condition of those who give them is higher in the social scale.

27. We exhort you, venerable brethren, to provide for all this, as the necessities of men and of places may require, according to your prudence and your zeal, meeting as usual in council to combine with each other in your plans for the furtherance of these projects. Let your solicitude watch and let your authority be effective in controlling, compelling, and also in preventing, lest anyone under the pretext of good should cause the vigor of sacred discipline to be relaxed or the order which Christ has established in His Church to be disturbed. Thus, by the rightful, harmonious and ever-increasing labor of all Catholics, let it become more and more evident that the tranquility of order and the true prosperity flourish especially among those peoples whom the Church controls and influences; and that she holds it as her sacred duty to admonish every one of what the law of God enjoins, to unite the rich and the poor in the bonds of fraternal charity, and to lift up and strengthen men's souls in the times when adversity presses heavily upon them.

28. Let Our commands and Our wishes be confirmed by the words so full of apostolic charity which the blessed Paul addressed to the Romans: "I beseech you therefore brethren, be reformed in the newness of your mind; he that giveth, with simplicity; he that ruleth, with carefulness; he that showeth mercy, with cheerfulness. Let love be without dissimulation. Hating that which is evil; cleaving to that which is good; loving

one another with the charity of brotherhood; with honor preventing one another; in carefulness, not slothful; rejoicing in hope; patient in tribulation; instant in prayer. Communicating to the necessities of the saints. Pursuing hospitality. Rejoice with them that rejoice; weep with them that weep; being of one mind to one another; to no man rendering evil for evil; providing good things not only in the sight of God but also in the sight of men."[40]

29. As a pledge of these benefits receive the apostolic benediction which, venerable brethren, We grant most lovingly in the Lord to you and your clergy and people.

---

40   Rom. 12:1, 2, 8–13, 15–17.

CONCLUSION

IN 1902, POPE LEO XIII REACHED THE TWENty-fifth year of his pontificate. On this occasion he published, in both Italian and French, an apostolic letter addressed to the patriarchs, archbishops and bishops of the world. The occasion was a happy one, but the Pope could find in the general situation obtaining at that time no cause for rejoicing. The temporal power of the Popes had not yet been restored; as to the nations, since they were more and more abandoning their Christian traditions, it was easy to foresee that they were headed for catastrophes still worse than those which they had undergone in the past. Looking for the cause of so many evils, Leo XIII could only find it in the sane war waged against the Church by modern States. In a way, there was nothing radically new in this situation. Christ Himself has warned His disciples that they should be ready to suffer persecution for the sake of justice (John 15:18). It is a fact, however, that the kind of persecution suffered by the Church in our own days differs in many ways from the early attacks directed against the Christians by the heathen emperors of Rome.

From this point of view, the influence exercised by the Protestant Revolution has been of decisive importance. True enough, the first reformers never intended to exclude Christianity from the life of the nation that had received it. Nevertheless, by rebelling against the authority of the Popes and by proclaiming the principle of free examination applied to all domains, they opened the way to later developments whose results are now visible to all. The spirit of free examination in matters of religious faith is nothing else than the spirit of philosophism. No wonder then that the so-called "Philosophers" of the eighteenth century simply rejected the authority of even Scripture, denied the possibility of divine revelation, and finally uprooted all Christian beliefs from the conscience of their own people. All the errors denounced by the Pope in the many encyclicals he had published during the twenty years of his pontificate can be considered as flowing from this common source. The spreading of practical atheism has finally shaken up to the very foundations of morality. The so-called lay State is the very embodiment of this progressive dechristianization of private and public life, and it is worthy of note that, confronted as it is with the tragic consequences of its own doctrine, the modern State is unable to discover the perils that threaten it with destruction.

All conceivable remedies have been imagined and tried, except the only effective one, that is, the returning of modern States to the principles of Christianity. Men have trusted "liberty", but, since they conceived it as granted indifferently to truth and error, the results have been an extreme confusion. They have trusted the spreading of "public instruction," but instruction without religion and morality only breeds pride and the spirit of rebellion. They have put their trust in "scientific progress," but this progress, whose reality cannot be denied, has been attended by a too visible regression of morality. Science has been divorced from Wisdom; the answer to our problems is not to reject science nor to refuse the advantages which accrue from it; the true answer to the problem is to subordinate the use of science to the religious ends established by the Creator.

At the end of his long pontificate, Pope Leo XIII could see more clearly than ever that the divorce of modern society and Christianity was the origin of the evils he had denounced ever since the very first year of his reign. Now, the return to Christianity is nothing else that a return to the Catholic Church in which Christianity is incarnate. Such is the reason why, in the mind of Pope Leo XIII, the defense of the Catholic Church and of her liberty has always been identical with the defense of the familial order, of the political order, of the social order, and of the economic order.

Looking backwards to the long series of encyclicals he devoted to these problems, the Pope could see in the mere list of their titles the concrete proof of the unity and continuity of his doctrinal apostolate: "In the full awareness of this divine efficacy,

Conclusion

We, from the very beginning of Our pontificate, have carefully endeavored to place in full light and to stress the helpful designs of the Church as well as to increase as far as possible, together with the treasure of her teachings, the field of her salutary action. Such has been the object of the principal acts of Our pontificate, especially of the encyclicals *On Christian Philosophy, On Human Liberty, On Christian Marriage, On Freemasonry, On Civil Government, On the Christian Constitution of States, On Socialism, On the Labor Question, On the Duties of Christian Citizens*, and on other similar subjects." These encyclicals (which have been collected here in this volume) obviously represent the core of the social teachings of Pope Leo XIII.

Not without a touch of melancholy did the Pontiff observe, after this twenty-five-year-long effort, that the same accusations leveled at the Church during the early years of his pontificate were still being directed against her: that the Church is the enemy of scientific progress; the Church is the enemy of liberty; the Church is usurping the rights of the State. As a matter of fact, it is to the Church that we are indebted for having defended and spread that Christian wisdom without which we would still be in the darkness of barbarity; it is the Church that has liberated the world from slavery and everywhere defended the feeble and the oppressed against the tyranny of the strong; and it is the State which has everywhere usurped the rights of the Church, not inversely!

Were he with us still today, Pope Leo XIII would find little encouragement in the latest developments which have taken place since the seizure of power by Marxism in central Europe and in Russia. But he would find in contemporary history countless verifications of his predictions and as confident as ever in the ultimate triumph of the truth, he would still predict the day when, through his Church, God will spread again the spirit and the life of the Gospel in the perishing members of our corrupt society. The duty of Catholics is clear. As to the final success, it depends on Him of whom it has been written (Heb. 13:8): "Jesus Christ, yesterday, and today; and the same for ever."

BIBLIOGRAPHICAL NOTE

WORKS OF LEO XIII:

Acta Leonis XIII, 26 vols., Rome, 1878–1903. Each encyclical is found in its chronological place in this collection of the complete works.

Acta Sanctae Sedis, Vols. 11–25, Rome, 1878–1903.

Actes de Léon XIII.... Texte latin avec traduction française en regard, Paris, Maison de la bonne presse, 7 vols., no dates.

There is no English translation of the complete writings of Pope Leo XIII. Translations of his encyclicals have been published in the London *Tablet* soon after issuance, but complete collections of the *Tablet* are not easy to find in the United States or in Canada. Separate encyclicals are easier to find in English translation. Among those that are known to us we cite:

The Paulist Press pamphlet series, consisting of *Anglican Orders (Apostolicae Curae)*; *Freemasonry (Humanum Genus)*; *The Condition of Labor (Rerum Novarum)*; *The Christian Constitution of States (Immortale Dei)*; *Christian Democracy (Graves de Communi)*; *Chief Duties of Christians as Citizens (Sapientiae Christianae)*; *Human Liberty (Libertas Humana)*; *Christian Marriage (Arcanum Divinae Sapientiae)*; *Civil Government (Diuturnum)*; *Scholastic Philosophy (Aeterni Patris)*; *Holy Scripture (Providentissimus Deus)*; *and Holy Spirit (Divinum Illud)*. Each of these contains the English translation of an encyclical, with a discussion club outline divided into lesson, prepared by Gerald C. Treacy, S. J. Each lesson covers a certain number of paragraphs, sums up their doctrine, and lists a series of relevant questions.

The National Catholic Welfare Conference (Washington 5, D. C.) has published several encyclicals of Pope Pius XI and of Pope Pius XII, but the only encyclical of Pope Leo XIII included in their publication is: *On the Condition of Labor (Rerum Novarum)*, or "A Magna Charta of Social Order." This is a publication in pamphlet form of the English translation contained in the book *Two Basic Social Encyclicals—'On the Condition of Workers' by Leo XIII, and 'On Reconstructing the Social Order' by Pius XI*, Latin text with English translation, Benziger Bros., New York.

OTHER TRANSLATIONS ARE:

J.J. Wynne, S.J., *The Great Encyclicals of Pope Leo XIII*. Translations from approved sources. New York, Benziger Bros., 1903.

J. Husslein, S.J., *Social Wellsprings: Fourteen Epochal Documents by Pope Leo XIII*. The Bruce Publishing Co., Milwaukee, 1940 (3rd

printing, 1949). The second volume of *Social Wellsprings* contains eighteen encyclicals of social reconstruction of Pope Pius XI. Extended bibliographies accompany each encyclical.

1. GENERAL BIBLIOGRAPHY UP TO 1907:

M. Claudia Carlen, I.H.M., *A Guide to the Encyclicals of the Roman Pontiffs, from Leo XIII to the Present Day: 1878-1907*, New York, Wilson, 1939.

2. LIFE AND WORKS OF POPE LEO XIII:

U. Benigni, "Leo XIII," *The Catholic Encyclopedia*, 9 (1910) 169-73.

G. Goyau. "Léon XIII," *Dictionnaire de theologie catholique*, 9 (1926) 334-59.

Mgr. T' Serclaes, *Le pape Léon XIII, sa vie, son action religieuse, politique et sociale*, 3 vols. Lille, 1895-1906.

P. Tischleder, "Leo XIII," Staatslexikon III (5), pp. 926-60.

3. CHRISTIAN PHILOSOPHY:

Many commentaries have been published on each encyclical at, or about the time of its publication. Most are contained in foreign reviews or journals difficult of access and, moreover, they seldom were written in view of introducing a larger public to the meaning of these documents. The encyclicals of Leo XIII are themselves their best commentary. Carefully read, especially with the help of an index referring the readers to the parallel passages, they will ultimately unveil their meaning to most of us. To become acquainted with the doctrinal background of Leo XIII's social teaching, one would do well to follow the advice given by the Pope himself, that is, to proceed to a direct study of Christian philosophy, such as, for instance:

E. Gilson, *The Spirit of Mediaeval Philosophy* (Gifford Lectures 1931-1932), trans. A. H. C. Downes, New York, Charles Scribner's Sons, 1940; Student's edition, 1953.

On the doctrine of St. Thomas Aquinas in particular:

A.C. Pegis, *Basic Writings of St. Thomas Aquinas*, 2 vols., New York, Random House, 1945.

A.C. Pegis, *Introduction to St. Thomas Aquinas*, New York, Modern Library, 1948.

Absolutely essential is the section devoted to the notion of Law (natural, human and divine) in *Basic Writings*, Vol. II, pp. 742-805; in *Introduction*, pp. 609-50. The whole doctrine of these encyclicals rests upon the notion of law developed in the *Summa theologiae* by Thomas Aquinas.

4. SOCIAL ETHICS AND NATURAL LAW:

On the social and political teachings of St. Thomas Aquinas see:

V.J. Bourke, *Ethics, A Textbook in Moral Philosophy*, New York, The Macmillan Company, 1951.

C. Riedl, "The Social Theory of St. Thomas Aquinas," *Proceedings of the American Catholic Philosophical Association*, 9 (1933) 24–34.

Y. Simon, *The Nature and Functions of Authority*, Milwaukee, Marquette University Press, 1940.

A. Beck, "The Thomist Approach to Natural Law," *Clergy Review*, London, 27 (1947) 217–27; 28 (1947) 73–91.

J. Messner, *Social Ethics: Natural Law in the Modern World*, trans. J.J. Doherty, St. Louis, B. Herder, 1949.

A. Rzadkiewicz, O.F.M., *The Philosophical Bases of Human Liberty according to St. Thomas Aquinas. A Study of Social Philosophy*, Washington, The Catholic University of America Press, 1949.

Huntington Cairns, *Legal Philosophy from Plato to Hegel*, Baltimore, The Johns Hopkins Press, 1949, ch 5, pp. 162–204.

C.A. Hart (ed.), "The Natural Law and International Relations," *Proceedings of the American Catholic Philosophical Association*, 1950.

M.B. Crowe, "The Natural Law before St. Thomas," *Irish Ecclesiastical Record*, 76 (1951), 193–205.

M.B. Crowe, "St. Thomas and the Natural Law," *Irish Ecclesiastical Record*, 76 (1951), 293–305.

5. SOCIAL AND ECONOMIC DOCTRINES:

W.J. McDonald, *The Social Value of Property according to St. Thomas Aquinas*, Washington, The Catholic University of America Press, 1939.

J.A. Ryan, "The Economic Philosophy of St. Thomas," *Essays in Thomism*, ed. R.E. Brennan, New York, Sheed & Ward, 1942, pp. 239–260.

J.P. Kelly, *Aquinas and Modern Practices of Interest Taking* (Thomas Aquinas Lectures), Brisbane, Aquinas Press, 1945.

D. MacLaren, O.P., *Private Property and the Natural Law* (Aquinas Papers, 8) Oxford, Blackfriars, 1948.

V.J. Bourke, "Material Possessions and Thomistic Ethics," *Philosophic Thought in France and in the United States*, ed. M. Farber, Buffalo, University Press, 1950, pp. 613–27.

W.J. McDonald, "Toward a Philosophy of Economics," *Philosophical Studies in Honor of the V.R. Ignatius Smith O.P.*, ed. J.K. Ryan, Westminster, Md., Newman Press, 1952, pp. 222–32.

6. POLITICAL AUTHORITY:

Y. Simon, *The Nature and Functions of Authority*, Milwaukee, Marquette University Press, 1940.

H. Rommen, *The State in Catholic Thought*, St. Louis, Herder, 1945.

J. Maritain, *Man and the State*, Chicago, University of Chicago Press, 1951; chs. 1–2 pp.1–53.

7. CHRISTIAN CITIZENSHIP :

H. Clérissac, O. P., *The Mystery of the Church*, New York, Sheed & Ward, 1937.

W. Parsons, S. J., *The First Freedom*, New York, McMullen, 1948.

I. Smith, O. P., "Aquinas and Some American Freedoms," *New Scholasticism*, 21 (1947) 105–35.

A. P. Stokes, *Church and State in the United States*, New York, Harper & Bros., 1950.

8. RERUM NOVARUM:

Among the many studies devoted to the encyclical *Rerum Novarum*, or directly concerned with its doctrine, the following can be usefully consulted:

H. E. Cardinal Manning, "Leo XIII on the Condition of Labour," *Dublin Review*, 109 (1891, 153–67.

J. Rickaby, S. J., "A Commentary on the Encyclical Letter of May 15, 1891, On the Condition of the Working Classes," *The Month*, 91 (1898), 368–74; 481–91.

L. Watt, S. J., *Catholic Social Principles, A Commentary on the Papal Encyclical Rerum Novarum*, London, Burns, Oates & Washbourne, 1929.

J. Husslein, S. J., *The Christian Social Manifesto, An Interpretative Study of the Encyclicals Rerum Novarum and Quadragesimo Anno*, 5th ed., Milwaukee, The Bruce Publishing Co., 1939.

For a comparison with *Quadragesimo Anno* consult:

O. von Nell-Breuning, S. J., *Reorganization of Social Economy*, Milwaukee, The Bruce Publishing Co., 1936.

INDEX

Academy of St. Thomas Aquinas, xviii
Aeterni Patris, xxii–xxiii, 3–29, 318
Alms, 183, 208, 318
Ancora Una Volta, 140
Apostolate, to be carried by Laymen, 245–246
Arcanum, 66–91, 100
Associations, 226–227, 229, 280, 323
    how they should be organized, 228–230
    rest upon religion, 230–231
Authority, its divine origin, xxvi, xxix–xxx, 45–46, 125–127, 146–147, 177, 179–182
    its sacredness, 154, 244
    domestic, xxvi, xxxiv–xxxv, 74–75, 182, 200–201, 264–265
    political, xxvii–xxviii
    must be obeyed, 43, 128–129
    must not reign by fear, 135
    protects man against States, 43–44
    of God, 157–158
    God to be obeyed rather than men, 129–130, 133, 150, 244

Bishops, 149–150, 322–323
Body Politic, xliii–xliv

Capital, and labor, 204, 311
Catholicae Ecclesiae, 284
Catholics, their duties, 241–242
    Catholic citizens, 167–169
    loyal to both Church and country, 242–243
    should preserve union of minds, 257–258
    how to take part in public affairs, 258–261
Charity, 206–208
    queen of virtues, 233
    bond of perfection, 263
    better than State relief, 212
    opposed to slavery, 290–291
Children, and parents, 200–201
Christ, Savior of the world, 6–7, 34, 177, 249, 291, 302
    His Sacred Heart, 213
    His love for men, 264
    the new Adam, 291
    has renewed the world, 66–67, 177–178
    became poor for our sake, 183, 208
    the sole guardian of morals, 161
    Son of a carpenter, Himself a Carpenter, 208
    His teachings, 316–317
    hater of idleness, 324
Christian action for the people, 313, 320
Christian citizens, 131–132
    not subjected to conflicting obligations, 154–155
Christian Constitution of States, 144–171, 193, 213
    coordinates divine and human rights, 154
    common good insured by laws, 154
Christian Democracy, 312–317, 321
Christian Democrats, 312
Christian Doctrine, should be studied by all, 246–247
Christian form of civil government, 131

Christian morals, should be
  reestablished, 233
Christian Philosophy, xxi–xxii,
  xxxvii, 3–4, 7–15, 19–20
  philosophy of the Gospel, 155
Christian Socialism, 312
Christian Society, described by
  Augustine, 154
Christian Wisdom, 88, 155, 166,
  239–240
Christians, must fight for Christ,
  266
  must unite, 321
  should avoid useless questions,
    321
Church, and defense of Christian
  faith, 54
  and the salvation of souls, 144
  is a perfect society, 59–60, 249
  is the City of God, 97
  is the Kingdom of Christ, 98
  established by Christ, 149,
    248–249
  never deserted by God, 262
  and State, xxxiii, 156, 254–257
  is the safest ally of the State,
    114, 136–137
  promotes progress and
    civilization, 144
  holds the answer to social
    problems, 202
  both teaches and educates,
    209–211
  her enemies, 245–246
Civilis potestas, xliv
Civilization, true and false, 273–274
Civitas, xliii–xliv
Commonwealth, xliv
Communism, Communists, 135,
  175, 329
  community of goods, 200–202
  propaganda, 176

Confraternities, 226
Corpus Leoninum, xl–xliv, 329

Deacons, 212
Democracy, legitimate form of
  government, 61–62, 125
Disasters, past and future, 241
Diuturnum, xxix, 93, 101
Divini Illius Magistri, 280
Divini Redemptoris, 173
Divorce, 69, 83–87
  and second marriage, 88–90
Domestic society, *see* Family

Ecclesiastica potestas, xliv
Employers, their duties, 204–205
Encyclicals, their nature, xix
  their object, xx
  their authority, xx–xxi
  character of their teaching, xxi
  choice made by Leo XIII, xxi,
    xl, 325
  how to read them,
    xxxvii–xxxviii
  their language, xli–xlii
  their effect, 310–311
Equality, of origin and nature, 112
  true and false, 178–179
  an impossible ideal, 203

Faith, should be professed and
  defended, even by private
  individuals, 246–249
  is one, 252
  helps reason, 250–251
  rests upon divine authority, 251
  achieves the union of minds, 251
Family, older than political society,
  xxxv
  springs from marriage, 75
  domestic society, 240–241
  owes its solidity to the

holiness of marriage, 154
and government, 199
Christian family training, 279
Fatalism, 36
Fear, *see* Authority
Freemasonry, 97–119
and fellow travelers, 100–103
and breakdown of morals, 108
aims to control public education, 109
opposed to the Church, 110–111
threatens both domestic and civil society, 111
should not be joined by Catholics, 115–117
Fundamental error, xxiii–xxiv
Fundamental truth, xxiv–xxvii

God, existence and attributes, 9–11
Creator and father of all, 117
teacher of mankind, 53
source of light, 7–10
supreme authority, 157–158
supreme ruler of the States, 147–149
Gospel, superior to pagan wisdom, 42
Grace, and nature, xxiv–xxv
and liberty, 39–40
Graves des Communi, 307, 310–325
Guilds, 117, 224–225

Heaven, loved more than earth, 248–249
Humanum Genus, 97–119

Immortale Dei, 35, 144–171
Inequality; essential to nature, xxv–xxvi, 112–113, 180
hierarchy, 180

Innovations, innovators, 176
In Plurimus, 286–305
Inscrutabili, xxiii, 271–285
In Supremo Apostolatus Fastigio, 300
Institute controlling the national Catholic welfare societies, 322
Intellect, ennobled by Christian faith, 87

Judgment, work of the intellect, 37
Jus, 40
Justice, and natural right, 195–196

Kings, hold their authority from God, xxvii–xxxi
consecrated by the popes, 133

Lateran Council, 13
Law, definition, 38
natural law, 39
human law, 40
eternal law, 39, 41
rules the States, 47–51
Liberalism, xxiv, 44, 46, 54–55
its intolerance toward the Church, 57–58
Liberals, 44
Libertas Praestantissimum, 34–62
Liberties, modern, xxxi, 48–51
of speech, 51–52
of teaching, 52, 160
of publishing, 160
of conscience, 55
of worship, 162
Liberty, its definition, 160
natural, 35–36
moral, 35
evangelical, 299
and intellect, 35–36
presupposes law, 41–42

in civil society, 42
fraternity and equality, 298–299
Longinqua Oceani, xix
Loyalty, to church and country, 245

Magistery of the Church, ordinary and extraordinary, xix–xx
Majority, *see* Sovereignty of the people
Man, must live in society, 145–146
his nature justifies his rights, 196–197
Marriage, xxxv, 66–91
was a sacrament amongst unbelievers, xxxvi, 76
ennobled by Christ, 70, 77
raised by Him to the dignity of a sacrament, 279
its final cause, 72–73, 81
debased by socialists and communists, 175
consequences, 280
and abolition of slavery, 74
no civil marriage, 75–77, 89
but consequences of marriage can be regulated by States, 87
mixed marriages, 90
Matrimonial contract, 80
Mirari Vos, 162
Mit Brennender Sorge, 141
Monogamy, a divine institution, 68–69
Morality, independent, 44

Nations, made for health, 281
see Sin
Naturalism, xxiii–xxiv, 44, 76, 93–95, 103–108, 110, 169
Naturalists, *see* Naturalism

Nature, and grace, xxiv–xxv, 67
its divine origin, xxv–xxvi
Neutral schools, xxxiii–xxxiv
Nihilism, 135, 175

Obedience, *see* Authority
Oppression, justifies legal action for a change of government, 61–62
Ownership, *see* Property

Parents, *see* Authority
Patience, xxxi, 181, 293
Patrimony, of the poor, 212–213
Paulist Press, xli–xlii, 86, 141,
Philosophers, self-styled, 178, 328
Philosophy, and revelation, 13–15
civil (i.e., non religious) philosophy of life, 160–161
Political opinions, can be different, 169–170
Political power, cannot be removed, 125
does not come from people, 125
should be carried after the example of God, 129–130
Polygamy, 69
Poor, xlii–xliii
are blessed, 208–209
helped by the Church, 212
need protection from the State, 216–217
see Poverty
Popes, supreme religious authority, 149–150
doctrinal authority, 251–253
political prudence, 260–262
have saved civilization, 274–275
Italy's debt to the papacy, 275–276
Popular Christian Movement, 312
Poverty, is no disgrace, 208

Power, comes from God, xxxi, 179
  the two powers, 151–153, 158
  their concord, 152, 155–157
  necessity of the temporal
    power, 276–277
Praeclara Gratulationis, xxix,
  xxxi, 94
Prelates, should be respected,
  260–262
Presidents, hold their power from
  God, xxviii
Principatus, xliv
  Proletarians, proletariat, *see*
  Working men,
Property, xxxvi, 224
  right to private property, 183
  is a right grounded in human
    nature, 195–199; and in the
    needs of domestic society,
    199–201
  should be better distributed,
    223–224
Prudence, political and personal,
  260–261

Quanta Cura, xviii, 162
Quod Apostolici Muneris, xxvi,
  100, 175–186

Race, human race, 287
  races united by Christ, 289–290
  their brotherly equality in
    Christ, 292–293
Rationalism, xxiii, 44, 169
  usurps the name of reason, 178
Reformation, and popular
  rebellions, and dechristianization, 134
Religion, links States to God,
  147–148
  true religion, 149
  and the State, 162

Religious associations, 117–118
  of St. Vincent de Paul, 118
Rerum Novarum, xxxvi, 193–233
Respublica, xliv
Rest, on Sundays, and feast of
  obligations, 219
Revolutions, to be avoided, xxxi,
  136–137, 154, 176, 193, 322–323
  promoted by socialism, 178
Rich, 183, 194–195, 206
  their duties, 204
Rulers, should rule as father, 146
  see Authority

Sancta Dei Civitas, 235
Sapitentiae Christianae, 235,
  239–266
Schism, and eastern civilization,
  276
Scholastics, 27–28
Secret Societies, *see* Freemasonry
Separation of Church and State,
  59
  is a fatal principle, 59–60
  is a false opinion, 161–163, 165
Sin, makes nations miserable, 262
  cause of all evils, 288
  is slavery, 37, 287
  and the cause of slavery, 288
  original sin, 107, 203
Slavery, abolished in Brazil, 286,
  303
  reproved by the Church,
    286–291
  a consequence of original sin,
    288
  wiped out by Christ, 291–294
  eliminated by Christians,
    296–297
  especially opposed by the
    popes, 297–298

Slaves, xxxi
  exhorted to patience, 293–294;
    and to moderation, 304
  their dignity, 294, 296
Social Christians, 312
Social classes, not necessarily
    hostile, 203–204
  all necessary to the State, 215
  bound in friendship by the
    Church, 206
  and in brotherly love, 210
Social Contract, or pact, xxx, 128,
  157, 159, 178
Social Democracy, 312–313
Social Question, not merely an
  economic one, 316
Socialism, 135, 175–186, 321
  an abominable sect, 185
  to be avoided by Christians,
    185
Socialists, 46, 175
  distort the Gospel, 179
Societas, xliii
Societies, 224–226
Society, its last end, 240
  domestic and civil, 240
Sovereignty of the People, 159–160
  see Social Contract
State, its various names, xliii
  definition, 213
  pretends to dominate the
    Church, 158–159
  its functions, 213–214
  must not absorb individuals
    nor families, 216
  cause of the evils that affect it,
    271–272

Strikes, 217–218
  should respect property, 218
Summi Pontificatus, 140
Syllabus, xviii, 162

Testem Benevolentiae, xix
Third Order of St. Francis, 116
Thomism, 19–29
Tolerance, its nature, xxxiii, 57–58
  of God, 57
  of the Church, 57
  of the State, 57

Unions, of workers, 117–118

Vatican council, xviii, xx, 11–13,
  15, 248, 253
Vis, xlii

Wages, 221–222
Will, can be constrained solely
  by God, xxviii–xxix, 127
Woman, in Christian family, 153
Woman's duties in social and
  political life, 141
Working classes, 193–194
Working men, their duties, 204
  necessary to the State, 214–215
  their rights, 216
  their unions, 224, 227
  their spiritual interests,
    218–220
  their material condition, 316
  should not be exploited,
    220–221
  should be helped, 227–229
  pressing question of the hour,
    231

INDEX OF PROPER NAMES

Adam, 68
Albert the Great, Saint, 28
Alembert, Jean le Rond d', 125
Alexander II, Emperor of Russia, 121, 123
Alexander III, Pope, 276, 297
Alphonsus of Leon, 86
Ambrose, Saint, 22, 86, 296
Anselm of Canterbury, Saint, 4, 18
Aristides, 10, 16
Arnobius, 17, 69
Athanasius, Saint, 17
Athenagoras, 16, 78, 132
Attila, 276
Augustine, Saint, xlii, 4, 8, 10, 12–13, 18, 22, 37, 42, 56, 67, 86, 97, 114, 126, 137, 145, 154, 164, 278, 279, 287, 297

Basil the Great, Saint, 10, 17–18,
Beck, A., 333
Benedict XIII, Pope, 22
Benedict XIV, Pope, 23, 85, 98–99, 136, 178, 300
Benigni, U., 332
Boethius, Manlius Severinus, 18
Bonaventure, Saint, 4, 19
Bourke, V.J., 333

Cairns, Huntington, 333
Cajetan, 20
Caligula, 77
Carlen, Sister M. Claudia, I.H.M., 332
Cary, E., 70
Celestine III, Pope, 86
Charlemagne, 298
Chrysostom, *see* John Chrysostom,
Clement of Alexandria, 9, 12
Clement of Rome, 297

Clement VI, Pope, 22
Clement VII, Pope, 86, 136
Clement XI, Pope, 136
Clement XII, Pope, 22, 98–99, 178
Clérissac, H., O.P., 334
Commodus, *see* Lucius A.
Crowe, M.B., 333
Cyprian, Saint, 10
Cyril of Alexandria, 154

Damascene, John, 18
De Aguirre, 78
Decurtins, Gaspard, 189
Diderot, Denis, 125
Diognetus, 132
Dionysius Halicarnassus, 70
Dominic, Saint, 21

Eligius, 297
Eugene IV, Pope, 85
Eusebius, Saint, 294

Fejer, 79
Felix of Valois, 297
Ferdinand, King of Bohemia, 136
Fourier, Charles, 74
Francis of Assisi, Saint, 95, 116, 308, 323
Frederick Barbarossa, 276
Friedberg, E., 298

Gibbons, James Cardinal, xix
Gilson, Etienne, xi, xiv–xv, 332
Goossens, Peter-Lambert Cardinal, 189
Goyau, G., 332
Gratian, 298
Gregory IX, Pope, 297
Gregory XVI, Pope, xvii–xviii, 85, 99, 162, 300

341

Gregory the Great, Saint, 22, 127, 208, 261, 287, 298
Gregory Nazianzen, 10, 18
Gregory of Neocaesaraea (or Thaumaturgus), 9
Gregory of Nyssa, 10
Gregory Thaumaturgus, *see* Gregory of Neocaesarea

Hadrian I, Pope, 297
Harduin, J., 78
Harney, John B., 141
Hart, C.A., 333
Henry VIII, 86
Hermias, 16
Hilary, Saint, 10, 297
Hippolytus, 78
Honorius III, Pope, xxxv, 76, 297
Husslein, J., S.J., xxxviii, xli, 86, 173, 189, 331

Ignatius the Martyr, Saint, 78
Innocent III, Pope, xxxv, 76, 86, 276, 297
Innocent VI, Pope, 23
Innocent XII, Pope, 22
Irenaeus, Saint, 10, 16
Ivo of Chartres, 156

James, Saint, 29
Jansenius, 36
Jerome, Saint, 10, 12, 16–17, 22, 69, 74, 86, 296
Jesus Christ, xxxv, 34, 37, 43, 54, 66, 68, 70, 72, 87, 97–98, 111, 117, 121, 126, 129, 149–150, 152, 155, 158, 163, 168, 199, 206–207, 209–210, 213, 237, 241, 243–245, 247–251, 254, 264–266, 279, 282, 284, 287, 290, 294, 309, 329
John the Baptist, Saint, 317

John Chrysostom, Saint, 17, 126, 295–296
John de Matha, 297
John of Medici, *see* Leo X
Joseph, Saint, 29, 119, 138, 186, 282
Justin, Saint, 4, 10, 16, 78
Justinian, 79, 289

Kelly, J.P., 333

Labbeus, P., 154
Lactantius, 10, 17, 296
Lauchert, Fr., 78
Leo X, Pope, 276, 299, 303
Leo XII, Pope, 99, 136
Leo XIII, Pope, xi, xiii–xvi, xvii–xliv, see introductions and conclusion
Leo the Great, Saint, 276
Lingenthal, C.E.Z., 79
Lothair, 86
Lucius Aurelius Commodus, 132
Luther, Martin, 134

MacLaren, D., O.P., 333
Magnus, 12
Mahomet, 301
Mani (or Manes), 73
Manning, H.E. Cardinal, 334
Marcellinus, Saint, 278
Marcus Aurelius Antoninus, 132
Maritain, J., xliii, 334
Marius Victorinus, *see* Victorinus
Mary, Blessed Virgin, 29, 91, 119, 137, 186, 208
Marx, Karl, 74
McDonald, W.J., 333
Messner, J., 333
Montanus, 73
Moses, 68, 70

Index of Proper Names

Napoleon I, 86
Nell-Breuning, O. von, S.J., 334
Nero, 77
Nicholas I, Pope, 86
Nicholas V, Pope, 22
Noe, 288
Nolasco, Peter, 298

Oceanus, 86
Onesimus, 293
Optatus, 10
Origen, 9, 17

Parsons, Wilfred, S.J., 334
Paschal II, Pope, 86, 156
Patrick, Saint, 297
Paul, Saint, xxx–xxxi, 3, 12, 29, 66,
    71, 73, 77, 91, 119, 121, 126, 129,
    131, 138, 141, 181, 186, 212, 233,
    244, 250–251, 258, 260, 263, 282,
    285, 290–291, 293, 295, 324
Paul III, Pope, 86, 300
Pecci, Vincent Joachim, *see* Leo
    XIII
Pegis, A.C., 332
Peter, Saint, xix, 6, 11, 26, 29, 91,
    119, 129, 138, 164, 186, 243, 254,
    257, 282, 291, 294
Peter Claver, Saint, 302
Philemon, 293, 295
Philip Augustus, King of France,
    276
Philip I, King of France, 86
Philip II, King of France, 86
Pius II, Pope, 299
Pius V, Saint, 22, 276
Pius VI, Pope, 85, 178
Pius VII, Pope, 85–86, 98–99, 178,
    300
Pius VIII, Pope, 85, 99
Pius IX, Pope, xviii, 85, 99, 162,
    178, 269, 277–278

Pius XI, Pope, 86, 141, 173, 189,
    269, 280, 331–332
Pius XII, Pope, xxi, 86, 140–141,
    189, 331
Polycarp, 78
Potamiana, 294

Quadratus, 10, 16

Rampolla, Cardinal, 32
Rickaby, J., S.J., 334
Riedl, C., 333
Rommen, H., 334
Rousseau, Jean-Jacques, xxx, 128
Ryan, J., 333
Rzadkiewicz, A., O.F.M., 333

Salvian, 297
Saint-Simon, Claude H., 74
Schmiedeler, Edgarm, O.S.B., 86
Simon, Y., 333–334
Sixtus V, Pope, 18, 25
Smith, Joseph, 74
Smith, G.D., 86, 140, 173
Smith, I., O.P., 334
Stokes, A.P., 334

Tertullian, 17, 78, 132, 168, 212
Theodosius, 79
Thomas Aquinas, Saint, xiv, xviii,
    xxii–xxiii, xxxi, xxxvii, xl, xlii,
    3–5, 8, 20, 22–23, 25–26, 28, 31,
    38, 139, 201, 207, 214–215, 226,
    252, 260–261, 322, 332–333
Tiberius, 77
Timothy, Saint, 291
Tischleder, P., 332
Titus, Saint, 26, 185, 244, 292
Treacy, Gerald C., 141, 173, 189, 331
T'Serclaes, Charles de, Msgr., 332

Urban II, Pope, 86
Urban V, Pope, 22–23
Urban VIII, Pope, 300

Victor Emmanuel II, King of
  Italy, 272, 277
Victorinus, Marius, 10

Vincent de Paul, Saint, 118, 308, 323
Voltaire, François, M.A., 125
Volusianus, 114

Watt, L., S.J., 334

www.ingramcontent.com/pod-product-compliance
Ingram Content Group UK Ltd.
Pitfield, Milton Keynes, MK11 3LW, UK
UKHW041952230426
12048UKWH00008B/286